W9-BMN-683

Beginning AppleScript®

Stephen G. Kochan

WILEY

Wiley Publishing, Inc.

Beginning AppleScript®

Published by
Wiley Publishing, Inc.
10475 Crosspoint Boulevard
Indianapolis, IN 46256-5774
www.wiley.com

Copyright © 2005 by Wiley Publishing, Inc., Indianapolis, Indiana

Published simultaneously in Canada

ISBN: 0-7645-7400-0

Manufactured in the United States of America

10 9 8 7 6 5 4 3 2 1

1MA/RX/RR/QU/IN

No part of this publication may be reproduced, stored in a retrieval system or transmitted in any form or by any means, electronic, mechanical, photocopying, recording, scanning or otherwise, except as permitted under Sections 107 or 108 of the 1976 United States Copyright Act, without either the prior written permission of the Publisher, or authorization through payment of the appropriate per-copy fee to the Copyright Clearance Center, 222 Rosewood Drive, Danvers, MA 01923, (978) 750-8400, fax (978) 646-8600. Requests to the Publisher for permission should be addressed to the Legal Department, Wiley Publishing, Inc., 10475 Crosspoint Blvd., Indianapolis, IN 46256, (317) 572-3447, fax (317) 572-4355, e-mail: brandreview@wiley.com.

LIMIT OF LIABILITY/DISCLAIMER OF WARRANTY: THE PUBLISHER AND THE AUTHOR MAKE NO REPRESENTATIONS OR WARRANTIES WITH RESPECT TO THE ACCURACY OR COMPLETENESS OF THE CONTENTS OF THIS WORK AND SPECIFICALLY DISCLAIM ALL WARRANTIES, INCLUDING WITHOUT LIMITATION WARRANTIES OF FITNESS FOR A PARTICULAR PURPOSE. NO WARRANTY MAY BE CREATED OR EXTENDED BY SALES OR PROMOTIONAL MATERIALS. THE ADVICE AND STRATEGIES CONTAINED HEREIN MAY NOT BE SUITABLE FOR EVERY SITUATION. THIS WORK IS SOLD WITH THE UNDERSTANDING THAT THE PUBLISHER IS NOT ENGAGED IN RENDERING LEGAL, ACCOUNTING, OR OTHER PROFESSIONAL SERVICES. IF PROFESSIONAL ASSISTANCE IS REQUIRED, THE SERVICES OF A COMPETENT PROFESSIONAL PERSON SHOULD BE SOUGHT. NEITHER THE PUBLISHER NOR THE AUTHOR SHALL BE LIABLE FOR DAMAGES ARISING HEREFROM. THE FACT THAT AN ORGANIZATION OR WEBSITE IS REFERRED TO IN THIS WORK AS A CITATION AND/OR A POTENTIAL SOURCE OF FURTHER INFORMATION DOES NOT MEAN THAT THE AUTHOR OR THE PUBLISHER ENDORSES THE INFORMATION THE ORGANIZATION OR WEBSITE MAY PROVIDE OR RECOMMENDATIONS IT MAY MAKE. FURTHER, READERS SHOULD BE AWARE THAT INTERNET WEBSITES LISTED IN THIS WORK MAY HAVE CHANGED OR DISAPPEARED BETWEEN WHEN THIS WORK WAS WRITTEN AND WHEN IT IS READ.

For general information on our other products and services or to obtain technical support, please contact our Customer Care Department within the U.S. at (800) 762-2974, outside the U.S. at (317) 572-3993 or fax (317) 572-4002.

Wiley also publishes its books in a variety of electronic formats. Some content that appears in print may not be available in electronic books.

Library of Congress Cataloging-in-Publication Data:
Kochan, Stephen G.
  Beginning Applescript / Stephen Kochan.
    p. cm.
  Includes index.
  ISBN 0-7645-7400-0 (paper/website)
  1. AppleScript (Computer program language) I. Title.
  QA76.73.A67K63 2004
  005.13'3--dc22

2004022630

Trademarks: Wiley, the Wiley Publishing logo, Wrox, the Wrox logo, Programmer to Programmer and related trade dress are trademarks or registered trademarks of John Wiley & Sons, Inc. and/or its affiliates, in the United States and other countries, and may not be used without written permission. AppleScript is a registered trademark of Apple Computer, Inc. in the U.S. and other countries. All other trademarks are the property of their respective owners. Wiley Publishing, Inc., is not associated with any product or vendor mentioned in this book.

About the Author

Stephen G. Kochan has been developing software and writing books for over 20 years. He is the author and coauthor of several best-selling titles on the C language, including *Programming in C* and *Programming in ANSI C* (both from Sams Publishing), *Programming C for the Mac* (Macmillan Computer Publishing), and *Topics in C Programming* (Wiley Publishing), as well as several Unix titles, including *Exploring the Unix System* and *Unix Shell Programming* (both Sams Publishing), and *Unix System Security* (Hayden Books). His most recent title on Mac programming is *Programming in Objective-C* (Sams Publishing), which is a tutorial on the primary programming language used on the Mac for application development.

Credits

Acquisitions Editor
Katie Mohr

Senior Development Editor
Jodi Jensen

Production Editor
Pamela Hanley

Technical Editor
Terrence Talbot

Copy Editor
Mary Lagu

Editorial Manager
Mary Beth Wakefield

Vice President & Executive Group Publisher
Richard Swadley

Vice President and Publisher
Joseph B. Wikert

Project Coordinator
April Farling

Graphics and Production Specialists
Carrie Foster, Denny Hager, Joyce Haughey,
Jennifer Heleine

Quality Control Technician
John Greenough, Carl William Pierce

Media Development Specialist
Kit Malone

Proofreading
Sossity R. Smith

Indexing
TECHBOOKS Production Services

To my friends Allan, Cesar, Ramon, Lev, and Adrian
for always being there

Contents

Contents

Contents

Contents

Contents

Contents

Contents

Contents

Contents

Contents

Contents

Contents

Contents

Acknowledgments

After all the books I've written, you would think I would have this time-management thing down to a science by now. Not a chance! I still haven't been able to judiciously ration my time so that I don't end up putting a lot of pressure on myself and the ones around me as I approach my deadline. To those around me who put up with this, I am eternally grateful. This includes my wonderful kids, Julia, Linda, and Greg, who were once again unfortunate enough to have their father work on a book during their summer break.

My contacts at Wiley were equally patient and professional. I'd like to thank my acquisitions editor, Katie Mohr, for her continued support throughout this project. My development editor, Jodi Jensen, was remarkable! Thanks Jodi, for all your hard work and attention to detail. It was a real pleasure working with you on this book. Finally, I'd like to thank Terrence Talbot, my technical editor, for his thoroughness in reviewing my manuscript.

Introduction

The AppleScript language evolved from a revolutionary language called HyperTalk, which was developed in 1987 by Bill Atkinson. HyperTalk, which was part of the programming environment called HyperCard, allowed you to write English-like sentences to accomplish your tasks. Several commercial applications, most notably the popular game *Myst*, were developed in HyperCard. However, due to various marketing decisions, HyperCard and HyperTalk never gained widespread popularity and support.

Like HyperTalk, AppleScript remained a language embraced by a relatively small circle of enthusiasts. With the surge in popularity of Mac OS X, a powerful operating system based on UNIX, came a surge in the popularity of AppleScript. This was partly due to the fact that more and more applications became *scriptable*, meaning you could talk to them from an AppleScript program. AppleScript was also found to be well suited for automating repetitive tasks in the workplace, a process known as *workflow automation*. Finally, AppleScript's growth in popularity was partly owed to Apple's recognition and adoption of AppleScript as a key technology component in Mac OS X.

AppleScript is called a *scripting* language. Scripting languages are programming languages designed primarily to control or coordinate the operation of other programs. Examples of other popular scripting languages include JavaScript, Perl, Ruby, VBScript, the UNIX shell, and Python.

On your Mac, a scripting language might ask the Safari browser to display a particular web page. Or it might ask iTunes to play a particular song. Scripting languages are also often used to coordinate the transfer of data between multiple applications to accomplish a task. So a script might contain code to go to the website for some data, put it into an Excel spreadsheet, and then email the spreadsheet to your boss.

In the past, scripting languages were not well suited for accomplishing general-purpose programming tasks because they either lacked sufficient programming capabilities or were simply too inefficient. However, the line between a scripting language and a general purpose programming language has become blurred over the years. In some situations, AppleScript can work just fine as a way to implement a solution to a general programming problem.

Who This Book Is For

This book is a tutorial on the AppleScript language. Most of the existing books on AppleScript concentrate on its use in the workplace for workflow automation. However, AppleScript is a great language for the hobbyist and computer enthusiast to learn, and those groups are the intended audience for this book. Instead of focusing on how to use AppleScript to format data for an Excel spreadsheet, edit some images in PhotoShop, or create a document with FrameMaker, this book shows how easy it is to use AppleScript to control some of the fun applications on your system. As a result, the programs in this book show you how do things like write a simple alarm clock program, create a simple iTunes player, or take a folder of images and make a DVD slide show.

That's not to say that programmers who intend to use AppleScript for workflow automation should not read this book. This book teaches you what you need to know to get started and how to write your scripts. However, be forewarned: you will be having some fun along the way!

How This Book Is Structured

As I just noted, the purpose of this book is to teach you how to write programs in AppleScript. It is designed to appeal to both the novice and experienced programmer alike and assumes no prior programming experience. Readers with prior programming experience will find that AppleScript has a unique way of doing things that most likely differs significantly from any other programming language you have used.

The approach taken in this text is to teach by example, using small, well-chosen, complete programming examples. These are presented using the Wrox trademark "Try It Out" format. By typing each example, running it, and examining the results, you gain experience with the entire process of entering, running, and debugging programs. Experience has shown that this hands-on approach is one of the most effective ways to learn.

You will find that most of the programs in this book illustrate a specific concept, such as how to write a loop, how to get a list of files, and so on. These examples are not designed for industrial use. That is, they do not avoid all possible errors in all possible situations. In many cases, that would make the programs too hard to follow. However, defensive programming is taught in the text, and an entire chapter is devoted to error handling.

At the end of each chapter, you will find exercises. To gain maximum benefit from this book, I strongly suggest that you work through each exercise before proceeding to the next chapter. Not only will this help to solidify the concepts presented in the chapter, but also it will help prepare you for the material covered in the following chapter. Answers to the exercises are supplied in Appendix A, but I urge you to first try solving the problems on your own before you consult the appendix.

Here's a rundown of what you'll find in the each chapter:

In Chapter 1, "Writing You First AppleScript Program," you waste no time getting started. Right off the bat, I show you how to start up the Script Editor application, type in a program, and run the program to see your results. The chapter then shows you how to write a program that puts up a simple dialog using the `display dialog` command. You use this command extensively throughout the book.

Chapter 2, "Variables, Classes, and Expressions," covers some of the more mundane aspects of the language, but these are concepts you need to learn to master the language. In this chapter, you learn the rules for forming variable names, writing arithmetic expressions, and working with many of AppleScript's built-in classes. One unique aspect of AppleScript is its support for a built-in date class, which allows you to easily work with dates in your programs.

In Chapter 3, "Making Decisions," you learn how to use the if statement to make comparisons and affect the flow of control in your program based on the result of your comparisons. In this chapter, you also learn how to get input from the user.

Chapter 4, "Program Looping," covers the many forms of AppleScript's repeat statement. This is the fundamental statement for repeatedly executing a group of statements. You see how to write a simple guessing game program that allows a user to try to guess a number between 1 and 10 that has been randomly selected by your program.

In Chapter 5, "Working with Strings," I show you how to work with character strings. You learn how to get elements such as characters and words from a string, how to get the length of a string, and how to compare two strings.

Chapter 6 is titled "Working with Lists and Records." List and Records are the fundamental data structures supported in AppleScript. This chapter shows you how to use them effectively in your programs, how to access elements from them, and how to form more complex data structures such as lists containing lists and lists containing records.

In Chapter 7, "Working with Files," you learn about file name paths and POSIX paths. The chapter shows you how to use AppleScript's built-in commands to open a file, read data from it, and write data to it. You also learn how to get information about a file, such as its size, its modification date, and its type. The chapter shows how to use commands to allow a user to choose a file or a folder on the system and how you can enumerate the contents of a folder in your program.

A handler is AppleScript's equivalent of a function or subroutine in other languages. In Chapter 8, "Handlers," this topic is covered in detail. You learn the different ways you can write a handler, how to pass arguments to and return values from a handler, and the differences between local and global variables. In this chapter, you also develop a set of handlers for performing common operations with lists.

Sometimes errors can occur in your program at unexpected times and in unexpected places. In Chapter 9, "Error Handling," you learn how to plan for such events and how to intelligently handle them when they occur. You learn how AppleScript provides a mechanism so that you can "catch" an error when it occurs and handle it accordingly.

Because AppleScript is a scripting language, it was designed to enable you to easily communicate with other applications. This is done primarily through a feature of the language called the tell statement. In Chapter 10, "Working with Applications," you learn how to use this statement in detail. The Finder is the primary application illustrated in this chapter. You learn how to ask the Finder to do things that you can't handle directly in AppleScript, such as renaming, moving, or deleting a file. The chapter also shows you how to write a *droplet*, which is an application that gets executed whenever someone drops files onto its icon.

Chapter 11, "Scripting iLife Applications," provides the most fun of any chapter in the book! iLife is a suite of applications that includes iTunes, iPhoto, iDVD, iMovie, and GarageBand. Of these five applications, only the first three were scriptable as of the writing of this book. In this chapter, you develop a simple application that allows you to prompt the user for a song title and then ask iTunes to play it. The iPhoto example shows you how to create a new album in your photo library from a folder of image files. Finally, The iDVD example shows you how to write an AppleScript program to create a DVD slide show presentation from a folder of images.

Chapter 12, "Script Objects," goes into detail about script objects, showing you how to store them in a file and subsequently load them into your programs. You also learn how defining a script object inside a handler allows you to write programs that are consistent with an object-oriented programming (OOP) style.

Chapter 13, "Loose Ends," serves the purpose implied by its name: to tie up some loose ends. Topics covered in this chapter are those that are either of a more advanced nature or did not fit neatly into the structure of earlier chapters. These include web services, the Script Menu, GUI scripting, and recording scripts.

Chapter 14 is the last chapter in the book and is titled "Introducing AppleScript Studio." AppleScript Studio was released with the Panther version of Mac OS X (v. 10.3). AppleScript Studio, makes the bridge between AppleScript and GUI applications. With AppleScript Studio, you can develop a sophisticated user interface and have AppleScript as the underlying code to respond to events like the clicking of a button or the movement of a slider. Chapter 14 is an introduction to AppleScript Studio and guides you through the steps involved in creating a simple application.

There are also three appendices provided in this book: Appendix A, "Exercise Answers," provides solutions for the exercises presented in the text. Appendix B, "Language Reference," provides a quick reference to AppleScript's operators and commands. Appendix C, "Resources," contains a list of resources and places you can look for more information about AppleScript and some of the tools mentioned in the text.

What You Need to Use This Book

This book covers the latest version of AppleScript. At the time of this writing, the latest version was 1.9.3. You use a separate program to enter and run AppleScript programs. On the Mac, Script Editor is the primary tool used for such purposes. The version of Script Editor I cover in this book is 2.0. There are other third-party script editors available for use with AppleScript, including Smile and Script Debugger. These are mentioned throughout the text but are not covered in detail.

The chapter covering scripting iLife applications was developed using the following versions: iTunes v4.6, iPhoto v4.0.3, and iDVD v4.0.1. The iLife suite comes preinstalled on many Mac systems. Alternatively, you can buy iLife from Apple's website. iTunes is also available for no charge from that website if you don't want to purchase the entire iLife suite.

The chapter on AppleScript Studio is based on version 1.5 of Xcode. The latest version of Xcode can be obtained at no charge from Apple's website. You just need to register there as an online developer, again, at no cost to you.

Although AppleScript is a fairly stable programming language that has not changed much, it is widely recommended that you use the latest versions of the software with this book. In that way, you are assured that the features used in the examples are supported by the applications being used.

All the programs in this book were tested on my Titanium PowerBook G4 running Mac OS X version 10.3.5. Compatibility with earlier versions of OS X or the applications cited previously is not guaranteed.

Conventions

To help you get the most from the text and keep track of what's happening, we've used a number of conventions throughout the book.

Tips, hints, tricks, and asides to the current discussion are offset and placed in italics like this.

As for styles used in the text

❑   We *highlight* important words when we introduce them

❑   We show keyboard strokes like this: Ctrl-A

❑   We show file and folder names, URLs, and code within the text in a special monofont typeface, like this: `persistence.properties`

❑   We present code in two different ways:

```
In code examples we highlight new and important code with a gray background.
```

```
The gray highlighting is not used for code that is less important in the present
context or has been shown before.
```

Source Code

As you work through the examples in this book, you may choose either to type in all the code manually or use the source code files that accompany the book. All of the source code used in this book is available for download at `http://www.wrox.com`. Once at the site, simply locate the book's title (either by using the Search box or by using one of the title lists) and click the Download Code link on the book's detail page to obtain all the source code for the book.

Because many books have similar titles, you may find it easiest to search by ISBN; for this book the ISBN is 0-7645-7400-0.

After you download the code, just decompress it with your favorite compression tool. Alternatively, you can go to the main Wrox code download page at `http://www.wrox.com/dynamic/books/download.aspx` to see the code available for this book and all other Wrox books.

Errata

We make every effort to ensure that there are no errors in the text or in the code. However, no one is perfect, and mistakes do occur. If you find an error in one of our books, like a spelling mistake or faulty piece of code, we would be very grateful for your feedback. By sending in errata you may save another reader hours of frustration; at the same time, you are helping us provide higher quality information.

To find the errata page for this book, go to `http://www.wrox.com` and locate the title using the Search box or one of the title lists. Then, on the Book Search Results page, click the Errata link at the bottom of the book entry. On this page, you can view all errata that has been submitted for this book and posted by Wrox editors. A complete book list, including links to each book's errata, is also available at www.wrox.com/misc-pages/booklist.shtml.

If you don't spot "your" error on the book's Errata page, go to www.wrox.com/contact/techsupport.shtml and complete the form there to send us the error you have found. We'll check the information and, if appropriate, post a message to the book's errata page and fix the problem in subsequent editions of the book.

p2p.wrox.com

For author and peer discussion, join the P2P forums at p2p.wrox.com. The forums are a Web-based system for you to post messages relating to Wrox books and related technologies and interact with other readers and technology users. The forums offer a subscription feature to e-mail you topics of interest of your choosing when new posts are made to the forums. Wrox authors, editors, other industry experts, and your fellow readers are present on these forums.

At http://p2p.wrox.com you will find a number of different forums that will help you not only as you read this book, but also as you develop your own applications. To join the forums, just follow these steps:

1. Go to p2p.wrox.com and click the Register link.

2. Read the terms of use and click Agree.

3. Complete the required information to join as well as any optional information you want to provide and click Submit.

4. You will receive an e-mail with information describing how to verify your account and complete the joining process.

   You can read messages in the forums without joining P2P but in order to post your own messages, you must join.

After you join, you can post new messages and respond to messages other users post. You can read messages at any time on the Web. If you would like to have new messages from a particular forum e-mailed to you, click the Subscribe to this Forum icon by the forum name in the forum listing.

For more information about how to use the Wrox P2P, be sure to read the P2P FAQs for answers to questions about how the forum software works as well as many common questions specific to P2P and Wrox books. To read the FAQs, click the FAQ link on any P2P page.

Writing Your First AppleScript Program

There's no point in wasting time. You are reading this book because you want to learn how to write programs in AppleScript. So instead of wading through theory and terminology, I want you to begin by typing an AppleScript program, running it, and looking at the results. I introduce terminology as it is necessary along the way. If you begin this way, you'll have more fun and you won't get overwhelmed.

Starting with Script Editor

Your Mac OS X system comes with some preinstalled tools that you'll be using in this book. One of the most useful ones (as far as AppleScript programming goes) is an application called Script Editor. This application allows you to enter, compile, debug, and run your AppleScript programs in an interactive environment. It is a simple and effective tool.

The Script Editor application is stored in your `Applications` folder inside a subfolder called `AppleScript`. Its icon looks like the one shown in Figure 1-1.

Figure 1-1

Locate the Script Editor application and double-click it to start it. You should get a window on your screen that looks similar to the one shown in Figure 1-2. This window is where you type your AppleScript program. I show you how in the following Try It Out.

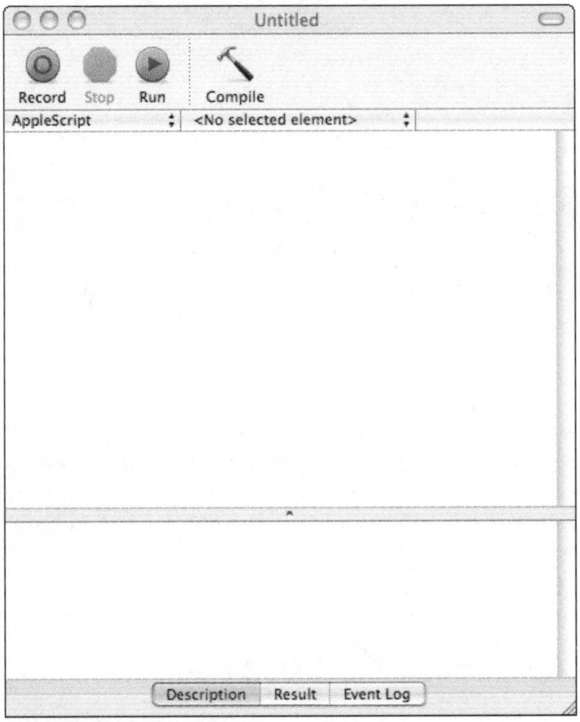

Figure 1-2

Try It Out   Typing Your First Program

Click inside the Script Editor window and type the following:

```
100 * pi
```

Your window should look like Figure 1-3.

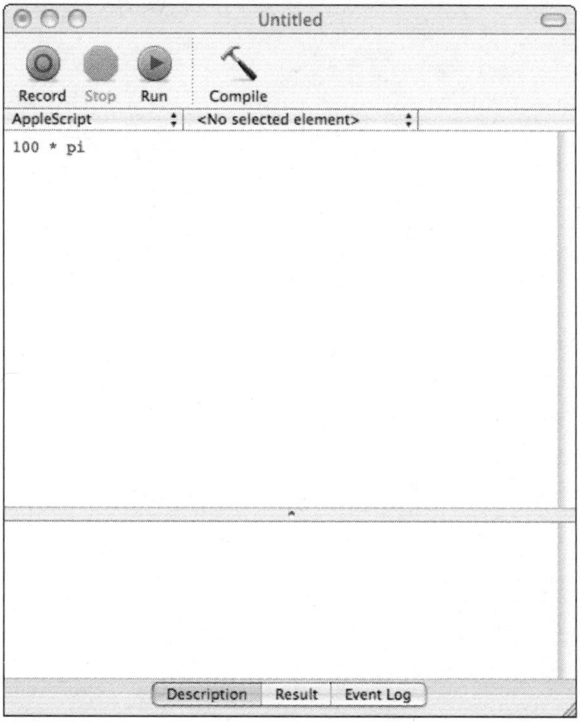

```
○ ○ ○                    Untitled
   ○        ○        ▶             ⟍
 Record   Stop     Run       Compile
 AppleScript            ⇕   <No selected element>   ⇕
 100 * pi








                              ▲


                    Description   Result   Event Log
```

Figure 1-3

Compiling and Running Your Program

Try It Out   Running Your First Program

After typing the indicated line in the window, move your pointer to the top of the window and click the button labeled Run, as depicted in Figure 1-4.

Figure 1-4

You'll notice that two things change in your Script Editor window, as depicted in Figure 1-5.

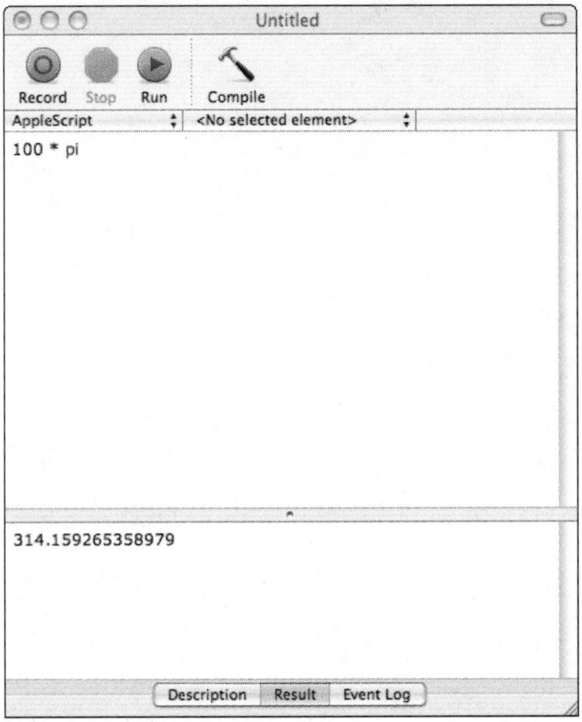

Figure 1-5

The first thing you may have noticed is that the color of your text changed in the window. Previously, when you typed the line

```
100 * pi
```

the text appeared in purple. After you clicked the Run button, the number `100` and the asterisk character `*` changed to black, and the word `pi` changed to blue. You may have noticed that the font changed as well, from Courier to Verdana.

This book is printed in black and white, so you obviously can't see the colors in Figure 1-5 or in any screen shots in this text. But if you're following along, you should see these color and font changes on your screen.

Script Editor automatically displays any special words, known as *keywords*, in blue by default (you can select other colors to use if you like). This is done to visually aid you when you look at your program. As you'll see later, other colors and font styles are used to indicate program elements such as comments, variables, and operators.

At the bottom of the window, you should see the number `314.159265358979` (or something very close to it). Congratulations, this number represents the output (or the result) from running your first AppleScript program!

Make sure that the Result tab button is highlighted at the bottom of the window. If it isn't, click it so that the result of the operation can be seen.

How It Works

When you start up Script Editor, a window labeled Untitled is automatically created for you. In this window you can enter your AppleScript program. In the simplest case, a program can simply be an expression to evaluate, as in

```
100 * pi
```

This expression uses the multiplication operator, which is the asterisk (as it is in every other programming language I know of) to multiply the number 100 by something called pi. Recalling your high school mathematics, pi or π (as it's written using mathematical notation) is a number frequently used when performing calculations with circles. It's roughly equal to the value 3.14159. As you learn in greater detail in Chapter 2, the keyword `pi` is used in AppleScript as an approximation of the value of π.

So the expression

```
100 * pi
```

is an AppleScript expression that multiplies 100 by the value specified by the keyword `pi`, which explains the result you obtained.

After you type your program into Script Editor, you click the Run button. Clicking that button initiates the following actions:

❏ Analyzes your AppleScript code to make sure it conforms to the rules for writing commands and expressions. (This process is described in detail throughout this book and actually involves more than just a conformance check.) The result of this *compilation* process is the translation of your AppleScript program into another format that is more optimal for execution

❏ Indents your AppleScript code according to certain stylistic rules

❏ Changes the color of your words, operators, and expressions according to certain rules

❏ Runs your program and displays the result in the lower portion of your window, provided no errors are detected during the compilation phase.

Now that you've run your first program, you should save it. The following Try It Out walks you through doing just that.

Try It Out   Saving Your First Program

Even though this was an extremely simple first program, you should save it anyway.

1.   Go to the menu bar at the top of your screen and choose File ⇨ Save. A dialog box like the one shown in Figure 1-6 appears.

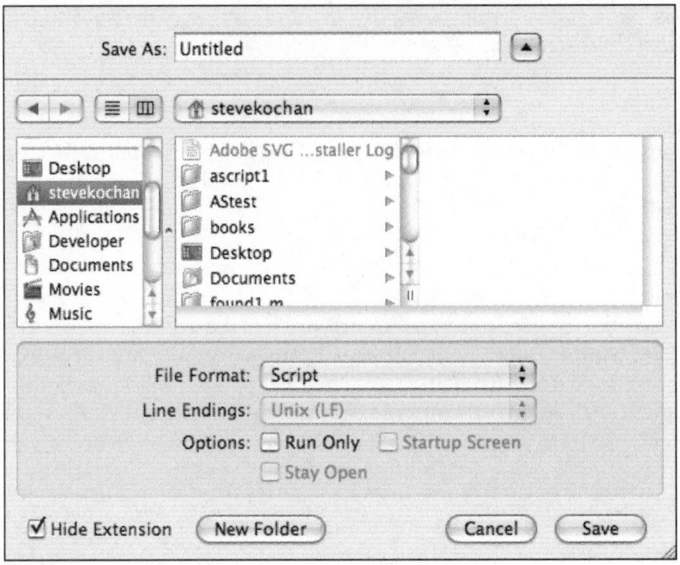

Figure 1-6

2. Your dialog box may look a little different based on the files stored on your system and which version of OS X you're running. In any case, in the box labeled Save As, replace the name Untitled with a more meaningful name such as My First AppleScript Program.

3. The other settings in the dialog box should remain as shown in Figure 1-6. After entering the file name, click the Save button. This causes your program to be saved to the specified file name.

When you go to save your program, Script Editor tries to compile it before saving. In that respect, it forces you to correct any errors before you can save your program to a file.

Later, if you want to make changes to your program, you can double-click the file name in the Finder to launch Script Editor with the specified file open. Alternatively, if Script Editor is already running, you can open the file for editing by choosing File ⇨ Open.

You now know how to start the Script Editor application, type an expression (which represents a complete AppleScript program), compile and run the program, view the results, and save the program to a file.

Extending Your First Program

You're not quite finished with your first program. In this section, you see how Script Editor reports errors. Then you learn how to add a description to your program and how to use a command that opens a simple dialog box.

Reporting Errors in Your Programs

First, let's see what happens if you make a mistake. Erase the contents of your window (one way is by highlighting all the text using your mouse and pressing the Delete key).

Now type the following into an empty window:

```
100 * pie
```

Click Run to compile and run your program, as you did previously. A dialog box like the one shown in Figure 1-7 should appear.

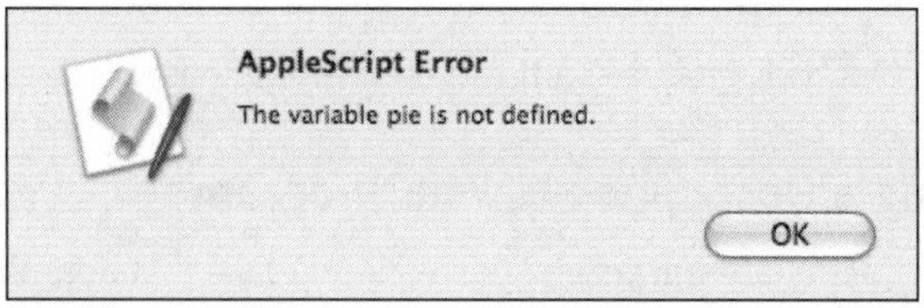

AppleScript Error

The variable pie is not defined.

OK

Figure 1-7

The Script Editor application is telling you that it doesn't know about a variable called `pie`; that is, `pie` is not defined. You learn about variables shortly; but essentially, a *variable* is a place in memory that you assign a name to and use for storing data. For now, just click OK to dismiss the dialog box. Your window should now look like the one shown in Figure 1-8.

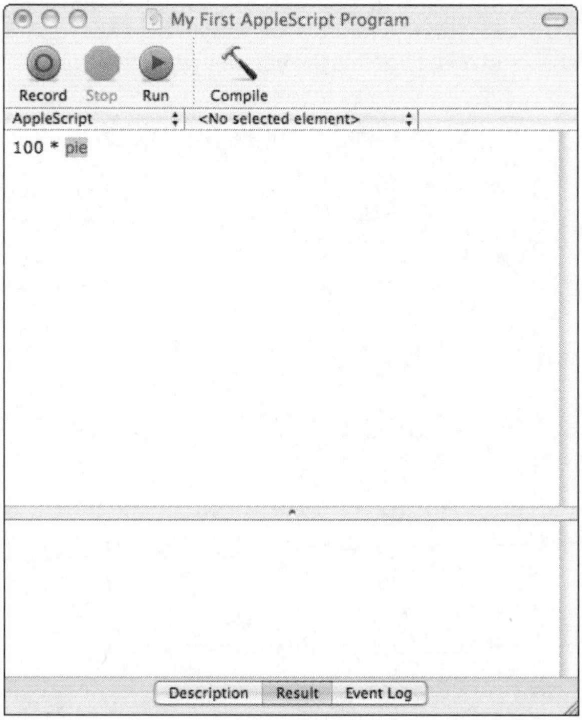

My First AppleScript Program

Record   Stop   Run   Compile

AppleScript   <No selected element>

```
100 * pie
```

Description   Result   Event Log

Figure 1-8

Notice that `pie` is highlighted. That's where the error occurred. Unlike the keyword `pi`, the word (or variable) `pie` does not have a special meaning in AppleScript, thus explaining the error message. In this case, you can simply delete the trailing `e` in `pie` and run the program again to remove the error.

Sometimes it's easy to decipher the error messages reported by Script Editor. At other times, the messages can seem quite cryptic. With experience, you will be able to readily understand the messages and the types of errors that cause them.

In the following Try It Out, you practice adding a description to your program.

Try It Out   Adding a Description to Your Program

You may be wondering about the purpose of the two other tabs that abut the Result tab at the bottom of your window. One is labeled Description, and the other is labeled Event Log, as you can see in Figure 1-8. I describe the Event Log tab in Chapter 2. You can use the Description tab to enter a description about what your program does, that is, to add notes about its operation.

1. Click the Description tab and then click in the lower pane of your window. Script Editor waits for you to enter your description.

2. Type the following line into the pane:

```
This is my first AppleScript program to multiply two numbers.
```

Your window should now resemble the one shown in Figure 1-9.

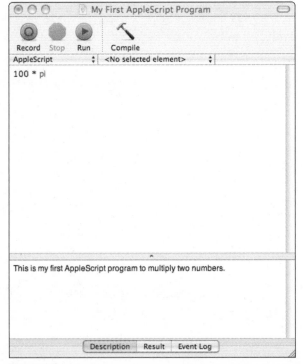

Figure 1-9

3.   Now save your program by choosing File ⇨ Save, and the description you entered is saved along with it.

You've already given your program a name (you called it My First AppleScript Program when you initially saved it), so you can simply choose File ⇨ Save to subsequently save any changes you make under the same name.

In Chapter 3, you see how the description you entered can be automatically displayed when you run your program as an application.

An AppleScript Command to Display a Dialog

Your first program shows the result of the expression evaluation in the Result pane. You use this Result pane (and the Event Log pane) to examine results throughout this book. However, to create an AppleScript program to talk to the user or to interactively display information, you need to do more. The simplest way to do this is to use an AppleScript command called `display dialog`.

For your second program, you put up a dialog box that says `Programming in AppleScript is fun.` If you still have your first program open in Script Editor, close the window by selecting File ⇨ Close or by simply clicking the red dot in the top-left corner of the window. If you've made any changes to the program since the last time you saved it, Script Editor gives you a chance to save the changes before closing the window.

Now open a new window by choosing File ⇨ New. You get a new empty window. Inside that window, type the following text:

```
Display Dialog "Programming in AppleScript is fun."
```

Your window should look like the one shown in Figure 1-10.

Now, instead of clicking the Run button, click the Compile button. This has the effect of analyzing your program and reporting any errors to you without actually running your program. Notice that the colors and formatting are changed by Script Editor, as depicted in Figure 1-11.

The `display dialog` command changes to blue and also to all lowercase letters. The blue color indicates special keywords, just as the keyword `pi` was displayed in blue earlier. And the conversion to all lowercase is done because, in general, AppleScript does not distinguish between upper- and lowercase letters. In later examples you see how, after compiling your program, Script Editor not only performs this case conversion, but it also may change and even rearrange some words in your commands! Finally, as noted before, the font of your small program changes from Courier to Verdana.

No error messages resulted from compiling your program, so you can now run the program by clicking the Run button.

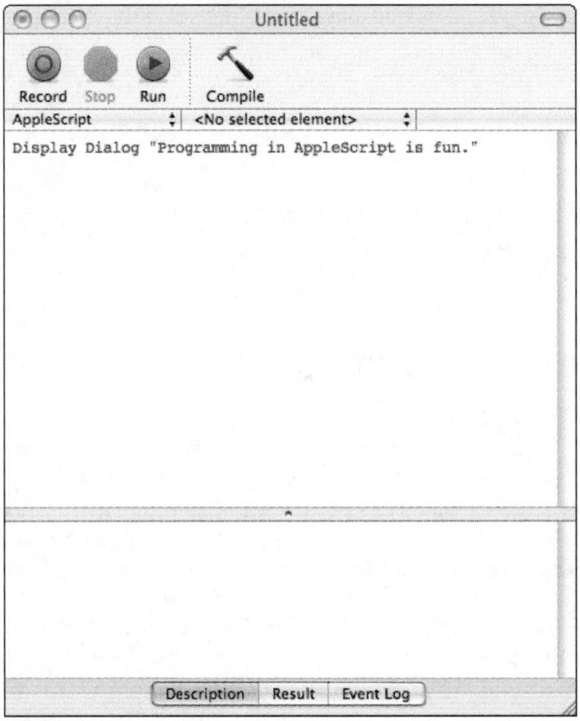

Figure 1-10

Figure 1-11

So that you don't get confused, remember the Compile button compiles your program but does not run it. The Run button also compiles your program if it has changed since the last time it was compiled. Then, if no errors are detected, it runs your program.

When you run your program, the dialog box shown in Figure 1-12 appears on your screen.

Programming in AppleScript is fun.

Cancel   OK

Figure 1-12

As you can see, the phrase `Programming in AppleScript is fun.` is displayed in the dialog box, without the quotes you typed around those characters. Those double quotes are used to define the beginning and end of your *character string*. Whatever is contained inside those quotes gets displayed by the `display dialog` command. You are also shown two buttons, one labeled Cancel, and the other OK. The OK button is highlighted, indicating that the default action that will be taken if you press the Return key. Click the OK button (or press the Return key) to return control back to Script Editor. Notice that the following appears in the Result pane:

```
{button returned:"OK"}
```

You see that this window doesn't just display the results of performing arithmetic operations. This time the window tells you that the OK button was clicked. This may not seem important now, but later you learn how to test which button is clicked in your program and how to take appropriate action based on that test. As a quick note, if you click the Cancel button instead of OK, no result is displayed in the Result pane. That's because, unless you take special action, the program is immediately terminated when you cancel it.

Understanding the Buttons Parameter in the display dialog Command

In the example shown in the preceding section, the Cancel button served no purpose. You can get rid of the Cancel button by using a `buttons` parameter with the `display dialog` command. The following Try It Out shows you how.

Try It Out   **Using the display dialog's Buttons Parameter**

Follow these steps to eliminate the Cancel button from the previous dialog box:

1.   Go back to the program you saved in the preceding Try It Out and add the following characters to the end of the `display dialog` command.

```
buttons {"OK"}
```

Your complete command line should look like this:

```
display dialog "Programming in AppleScript is fun." buttons { "OK" }
```

2. Compile and run the program. You see the dialog box shown in Figure 1-13.

> Programming in AppleScript is fun.
>
> OK

Figure 1-13

Because of the changes you made to the code, the dialog box no longer contains a Cancel button but just the single button labeled OK.

How It Works

The word `buttons` that you added to your program is an optional *parameter* to the `display dialog` command. AppleScript commands often accept parameters that enable you to extend the functionality of a command.

> *You can see that AppleScript, unlike any other programming language you probably have used, employs English words in its vocabulary. This allows you to write commands that are easy to read. However, it's also a trap that may mislead you into thinking you can write just about any English sentence in your program. That's not the case; the AppleScript language has a fairly rigid structure and, generally, likes its words to be in the expected places. Through practice, you can learn this syntax and begin to understand where words are acceptable and where they're not.*

Following the keyword `buttons` is the string `"OK"` enclosed inside a pair of curly braces { and }. These curly braces have special meaning in AppleScript: They define a *list*. Lists are discussed in full in Chapter 6. Between now and then, however, you learn some basic concepts for working with lists in your programs.

The list in this program contains just one *item*, which is the character string `"OK"`. You can include additional items in a list by placing them inside the curly braces and separating one item from the next with a comma. For example, here is a list containing seven strings:

```
{ "Sun", "Mon", "Tue", "Wed", "Thu", "Fri", "Sat" }
```

And here is a list containing three numbers:

```
{ 1, 2, 3 }
```

Finally, because lists can contain just about anything, here's one that contains a string and three numbers:

```
{ "DOB", 8, 8, 1986 }
```

Changing the Labels on a Button

Your program does not have to have a button labeled OK. In fact, you can choose any labels you want for your buttons. Simply specify the label in the list after the `buttons` parameter like this:

```
display dialog "Programming in AppleScript is fun." buttons { "You're so right!" }
```

When you run a program containing this command, the dialog displays a button with the label `You're so right!`.

The following Try It Out shows you how to set a default button.

Try It Out   Setting the Default Button in a Dialog

Follow these steps to set a default button in a dialog:

1. Go back to your program and change the command to the following:

```
display dialog "Pick a color" buttons {"Red", "Yellow", "Blue"}
```

This change puts up a dialog box with the message `Pick a color` and buttons labeled Red, Yellow, and Blue, respectively.

2. Run your program containing this command, and you should get a dialog that looks like the one shown in Figure 1-14. The actual button you select should appear in the Result pane, as previously described.

Figure 1-14

You may have noticed that most standard dialogs on the Mac have a default button. A *default button* is one that is highlighted to indicate what will be selected if you press the Return key.

3. Make the default button the third button in the list, which is labeled Blue. You can write either

```
display dialog "Pick a color" buttons { "Red", "Yellow", "Blue" } default button 3
```

or

```
display dialog "Pick a color" buttons { "Red", "Yellow", "Blue" } default button
    "Blue"
```

4. Compile and run your program. You should get the dialog shown in Figure 1-15.

Figure 1-15

How It Works

By using the `default button` parameter, you can specify the default. The value that follows this keyword is either the number of the button in the list (that is, 1, 2, or 3) or the button's label. It doesn't matter which you choose. The label may be a better choice because it makes the command easier to read.

If you type a long line into Script Editor, the editor automatically wraps your line at an appropriate point. This is fine. Script Editor knows that this continuation is part of the previous line when compiling your program. This is important because you cannot extend an AppleScript command over multiple lines simply by pressing the Return key to break the line. Instead, if you want to manually break a line (perhaps at a place you find more meaningful than where Script Editor breaks it for you), you have to press Option-Return to continue the command on the following line. Pressing Option-Return shows up as the character ¬ on your screen, as in the following example:

```
display dialog "Pick a color" buttons {"Red", "Yellow", "Blue"} ¬
    default button "Blue"
```

As you can see in Figure 1-15, shown earlier, the button labeled Blue is highlighted in the dialog. If you simply press the Return key, notice that Blue is shown in the Result pane as the button returned.

You can have up to three buttons in your `display dialog` *command. In Chapter 6, you learn about the* `choose from list` *command, which you can use to present any number of choices to the user.*

Adding an Icon to Your Dialog Box

As the last extension to your dialog, add a special symbol, known as an *icon*. You can add any icon you want, but three of them are predefined, as shown in the following table.

Icon Name	Symbol
stop	![stop icon]
note	![note icon]
caution	![caution icon]

The parameter you use to add an icon is called with icon. It is followed by a name, a string, or a number. The following Try It Out shows you how to add an icon to a dialog.

Try It Out   **Adding a Note Icon to Your Dialog**

Follow these steps to add a note icon to the dialog you generated earlier:

1. Go back to the program you created and revised earlier and add a note icon to the dialog so that your display dialog command looks like this:

```
display dialog "Pick a color" buttons {"Red", "Yellow", "Blue"}
    default button "Blue" with icon note
```

2. Run this program, and you should see the dialog shown in Figure 1-16.

Figure 1-16

Multiple AppleScript Commands

So far, your programs have done only a single thing: either perform a multiplication or display a dialog. It's obvious that you can do a lot more in your programs. Each line can contain another AppleScript command, which is executed sequentially, in turn, when the program is run.

The following Try It Out shows you how to add a sound effect to your program.

Try It Out   **Add a "Beep"**

Suppose you're running a program and you detect that an error has occurred. For example, suppose the program can't locate a file it wants to use called myFavorites. It would be reasonable to put up a dialog box telling the user that the error occurred. Adding a beep can help get the user's attention.

Follow these steps to add a sound effect with AppleScript's beep command:

1. Create a new AppleScript program with the following code:

```
beep
display dialog "Couldn't find myFavorites" buttons { "OK" } default button "OK"
    with icon stop
```

2. Run the program. A beep will sound, and then a dialog is displayed with a stop icon and a single default button labeled OK. This is depicted in Figure 1-17.

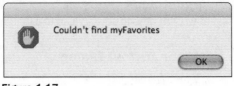

Figure 1-17

Adding Comments to Your Programs

As you start writing larger AppleScript programs, it is a good habit to document your program. You can do this directly in the program by inserting *comments*. A comment describes to the reader of the program the intentions of a particular sequence of code. Not only is this helpful when you go back months later to look at code that you wrote, but it can also aid the person who has to maintain your code.

You can insert a comment into an AppleScript program in one of two ways:

❑ By typing two consecutive hyphen characters (--) followed by any characters you want. Any characters that appear on the line after the two hyphens are ignored when the code is compiled.

❑ By typing an open parenthesis and an asterisk [(*] followed by your comments spread out over as many lines as you like. You terminate this comment style by typing an asterisk and close parenthesis [*)].

Here's an example of the first type of comment:

```
-- This program will resize all selected images to a specified size
```

And here's an example of the second type of comment:

```
(*
    This program creates an alphabetized list
    of all of the songs in someone's iTunes library

    Version 1.1 created 2/22/05
    Stephen Kochan
*)
```

You can mix and match your comment styles. And the second form of commenting can itself include comments. That is, comments can be nested.

The double hyphen is often used to add a single-line comment or a comment at the end of a line. In addition to its use for multiline comments, the paren-star comment is often used to "comment-out" a section of your program that is not yet finished or for debugging purposes.

Figure 1-18 shows how the previous program example appears in Script Editor after adding a comment and compiling it. Notice that Script Editor italicizes both types of comments.

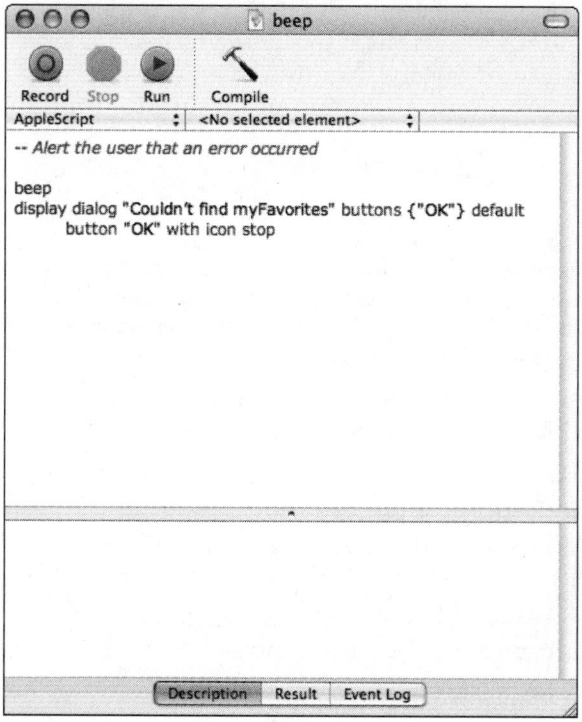

Figure 1-18

Summary

In this chapter, you learned how to do the following:

- ❏ Start up Script Editor
- ❏ Type a simple AppleScript program, compile it, and run it
- ❏ Look at the results of the program in the Result pane
- ❏ Save your AppleScript program to a file
- ❏ Add a description to your program
- ❏ Use the `display dialog` command to display a message to the user
- ❏ Define a character string
- ❏ Set up a simple list
- ❏ Use optional command parameters; in particular, use some of the `display dialog` command's parameters to change the labels on buttons, specify a default button, and display an icon
- ❏ Write an AppleScript program containing more than one command
- ❏ Add comments to your program

In the next chapter, you learn more about writing expressions, the different types of data that AppleScript supports, and how to work with variables in your programs. Before proceeding, however, try the exercises that follow to test your understanding of the material covered in this chapter. You can find the solutions to these exercises in Appendix A.

Exercises

1. Modify the expression from your first program so that it calculates the circumference of a circle with a radius of 1.48. As a hint, recall that the circumference of a circle with radius r is expressed by the formula $2\pi r$. Have the program perform the entire expression evaluation (that is, don't calculate $2r$ yourself!).

2. Write a program that poses the following question: "Do you think this is a great book?" Have two buttons labeled Yes and No, with Yes as the default.

3. Add a comment to the beginning of the program you created in Exercise 2 that describes the purpose of the program.

4. Add the following description to the program created in Exercise 2: "A program to ask a profound question!"

5. Modify the display dialog example (used earlier in this chapter) that presented the three color choices to make "Red" the default button.

6. Can you alter the order of the display dialog parameters? Experiment and see.

7. The beep command takes an optional numeric parameter that specifies the number of times to beep your system. For example, beep 2 causes two beeps. Modify the last program in this chapter to beep 3 times before the dialog is displayed.

8. The AppleScript say command can be used to speak text. The command is followed by the character string to be spoken. Write an AppleScript program that speaks the phrase "Programming in AppleScript is fun."

Variables, Classes, and Expressions

In this chapter you learn about how to work with variables in your programs. You also learn about many of the built-in AppleScript *data types* or *classes*. The basic arithmetic operators are covered in this chapter, and you see how to write arithmetic expressions and perform basic conversions between data types.

Working with Variables

Variables allow you to store data during your program's execution and give you the ability to refer to that data by a convenient name. You can store a value in a variable using the set or copy command, although I now introduce only the set command.

Variable Names and the set Command

The general format of the set command is as follows:

```
set   variable to value
```

Executing this command has the effect of storing the specified value (value) inside the variable (variable). As an example, the statement

```
set fileCount to 0
```

stores the value 0 inside the variable fileCount.

Variable names must begin with a letter (upper- or lowercase) or underscore character (_), and can be followed by any number of letters, digits (0-9), or underscore characters. You can't use a name that otherwise has a special meaning, such as the name of a command. Also, when talking to an application (see Chapter 10), you can't use a variable name that's part of that application's dictionary.

> *You actually can use a reserved word as a variable name, but the syntax is a little awkward. The method is described later in this section. So many words are significant AppleScript including command names, class names, operator names, and so on. Sometime the best way to see if a word has a special meaning is to type it into a statement in Script Editor and notice its color after compiling. If it's blue, it has a special meaning. If it's green, you can safely use it as a variable name in your program.*

Following are examples of valid variable names:

```
last_name        -- underscore characters are ok
lastName         -- some people prefer to capitalize words in a name
_errorMessage    -- can start with an underscore character
textFile101      -- can contain digit characters
```

Following are examples of invalid variable names for the stated reasons:

```
101textFile      -- can't start with a digit
set              -- can't use a command name
last name        -- can't contain spaces
myAccount$       -- can't use special characters
last-name        -- can't use dash, only underscore
```

When choosing names for your variables, don't be lazy. Pick names that reflect the intended use of the variables in your program. This helps make your program more self-documenting. That is, if the variable names are wisely-chosen, it's easier for you or someone else to figure out what's going on in your code. So it is much clearer if you write a statement like the following:

```
set fileCount to 0
```

than if you write a statement like

```
set i to 0
```

to express the intended use of this variable.

> *If you're used to programming in other languages like C++ or Java, you realize that you don't declare variables before they're used in a program; you simply assign a value to them when you want to use them. Also, variables do not have a particular type associated with them. That means you can store any type of data in a variable.*

Accessing the Value of a Variable and the get Command

After you've stored a value in a variable, you can subsequently retrieve its value using the get command, whose general format is shown here:

```
get variable
```

When this command is executed, the value of the specified variable is retrieved and substituted.

Variables have no default values in AppleScript, and they must be assigned a value before they can be used in an expression. If you don't assign a value to a variable but try to access its value, AppleScript gives you the error: "The variable `variable` is undefined."

In the next Try It Out, you set the value of a variable using the `set` command and then retrieve its value using the `get` command.

Try it Out   Working with Variables

These steps give you practice in working with variables.

1. Type the following program into Script Editor:

```
-- Working with variables

set myFirstVar to 1000
get myFirstVar
```

2. Click the Result tab and run the program. The following output should be displayed in the Result pane:

```
1000
```

How It Works

The first statement in the program stores the value 1000 in the variable `myFirstVar`. The next statement uses the `get` command to retrieve its value. Because this is the last statement executed in the program, it is the value of this statement that gets recorded in the Result pane.

The use of the keyword `get` is actually optional in almost all situations. In fact, most programmers don't use it. When AppleScript sees a variable used in a statement, it simply substitutes its value there, making the use of the keyword `get` superfluous.

The next Try It Out shows how the values of variables can be accessed without using the `get` command. It also illustrates the addition operator, which you can use to add two numbers.

Try It Out   More on Working with Variables

The following steps enable you to continue your practice with variables.

1. Type the following program into Script Editor:

```
-- More on working with variables

set a to 100
set b to 200
set sum to a + b
sum
```

2. Click the Result tab and run the program. The following output should be displayed in the Result pane:

```
300
```

How It Works

The following two statements set the values of the variables a and b to 100 and 200, respectively:

```
set a to 100
set b to 200
```

Next, the program adds the values stored inside these two variables, assigning the result to the variable sum. This is done with the following statement:

```
set sum to a + b
```

Note that you could have written this statement this way:

```
set sum to (get a) + (get b)
```

but nobody ever does that!

Finally, the program just lists the variable sum, which causes its value to be entered into the Result pane:

```
sum
```

As a point of information, you could have omitted this last statement and obtained the same result. That's because the value of the statement

```
set sum to a + b
```

is the result of the addition, which would appear in the Result pane anyway. Try it and see!

AppleScript does not distinguish uppercase from lowercase letters in variable names. So the following variable names are all considered the same:

```
currentDocument
CURRENTDOCUMENT
currentdocument
```

When Script Editor sees the variable used the first time in a script, it changes all subsequent spellings to that of the first use of the variable. This happens when you compile the script. In fact, if you open other windows in Script Editor, you can see that they use that same spelling in the other windows.

The following Try It Out helps illustrate these points.

Understanding Case in Variable Names

To help further your understanding of how case works in variable names, follow these steps:

1. In Script Editor, choose FileType ⇨ New and type the program exactly as shown in Figure 2-1.

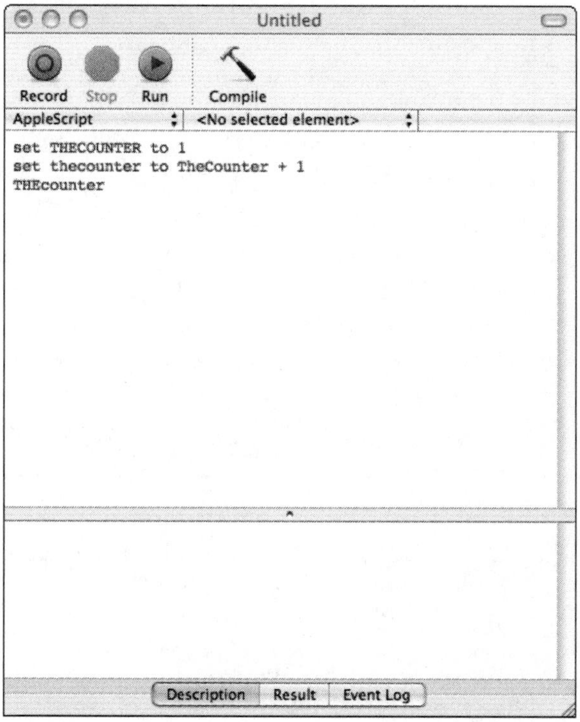

Figure 2-1

2. Run the program. Your window should look like Figure 2-2. Notice what happened to the upper- and lowercase letters in your variable name.

3. Choose File ⇨ New to create a new Editor window. Type the program into the window precisely as shown in Figure 2-3.

4. Run the program. Your window should look like Figure 2-4. Again, notice what happened to your variable name.

Figure 2-2

Figure 2-3

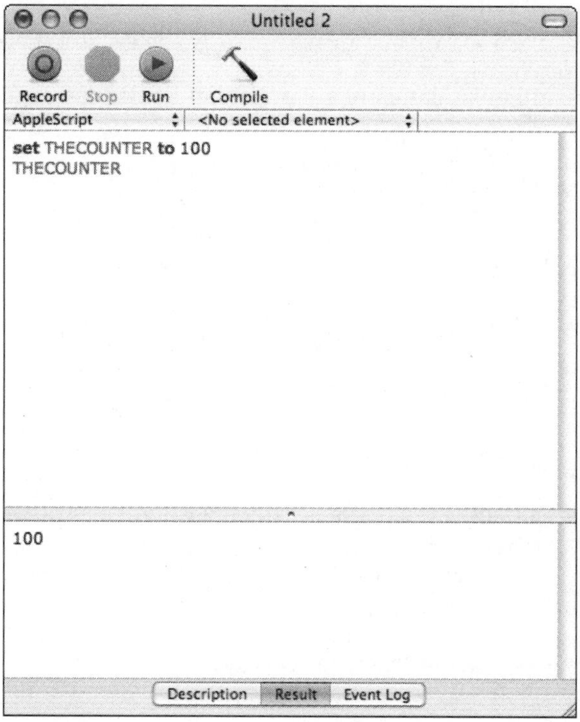

Figure 2-4

How It Works

The first time you used the variable THECOUNTER, you wrote it entirely in caps. Script Editor, therefore, changed all subsequent occurrences of that variable to all caps. When you opened a new script editor window and wrote the variable names thecounter and ThEcOuNtEr, Script Editor changed those to all caps as well when you compiled the program.

Don't get confused here, the variable is not shared across multiple windows, only its spelling. In other words, you couldn't set the value of THECOUNTER to 100 in one window and then access its value in another.

Writing Special Variable Names

AppleScript allows you to define variables that can contain any characters you like, including space characters, return characters, dollar signs, and so on. You define the variable by enclosing the variable name within a pair of vertical bar characters (|). All subsequent uses of that variable in the program must also specify the variable name within the vertical bar characters.

In the statement

```
set |greg's birth year| to 1996
```

the variable is `greg's birth year`. The vertical bars are needed because you're using three characters here (an apostrophe and two spaces) that are not normally allowed in variable names.

AppleScript does not perform its normal case conversion for variables defined with vertical bars. So these two statements define two different variables:

```
set abc to 100
set |ABC| to 200
```

You can use reserved words as variable names using the vertical bars, like so:

```
set |set| to 100
```

This sets the value of a variable called `set` to 100.

The Special result Variable

Every time you execute a statement, AppleScript stores the result of that statement—which could be the result of a command or the evaluation of an expression—inside a special variable called `result`. If the command does not produce a value, the value of `result` is undefined, which means you get an error if you subsequently try to access its value.

When you execute a program containing these two statements

```
pi * 100
result
```

the expression `pi * 100` is evaluated first. The result of the multiplication is then automatically stored in the special `result` variable. The second statement retrieves this value, which is then displayed in the Result pane.

Earlier in this chapter, I noted that if the statement

```
set sum to a + b
```

appears last in your program, you get the value of `sum` in the Result pane. That's because the value stored in the variable `sum` is also the result of the statement. So that's the value stored in the variable `result`.

Given the following two statements

```
set x to 100
set y to result + 200
```

the value assigned to `y` is 300. This represents the value of the `result` variable (which is set to 100 from the previous statement) added to the value 200.

The previous two-line program illustrates a serious pitfall when you use the `result` variable. If you add another statement to the program later, so that it looks like this:

```
set x to 100
set z to 500
set y to result + 200
```

the value assigned to `y` in this case is now `700`. This change might be an unintended side effect of adding that additional line to the program; it is easy to forget that the next statement depends on the previous statement. So, just be careful when you use the `result` variable in your program.

More on Commands and Statements

In this section, you learn more about commands, statements, and compound statements. You also learn about the Event Log, which is a valuable tool that allows you to trace a program's execution. It makes it easier for you to debug your programs — that is, to figure out what's going wrong.

Commands

A command is a reserved word in AppleScript (or in an application's dictionary) that asks for some action to be taken. Up to this point in the book, you have used four commands:

```
display dialog
set
get
beep
```

As you saw with the case of `display dialog`, sometimes a command takes optional *parameters* that alter the command's behavior. For example, the `display dialog` command accepts a parameter called `buttons` that is followed by a list of labels for the dialog's buttons.

Statements

A *statement* is just a single line of code in AppleScript that contains one or more commands or expressions. The line may extend over several physical lines in your editor window if it is very long (or if you make your Script Editor window very narrow!). As I noted in Chapter 1, statements are automatically continued on subsequent lines if necessary. These continuation lines are automatically indented for you so you know they belong to the previous line. In Chapter 1, you learned that you can break a line by pressing Option-Return at the end of any line that you want to continue on the following line. This puts the special character ¬ at the end of the line to tell you that the line is being continued.

Compound Statements

As you learn in Chapter 3, statements that span more than a single line and have the capability to contain any number of other statements are called *compound* statements. All compound statements are terminated by the keyword `end`, followed by the name of the compound statement.

As an example of a compound statement, the following code tests whether a variable `count` is equal to `100` and displays a message if it is. Don't try to fully understand how this works; I show it here only to illustrate a compound statement:

```
if count is equal to 100 then
    display dialog "Count equals 100"
end if
```

The name of this compound statement is `if`. It contains one other statement, which executes a `display dialog` command. This statement is indented from the left margin to visually indicate to you that it is part of the compound `if` statement. Additional statements could follow the `display dialog`, but in this example, only one such statement is shown.

The compound `if` statement is terminated by a line containing the reserved word `end`, followed by the statement name, which is `if`. Script Editor makes it easy for you to key in compound statements. All statements that are part of the compound statement are automatically indented for you when you compile the statement. And you can terminate any compound statement by typing `end`; Script Editor automatically fills in the statement's name when the program is compiled. Therefore, you can type the previous compound statement into Script Editor like this:

```
if count is equal to 100 then
display dialog "Count equals 100"
end
```

The indentation and the completion of the `end` to `end if` are done automatically.

The log Command and the Event Log

You have seen how useful it is to see the result of your last operation in the Script Editor's Result pane. However, when you're trying to get all the kinks out of your programs, you may want to see what's happening *inside* the program. You want to see the results of variables and operations throughout your program's execution, not just at the end. As shown in the following Try It Out, that's where the Event Log comes into play.

Try It Out   **Using the Event Log**

Follow these steps to practice using the Event Log.

1.   Type the following program into Script Editor:

```
-- Illustrate the log command and the Event Log

log "Put this into the log."
log "And then put this in as well."
log 100 -- Log an integer
log 100 * pi -- And the result of an expression

set x to 100
log x -- log the value of a variable
```

2.   Click the Event Log tab at the bottom of the window. Make sure this tab is highlighted and then run your program. You should see the following results in the lower pane of your window:

```
  (*Put this into the log.*)
 (*And then put this in as well.*)
 (*100*)
 (*314.159265358979*)
 (*100*)
```

How It Works

Script Editor maintains a special log of your program's execution. This is called the Event Log. Certain actions (that you learn about later) automatically add entries to the log. In addition, you can use the `log` command to put anything you want into the log. Each time you execute the `log` command, the specified value that follows is added as a new line to the log, delimited by the characters (* and *).

The program first adds two strings to the log with these statements:

```
log "Put this into the log."
log "And then put this in as well."
```

Notice that the double quotes are not displayed when a string is entered into the log:

```
(*Put this into the log.*)
(*And then put this in as well.*)
```

Next, the program logs the value 100, followed by the result of multiplying 100 by the value of `pi`:

```
log 100 -- Log an integer
log 100 * pi -- And the result of an expression
```

This results in the following two lines being added to the Event Log:

```
(*100*)
(*314.159265358979*)
```

The last statement in the program shows how you can log the value of a variable, which is a very useful feature. The statement

```
log x -- log the value of a variable
```

adds the value of the variable x, which was previously set to 100, to the log. You can see how this feature might come in handy if you are debugging a program and want to know the values of your variables during your program's execution. By interspersing `log` commands throughout the program, you can get a peek into the program's execution and the intermediate values assigned to your variables.

It's important to always make sure the Event Log tab is highlighted before you run your program by clicking the tab if necessary. Otherwise, the Event Log pane will not be updated.

Not only can you log the results of your program's execution, but you can also save those results in a place known as the Event Log History. The Event Log History, which you work with in the following Try It Out, is useful when you want to go back and examine the results you obtained from prior runs of your program.

Chapter 2

Try It Out **Using the Event Log History**

To practice working with the Event Log History, follow these steps:

1. Type the program from the previous Try it Out ("Using the Event Log").

2. Choose Script Editor ➪ Preferences, and you should see a window like the one shown in Figure 2-5 (you may see a different window if you've set Preferences before).

Figure 2-5

3. Click History to open a window like the one shown in Figure 2-6 (your current settings may differ from those shown).

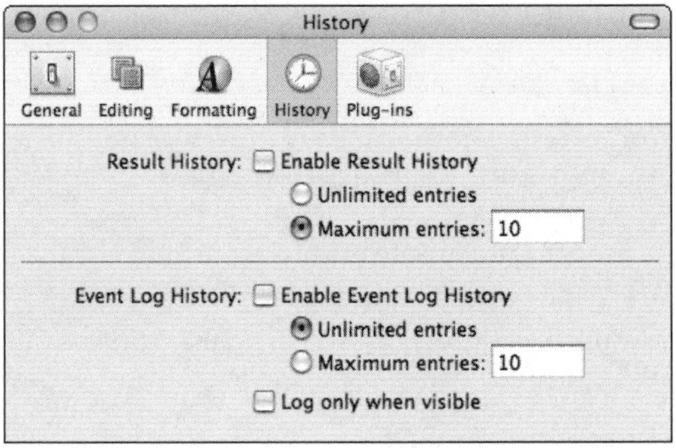

Figure 2-6

4. Click to place a check mark in the Enable Event Log History box.

5. Click the Maximum Entries button. The number 10 should be in the text box. A different number is displayed if you've changed it before.

6. Close the History window.

7. Run the program you typed in Step 1 three times in succession.

8. Choose Window ➪ Event Log History. You should see a window like the one shown in Figure 2-7. If your window differs significantly from the figure, make sure that the option Log Events and Results is selected in the drop-down box at the top of the window. If it isn't, select that option and return to the previous step.

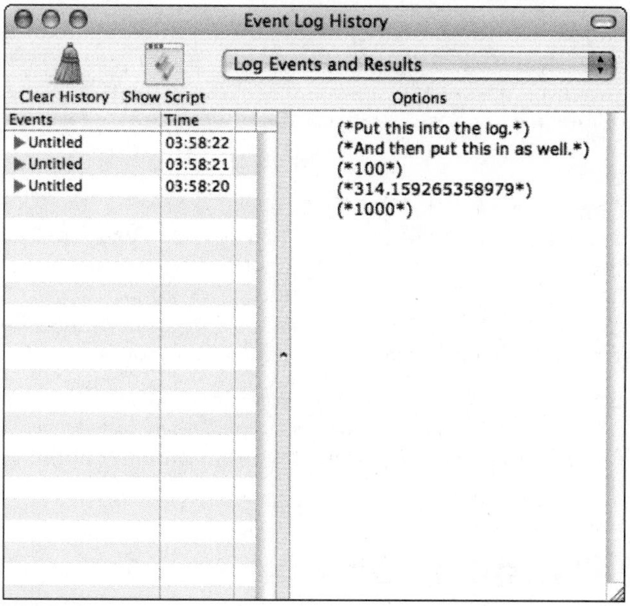

Figure 2-7

9. Click the first right-pointing arrow ▶ that appears in front of Untitled in the left pane. Your window should now look like Figure 2-8.

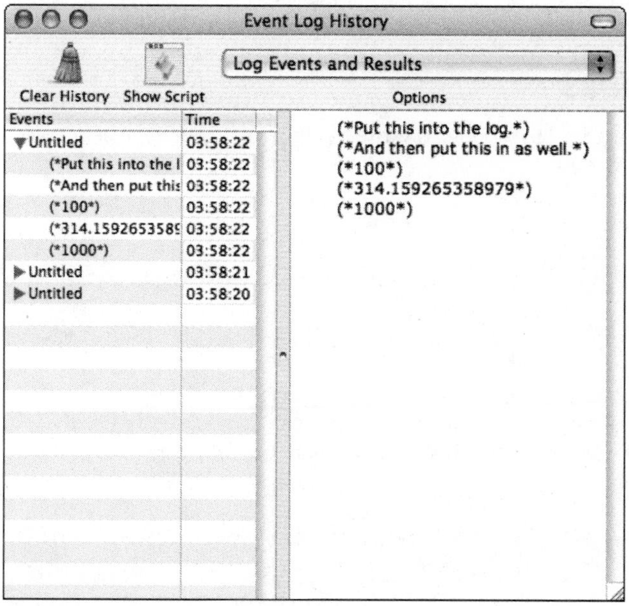

Figure 2-8

How It Works

The Event Log History keeps track of previous executions of your program. This can come in handy when you need to look back at what happened in the past. You can specify the maximum number of entries you want to store in the history, or you can specify that the log be of unlimited size (which is not recommended).

When you click the right arrow ▶ in the Events pane, you see precisely when an event was logged. This is not useful to you now, but it can be handy when you develop more sophisticated programs and work with other applications.

> *As your programs get larger, you may also want to check the Log Only When Visible option in the History window (see Figure 2-6) so the log is updated only when the Event Log History window is open.*

> *For a more sophisticated approach to debugging applications, you should investigate the Script Debugger application from Late Night Software, Ltd. This application lets you trace through a program's execution, insert break points, and monitor the values of variables. For more information, consult Appendix C.*

Basic Data Type Classes

AppleScript has built-in support for some basic data types that enable you to easily work with numbers, true/false values, strings, and dates in your programs. Many of these *classes* are described in the following sections. Lists and records are covered in detail in Chapter 6.

> *When I use the term* data type *or just* type *in this book, I'm referring to the class. For example, when I use* integer data type *and* integer type, *these terms are synonymous with the term* integer *class.*

The string Class

In Chapter 1, you learned that you can write a string by enclosing a sequence of characters inside a pair of double quotes, like this:

```
"Programming in AppleScript is fun."
```

It makes sense that you can assign such a literal character string to a variable in your program, like so:

```
set myFirstMessage to "Programming in AppleScript is fun."
```

This statement has the effect of storing the literal character string `"Programming in AppleScript is fun."` inside the variable `myFirstMessage`. You can subsequently use this variable in situations where a string is required. For example, this program produces the same output as your second program in Chapter 1:

```
set myFirstMessage to "Programming in AppleScript is fun."
display dialog myFirstMessage
```

Here the string you stored inside the variable `myFirstMessage` in the first statement of the program is given to the `display dialog` command to be displayed. It's as if you typed the literal string right on the `display dialog` command line.

An entire chapter, Chapter 5, is devoted to teaching you all about strings.

The Integer Class

An integer is a value without any decimal places. If you were counting the number of files in a folder, for example, you would use an integer.

You write a literal integer constant as a sequence of digits 0-9, optionally preceded by a minus sign.

You can place a plus sign in front of an integer constant if you like (as in +100), but it gets removed anyway when you compile your script.

Integer values can be in the range of $-(2^{29} - 1)$ to $(2^{29} - 1)$, or from -536870911 to 536870911. If you write an integer constant outside of this range, AppleScript changes it to a real number (see the next section).

The following are examples of integer constants:

```
100
-933
32767
0
```

The following are not integer constants for the stated reasons:

```
100.25      -- integers don't contain decimals
100.0       -- still not an integer because of decimal point
100.        -- ditto (and gets changed to 100.0 after compiling)
1000000000  -- Greater than 229-1, so gets changed to a real number
```

Small and Double Integer Classes

When you're working with other applications, you may find references to `small integer` or `double integer` types. Technically, AppleScript uses four bytes (32 bits) internally to store integer values. A `small integer` is stored in 16 bits, whereas a `double integer` is stored in 64 bits. AppleScript treats `small integer` values as integers in your program, and it treats `double integer` values as real numbers.

The real Class

A *real* number can contain decimal places, even if they're all zero.

You write a literal real number by writing an optional plus or minus sign, followed by a sequence of zero or more digits, followed by a decimal point and a sequence of zero or more digits. At least one digit must appear (either before or after the decimal point).

You can also express a real number in *scientific notation*. To do that, you write a number followed immediately by the letter e or E, followed by an optionally signed number, called the *exponent*. The number before the letter E (known as the *mantissa*) is raised to the power of 10 specified by the exponent.

These are examples of valid literal real numbers:

```
100.25
-933.
-7.995e+15
0.0
1.23e-3     -- gets changed to this after compiling: .00123
```

Be advised that when your script is compiled, AppleScript sometimes converts numbers typed in scientific notation to real numbers without exponents and vice versa. For example,

```
1.23e-3
```

is changed to

```
0.00123
```

And if you type the number

```
.001
```

it is changed after compilation to

```
1.0E-3
```

AppleScript also changes a lowercase e to an uppercase E, inserts a sign before the exponent (if one wasn't typed), and *normalizes* the mantissa (that is, makes sure that just one digit appears before the decimal point).

So when you type

```
455.66e5
```

you end up with this after compilation:

```
4.5566E+7
```

A real variable can store a value in the range from $-1.797693 \times 10^{308}$ to 1.797693×10^{308}.

The Boolean Class

A Boolean value is either true or false. You use Boolean variables in programs when you want to store an on/off, yes/no, or true/false condition in a variable. Some types of expressions also produce Boolean results. For example, if you compare two numbers in AppleScript, the result is a Boolean value, or a value that is either true or false.

The following Try It Out gives you some practice in working with Boolean values.

Understanding Boolean Values

These steps help you understand the Boolean class.

1. Type the following program into Script Editor:

```
-- Boolean values and expressions

set bool to true
log bool

set bool to false
log bool

set bool to not bool
log bool

log 100 is less than 200    -- comparison
```

2. Click the Event Log tab and run the program. You should see the following displayed in the Event Log pane:

```
(*true*)
(*false*)
(*true*)
(*true*)
```

How It Works

The program begins by assigning the value true to the variable bool as follows:

```
set bool to true
```

AppleScript defines the keywords true and false as built-in constants. That means you can use them in any programs where you want to assign or test for these values. As you can see from the log's output, the value logged for bool is true

> *Unlike some other programming languages that treat nonzero values as* true *and zero values as* false, *AppleScript maintains this separate Boolean class distinct from a numeric class. However, you can coerce Boolean values into integers and vice versa, as you see in the next section.*

In the next two statements in the program the value false is first assigned to bool and then its value is logged. Here, the built-in constant false is used in the assignment:

```
set bool to false
log bool
```

In the next set of statements, the logical negation operator not is introduced. It is a *unary* operator, meaning that it operates on a single value. The not operator is followed by a Boolean expression, and the result of the operation is to turn a true value into a false value and vice versa.

In the program, the value of `bool` has been previously set to `false`, so the statement

```
set bool to not bool
```

will "flip" its value or set it to `true`. This is verified by the output added to the log.

The last statement in the program is put there as a preview to Chapter 3. As noted at the start of this section, comparisons in AppleScript produce a Boolean result. The expression

```
100 is less than 200
```

uses the relational operator `is less than` (which can be equivalently written with the less than symbol `<`) to test if the first value (`100`) is less than the second value (`200`). The result of the comparison is a true/false value. In this case, because `100` is, in fact, less than `200`, the result is `true`, and that value is logged.

The class Command

The `class` command is used for determining the class of the value stored in a variable or of the result of evaluating an expression. This is useful when you want to test a value to make sure it belongs to a particular class so that you can avoid potential errors from occurring when your program is running.

The `class` command is also very helpful when debugging programs. You can use it to check the class of a value stored in a variable, the class of a value returned by a command, or the class of a value produced by an expression.

The `class` command is followed by the keyword `of` (or `in`) and the value whose class you want to determine. So, given the following statement

```
class of 100
```

the result is the class name `integer` because that's the class of the literal number `100`.

Work through the following Try It Out to get some practice using the `class` command.

Try It Out   Using the Class Command

These steps show you how you can use the `class` command to determine the class of different data types.

1. Type the following program into Script Editor:

```
-- Illustrate the class command

log class of 100
log class of 100.25
log class of true
log class of "Programming in AppleScript is fun."

set x to 100
log class of x
```

2. Click the Event Log tab and run the program. You should see the following results in the Event Log pane:

```
(*integer*)
(*real*)
(*boolean*)
(*string*)
(*integer*)
```

How It Works

The output from this program should be self-explanatory. The program uses the `class` command directly on a literal integer, real number, Boolean value, and character string. The output in the log verifies the correct class identifications. In the last case, the integer `100` is first assigned to the variable x; then the `class` command is executed on x:

```
set x to 100
log class of x
```

Because x contains an `integer` value, it should come as no surprise that `integer` is returned by the `class` command.

Basic Data Type Conversions

AppleScript allows you to freely store different types of data in your variables. As a result, it is good programming practice to always know what type of value you have stored in a variable at any point in time. Does the variable contain an integer, a real, a string, or perhaps a date? The answer to this question determines how you can use the variable in expressions and pass its value as an argument to a command.

Some AppleScript commands automatically convert values for you. For example, the `display dialog` command displays the string specified after the command in a dialog:

```
display dialog "Programming in AppleScript is fun."
```

What you may not know is that the following works as well:

```
display dialog 100
```

and produces the output shown in Figure 2-9.

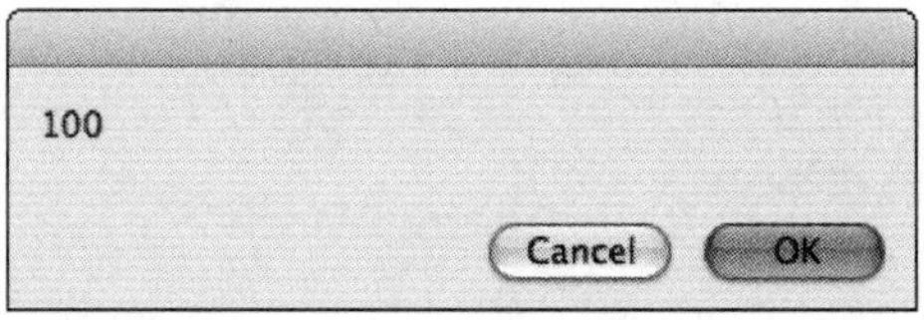

Figure 2-9

Here, the `display dialog` command sees an `integer` as its argument and, realizing that, converts it to a `string` to be displayed. The `display dialog` command does the conversion for you. Although that may work in this case, in similar cases with other commands, it may not. It's usually better to know what types of values your commands expect and not to rely on the command to do the conversions for you. If you make sure that you provide the correct types, you can avoid problems that might occur when a command cannot or does not perform the correct conversions for you.

Coercing a Data Type Using the as Operator

You can explicitly convert one data type to another in your program. You do this, when it makes sense, by using the `as` operator. The basic format of this operator is as follows:

```
value as class
```

Here, the specified `value` is converted to the specified `class`. If `value` is a variable, the value in the variable is retrieved and converted to the specified class, leaving the value stored inside the variable unaltered.

In AppleScript terminology, a value that is converted from one data type to another is said to have been coerced.

A program example is the best way to see how the `as` operator works. The following Try It Out lets you see the `as` operator in action.

Try It Out   **Basic Data Type Conversions with the as Operator**

Follow these steps to use the `as` operator to convert `integers`, `reals`, `strings`, and `Boolean` values.

1. Type the following program into Script Editor:

```
-- Conversions using the "as" operator

set R to 100.25
set I to 9800
set B to true
set S to "  15.387"

-- real to integer conversion

set O to R as integer
log O

-- integer to real conversion

set O to I as real
log O

-- integer to string
```

```
set O to I as string
log O
log class of O

-- real to string

set O to R as string
log O

-- string to number conversion

set O to S as real
log O
set O to S as number  -- Can be either an integer or real
log O

-- boolean to integer

set O to B as integer
log O

set O to (not B) as integer
log O

-- integer to boolean

set O to 0 as Boolean
log O
set O to 1 as Boolean
log O

-- boolean to string

set O to B as string
log O
```

2. Click the Event Log tab and run the program. You get the following output:

```
(*100*)
(*9800.0*)
(*9800*)
(*string*)
(*100.25*)
(*15.387*)
(*15.387*)
(*1*)
(*0*)
(*false*)
(*true*)
(*true*)
```

How It Works

When you write a statement like this in your program:

```
set O to R as integer
```

AppleScript attempts to coerce the value stored in the specified variable into the particular class, which in this case is `integer`. Previously, R has been set to the real number 100.25. When converting a real number to an `integer`, the number is rounded before it is coerced into an `integer`. You should understand how rounding works in AppleScript. This is particularly important for the *borderline* cases where the value is 0.5 or a multiple thereof. When AppleScript rounds one of these values, it *rounds to the next even* `integer`. This is done to minimize the accumulation of errors that can occur when many values get rounded. The following table shows examples of real numbers and their rounded `integer` values.

Real Number	Coerced Integer Value
100.25	100
100.5	100
100.6	101
101.25	101
101.5	102
101.6	102

Notice that the value 100.5 gets rounded down to 100, whereas the value 101.5 gets rounded up to 102. This conforms to the previously described rounding strategy. If you need all your numbers rounded in the same direction, use the `round` command, which I describe shortly.

Returning to your program, you can see that real numbers are readily converted to `integers`, and either `reals` or `integers` can be converted to `strings`. This latter information is useful for commands that take `strings` as arguments. So, the following sequence is illustrative (if not very practical):

```
set maxFiles to 1000
display dialog (maxFiles as string)
```

The `integer` value of `1000` that is stored in `maxFiles` is coerced into a `string` and then passed to the `display dialog` command. (The parentheses around the expression `maxFiles as string` are not required.)

As previously discussed, this would work as well:

```
display dialog maxFiles
```

In the first case, you're doing the coercion yourself. In the second case, you're relying on `display dialog` to do it for you. In general, the first method is the preferred method.

When you convert the `integer` stored in I to a `string` using

```
set O to I as string
```

and then subsequently log its value, the following is entered into the log:

```
(*9800*)
```

Recall that the `log` command does not put double quotes around `strings` that are logged. So the next statement in the program logs the class of `O`:

```
log class of O
```

You can see that `string` gets logged, which verifies that `O` does in fact contain a `string`.

The number Class

The next six statements in the program demonstrate coercion of strings into numbers:

```
set O to S as real
log O
set O to S as number  -- Can be either an integer or real
log O
```

The first `set` statement says to look in the string `S` and to convert it to a real number. The string can have any number of leading spaces, but it must have a valid number or AppleScript generates an error. Because you previously set the value of `S` with the statement

```
set S to "  15.387"
```

AppleScript converts the string in `S` to the real number 15.387, which is then stored by the program in the variable `O`. Note that the following would generate an error

```
set O to S as integer
```

because `S`, in this case, does not contain a valid `integer` number. You can always convert to `real` if you're not sure if the number is an `integer`, but it still must contain a valid number to avoid an error. Alternatively, you can use the class name `number`, as an *umbrella* class for the classes `integer` and `real`. When you write this statement in your program

```
set O to S as number -- Can be either an integer or real
```

AppleScript looks at the specified `string` and converts it to either an `integer` or `real`, depending on the value it finds (its magnitude and format). In this case, the result of 15.387 is stored as a real number in the variable `O`. Remember, the coerced value does not belong to the class `number`; it's either a `real` or an `integer`.

You can see from the program that it's okay to coerce Boolean values into integers and vice versa. A `true` value gets coerced into the integer 1, and a `false` value gets coerced into the integer 0. In the other direction, an `integer` value of 1 gets coerced into the Boolean value `true`, and an `integer` value of 0 gets coerced into the Boolean value `false`. If you try to coerce an `integer` value other than 0 or 1 (or try to coerce a noninteger), you get an AppleScript error when you run the program.

The last two statements in the program show coercion of a `Boolean` to a `string`:

```
set O to B as string
log O
```

Again, even though the log output doesn't show the double quotes, when the value stored in B (which is s) gets converted to a `string`, the result is the string `"true"`.

The round Command

The `round` command is useful for converting real numbers to integers using rounding methods other than the one previously described. The optional rounding parameter to this command determines the direction of the rounding operation. These parameters are summarized in the following table.

Rounding Parameter	Meaning
rounding up	round to next largest integer
rounding down	round to next smallest integer
rounding toward zero	round toward zero
rounding to nearest	round to nearest integer, round .5 to nearest even integer
rounding as taught in school	round .5 away from zero

If a rounding parameter is not specified with the `round` command, `rounding to nearest` is used by default (which, as previously noted, is how AppleScript coerces a real number into an `integer`).

The following shows how some numbers are rounded using the `round` command with its various parameters:

```
round 1.5                                  -- 2
round 1.25 rounding up                     -- 2
round 1.25 rounding down                   -- 1
round 1.25 rounding toward zero            -- 1
round 1.5 rounding to nearest              -- 2
round 1.5 rounding as taught in school     -- 2

round 2.5                                  -- 2
round 2.25 rounding up                     -- 3
round 2.25 rounding down                   -- 2
round 2.25 rounding toward zero            -- 2
round 2.5 rounding to nearest              -- 2
round 2.5 rounding as taught in school     -- 2

round -1.5                                 -- -2
round -1.25 rounding up                    -- -1
round -1.25 rounding down                  -- -2
round -1.25 rounding toward zero           -- -1
round -1.5 rounding to nearest             -- -2
round -1.5 rounding as taught in school    -- -2
```

Arithmetic Operators and Expressions

AppleScript supports the basic operations of addition, subtraction, multiplication, and division. Several other operations are also supported, as you learn in the following Try It Out.

Try It Out   **Understanding Arithmetic Operations**

Follow these steps to get some practice with arithmetic operations.

1. Type the following program into Script Editor:

```
-- Basic arithmetic operations

set a to 10
set b to 3
set c to 25
set d to 4

log -a     -- negation
log a + b -- addition
log a - b -- subtraction
log a * b -- multiplication
log a / b -- division
log a div b -- integer division
log a mod b -- remainder
log a ^ b -- exponentiation

-- operator precedence

log a + b * c
log a * b + c * d
log a * (b + c) * d -- parentheses
log a ^ -b * c

log 100 mod 10 div 3
```

2. Click the Event Log tab and run the program. You get the following results in the lower pane:

```
(*-10*)
(*13*)
(*7*)
(*30*)
(*3.333333333333*)
(*3*)
(*1*)
(*1000.0*)
(*85*)
(*130*)
(*1120*)
(*0.025*)
(*0*)
```

How It Works

The following table summarizes AppleScript's arithmetic operators.

Operator	Meaning	Type of Result
–	unary minus	integer or real
^	exponentiation	real
*	multiplication	integer or real
/	division	real
div	integer division	integer
mod	integer remainder	integer or real
+	addition	integer or real
–	subtraction	integer or real

All operators except the unary minus operator are *binary* operators, meaning that they operate on two values, one listed before and the other after the operator. The unary minus operator is followed by the value you want to negate. The operators are ordered in the table by operator *precedence*, which is described shortly.

The program begins by assigning arbitrary values to the four variables a, b, c, and d:

```
set a to 10
set b to 3
set c to 25
set d to 4
```

The program then executes statements to exercise the various arithmetic operators. Following are these statements shown with the output from the Event Log pasted onto the corresponding line as a comment:

```
log -a          -- -10
log a + b       -- 13
log a - b       -- 7
log a * b       -- 30
log a / b       -- 3.333333333333
log a div b     -- 3
log a mod b     -- 1
log a ^ b       -- 1000.0
```

The result of each operation is straightforward. If two `integers` are added, subtracted, or multiplied, the result is an `integer`. However, if the result is too large (or too small) to be represented as an `integer`, the result is a `real`. If either or both of the operands are `reals`, the result is always a `real`.

In the case of the division operator /, a normal division operation is performed and the decimal places in the result are retained. The result is always a `real` data type. In the program, a is divided by b, or 10 is divided by 3. The result is logged as 3 followed by a long string of 3's. All those 3's are there because the computer can't exactly represent the fraction 1/3 internally. You've seen this happen on calculators when you perform similar types of operations.

The `div` operator is also used to divide two numbers. AppleScript converts both numbers to `integers` (if they're not already `integers`), performs the division, and discards any fractional remainder. The result is always an `integer`. In the program, the expression `10 div 3` produces an `integer` result of 3, as verified by the log.

The modulus operator `mod` gives the remainder after one number is divided by another. It can be used with either `integer` or `real` numbers. In the program, the remainder after dividing 10 by 3 is 1, as indicated by the output. One frequent use of the modulus operator is to test whether one `integer` is evenly divisible by another. In Chapter 3, for example, you see how to test if a number is even or odd by determining if there is a remainder after the number is divided by 2. So the expression

```
testNumber mod 2
```

produces a result of 0 if `testNumber` is even. A nonzero result (which has to be 1) indicates the number is odd. As noted, you can use the `mod` operator with real numbers as well as integers. So when you write the expression

```
100.22 mod .25
```

you get the remainder after dividing `100.22` by `.25`, which is `.22`.

The exponentiation operator `^` is used to raise a number to a power. The number is specified first, followed by the `^` operator, followed by the power to which you want the number raised. In the program, you raise the value of a, which is `10`, to the power of b, which is `3`. The result of 10^3, or 1000, is then entered into the log. Notice that the result of exponentiation is always a real number.

Operator Precedence

The following statements in the program introduce the notion of operator precedence. The precedence of an operator determines how an expression is ordered for evaluation when more than one operator is used. In the previous table of operators, the operators are listed from top to bottom in order of decreasing precedence. Operators listed together in the same box (like + and –) have the same precedence.

When you write this statement in your program:

```
log a + b * c
```

AppleScript compares the precedence of the + operator to that of the * operator. Because the latter operator has higher precedence than the former operator (that is, the * is listed above the + in the table), the expression

```
a + b * c
```

gets evaluated like this:

```
a + (b * c)
```

The multiplication of b and c is performed first and the result is then added to a.

In a similar way, the statement

```
log a * b + c * d
```

logs the result of evaluating the expression this way:

```
(a * b) + (c * d)
```

Of course, you can always use parentheses to override operator precedence, as in the program's next statement:

```
log a * (b + c) * d  -- parentheses
```

In the statement that follows next in the program

```
log a ^ -b * c
```

the unary minus has highest precedence, followed by the exponentiation operator, followed in turn by the multiplication operator. So the expression gets evaluated like this:

```
(a ^ -b) * c
```

Because the mod and div operators have the same precedence, it's not clear how this statement from the program will be evaluated:

```
log 100 mod 10 div 3
```

When you encounter two operators in an expression that have the same precedence, the notion of operator *associativity* comes into play. This property determines whether operators of the same precedence associate from left to right or from right to left. For example, multiplication and division have the same precedence. Those two operators, plus the other two having the same precedence (mod and div) associate from left to right. That means this expression

```
a * b / c mod d div e
```

is evaluated like this:

```
(((a * b) / c) mod d) div e)
```

The addition and subtraction operators also have the same precedence and also associate left to right, so the following expression

```
a - b + c
```

is evaluated left to right like this:

```
(a - b) + c
```

Finally, the exponentiation operator — even though it's by itself in terms of precedence — associates right to left, meaning this expression

```
2 ^ 3 ^ 4
```

is evaluated like this:

```
2 ^ (3 ^ 4)
```

In this case, AppleScript even inserts the parentheses for you to tell you how it will evaluate the expression.

Refer to the table in Appendix B for a list of the associativity property for all the operators.

Rather than relying on your knowledge of operator precedence and associativity, it's better to just freely use parentheses in any complicated expressions you write, particularly if it may be unclear to you how an expression will be evaluated.

The Date Class

AppleScript is unique with its special class for working with dates. You can store dates inside variables in your program and then manipulate those dates to find things such as the number of days between two dates, the day of the week a particular day falls on, or a list of files created within the last seven days.

The general format for a date in AppleScript is as follows:

Weekday, Month day, year hh:mm:ss ampm

where

Weekday	is the day of the week, with possible values of Sunday, Monday, Tuesday, Wednesday, Thursday, Friday, or Saturday
Month	is the month of the year, with possible values of January, February, March, April, May, June, July, August, September, October, November, or December
day	is the day number, with values from 1 through 31
year	is the four-digit year number
hh:mm:ss	is the time expressed in hours, minutes, and seconds
ampm	is AM, PM, or omitted if a 24-hour clock is being used

The following Try It Out gives you some practice in working with the format of a date in AppleScript.

Try It Out   **Understanding the Date Format**

Follow these steps to work with the date format.

1. Type the following program into Script Editor:

```
current date
```

2. Click the Result tab and run the program. Your result should look like the following except that your date will reflect when you run the program:

```
date "Wednesday, September 22, 2004 6:29:10 PM"
```

If you have your International settings under System Preferences set to use a 24-hour clock (which you do by setting 24-hour clock under Personal ⇨ International ⇨ Formats ⇨ Times ⇨ Customize), the output from the program will not show an AM or PM indication, but a 24-hour time like this:

```
date "Wednesday, September 22, 2004 18:29:10"
```

The output you get also reflects your regional settings. For example, with the Region set to France (French under Personal ⇨ International ⇨ Formats), the output from this program looks like this:

```
date "mercredi 22 septembre 2004 18:29:10"
```

Unless otherwise noted, the remaining examples in this chapter assume you have set your clock to a 12-hour clock and the region is the United States.

How It Works

AppleScript's `current date` command can be used in a program to obtain the current date and time. The date and time returned reflects the date and time that the command was executed. You can assign the value to a variable if you like, as you learn to do in the next section.

Getting Date Properties

You can get direct access to various fields or attributes of a date value. These are known as *properties*. You access a property of a value by writing the following expression in AppleScript:

```
property of value
```

You are also permitted to substitute the word `in` for `of`, but most people tend to use `of`.

In the following Try It Out, you practice getting the properties for a `date` value.

Try It Out   **Getting the Properties of a Date**

In the following steps, you first store the current date and time in a variable and then access and log its properties.

1. Type the following program into Script Editor:

```
-- Get various properties of a date

set D to current date

log weekday of D
log month of D
log day of D
log year of D
log time of D

-- these are strings

log date string of D
log time string of D
log short date string of D
```

2. Click the Event Log tab and run the program. The output in your Event Log pane should be similar to what's shown, except it is based on the date and time you run the program.

```
tell current application
    current date
        date "Thursday, July 22, 2004 7:02:17 PM"
    (*Thursday*)
    (*July*)
    (*22*)
    (*2004*)
    (*68537*)
    (*Thursday, July 22, 2004*)
    (*7:02:17 PM*)
    (*7/22/04*)
end tell
```

How It Works

The properties that you can obtain from a date value are summarized in the following table.

Property	Value
weekday	day of the week (Sunday – Saturday)
month	month of the year (January – December)
day	day of the month (1 – 31)
year	four digit year number
time	integer time in seconds since midnight
date string	string in the format "Weekday, Month day, year" or a different format depending on the International settings in System Preferences
time string	string in the format "hh:mm:ss AM or PM" or a different format depending on the 24-hour clock and Region settings in System Preferences
short date string	string in the format "mm/dd/yyyy" or a different format depending on the International settings in System Preferences

The program starts by assigning the current date to the variable D in the program using the following statement:

```
set D to current date
```

As you can see from the log, this was the current date and time when the program was run:

```
date "Thursday, July 22, 2004 7:02:17 PM"
```

This line was added to the log for you, even though you didn't explicitly log the value of D. You can also see that the line tell current application *appears at the beginning of the log, and the line* end tell *appears at the end of the log. You did not directly add these lines. Just ignore these lines for now. They make sense later when you learn about the* tell *statement in Chapter 10.*

After storing the current date in the variable D, various properties are extracted from the date stored in D and are logged. A couple of points are worth noting:

❑ The weekday property of a date (in this example, Thursday), and the month property of a date (in this example, July), *are not strings*. They are actually *classes*. You can convert them to strings if you need to, and I show you how to do that shortly.

❑ Even if you have your International settings set to Français, for example, the weekday property always returns a value (from Sunday through Saturday) in English. Likewise, the month property always returns a value (from January through December) in English.

❑ You can extract a property directly from the current date, for example by writing an expression like this:

```
weekday of (current date)
```

The parentheses are required here to tell AppleScript that the of operator applies to the result of the command current date (and not just to the word current). Realize that every time you use current date in an expression, it will be reevaluated. So if you use it more than once in your program, the date may actually change if your program crosses midnight while it's executing! That's a good motivation for capturing the current date in a variable first and then using the value of that variable.

When you get the time property from D, you get the integer value 70326 returned. This represents the time expressed as the number of seconds since midnight. Because there are 60 seconds in a minute, and 60 minutes in an hour, or 3600 seconds in an hour, the expression

```
(time of D) div 3600
```

gets the hour number from the date D. Obtaining the minutes and seconds are left as exercises for you to work on at the end of this chapter.

Setting Date Properties

You can set the weekday, month, day, year, and time properties of a date in your program using the set command. When performing date calculations in the past or future, or setting the time property, you should do all your work in seconds. To make things a little easier for you, AppleScript defines the values listed in the following table.

Property	Value
minutes	60
hours	3600
days	86400
weeks	604800

These values represent the corresponding time in seconds: 60 seconds in a minute, 3600 seconds in an hour, 86400 seconds in a day, and 604800 seconds in a week. You can see how they're used in the following Try It Outs.

Try It Out   Setting Date Properties

The following steps show you how to set the properties of a date.

1.   Type the following program into Script Editor:

```
-- Set various properties of a date

set D to current date

set weekday of D to Friday -- this doesn't do anything
log D

set month of D to February
log D

set day of D to 1
log D

set year of D to 2007
log D

set time of D to 12 * hours + 30 * minutes
log D

-- set complete dates

set D to date "12/17/2006"  -- can use this format
log D

set D to date "12/17/2006 5:35 PM"  -- can specify a time too
log D

set D to date "December 17"  -- of this year
log D

set D to date "10:40 PM"  -- of today
log D
```

2. Compile the program. Notice what happens to the last four dates you keyed into the program.

3. Click the Event Log tab and run the program. You see output similar to the following. Your output may differ slightly because your program is run on a different date and at a different time.

```
tell current application
    current date
        date "Thursday, July 22, 2004 8:12:32 PM"
    (*Thursday, July 22, 2004 8:12:32 PM*)
    (*Sunday, February 22, 2004 8:12:32 PM*)
    (*Sunday, February 1, 2004 8:12:32 PM*)
    (*Thursday, February 1, 2007 8:12:32 PM*)
    (*Thursday, February 1, 2007 12:30:00 PM*)
    (*Sunday, December 17, 2006 12:00:00 AM*)
    (*Sunday, December 17, 2006 5:35:00 PM*)
    (*Friday, December 17, 2004 12:00:00 AM*)
    (*Thursday, July 22, 2004 10:40:00 PM*)
end tell
```

How It Works

When you set a property of a date, it has to make sense. It never makes sense to set the weekday property. The current date in this program example is logged as

```
date "Thursday, July 22, 2004 8:12:32 PM"
```

So attempting to set the weekday of this date to Friday with the following statement

```
set weekday of D to Friday -- this doesn't do anything
```

results in AppleScript simply ignoring the statement, and no error message is provided. July 22, 2004, falls on a Thursday; therefore, you cannot set it to Friday.

The program subsequently sets the month, day and year properties of D to February 1, 2007, respectively, and logs the value of D each step along the way.

The time property is stored as an integer, so you can't set the time to 12:30 PM by writing a statement like this:

```
set time of D to "12:30 PM"    -- Don't try this at home!
```

It would be nice if you could do that, but AppleScript doesn't support it. Instead, you calculate the number of seconds since midnight for the time 12:30 PM by using the properties listed in the previous table and writing an expression like this:

```
12 * hours + 30 * minutes
```

Notice that you have to do the multiplication here. You may be tempted, but you cannot write your expression like this:

```
12 hours + 30 minutes    -- No! No! No!
```

Now, you can cheat a little here and create a date whose time is 12:30 PM, extract the time property from that date, and assign it to D. You see how to do that after the discussion of the remaining statements in your program.

Notice what happens in the section of code that sets entire dates. AppleScript allows you to create a date from a string on the fly in your program by simply writing an expression like this:

```
date "date-string"
```

Here *"date-string"* can be a literal string, or it can be a variable containing a string representing a date.

The last four set statements in the program are entered like this:

```
set D to date "12/17/2006"  -- can use this format
set D to date "12/17/2006 5:35 PM" -- can specify a time too
set D to date "December 17"  -- of this year
set D to date "10:40 PM"  -- of today
```

After compiling, AppleScript converts each date into a full date specification. So the previous four set statements are changed to the following after they are compiled:

```
set D to date "Sunday, December 17, 2006 12:00:00 AM" -- can use this format
set D to date "Sunday, December 17, 2006 5:35:00 PM" -- can specify a time too
set D to date "Friday, December 17, 2004 12:00:00 AM" -- of this year
set D to date "Thursday, July 22, 2004 10:40:00 PM" -- of today
```

In general, if you don't give a full date specification, AppleScript assumes you are specifying a date that is relative to the current date. So if you specify just a time, it's assumed to be the time of the current date, even if the time has already elapsed. If you specify just a month, it's the first day of the specified month of the current year. And if you specify just a day, it's the day of the current month of the current year. If you don't specify a time when setting a date, AppleScript sets the time to midnight.

You can specify two digits for the year number if you like, as in

```
set D to date "12/17/06"
```

but you shouldn't! AppleScript uses an algorithm to produce a four-digit year number from a two-digit year number. The algorithm is based on the value of the two-digit year and the current year. It tries to make an intelligent choice. So if you execute the following:

```
set D to date "12/17/96"
```

and the current year is 2005, AppleScript converts your two-year specification into the year 1996. However, if you execute this statement in 2005

```
set D to date "12/17/89"
```

AppleScript picks the year 2089 and not 1989! So again, without getting into the gory details here, just remember to use a four-digit year specification.

Getting back to setting the time of a date, you may know that you can set the time of the date D to 12:30 PM by writing a statement like this:

```
set time of D to time of date "12:30 PM"
```

This works and is perfectly valid. The time "12:30 PM" will get expanded when it's compiled, and you'll end up with a funny-looking statement like this:

```
set time of D to (time of date "Thursday, July 22, 2004 12:30:00 AM")
```

Performing Arithmetic with Dates

In the following Try It Out, you see how to write expressions to perform arithmetic with dates. You do that in order to see the number of elapsed days between two dates for example, or to see if a file is older or newer than a certain number of days.

<table>
<tr><td>Try It Out</td><td>Understanding Arithmetic with Dates</td></tr>
</table>

The following program defines two dates. One date is July 16, 2006, and the other is February 22, 2006. In the following steps, you perform various calculations with these dates.

1. Type the following program into Script Editor:

```
-- Performing Arithmetic on Dates

set D1 to date "7/16/2006"  -- This gets changed when compiled
set D2 to date "2/22/2006"  -- This gets changed when compiled
log D1
log D2

-- difference between two dates

set elapsedTime to D1 - D2

log elapsedTime -- gives seconds as difference
log elapsedTime div hours -- difference in hours
log elapsedTime div days --  difference in days
log elapsedTime div weeks -- difference in weeks

-- relative dates

log D1 + 10 * minutes -- 10 minutes later
log D1 + 1 * hours + 30 * minutes -- 1 1/2 hours later
log D1 - 5 * days -- five days earlier
log D1 + 1 * weeks -- one week later

-- how many days until we reach D1?

log (D1 - (current date)) div days
```

2. Click the Event Log tab and run the program. You get the following output:

```
(*Sunday, July 16, 2006 12:00:00 AM*)
(*Wednesday, February 22, 2006 12:00:00 AM*)
(*12441600*)
(*3456*)
(*144*)
(*20*)
(*Sunday, July 16, 2006 12:10:00 AM*)
(*Sunday, July 16, 2006 1:30:00 AM*)
(*Tuesday, July 11, 2006 12:00:00 AM*)
(*Sunday, July 23, 2006 12:00:00 AM*)
tell current application
    current date
        date "Thursday, July 22, 2004 9:01:31 PM"
    (*723*)
end tell
```

How It Works

The program starts by assigning two dates to the variables D1 and D2, as follows:

```
set D1 to date "7/16/2006"  -- This gets changed when compiled
set D2 to date "2/22/2006"  -- This gets changed when compiled
```

As noted in the comments, these two dates get expanded when compiled, so the resulting two lines look like this:

```
set D1 to date "Sunday, July 16, 2006 12:00:00 AM"
set D2 to date "Wednesday, February 22, 2006 12:00:00 AM"
```

After logging the values of these two variables, the program subtracts the two dates represented by D1 and D2:

```
set elapsedTime to D1 - D2
```

The result of subtracting two dates is an integer value (either positive or negative) representing the number of seconds that separate the two dates. You can't add, multiply, or divide two dates; you can only subtract them.

The output recorded in the log indicates that 12,441,600 seconds separate the two dates! Obviously, you may want a more meaningful difference than seconds. The next three lines in the program use the built-in properties to express this difference in hours, days, and weeks, respectively:

```
log elapsedTime div hours -- difference in hours
log elapsedTime div days -- difference in days
log elapsedTime div weeks -- difference in weeks
```

According to the log output, the difference between the two dates represents about 3,456 hours, or about 144 days, or about 20 weeks (recall that the integer division operator div is being used here; for fractional amounts the / operator could be used instead).

A series of statements executed by the program shows how to calculate dates and times in the past or in the future:

```
log D1 + 10 * minutes -- 10 minutes later
log D1 + 1 * hours + 30 * minutes -- 1 1/2 hours later
log D1 - 5 * days -- five days earlier
log D1 + 1 * weeks -- one week later
```

These are useful operations. Remember, however, they must all be done in seconds.

The last example shows how to calculate the number of elapsed days between a given date (D1) and the current date:

```
log (D1 - (current date)) div days
```

As you can see from the log's output, when this program is run that there are 723 days between the current date and July 16, 2006.

Classes of Weights and Measures

AppleScript has built-in classes for weights and measures. These include classes for distance, area, volume, weight, and temperature. Each of these classes is listed in the following table.

Category	Class
Distance	inches
	feet
	yards
	miles
	meters
	centimeters
	kilometers
Area	square feet
	square yards
	square miles
	square meters
	square kilometers
Liquid Volume	liters
	gallons
	quarts

Category	Class
Cubic Volume	cubic meters
	cubic centimeters
	cubic inches
	cubic feet
	cubic yards
Weight	kilograms
	grams
	ounces
	pounds
Temperature	degrees Celsius
	degrees Fahrenheit
	degrees Kelvin

In the following Try It Out, you use weights and measures in your program.

Try It Out   Using Weights and Measures

In the following steps, you practice using most of the weights and measures from the preceding table.

1. Type the following program into Script Editor:

```
-- Try various weights and measures

-- distance

set D to 9000 as inches
log D
log class of D
log D as feet
log D as yards
log D as miles
log D as meters
log D as metres -- alternate spelling - gets changed when compiled

-- area

set a to 10000 as square feet
log a
log a as square yards
log a as square kilometers

-- liquid volume
```

```
set Q to 2 as gallons
log Q
log Q as liters
log Q as quarts

-- subtract 1/2 gallon from Q

set Q to ((Q as number) - 0.5) as gallons
log Q

-- cubic volume

set C to 1 as cubic yards
log C
log C as cubic meters
log C as cubic feet
log C as cubic inches

-- weight

set W to 100 as pounds
log W
log W as kilograms
log W as ounces

-- temperature

set C to 100 as degrees Celsius
log C
log C as degrees Fahrenheit
log C as degrees Kelvin
```

2. Click the Event Log tab and run the program. You should see the following output in the Event Log pane. Your output may differ slightly in some of the less significant decimal places because of your processor (for example, G4 or G5) and the version of Mac OS X you're using.

```
(*inches 9000.0*)
(*inches*)
(*feet 750.0*)
(*yards 250.0*)
(*miles 0.142045454545*)
(*meters 228.600000000043*)
(*meters 228.600000000043*)
(*square feet 1.0E+4*)
(*square yards 1111.111111111111*)
(*square kilometers 9.29030397175748E-4*)
(*gallons 2.0*)
(*liters 7.57*)
(*quarts 8.0*)
(*gallons 1.5*)
(*cubic yards 1.0*)
(*cubic meters 0.764554854498*)
(*cubic feet 27.0*)
```

```
(*cubic inches 4.6656E+4*)
(*pounds 100.0*)
(*kilograms 45.359249794296*)
(*ounces 1600.0*)
(*degrees Celsius 100.0*)
(*degrees Fahrenheit 212.0*)
(*degrees Kelvin 373.15*)
```

How It Works

The program sets various variables to arbitrary weights and measures and then uses the as operator to convert them to different units of measure. In the first set of conversions, the variable D is set to 9000 inches with the following statement:

```
set D to 9000 as inches
```

The class D after this assignment is not a number but inches. This is verified by the two log statements that immediately follow in the program:

```
log D
log class of D
```

The first statement places inches 9000.0 into the log (and not just 9000.0), whereas the second verifies that the class D is indeed inches.

The program then proceeds to log various equivalents for D with the following statements:

```
log D as feet
log D as yards
log D as miles
log D as meters
```

If you look at the next four lines of output in the log, you can see that 9000 inches = 750 feet = 250 yards = .142 meters.

The line that follows in the program illustrates that AppleScript allows you to spell weights and measures that ends in *ers* as *res*.

```
log D as metres -- alternate spelling - gets changed when compiled
```

So you can write meters or metres, kilometers or kilometres, cubic centimeters or cubic centimetres, and so on. When you compile your script, the *res* spelling is automatically changed to the *ers* spelling, meaning the previous code line looks like the following after it's compiled:

```
log D as meters -- alternate spelling - gets changed when compiled
```

The program then proceeds to perform some conversions with area and liquid volume. In this latter case, the following statement is of particular note:

```
set Q to ((Q as number) - 0.5) as gallons
```

The idea here is to subtract one half gallon from the number of gallons stored in the variable Q. Unfortunately, AppleScript does not allow you to directly use any weights and measures as numbers. That means, you can't just write

```
set Q to Q - .5    -- Not allowed!
```

because you'll get an AppleScript error. You also can't do something like this

```
set Q to Q - (.5 as gallons)    -- Not allowed!
```

or this:

```
set Q to Q - (2 as quarts)      -- Not allowed!
```

The only option is to convert your unit into a number, perform the numeric operation, and then convert it back to the original unit of measure.

Summary

In this chapter, you learned

- ❏ How to define variables that you can use in your programs to store values

- ❏ How the set command is used to set the value of a variable

- ❏ How the get command can be used to retrieve the value of a variable

- ❏ The get command is implied when you use a variable in an expression and, therefore, is often omitted.

- ❏ How you can use the log command to enter values into the Event Log, which is a useful tool for tracing the execution of your program and displaying intermediate results

- ❏ In AppleScript, data types are called classes. You also learned how to work with the basic integer, real, string, boolean, and date classes.

- ❏ That you can use parentheses freely in expressions to alter the order of evaluation

- ❏ That you can use the as operator to coerce one data type into another when it makes sense to do so

- ❏ That AppleScript has many built-in classes for working with weights and measures. You saw how you can use these classes to perform your own conversions.

Other classes built into AppleScript were not described here. These include the following: point, RGB color, machine, data, list, record, handler, script, and file. Many of these classes are described later in this book.

In the next chapter, you learn to use AppleScript's relational and logical operators to make decisions in your programs. Before proceeding, however, try the exercises that follow to test your understanding of the material covered in this chapter. You can find the solutions to these exercises in Appendix A.

Exercises

1. Which of the following are invalid variable names? Why?

```
integer
6_05
month
XxX
a$
_count
file extension
file_extension
FILENAME
_100
```

2. Which of the following are invalid constants? Why?

```
123.456
+1.23e+02
0005
+.00004
e-02
-1e-1
2.44  e -03
```

3. Calculate the results and type of each of the following expressions. Then enter them into a program to verify your answers.

```
          200 mod 7
100 / 25 * 4
          ((100.5 as integer) - (50.99 as integer) ) ^ 2
          (1.234e+2 + 2.345e+3)
          2 ^ 0.5  -- what does this do?
          (6 ^ 2 + 8 ^ 2) ^ 0.5
          100.25 + 7.5 div 5 - 29 mod 8
```

4. Given the following formula for converting degrees Fahrenheit (*F*) to degrees Celsius (*C*)

```
C = 5 ( (F - 32) / 9
```

calculate the equivalent Celsius temperatures for the following Fahrenheit temperatures:

100° F

32° F

0° F

55° F

First perform the calculation using the formula. Then use the built-in classes `degrees Fahrenheit` and `degrees Celsius` to do the conversions.

5. Write a program that evaluates the following expression:

```
(3.31 ( 10-8 + 2.01 ( 10-7) / (7.16 ( 10-6 + 2.01 ( 10-8)
```

6. To round off an integer `i` to the next largest even multiple of another integer `j`, the following formula can be used:

```
NextMultiple = i + j - i mod j
```

For example, to round off 256 days to the next largest number of days evenly divisible by a week, values of `i = 256` and `j = 7` can be substituted into the preceding formula as follows:

```
NextMultiple   =   256 + 7 - 256 mod 7
               =   256 + 7 - 4
               =   259
```

Write a program to find the next largest even multiple for the following values of `i` and `j`:

i	*j*
365	7
12,258	23
996	4

7. Given that you have two dates stored in the variables `D1` and `D2`, calculate the number of weeks, minutes, hours, and seconds that separate the two dates. For example, given these two dates:

```
date "Friday, July 22, 2005 8:34:35 PM"
date "Sunday, August 14, 2005 8:44:50 PM"
```

the program should log that 3 weeks, 2 days, 10 minutes, and 15 seconds separate the two dates. You can assume the date stored in `D2` occurs after the date stored in `D1`. (*Hint:* Remember the `div` and `mod` operators.)

Making Decisions

You know how to write simple AppleScript programs to evaluate expressions, assign the results to variables, and display dialogs. Now you learn how to make decisions in your programs. Decision-making is a fundamental characteristic of any programming language. AppleScript's relational and logical operators provide the means for asking questions, and the `if` statement and its variants enable you to alter the flow of execution based on the answers to those questions.

Predicting errors that can occur during a program's execution and taking preventive measures to handle them are two components of good programming discipline. The `try` statement, which allows you to catch errors that might otherwise cause your program to terminate, is also covered in this chapter.

The if Statement

When someone asks if you are going to the Yankees' game and you tell them, "Only if it's not raining," you've expressed a condition for attending the game. The result of that condition determines whether you go. In other words, if it doesn't rain, then you'll go to the ballgame. If it does rain, then you won't go.

AppleScript has a special statement called the `if` statement that allows you to take action based on a condition. Here is the general format of the `if` statement:

```
if Boolean-expression then
    statement
    statement
    ...
end if
```

A *Boolean-expression* is an expression that produces a *true* or *false* result. It may be the result of a comparison, such as one between two numbers or two strings.

If the result of evaluating *Boolean-expression* is true, then the statements that follow — up to the `end if` — are executed. If the result of the evaluation is false, these statements are skipped. If they are skipped, execution continues with the statement that immediately follows the `end if` in the program.

If you were to express your condition for attending the ballgame in AppleScript-ese, it might look something like this:

```
if it's not raining then
    display dialog "Take me out to the ballgame!"
end if
```

If it is not raining, the `display dialog` that follows is executed, presumably to announce your intentions to attend the ballgame. If it is raining, the `display dialog` that follows is skipped.

Here's an actual AppleScript `if` statement that sets the number stored in the variable x to its absolute value:

```
if x is less than 0 then
    set x to -x
end if
```

The statements that occur between the `if` and the `end if` are normally indented to show that they belong to the `if` statement. You don't have to enter them that way because Script Editor automatically indents them for you when you compile your program. It also suffices to simply type `end` to terminate the `if` statement. When you compile your program, Script Editor matches the `end` with the `if` statement, changing it to the words `end if`.

If the value of x is less than zero, the following statement is executed:

```
set x to -x
```

This has the effect of negating the value of x and storing it back in the same variable. If the value of x is not less than zero (that is, it's greater than zero), the statement to negate its value gets skipped. In either case, after the `end if`, the value of x is positive.

A Single Line Form of the if Statement

The `if` statement is a *compound* statement, in that it encapsulates the execution of other statements. As you see later in this chapter, the `if` statement can even include other `if` statements. In the general form of the `if` statement, the statement or statements that follow the `if` must appear on separate lines. If you want to carry out just one action based on the result of a test, you can use an abbreviated form of the `if` statement whose general format is

```
if Boolean-expression then statement
```

Note that in this case no `end if` is used. Returning to the absolute value example, you could equivalently express the `if` statement

```
if x is less than 0 then
    set x to -x
end if
```

in a single line like this:

```
if x is less than 0 then set x to -x
```

Feel free to use this single line form of the `if` statement in your programs.

AppleScript's Relational Operators

A little earlier, I showed you how to test whether the value of a variable x was less than zero. You can do so by using the English phrase: *is less than*. This phrase is actually an operator in AppleScript and is more formally known as a *relational* operator. You use a relational operator to compare two expressions, one to the left of the operator and the other to the right. If the relation is valid, the result of the Boolean expression is true; otherwise, the relation does not hold and the result is false. When used in an `if` statement, the result of the comparison is tested to determine whether the statements that follow are to be executed.

As you might expect, AppleScript provides an assortment of relational operators. These operators exist in English word forms, but they also have their symbolic counterparts. For example, you can use the less than symbol < in place of the words and write an `if` statement that looks like this:

```
if x < 0 then set x to -x
```

The relational operators built-in to AppleScript are summarized in the following table. These operators can be used to compares numbers, strings, and dates (the equality and inequality operators can also be used to compare other data types like lists and records).

Relational Operator	Symbol	Examples
is less than is not greater than or equal to comes before	<	x is less than 0 x < 0 "a" comes before "b"
is less than or equal to is not greater than does not come after	≤	(x + 5) is less than or equal to maxItems (x + 5) ≤ maxItems
is equal to is	=	currentIndex is equal to 100 favoriteArtist = "George Harrison"
is not equal to is not	≠	numberOfFiles is not equal to maxFiles year of (current date) ≠ 2006
is greater than is not less than or equal to comes after	>	pixelHeight is greater than 480 folderName > prevFolderName
is greater than or equal to is not less than does not come before	≥	age is greater than or equal to 21 age ≥ 21

You can create the special symbols ≤, ≠, and ≥ by holding down the Option key while pressing the <, =, or > key, respectively. You can also enter ≤ by typing <= and ≥ by typing >=. Script Editor replaces the two-character sequence with the equivalent single character when you compile your program.

Whether you use the words or the symbols is up to you. In either case, the result of the test is the Boolean value `true` or `false`. Additional English equivalents (or synonyms) can be used that are not shown in the preceding table. For example, for the equality test, you can write

```
n equals 100
```

But when you compile your program, Script Editor changes it to

```
n is equal to 100
```

For this reason, I don't show these synonyms here and I don't use them elsewhere in this book.

You can perform additional tests with strings. For example, you can test to see if one string is contained inside another string. These tests are covered in Chapter 5.

The following Try It Out has you type a program that performs a number of tests on numbers, strings, and dates and then logs the result of each test.

Try It Out   Testing the Various Relational Operators

Work through this program to test the different relational operators.

1.   Type the following program:

```
-- Try out various relational tests

-- numeric tests

set n to 100
set maxFiles to 99

log "*** Numeric Tests ***"
log n < 200
log n is less than or equal to 99
log n mod 2 = 0
log n ≠ 100.0
log n > maxFiles
log n ≥ 0

-- string tests

set bookName to "Beginning AppleScript"
set firstWord to "Aardvark"
set startupDisk to "Macintosh HD"

log "*** String tests ***"
log firstWord comes before "Apple"
log bookName is equal to "Beginning AppleScript"
log firstWord = "AARDVARK"
log "100" < "alpha"
log startupDisk ≠ "Macintosh HD"

-- date tests
```

```
set today to current date
set thisMonth to month of today

log "*** Date tests  ***"
log thisMonth
log thisMonth < June
log thisMonth = April
log today > date "Saturday, January 1, 2000 12:00:00 AM"
log year of today = 2005
```

2. Click the Event Log tab and run the program. The following output appears in the Event Log pane (the actual date shown will reflect the date on which you run the program):

```
(**** Numeric Tests ****)
(*true*)
(*false*)
(*true*)
(*false*)
(*true*)
(*true*)
(**** String tests ****)
(*true*)
(*true*)
(*true*)
(*true*)
(*false*)
tell current application
    current date
        date "Friday, April 23, 2004 12:23:09 PM"
    (**** Date tests  ****)
    (*April*)
    (*true*)
    (*true*)
    (*false*)
end tell
```

How It Works

Now take a look at each section of output in detail, starting with the numeric tests.

Numeric Tests

The program begins by setting the variable n to 100 and the variable maxFiles to 99. The program then places a string in the Event Log with the following statement:

```
log "*** Numeric Tests ***"
```

This string marks the start of the numeric tests in the output. Similar log commands are used later in the program to mark the start of the string and date tests.

Next, the program performs six numeric comparisons using the log command to enter the result of each test in the Event Log. The results from the log have been pasted onto the comparison lines that follow for easy reference.

```
n < 200                            (*true*)
n is less than or equal to 99      (*false*)
n mod 2 = 0                        (*true*)
n ≠ 100.0                          (*false*)
n > maxFiles                       (*true*)
n ≥ 0                              (*true*)
```

Recalling that the value of n is 100, the first test, which asks if n is less than 200, is true. This can be verified by looking at the second line in the Event Log pane. Here you see that the value true was in fact logged there.

Because n is not less than or equal to 99, the result of the test

```
n is less than or equal to 99
```

is false, as is verified from the log. The test that follows next

```
n mod 2 = 0
```

takes the remainder of n divided by 2 and compares it for equality to zero.

> *As pointed out in Chapter 2,* the = *operator is not an assignment operator and can only be used to test for equality.*

Because n is an even number (its value is 100), there is no remainder when it is divided by 2, and so the result of the comparison for equality to 0 is true. The equality operator = has lower precedence than the mod operator, so parentheses are not required in this case.

> *The relational operators have lower precedence than the arithmetic operators. Parentheses can always be used to aid readability or if you're in doubt about operator precedence.*

The fourth numeric test in the program,

```
n ≠ 100.0
```

shows that it's okay to compare an integer (the value stored inside n) to a real number (the constant 100.0). Because the two values are numerically equivalent, the result of the test is false.

The results of the last two numeric tests, which use the > and ≥ operators, are self-explanatory. The variable n is greater than 99 (the value of maxFiles) and is greater than or equal to zero. As a result, true gets logged for both tests.

String Tests

Your program performs six string comparisons. Before doing so, three string assignments are made:

```
set bookName to "Beginning AppleScript"
set firstWord to "aardvark"
set startupDisk to "Macintosh HD"
```

Here are the tests from the program with the corresponding lines from the Event Log pane pasted onto each line:

```
firstWord comes before "Apple"              (*true*)
bookName is equal to "Beginning AppleScript" (*true*)
firstWord = "AARDVARK"                       (*true*)
"100" < "alpha"                              (*true*)
startupDisk ≠ "Macintosh HD"                 (*false*)
```

The first test compares the string stored in the variable firstWord to the string "Apple". Recall that even though the words comes before are used in the example, this is equivalent to writing the test as

```
firstWord < "Apple"
```

When comparing two strings, you're performing a lexical comparison. It's like asking the ordering of the strings if you were to look them up in a dictionary. For that reason, "Aardvark" is considered less than "Apple."

The equality test is used next on two strings, and since bookName was previously set to the string "Beginning AppleScript", the result of the test is true.

The test that appears next

```
firstWord = "AARDVARK"
```

demonstrates that the case of the characters in a string is irrelevant when performing comparisons. For that reason, the two strings compare as equal. In fact, this test also produces a true result:

```
"AaRdVaRk" = "aardVARK"
```

In Chapter 5, you learn how you can refine your string comparisons. For example, AppleScript allows you to ignore punctuation marks and hyphens and to consider upper- and lowercase characters when comparing two strings.

Returning to the program, the test

```
"100" < "alpha"
```

produces a true result, which demonstrates that numeric characters are considered *less than* alphabetic characters. The numeric characters are also ordered from 0 through 9, as you might expect, meaning that the string "image100" compares as less than the string "image101". However, the same string also compares as less than the string "image50". That's because you're doing a string comparison here, and the character 1 comes before the character 5. For the same reason, the numeric comparison

```
100 < 50
```

is obviously false, whereas the comparison

```
"100" < "50"
```

is true.

It really starts to get interesting when you compare a string with an integer, as in

```
"100" < 50
```

or an integer with a string, as in

```
100 < "50"
```

When comparing two values, the second operand is coerced into the type of the first. This does not happen, however, when testing for equality or inequality. In that case, no coercion is attempted. In the test "100" < 50, the second operand, or 50, is coerced into a string to match the type of the first operand. Because the string "100" is less than the string "50", the result is true. In the test 100 < "50", the second operand, or "50", is coerced into an integer. Because the integer 100 is not less than the integer 50, the result is false.

No coercion is done with equality and inequality tests, so the comparison "100" = 100 is false, and the comparison 50 ≠ "50" is true.

Finally, the last string comparison in your program is false because the variable startupDisk does equal the string "Macintosh HD". In Chapter 11, you see how you can use AppleScript to obtain the names of the disks on your system.

Date Tests

It's useful to be able to compare two dates. For example, you may want to schedule a backup to occur on the first day of every month. In that case, your program must determine if a day is, in fact, the first day of the month. You may also want to back up files that are, for example, less than 14 days old. That's another test you can do easily in AppleScript.

In your program example, the current date is first stored in the variable today. The program then gets the month from the date variable today and stores it in the variable thisMonth. After logging the value of this variable, the program performs four date comparisons:

```
thisMonth < June                                    (*true*)
thisMonth = April                                   (*true*)
today > date "Saturday, January 1, 2000 12:00:00 AM"   (*true*)
year of today = 2005                                (*false*)
```

The first comparison tests to see if the month stored in thisMonth is less than June. Again, you may prefer to express the comparison like this:

```
thisMonth comes before June
```

Because the month logged for thisMonth is April, which comes before June, the result of the first comparison is true. This explains why the result of the second comparison is also true. Obviously, if you run this script and April is not the current month, you may get different results.

The comparison

```
today > date "Saturday, January 1, 2000 12:00:00 AM"
```

is `true`, because the date stored in `today` is greater than January 1, 2000. This test was actually keyed-in as

```
today > date "1/1/2000"
```

but was changed to the expanded version by Script Editor when the program was compiled. You may recall that I discussed this expansion performed with dates in Chapter 2.

Finally, this program was run in the year 2004, so the last comparison

```
year of today = 2005
```

proves `false`.

> *As I noted in the previous section, AppleScript enables you to compare strings, dates, numbers, and to some extent, lists and records with each other according to specific data type coercion rules. Detailed coverage of this topic is deferred until Chapter 13.*

Getting Data from the User

Sometimes you want to get data from the user. You might ask for the user's name or the name of a file on the system. As long as you're looking for a single piece of data to be input, you can use a parameter to the `display dialog` command to get it. If your input requirements get more complex, you should learn how to use AppleScript Studio, which is introduced in Chapter 14.

The `default answer` parameter to the `display dialog` command enables you to display a text field in which the user can enter information. The default value that is filled into the field is whatever string follows the parameter. For example, the following dialog asks the user to enter her favorite artist, displaying a default value of `Beatles`:

```
display dialog "Who's your favorite artist?" default answer "Beatles"
```

When you run a program containing this command, you get a dialog like the one shown in Figure 3-1.

Figure 3-1

The user can then type anything into the dialog and click OK to have the result sent back to the program. If the user clicks OK without entering any text, the default value, which in this case is `Beatles`, is sent back.

If you don't want to display a value for the default, you specify a string containing no characters — referred to as a *null* string — after `default answer`, like this:

```
display dialog "Who's your favorite artist?" default answer ""
```

If the user enters the name *Eminem* in the text box shown in Figure 3-1, the dialog would look like Figure 3-2 before the OK button is clicked.

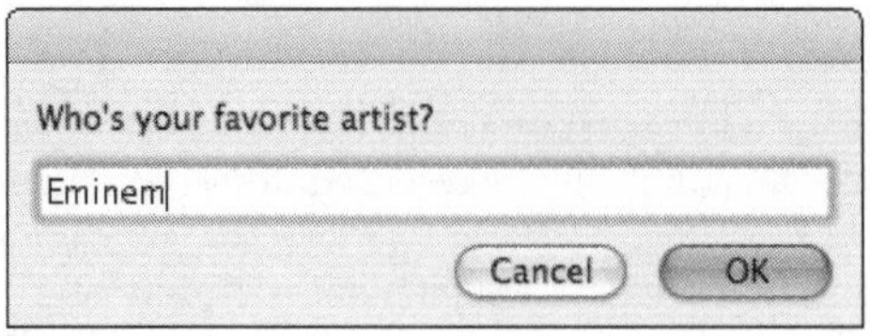

Figure 3-2

More Details on Getting Results

You may recall that the result of the `display dialog` is the button that is clicked. You've seen that result displayed in Script Editor's Result pane. When you enter data, not only is the button that is clicked returned, but the data entered into the text field is also returned. Both values are returned in the form of a *record*, which you learn about in more detail in Chapter 6. For now, you need to know how to get the information from the record that is returned.

To determine the button that was clicked, you write the expression

```
button returned of result
```

and to access the value entered into the text field, you write

```
text returned of result
```

The class of the value returned is Unicode *text, which you learn about more in Chapter 5. However, for now you can just treat it as a string.*

After OK is clicked in the dialog shown in Figure 3-2, the value of `button returned of result` is the string `"OK"`, and the value of `text returned of result` is the string `"Eminem"`.

Remember, the result from a command stored in the special variable `result` must be accessed *immediately* after the command is executed. So, if you write the `display dialog` command shown previously, you must follow it immediately by a command to access the result, as in the following:

```
display dialog "Who's your favorite artist?" default answer "Beatles"
set favArtist to text returned of result
```

What do you think would happen if you also tried to get the button that was clicked by adding an additional line like so:

```
display dialog "Who's your favorite artist?" default answer "Beatles"
set favArtist to text returned of result
set buttonHit to button returned of result
```

You're correct if you said this would generate an error. The third line tries to access the value of the variable `result` from the *last* command executed, which is the previous `set` command — not from the `display dialog` command! Make sure you understand that point. In fact, type these lines into Script Editor and verify the results.

If you need to get both the button and the text, you can assign `result` to a temporary variable, like so:

```
display dialog "Who's your favorite artist? " default answer "Beatles"
set dialogResult to result
set favArtist to text returned of dialogResult
set buttonHit to button returned of dialogResult
```

Realize that in this example it makes no sense to examine the button that was clicked because the dialog displays just the OK and Cancel buttons. If the user clicks Cancel, the statements following the `display dialog` command are not executed anyway because the program's execution is aborted.

Numbers from Strings

If you're looking for a number to be entered by the user in your dialog, remember that a string is returned. So in the following command

```
display dialog "Pick a number from 1-10" default answer "1"
```

the number entered is returned as a string, even if the user just enters 5, for example. Based on what you learned in the previous chapter, you can convert the text that is returned into a number with a statement like this:

```
set guess to text returned of result as number
```

If you are expecting an integer value to be entered, you write this instead:

```
set guess to text returned of result as integer
```

Be forewarned that in either case, if you enter a nonnumeric value such as `abc`, the following error is displayed when you try to coerce it into a number:

```
Can't make "abc" into a number.
```

This error causes your program to terminate. You can avoid this termination by using a `try` statement, as you see later in this chapter.

The next Try It Out walks you through writing a program using an `if` statement.

Try It Out   **Taking the Absolute Value of a Number**

This program asks you to enter a number; it then calculates the absolute value and displays the result.

1.   Type the following program:

```
-- Calculate the absolute value

display dialog "Enter your number:" default answer "0"
set x to text returned of result as number
```

```
if x < 0 then
    set x to -x
end if

display dialog (x as string) buttons {"OK"}
```

2. Click Run. A dialog appears asking you to enter your number.

3. Enter the number −200 and click OK. A dialog displaying the number 200 appears. Click OK to return to Script Editor.

4. Click Run again and this time enter 15.5 and click OK. A dialog displaying the result as 15.5 appears.

How It Works

As previously noted, the number you enter in the dialog is returned to the program in the variable result after you click OK. The statement

```
set x to text returned of result as number
```

converts that value to a number and assigns the result to the variable x. The if statement that follows next in the program

```
if x < 0 then
    set x to -x
end if
```

tests the value of x to see if it is less then zero, and negates it if it is. If the value is not less than zero, the statement that negates its value is skipped.

After execution of the if statement, the value of the number stored in x is coerced into a string and displayed with the following display dialog command:

```
display dialog (x as string) buttons {"OK"}
```

Execution of your program is then complete.

The if-else Statement

Suppose someone asks you if a number is even or odd. You just look at the last digit of the number. If it is 0, 2, 4, 6, or 8, you would say the number is even. Otherwise, if the last digit is 1, 3, 5, 7, or 9, you would say the number is odd. Because the computer doesn't have eyes, it must use other means to determine if a number is even or odd. One simple approach is to have the computer divide the number by 2 and check for a remainder. If there is a remainder, the number is odd; otherwise it is even.

Recalling that the mod operator gives the remainder of one integer divided by another, you can write two tests for a number n like this:

```
if n mod 2 = 0 then
    display dialog "The number is even"
end if

if n mod 2 ≠ 0 then
    display dialog "The number is odd"
end if
```

If the remainder is 0, the program reports that the number is even. If the remainder is nonzero, the program reports that the number is odd. Realize that, in either case, only one of the display dialog statements is executed. That's because the number is either even *or* odd; it can't be both.

This notion of one condition occurring or not occurring can be handled more succinctly with AppleScript's if-else statement. The general format of this statement is

```
if Boolean-expression then
    statement
    statement
       . . .
else
    statement
    statement
       . . .
end if
```

When this statement is executed, *Boolean-expression* gets evaluated first. If the result is true, the statements that follow get executed until the else is reached. The statements between the else and the end if get skipped. If the result is false, statements up to the else get skipped, and the statements between the else and the end if get executed instead. In any case, only one set of statements is executed.

Here's how you can rewrite your even-odd test using an if-else statement:

```
if n mod 2 = 0 then
    display dialog "The number is even"
else
    display dialog "The number is odd"
end if
```

Here's a complete AppleScript program that reads a number from the user and tests whether it's even or odd:

```
-- Program to test if a number is even or odd

display dialog "Enter your number:" default answer "0"
set n to text returned of result as integer

if n mod 2 = 0 then
    display dialog "The number is even"
else
    display dialog "The number is odd"
end if
```

Figure 3-3 shows the dialog that is displayed after you run this program.

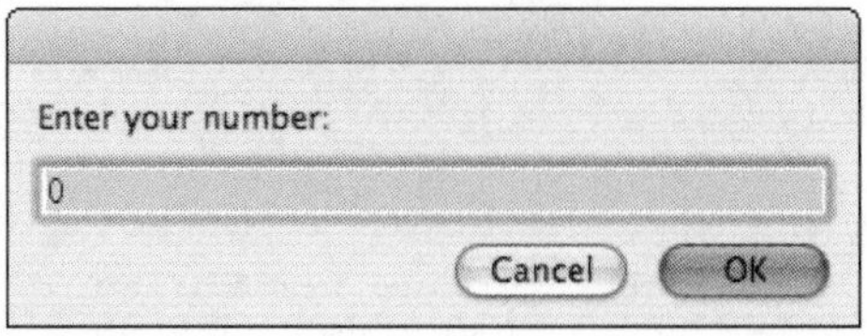

Figure 3-3

Figure 3-4 shows the result displayed by the program after the number 55 has been entered and the OK button is clicked.

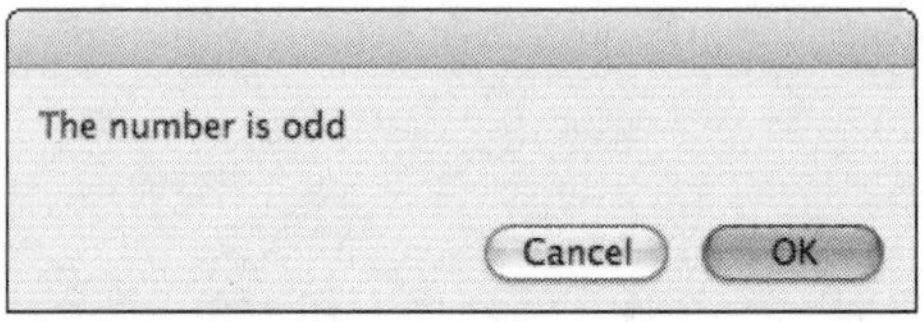

Figure 3-4

Nested if Statements

You may recall that the general format of the if statement is as follows:

```
if Boolean-expression then
    statement
    statement
    ...
end if
```

The statement that follows the if can be any type of statement at all, even another if statement. You often use additional if statements when you have to make more than just a two-way or simple if-else decision. For example, suppose you are processing some image files, and you want to take different actions depending on the image type. You want to do one thing if the file is a JPEG, another if it's a TIFF, and take a third action if it's a GIF (don't worry if these file types aren't familiar; it's not important).

You find out how to determine a file's type in Chapter 7. For now, assume that the type is stored as a string in a variable called imageType, and you want to test the type and take the appropriate action. You can write a three-way if statement like so:

```
if imageType = "JPEG" then
    -- perform actions for JPEG file
else
    if imageType = "TIFF" then
        -- perform actions for TIFF file
    else
```

```
            if imageType = "GIF" then
                -- perform actions for GIF file
            end if
        end if
    endif
```

If the image is a JPEG image, some action is presumably performed on the file. Otherwise, a test is made to see if it's a TIFF image. If it is a TIFF, some action is taken on the file. If it's not a JPEG image or a TIFF image, the final test is made to see if it is a GIF image. If it is, an appropriate action is then taken.

Each if statement must be balanced by a corresponding end if statement. And each if statement can contain an optional else clause. The indentation visually aids your recognition of the structure of the nested if statements.

You should note that if the image is none of the three tested file types, no statements in the nested if statement are executed. You can add an additional else clause as a "fall-through" case. The statements that follow this else are executed if none of the preceding conditions is satisfied. Those statements might generate an error message (you learn how to do that in Chapter 9) or throw up a dialog, as in the following:

```
if imageType = "JPEG" then
    -- perform actions for JPEG file
else
    if imageType = "TIFF" then
        -- perform actions for TIFF file
    else
        if imageType = "GIF" then
            -- perform actions for GIF file
            else
                display dialog "Unrecognized image type!" with icon stop
        end if
    end if
endif
```

Of course, it would be nice to display the unrecognized image type stored in imageType in the dialog as well, but you don't know how to do that yet!

The if-else if Statement

Writing nested if statements can become unwieldy, as you can see from the previous example. Luckily, a special form of the if statement comes to the rescue and enables you to combine the if with the else on the same line. The general format of the if-else if statement is

```
if Boolean-expression1 then
    statement
    statement
       . . .
else if Boolean-expression2 then
    statement
    statement
       . . .
```

```
else if Boolean-expression3 then
    statement
    statement
        . . .
else
    statement
    statement
        . . .
end if
```

Execution of the if-else if statement proceeds as follows:

❑ *Boolean-expression1* gets evaluated first. If the result is true, the statements that follow up to the first else if get executed, and all remaining statements up to the terminating end if get skipped. Otherwise, *Boolean-expression2* gets evaluated; if the result of its evaluation is true, the statements that follow up to the next else if get executed and the remaining statements up to the end if get skipped.

❑ This process of evaluating Boolean expressions continues until either one of the expressions evaluates true or the optional else clause is encountered. If the else is present and none of the preceding Boolean expressions evaluated true, the statements that follow the else up to the terminating end if get executed.

If the else is not included in the if-else if, it's possible that none of the statements in the if-else if will be executed.

Here's how you would rewrite the nested if statement from the previous section in the form of an if-else if:

```
if imageType = "JPEG" then
    -- perform actions for JPEG file
else if imageType = "TIFF" then
    -- perform actions for TIFF file
else if imageType = "GIFf" then
    -- perform actions for GIF file
      else
            display dialog "Unrecognized image type!" with icon stop
end if
```

If you compare the two versions, you'll agree that this one is much easier to read. The indentation doesn't creep off the page to the right, as can happen with a complex nested if. And, unlike the previous format, this is one long statement, so it is terminated by only a single end if at the end.

In the following Try It Out, you write an AppleScript program that tests the day of the week and displays a special message based on the day.

Try It Out   Displaying a Message Based on the Day of the Week

In the next example, you use an if-else if statement to test the day of the week, and you display a special message based on whether it's a Monday, Wednesday, or Friday. For any other day, the program gives a standard message.

1. Type the following program:

```
-- Program to give a greeting

set today to current date
set weekdayToday to the weekday of today

if weekdayToday = Monday then
    set message to "Hope you had a great weekend!"
else if weekdayToday = Wednesday then
    set message to "Happy Hump Day!"
else if weekdayToday = Friday then
    set message to "TGIF!"
else
    set message to "Have a Great Day!"
end if

display dialog message with icon note buttons {"Thanks!"}
```

Figure 3-5 shows the dialog I received when I ran this program on a Thursday.

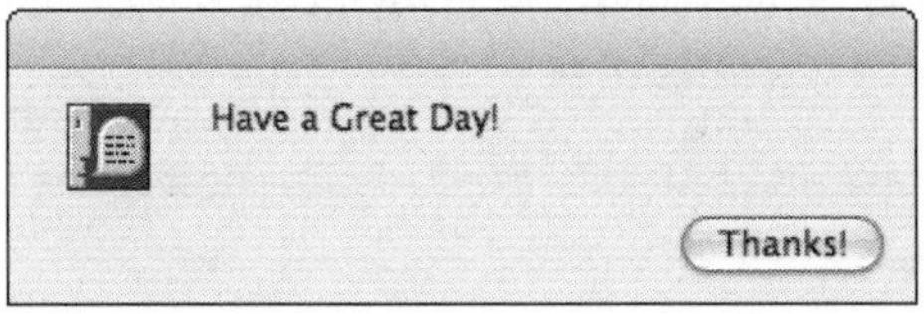

Have a Great Day!

Thanks!

Figure 3-5

Figure 3-6 shows the dialog I received when I ran it the next day (Friday).

TGIF!

Thanks!

Figure 3-6

How It Works

Because you want to determine the current weekday, you first determine the current date. The first statement of your program

```
set today to current date
```

does just that, and the statement that follows,

```
set weekdayToday to the weekday of today
```

sets the variable weekdayToday to the particular weekday represented by the date today. So after executing this statement, the variable weekdayToday contains one of the weekdays Sunday, Monday, . . ., or Saturday. You can consolidate the first two statements from the program into a single statement, like this:

```
set weekdayToday to the weekday of (current date)
```

Remember that the parentheses are needed around the current date command so that AppleScript sees the of applied to current date and not just to current, which would produce an error.

Instead of running your program on all seven days of the week to make sure it's functioning properly, you can "simulate" each day of the week. You simply insert a statement such as set weekdayToday *to* Sunday *right before the* if-else if *statement. This tests the code to see the effect when the weekday is, in fact, a Sunday. You can use a similar approach for the other weekdays as well.*

After assigning the current weekday to weekdayToday, the program executes an if-else if statement to test the value of this variable. In the first case, a test is made to see if the weekday is Monday. If it is, the program assigns the string "Hope you had a great weekend!" to the variable message. This variable is later used as the value displayed in the dialog.

If the weekday is not Monday, the program next tests to see if it's Wednesday. If it is, the string "Happy Hump Day!" gets assigned to the variable message.

If it's not Wednesday, the program tests to see if it's Friday. If it is, the string "TGIF!" gets assigned to the variable message.

Finally, if it's not Monday, Wednesday, or Friday, the else part of the statement gets executed. That has the effect of assigning the string "Have a Great Day! to message.

By the time you've reached the end of the if-else if statement, one of four possible strings is assigned to the variable message. The display dialog command that follows at the end of the program displays this string in a dialog and waits for the user to click OK. Execution of the program is then complete.

Compound Relational Tests

You might need to make more sophisticated decisions in your programs based on more than one comparison. For example, at the beginning of the chapter, you said you would go to the Yankees' game if it wasn't raining. Suppose you said that the temperature also had to be above 60° F. In other words, you're going to the ballgame only if both conditions are met: It's not raining and the temperature is above 60° F. Using what you've learned so far, you could express this in AppleScript notation by writing a statement like this:

```
if it's not raining then
    if the temperature's above 60 degrees then
        display dialog "Take me out to the ballgame!"
    end if
end if
```

An easier way to ask both of these questions at the same time is by using the and operator. You can use this operator to test if two Boolean expressions are *both* true; if they are, the result is true. If either is not true (that is, false), the result is false.

If you were to use this operator to rewrite the previous conditions, it would look like this:

```
if it's raining and the temp's above 60 then
    display dialog "Take me out to the ballgame!"
end if
```

The or operator tests to see if *either* of two Boolean expressions is true, and if so, the result is true.

The not operator is used to negate a Boolean expression, making a true value false, and a false value true.

These three Boolean operators are summarized in the following table.

Boolean Operator	Meaning	Example
boolean1 and boolean2	true if both expressions are true	x > 0 and x ≤ maxItems
boolean1 or boolean2	true if either expression is true	theDay = Saturday or theDay = Sunday
not boolean	negates the value of boolean	not endOfMonth

You can make these compound tests as lengthy as you like. For example, if theDay contains the current weekday, the test

```
theDay = Monday or theDay = Tuesday or theDay = Wednesday or
        theDay = Thursday or theDay = Friday
```

tests if it's a weekday, as will

```
not (theDay = Saturday or theDay = Sunday)
```

which just inverts the test by asking if it's not a weekend day.

In the case of the and operator, *boolean1*, the expression to the left of the and is evaluated first. If the result is true, *boolean2* (the expression to the right of and) is evaluated, and that is the result of the operation. However, if *boolean1* evaluates false, evaluation of *booolean2* gets skipped because the result of the and operation must be false.

A similar approach is taken for evaluation of the or operator. The first expression, *boolean1*, is evaluated. If it is true, *boolean2* does not get evaluated (it's not necessary). If it is false, *boolean2* is evaluated to determine the result of the operation.

Notice the last example of the previous table:

```
not endOfMonth
```

This assumes that endOfMonth is a variable that has been previously set to some true/false value, presumably based on whether it's the end of the month. The not operator simply inverts the value for purposes of evaluation of the expression, but it has no effect on the actual value stored inside the variable.

As for operator precedence, the not operator has higher precedence than the and and or operators, but lower precedence than all the other arithmetic and relational operators. The and operator has higher precedence than the or operator. Of course, you should use parentheses for clarity and to aid readability of your programs.

Based on this precedence, the expression

```
b1 or b2 and b3
```

is evaluated as

```
b1 or (b2 and b3)
```

The expression

```
b1 and not b2 or b3
```

is evaluated as

```
b1 and ((not b2) or b3)
```

because the not operator has higher precedence than the or, which, in turn, has lower precedence than the and. Finally, the expression

```
b1 and not b2 and not b3
```

is evaluated as

```
b1 and (not b2) and (not b3)
```

In the following Try It Out, you use a compound test to determine whether a particular year is a leap year.

Try It Out   Testing Whether a Year Is a Leap Year

If someone gives you a year and asks if it's a leap year, you base your answer on whether the year is evenly divisible by 4. However, what you may not realize is that years that are evenly divisible by 100 are not leap years unless they are also evenly divisible by 400. So the year 2000 was a leap year, but 2100 will not be.

Assume you have the year in question stored in your program in a variable called testYr. You can write a compound test that is true if testYr is a leap year and false if testYr is not a leap year, as follows:

```
testYr mod 4 = 0 and (testYr mod 100 ≠ 0 or testYr mod 400 = 0)
```

If the year is evenly divisible by 4, and it's either not divisible by 100 or is divisible by 400, it's a leap year. Think through this logic before proceeding to verify that this is the correct translation for the definition of a leap year. You may also want to determine why the parentheses are not necessary, even though the and operator has higher precedence than the or.

The following incorporates the preceding expression into a complete program to prompt the user to enter a year, test the year entered, and display a dialog indicating whether the year represents a leap year or not:

1. Type the following program into Script Editor.

```
-- Program to test for a leap year

display dialog "Enter the year:" default answer ""
set testYr to text returned of result as integer

if testYr mod 4 = 0 and (testYr mod 100 ≠ 0 or testYr mod 400 = 0) then
    display dialog "Remember that February has 29 days!"
else
    display dialog "Just another ordinary year!"
end if
```

2. Run the program. When prompted, enter a year and click OK. You get a dialog that tells you if the year you typed is a leap year.

3. Rerun the program several times, keying in different years each time. Verify proper operation of your program.

How It Works

After the year is entered in the dialog that is presented to the user, the year is coerced into an integer and stored in the variable testYr. The program then tests the value and, if the result of the test is true, it reminds the user that February has 29 days in that year. That is, the year represents a leap year. If the result of the test is false, it's just another ordinary year (as far as leap years go) and the user is so informed.

Creating Your First Application

You're now going to write a program to display a dialog containing the message "Good morning!" if it's before noon but after midnight; "Good afternoon!" if it's after noon but before 6 PM; and "Good evening!" otherwise. Just from reading the preceding sentence you can readily surmise that an if-else if statement will probably fit the bill.

As you may recall, the current date command not only gives you information about the date, but it also gives you the time, as well. You can get the time of the current date and store it in the variable secsSinceMidnight, for example, with this statement:

```
set secsSinceMidnight to time of (current date)
```

Remember that the parentheses are required here. The result of this statement is the number of seconds since midnight.

To conclude that it's the morning, you test for the time after midnight *and* before noon. If you're counting seconds since midnight, 0 represents midnight and the expression

```
12 * hours
```

represents noon. Remember that the special AppeScript variable hours is set to the number of seconds in an hour (which happens to be 3600).

You can now write your test for morning like so:

```
secsSinceMidnight ≥ 0 and secsSinceMidnight < 12 * hours
```

The fact of the matter is that secsSinceMidnight is always greater than or equal to zero, so the first part of the test is unnecessary and you can rewrite it like this:

```
secSinceMidnight < 12 * hours
```

If it's not morning, you want to test if it's afternoon. Using your variable secsSinceMidnight, and recalling that in military time 6 PM is actually 1800 hours, you can write a test like this

```
secsSinceMidnight ≥ 12 * hours and secsSinceMidnight < 18 * hours
```

If neither of these two tests is satisfied, it must be evening, according to the stated criteria.

You can also calculate the seconds from midnight to noon by letting AppleScript calculate it for you using a statement like this:

```
time of date "12 PM"
```

Similarly, to calculate the seconds from midnight to 6 PM, you can write

```
time of date "6 PM"
```

AppleScript contains a command that enables your words and sentences to be spoken to you, as the following Try It Out illustrates.

Try It Out   Speaking a Salutation

The following program shows you how to use the say command to speak a salutation and how to save your program as an application.

1. Type the following program into Script Editor.

```
-- speak salutation based on the time

set secsSinceMidnight to time of (current date)

if secsSinceMidnight < 12 * hours then
    say  "Good morning!"
else if secsSinceMidnight ≥ 12 * hours and secsSinceMidnight < ¬
        18 * hours then
```

```
      say "Good afternoon!"
else
      say "Good evening!"
end if
```

2. Run the program to make sure it runs correctly and displays the correct salutation.

3. Choose File ⇨ Save and type the file name `salutation` in the Save As box. Before you click Save, however, select Application as the option under File Format. Your dialog window should be similar to the one shown in Figure 3-7. Note that Run Only, Startup Screen, and Stay Open are all unchecked.

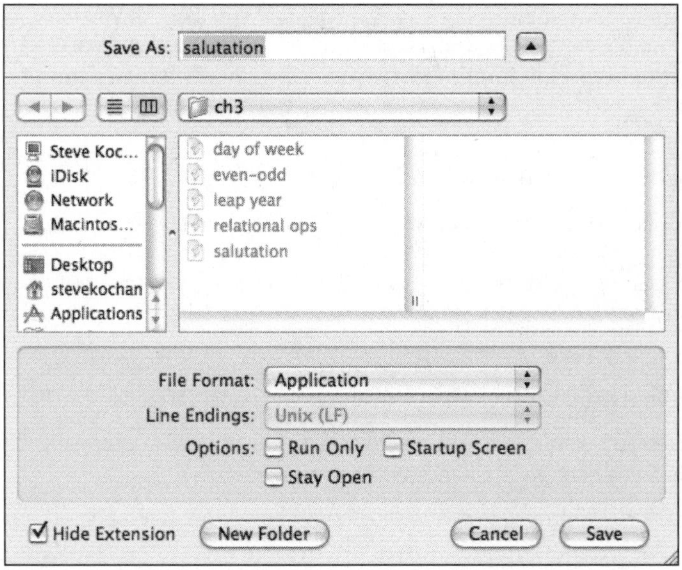

Save As: salutation

ch3

- Steve Koc...
- iDisk
- Network
- Macintos...
- Desktop
- stevekochan
- Applications

- day of week
- even-odd
- leap year
- relational ops
- salutation

File Format: Application

Line Endings: Unix (LF)

Options: ☐ Run Only ☐ Startup Screen
          ☐ Stay Open

☑ Hide Extension   (New Folder)   (Cancel) (Save)

Figure 3-7

4. Click Save. This saves the file under the specified name, only as an application this time and not as a script.

5. Locate the file you just saved in the Finder. If your options are set to display files as icons, your program should resemble Figure 3-8.

Figure 3-8

6. Double-click the `salutation` file icon and see what happens. If it's the morning when you run your program, you should get the phrase "Good Morning" spoken to you.

How It Works

The programs you have written so far were saved as script files (the file name's extension is scpt) on the disk. If you double-click a script file, the Finder launches whatever application is associated with files of this type. Unless you have changed the default, double-clicking causes Script Editor to run and open the specified file. This is the same action that occurs when you double-click any file that's not an application: The Finder opens the application associated with that file.

When you tell Script Editor to save your file as an application, however, it creates a standalone application from your program. So when you subsequently double-click the application file, the Finder doesn't look for an application associated with the file — it's already an application — it just runs the file.

You can have your applications display a startup screen if you like. All you have to do is check the Startup Screen option from the Save dialog (refer to Figure 3-7). The message displayed in the startup screen is whatever you enter for the program's description. If you didn't enter a description, you get the message Press Run to run this script, or Quit to quit. instead.

Try It Out   Displaying a Startup Screen

To have your application display a startup screen, follow these steps:

1. Return to the previous program. Click the Description tab and enter the following description for your program: Speaks a salutation.

2. Choose File ➪ Save.

3. Check the Startup Screen option and choose Application under File Format. Click Save.

4. Locate the application you just created (salutation) and double-click it. Your program is launched, and you get the window shown in Figure 3-9.

5. Click Run. An appropriate salutation should be spoken to you based on the time of day.

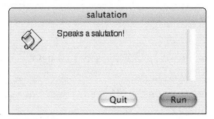

Figure 3-9

As you see, once you've created an application file, you can double-click the file's icon to execute it. You can still edit the file in Script Editor by choosing File ➪ Open from Script Editor's menu bar or by dragging your application's icon onto the Script Editor icon.

The following Try It Out shows you how to have your salutation program run automatically to greet you when you log in.

Try It Out   Have Some Fun: Get Your Salutation at Log In

To have your salutation program run automatically whenever you log in to your system, follow these steps:

1. Under the Apple Menu (🍎) select System Preferences.

2. Under System, click the Accounts icon. Your account should be selected in the left pane.

3. Click the Startup Items tab. This brings up a window similar to the one shown in Figure 3-10.

Figure 3-10

4. Click the + button inside the Startup Items pane. This drops down a sheet for you to locate your application file.

5. After you locate your `salutation` application, highlight it and click Add. You get a window similar to the one shown in Figure 3-11. You see that your application has been added to the list of programs that run whenever you log in.

6. Save all your changes, and then log out and back in again. Your salutation program should automatically run and talk to you!

Figure 3-11

Catching Errors with the try Statement

You may recall from earlier in this chapter that trying to coerce a string into a number produces an error and causes your program to terminate if the string does not contain a valid numeric representation. For example, writing

```
"Hello" as integer
```

causes as error when run because the string `"Hello"` does not represent an integer.

The following Try It Out shows what happens when you try to coerce a string that does not contain a valid numeric representation into a number. Then you use a `try` statement to catch the error that normally occurs.

Try It Out   Introducing the try Statement

Follow these steps to work with the `try` statement:

1.   Type the following program into Script Editor:

```
-- Introducing the try statement

"Hello" as integer
log "Got here!"
```

2. Click the Event Log tab and run the program. You get the error shown in Figure 3-12.

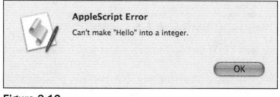

AppleScript Error
Can't make "Hello" into a integer.

OK

Figure 3-12

3. Modify the program by inserting the statement `try` before the coercion of the string and `end try` after the coercion (you can just type `end` if you like). Your program should now look like this:

```
-- Introducing the try statement

try
    "Hello" as integer
end try

log "Got here!"
```

4. Make sure the Event Log pane is still displayed and run the program. You should see the following in the Event Log pane:

```
(*Got here!*)
```

How It Works

When you run the first version of the program, AppleScript attempts to convert the string `"Hello"` into an integer. That fails, and so the error dialog shown in Figure 3-12 is displayed. After you acknowledge the dialog, the program's execution is terminated. So the `log` statement that follows never gets executed. That's why nothing appears in the Event Log.

When you put the coercion inside a `try..end try`, or inside a `try` *block* as it's often called, its failure does not cause the program to terminate. The error is ignored and execution continues with whatever statements follow the try block. In this case, just a single `log` statement follows the block, so it gets executed and the message gets logged.

You can have more than one statement inside a try block. However, once an error occurs in the block, any statements that occur before the `end try` are skipped. That means that writing your previous program this way

```
-- Introducing the try statement

try
```

95

```
        "Hello" as integer
        log "Got here!"
    end try
```

causes the `log` statement to be skipped and not executed when the coercion on the previous line fails.

The following Try It Out provides another example of the `try` statement in action.

Error Handling with the try Statement

Follow these steps to see how you can use the `try` statement for error handling:

1. Type the following modified version of the even/odd program into Script Editor:

```
-- Program to test if a number is even or odd - ver. 2

display dialog "Enter your number:" default answer "0"

try
    set n to text returned of result as integer

    if n mod 2 = 0 then
        display dialog "The number is even"
    else
        display dialog "The number is odd"
    end if
end try
```

2. Run the program. When the program runs, enter a valid integer number to verify its proper operation.

3. Rerun the program. This time, type a nonnumeric value when prompted by the dialog. Click OK.

How It Works

The entire set of statements after the first `display dialog` is enclosed in the `try` block. If you enter a noninteger, the statement

```
    set n to text returned of result as integer
```

fails, and all the remaining statements in the program are skipped. That's not too helpful. A better approach is to tell the user that he didn't enter a valid integer. One way to do that is to set n to some value before you try to coerce it. The special predefined constant `missing value` comes in handy for such purposes. If the coercion fails, the value of n is not changed.

More on the try Statement

The following program is another modification of the even/odd program.

1. Type the following program into Script Editor:

```
-- Program to test if a number is even or odd - ver. 3

set n to missing value
display dialog "Enter your number:" default answer "0"

try
    set n to text returned of result as integer
end try

if n ≠ missing value then
    if n mod 2 = 0 then
        display dialog "The number is even"
    else
        display dialog "The number is odd"
    end if
else
    display dialog "You didn't enter an integer!" with icon note
end if
```

2. Run the program and type the text Hello when prompted for a number by the program.

3. Click OK. You should get the dialog shown in Figure 3-13.

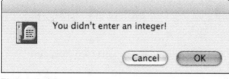

Figure 3-13

How It Works

You start by setting the variable n to the special constant missing value with the statement

```
set n to missing value
```

You don't have to use this constant; you could use a nonnumeric value instead, for example, and then test for it later.

After the dialog is displayed and you key in your number, the program coerces the value entered into an integer. This is done inside the try block:

```
try
    set n to text returned of result as integer
end try
```

If the text entered by the user can't be coerced into an integer, the statement fails. That means that a value is not assigned to n, and it retains its previous value of missing value.

After the `try` block, the program tests whether the coercion succeeded by testing the value of n. If n does not equal `missing value`, a valid integer was entered. In that case, a test is made to see if the number entered is even or odd, and an appropriate dialog is displayed as before.

If the value of n does equal `missing value`, the last `else` clause is executed. This puts up a dialog to inform you that you didn't enter an integer. Ideally, at this point, the program should go back and give you another chance to get it right. However, you don't know how to do that yet. You learn how it's done in Chapter 4.

> *If you put a* `display dialog` *command in a* `try` *block, you can catch the case where the Cancel button is clicked. Normally, clicking this button causes your program to terminate.*

You learn about another form of the `try` statement in Chapter 7. This form enables you to specify an action to take if any error occurs inside the `try` block.

Summary

AppleScript's `if` statement allows you to make decisions and alter the flow of execution based on the result of your decisions. In addition, you learned the following in this chapter:

❑   Relational operators allow you to easily compare numbers, strings, and dates. These operators can be expressed with English words or symbols, and they produce a Boolean result of either true or false.

❑   The operators `and` and `or` allow you to join two Boolean expressions and make more complex decisions.

❑   The `not` operator simply turns a true value false, and a false value true.

❑   The `if else` statement allows you to specify two sets of statements: one that is executed if the result of the test is true, and the other if it is false.

❑   The `if-else if` statement extends the `if else` statement so that you can specify any of a number of different paths to take based on the results of more than just a single test.

❑   A `try` block encapsulates statements whose failure might otherwise cause a program to terminate. It provides a more elegant way to handle errors.

In the next chapter, you learn how to work with variables, and you are introduced to the built-in AppleScript classes. You also see how to write arithmetic expressions and perform basic conversions between data types. Before proceeding, however, try the exercises that follow to test your understanding of the material covered in this chapter. You can find the solutions to these exercises in Appendix A.

Exercises

1.   Modify the program from this chapter that displays various messages based on the weekday to also display the message "What are you doing here on the weekend" if it's a Saturday or Sunday.

2. Using the result from the previous exercise, save your program as an application and then set it up to run every time you log in.

3. Determine the results of the following expression evaluations. Then type them into Script Editor to verify your answers.

```
true and true
true and false
true or false
false or false
not true and false
true and not false or true
true and not (false or true)
```

4. Run the leap year program presented in this chapter. Record whether the following years are reported as leap years: 1986, 1989, 2000, 2010, and 2100.

5. Predict what would happen if you ran the following program and clicked OK without entering a value. Then run the program to verify your prediction. What can you say about the null string and its conversion to a number?

```
display dialog "Pick a number between 1 and 10" default answer ""
set guess to text returned of result as number
```

6. Modify the `salutation` program from the "Creating Your First Application" section of this chapter. Use the technique described in the Note in that section, which explains how to calculate the seconds from midnight to noon and from midnight to 6 PM.

7. The `delay` command pauses execution of your program for a specified number of seconds, as in

```
delay 10
```

which will pause your program for 10 seconds.

Write a simple alarm clock program that asks the user to enter the number of seconds to pause before the alarm goes off. In a separate dialog, ask the user for a message to display. Then pause the program for the specified number of seconds. At the end of the pause, display the indicated message. Save your program as an application.

8. Modify the leap year program from this chapter to catch the error that occurs if a nonnumeric year is entered.

Program Looping

In Chapter 3 you learned how to make decisions in your program and how to alter its execution based on the results of those decisions. In this chapter, you learn about another fundamental feature of computer programming languages: the capability to repeatedly execute a set of statements.

In many instances, you'll want to iterate a group of statements. For example, you may want to print each file from a list of files. Or you may want to rename each file in a certain folder. Finally, you may have iPhoto images stored in an album that you want to resize. Each of these situations requires you to apply your process — whether it's printing, renaming, or resizing — to each file, in turn. This is done through the process of iteration.

The capability to repeatedly execute a group of statements is supported in AppleScript by a statement called, appropriately enough, the repeat statement. This statement takes different forms, which you learn about in this chapter. One form, the repeat...times statement, lets you repeat a set of statements a predetermined number of *times*. Two other forms, repeat while and repeat until, enable you to repeat a set of statements *while* a particular condition is satisfied or *until* a particular condition is satisfied. Finally, you can use the last form, repeat with, to repeatedly execute a set of statements for each element in a list.

The repeat...times Statement

The repeat...times statement is used to repeat a set of statements a specified number of times. You get a chance to use this statement in the following Try It Out.

Try It Out   Log a Message Five Times

To log a message five times, follow these steps:

1. Start up Script Editor and type the following program:

```
-- Log a message 5 times

repeat 5 times
    log "AppleScript rocks!"
end repeat
```

2. Click the Event Log tab and run the program. If you look at the Event Log pane, you see the following results displayed:

```
(*AppleScript rocks!*)
(*AppleScript rocks!*)
(*AppleScript rocks!*)
(*AppleScript rocks!*)
(*AppleScript rocks!*)
```

How It Works

Here is the general format of the `repeat...times` statement:

```
repeat expr times
    statement
    statement
    ...
end repeat
```

Execution of the `repeat...times` begins with evaluation of *expr*, which can be any expression that evaluates to an integer. The result of the expression determines the number of times the statements that follow up to the `end repeat` are executed. So if *expr* is 5, as it was in the preceding program, the statements get executed in turn five times. If *expr* is 100, the statements get executed 100 times. And if *expr* is less than or equal to zero, none of the statements that follow up to the `end repeat` get executed.

In this program, one statement is included in the body of your loop, namely

```
log "AppleScript rocks!"
```

This `log` statement was executed five times, as verified by the results in the log.

Note that you don't have to type the keyword `times`; it is automatically inserted when you compile your program. So the `repeat` statement from the preceding program could have also been keyed like this:

```
repeat 5
    log "Hello"
end repeat
```

The repeat with Statement

Two different versions of the `repeat with` statement are used. The first one repeats a set of statements a specified number of times; it is illustrated in the following Try It Out. The second version sequences through the elements in a list; it is described later in this chapter.

Try It Out   **Counting from 1 to 10**

To use the `repeat with` statement to count from 1 to 10, follow these steps:

1. Start up Script Editor and type the following program:

```
-- Count from 1 to 10

repeat with n from 1 to 10
    log n
end repeat
```

2. Click the Event Log tab and run the program. If you look at the Event Log pane, you should see the following results:

```
(*1*)
(*2*)
(*3*)
(*4*)
(*5*)
(*6*)
(*7*)
(*8*)
(*9*)
(*10*)
```

How It Works

Here is the general format of the `repeat with...from...to` statement:

```
repeat with loopvar from init-expr to end-expr
    statement
    statement
    ...
end repeat
```

Execution of the `repeat with...from...to` proceeds according to the following steps:

1. The integer expression `init-expr` is evaluated and assigned to the variable `loopvar`. The terminating integer expression `end-expr` is also evaluated.

2. The value of `loopvar` is compared to the value of `end-expr`. If the former is greater than the latter, the loop is immediately terminated. Execution then continues with whatever statement follows the `end repeat`.

3. The statements that immediately follow the `repeat`, up to the `end repeat`, are executed.

4. The value of the variable `loopvar` is incremented by 1.

5. The process returns to Step 2.

Note a couple of things about the `repeat with` statement:

1. The initial expression `init-expr` and the terminating expression `end-expr` are evaluated once when the loop begins.

2. If the value of the initial expression is greater than the value of the ending expression, the statements in the loop are skipped without being executed even once.

In your program, the `repeat with` statement starts by assigning the value of the initial expression to the variable n. This value is then compared to the ending expression, which is 10. Because 1 is not greater than 10, the loop continues executing. The body of your loop consists of a single `log` statement whose purpose is to log the value of the variable n. So the first time through the loop, the value of n, or 1, gets logged.

The program then goes to the top of the loop and increments the value of n by 1, changing its value to 2. Because 2 is still not greater than 10, the body of the loop—which logs the value of n—is executed again. This has the result of placing the value 2 into the log.

This process is repeated until the value of n reaches 11. Because this value is greater than 10, the loop is immediately terminated. If you had a statement in the program following the `repeat with`, execution would continue at that point.

When you're writing loops, you'll often find more than one way to do something. You can usually substitute one form of a `repeat` statement for another. For example, the following program uses `repeat . . . times` to count to 10:

```
-- Count from 1 to 10

set n to 1

repeat 10 times
    log n
    set n to n + 1
end repeat
```

Using this form of the `repeat` statement, you have to set the initial value of your variable before the loop starts and increment it each time inside the loop. Nevertheless, it is still perfectly valid.

Writing a Loop with an Increment

The `repeat with` statement actually has a more general form, which is as follows:

```
repeat with loopvar from init-expr to end-expr by incr-expr
    statement
    statement
    ...
end repeat
```

The integer expression *incr-expr* is evaluated once when the loop begins execution. It specifies the value to be added to *loopvar* after each iteration of the loop. If you don't use the optional `by` parameter, the default value of 1 is used, as you saw in the last Try It Out example. In fact, you could have written the `repeat with` from that example like so:

```
repeat with n from 1 to 10 by 1
    log n
end repeat
```

The result is the same.

Note that *incr-expr* can be a negative value. In that case, a negative value is added (or in a sense subtracted) from the variable *loopvar* for each iteration of the loop. Furthermore, the sense of the termination condition is inverted. That is, each time through the loop *loopvar* is compared again with *end-expr*, as before. In this case, however, the loop is terminated if the value of *loopvar* is *less than* the value of *end-expr*. This fact explains why the program illustrated in the following Try It Out counts down from 10 to 1 and why the loop is terminated when the value of the looping variable n reaches 0.

Try It Out   **Counting Down from 10**

The following shows you how to count down from 10 using repeat with.

1. Type the following program into Script Editor:

```
-- Count down from 10 to 1

repeat with n from 10 to 1 by -1
    log n
end repeat
```

2. Now click the Event Log tab and run the program. You see the following results displayed in the Event Log pane:

```
(*10*)
(*9*)
(*8*)
(*7*)
(*6*)
(*5*)
(*4*)
(*3*)
(*2*)
(*1*)
```

How It Works

The first time through the loop, the value of n is set to 10. Because this value is greater than 1, the body of the loop is executed. Remember, if the increment value is negative, the comparison against the ending expression is inverted.

The log statement, which constitutes the body of the loop, places the value 10 into the log. Execution then goes back up to the top of the loop. Because 1 is specified as the increment value, the value of n is decremented by 1, changing its value to 9. The loop body is then executed, and the value of n, which is 9, is logged. Execution of the loop continues until the value of n is decremented to 0, at which point the loop is terminated.

In the next Try It Out, you write a program to ask the user to enter a number, and then you add all the integers from 1 to that number. That number has a special name in mathematics; it's known as a *triangular* number. For example, when you rack up a set of pool balls, you arrange them in the shape of a triangle, as depicted in Figure 4-1.

Figure 4-1

The number of balls in the first row is 1, in the second row 2, in the third row 3, the fourth row 4, and the number of balls in the fifth row is 5. The total number of balls in all five rows is, therefore,

$1 + 2 + 3 + 4 + 5 = 15$

Now try writing a program to do this calculation for you.

Try It Out   **A Program to Sum the Integers from 1 to n**

These steps enable you to ask the user to enter a number and from that to calculate the specified triangular number.

1. Type the following into Script Editor:

```
-- Calculate a triangular number specified by the user

set triangularNumber to missing value
set sum to 0 -- the sum so far

display dialog "Enter your integer" default answer ""

-- make sure an integer was entered
try
    set triangularNumber to text returned of result as integer
end try

if triangularNumber = missing value then
    display dialog "You didn't enter an integer" with icon stop buttons {"OK"} ¬
            default button 1
else
    -- now calculate the requested number

    repeat with n from 1 to triangularNumber
        set sum to sum + n
    end repeat

    display dialog (sum as string)
end if
```

The line continuation character (¬) is shown at the end of the first line of the second display dialog *command in the preceding code. Recall that this indicates that I pressed Option-Return at the end of the line to force a line break and continue the statement to the next line. The wrapped line is then automatically indented when the program is compiled. Remember that Script Editor automatically breaks lines for you and does not insert the line continuation character when it does so. Throughout the rest of this chapter, I show long lines with the ¬ character at the end just to remind you that the line is being continued. However, in later chapters, this character is not shown at the end of such lines. By that time, you will have learned enough about AppleScript and its format to know when a line is being continued.*

2. Run the program. You get the dialog shown in Figure 4-2.

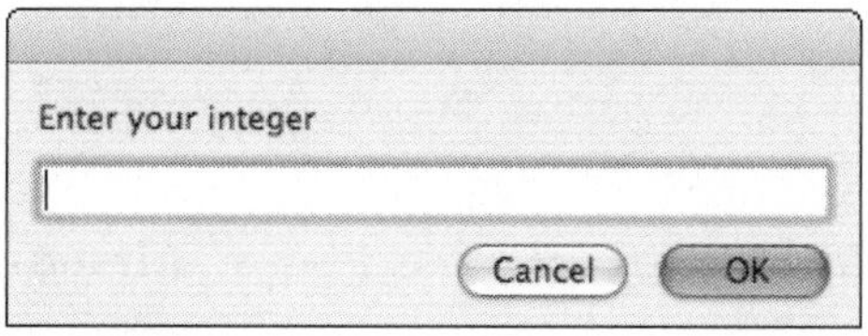

Figure 4-2

3. Enter the number 10 and click OK. You get the dialog with the result as 55, as shown in Figure 4-3.

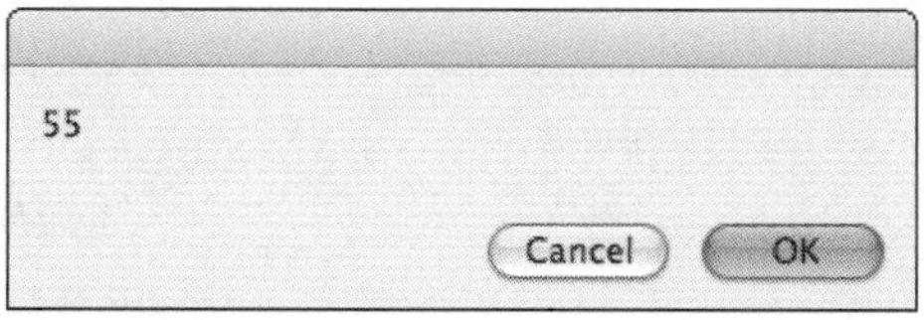

Figure 4-3

4. Run the program again. This time, type abc in the dialog and click OK. You get the dialog shown in Figure 4-4, and the program stops execution.

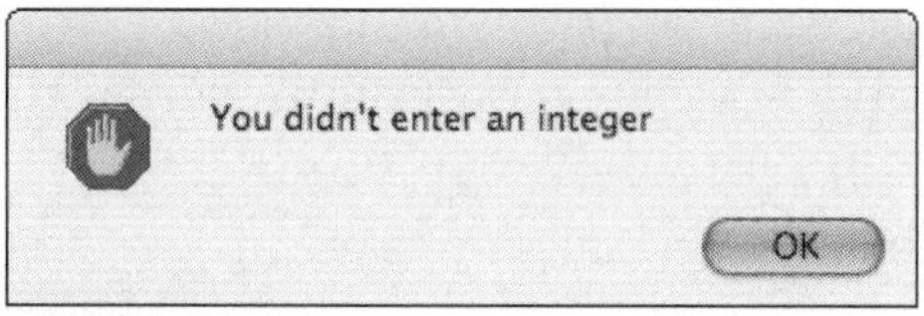

Figure 4-4

How It Works

The program begins by initializing two variables with the following statements:

```
set triangularNumber to missing value
set sum to 0 -- the sum so far
```

The variable `triangularNumber` stores the number whose triangular number you want to calculate. It's initially set to `missing value` so that you can test later to see if a valid integer was keyed.

The variable `sum` calculates the sum of the integers from 1 to the value stored in `triangularNumber`. The value is initially set to zero in the program.

The program then displays a dialog asking the user to enter an integer and tries to coerce the entered value into an integer inside a `try` block:

```
display dialog "Enter your integer" default answer ""

-- make sure an integer was entered
try
    set triangularNumber to text returned of result as integer
end try
```

If the coercion fails, the value of `triangularNumber` is not set; that is, it still has the value `missing value` that you initially assigned to it. This condition is tested by the `if` statement that follows next in the program. If the coercion fails, a dialog alerts the user to the error. Otherwise, the program proceeds to calculate the requested triangular number by using the following `repeat` statement:

```
repeat with n from 1 to triangularNumber
    set sum to sum + n
end repeat
```

The variable n goes from 1 to the value of `triangularNumber`. Each time through the loop, its value is added into the value of sum by the statement

```
set sum to sum + n
```

This statement says to take the current value of sum, add n to it, and store the result back into sum. When the `repeat` loop has finished execution, the display dialog command

```
display dialog (sum as string)
```

is executed to display the final answer, which is stored in the variable sum. Note that you coerce sum into a string before displaying the result. You do this because the `display dialog` command displays text in a dialog. So you coerce sum into a string before you give it to `display dialog` to display.

> Many commands like `display dialog` coerce values themselves. For example, if you give the `display dialog` command a number to display, it automatically converts it to text. However, it's best not to rely on commands to do the coercion for you because not all commands behave in a predictable manner.

Your First Look at a Dictionary

So, how would you know that the `display dialog` command shows a text message? And what about its other parameters. If you didn't know what they were, how could you find them easily?

The `display dialog` *command is known as a* Standard Addition *command. Standard Addition commands are not built directly into the AppleScript language, but they exist in the form of an* osax, *or an Open Script Architecture Extension. Because the Standard Addition commands are found in all AppleScript installations, this book treats them as part of the language.*

You can look in the Standard Additions Dictionary to learn more about the `display dialog` command. In the following Try It Out, you learn how to use this dictionary.

Try It Out   Looking Up a Command in a Dictionary

The following are steps to using the Standard Additions dictionary to look up a command:

1. Start up Script Editor and choose File⇨Open Dictionary. A dialog like that shown in Figure 4-5 appears.

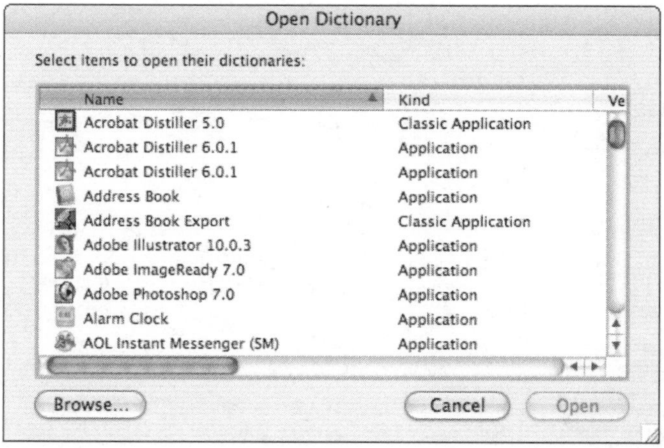

Open Dictionary

Select items to open their dictionaries:

Name	Kind	Ve
Acrobat Distiller 5.0	Classic Application	
Acrobat Distiller 6.0.1	Application	
Acrobat Distiller 6.0.1	Application	
Address Book	Application	
Address Book Export	Classic Application	
Adobe Illustrator 10.0.3	Application	
Adobe ImageReady 7.0	Application	
Adobe Photoshop 7.0	Application	
Alarm Clock	Application	
AOL Instant Messenger (SM)	Application	

Browse...   Cancel   Open

Figure 4-5

2. Scroll down in the window until you see `Standard Additions` and click to select this line (see Figure 4-6).

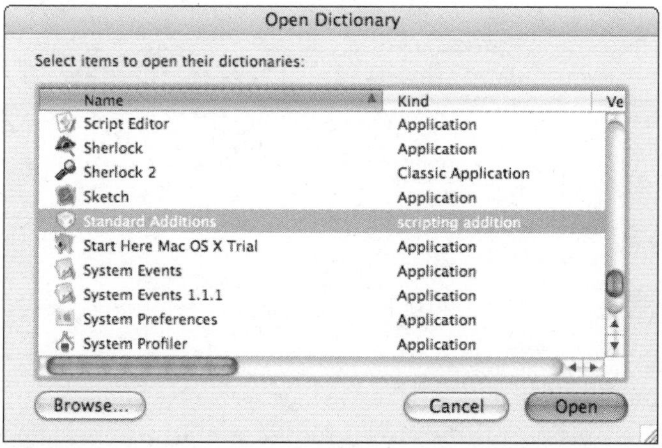

Open Dictionary

Select items to open their dictionaries:

Name	Kind	Ve
Script Editor	Application	
Sherlock	Application	
Sherlock 2	Classic Application	
Sketch	Application	
Standard Additions	scripting addition	
Start Here Mac OS X Trial	Application	
System Events	Application	
System Events 1.1.1	Application	
System Preferences	Application	
System Profiler	Application	

Browse...   Cancel   Open

Figure 4-6

3. Click Open. A window similar to that shown in Figure 4-7 appears.

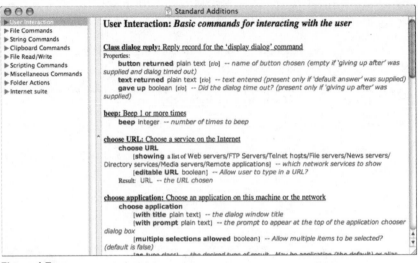

Figure 4-7

4. Scroll down the right frame of this window until you find the `display dialog` command. Your window should look like Figure 4-8. The information displayed here describes the syntax of the `display dialog` command and its parameters.

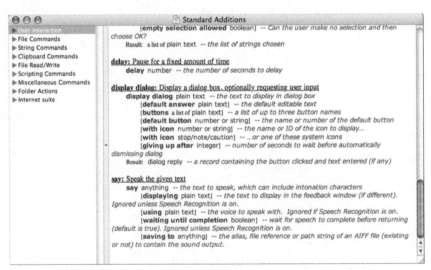

Figure 4-8

How It Works

Notice the first two lines of the `display dialog` command:

```
display dialog: Display a dialog box, optionally requesting user input
    display dialog  plain text  -- the text to display in dialog box
```

The first line gives a brief summary of what the command does. The second line shows the general format of this command: The command name is followed by plaintext to be displayed in the dialog.

The remaining lines shown for the display dialog command — excluding the last line — list optional parameters. You know they're optional because they're enclosed in a pair of brackets:

```
[default answer  plain text]  -- the default editable text
[buttons  a list of plain text]  -- a list of up to three button names
[default button  number or string]  -- the name or number of the default button
[with icon  number or string]  -- the name or ID of the icon to display...
[with icon  stop/note/caution]  -- ...or one of these system icons
[giving up after  integer]  -- number of seconds to wait before automatically
                                dismissing dialog
```

You are familiar with all these optional parameters except the last one, and Exercise 9 at the end of this chapter asks you to try out this last parameter.

The last line under the display dialog command is the following:

```
Result: dialog reply  -- a record containing the button clicked and text
                          entered (if any)
```

As you can surmise, this line tells you about the result that the display dialog command returns.

You learn a lot more about dictionaries in later chapters of this book. An application's dictionary provides information so that you can write AppleScript code to communicate with that application. For example, iTunes has a dictionary that contains many commands that enable you to do tasks such as list the songs in your music library, list the songs in a playlist, play a particular song, or delete a song.

Now that I've taken you on this little side trip about dictionaries, the next section continues the discussion of the repeat statement.

The repeat while Statement

You use the repeat while statement to repeat a set of statements while a specified condition is true. In the following Try It Out, you see how you can use the repeat while to count to 10.

Try It Out   Counting from 1 to 10

You can use the following program to count to 10 by using repeat while.

1.   Start up Script Editor and type the following program:

```
-- Count from 1 to 10: repeat while

set n to 1
repeat while n    10
```

```
        log n
        set n to n + 1
    end repeat
```

2. Click the Event Log tab and run the program. If you look at the Event Log pane, you see the following results displayed:

```
        (*1*)
        (*2*)
        (*3*)
        (*4*)
        (*5*)
        (*6*)
        (*7*)
        (*8*)
        (*9*)
        (*10*)
```

How It Works

Here is the general format of the `repeat while` statement:

```
repeat while Boolean-expression
    statement
    statement
    ...
end repeat
```

When this loop begins execution, `Boolean-expression` is evaluated. If the result of the evaluation is true, the statements that follow up to the `end repeat` are executed. If `Boolean-expression` is false, the loop is immediately terminated, and execution continues in the program with whatever statements follow the `end repeat`. In other words, the body of the loop is repeatedly executed as long as `Boolean-expression` is true.

In the Try It Out example, the variable n is initially set to 1 with this statement:

```
set n to 1
```

The `repeat while` loop follows next:

```
repeat while n    10
    log n
    set n to n + 1
end repeat
```

This loop is executed as long as the value of the expression

```
n ≤ 10
```

is true. Because n starts out at 1, you know that the loop is executed at least one time. Inside the loop, the value of n is logged and then 1 is added to n with this statement:

```
set n to n + 1
```

Execution of the loop then continues at the top, where the value of n is once again tested against 10. Because n is now 2, which is still less than 10, the loop continues execution. The process continues until the value of n is incremented to 11. At that point, n is no longer less than or equal to 10, and the loop is terminated.

Using Flags

A *flag* is simply a variable that contains the Boolean value true or false. This value is usually inverted (or flipped) during program execution based on some event occurring. For example, you might have a flag called endOfData that is used to keep track of whether the last data item has been processed. Initially, you set this flag false, using a statement like this:

```
endOfData = false
```

You might also have a statement that executes in a loop as long as you haven't reached the end of your data. You write such a loop this way:

```
repeat while not endOfData
    -- process the data
end repeat
```

Presumably, somewhere inside the repeat while statement a test appears to see if the end of data is reached. This is followed by a statement to set the flag true, like this:

```
endOfData = true     == signal we've reached the end
```

After this flag is set true, the expression not endofData at the top of the repeat while evaluates false. This causes the repeat while statement to terminate.

Another Look at the Triangular Number Program

Next, you revisit the triangular number program and modify it to handle the situation in which no valid integer value is entered when prompted. In the previous chapter, you saw how to catch such an error by using the try statement. In the following Try It Out, however, if you type a bad number, you get another chance. In fact, you keep getting the same dialog displayed over and over until you finally enter a number or click Cancel to end the program.

Try It Out   Getting Another Chance

The following gives you a second chance to provide an integer.

1.   Type the following program into Script Editor:

```
-- Calculate a triangular number specified by the user - Version 2

set sum to 0  -- the sum so far
set validNumber to false
```

```
repeat while not validNumber
    display dialog "Enter your integer" default answer ""
    try
        set triangularNumber to text returned of result as integer

        -- if this statement is reached, an integer was entered
        set validNumber to true
    end try

    if not validNumber then
        display dialog "You didn't enter an integer" with icon note
    end if
end repeat

-- now calculate the requested number

repeat with n from 1 to triangularNumber
    set sum to sum + n
end repeat

-- display the result
display dialog (sum as string)
```

2. Run the program.

3. Enter an invalid integer and see what happens.

4. Try it again. After entering an invalid integer several times, enter a valid number. In this case, you should get your triangular number calculated and displayed.

How It Works

The program uses the variable validNumber to indicate whether a valid integer has been keyed.

The program enters a repeat while loop next. This loop is repeatedly executed while the value of validNumber is not true (that is, false). This implies that somewhere inside the loop you should see at least one place where the value is set to true. Otherwise, your program would continue to loop forever. This is an *infinite loop*, and it's something you don't want to set up.

After entering the loop, a dialog is displayed to the user with a request to enter an integer. The following try block appears next in the program:

```
try
    set triangularNumber to text returned of result as integer

    -- if this statement is reached, an integer was entered
    set validNumber to true
end try
```

If the coercion of the value typed in the dialog to an integer succeeds, the statement that follows, which sets the value of validNumber to true, is executed. If the coercion fails, execution of the set is skipped, and the value of validNumber remains unchanged (that is, false).

If validNumber is false after exiting the try block, a message is displayed to indicate that an integer wasn't entered, and execution of the repeat while continues. However, if the value of validNumber is true after the try block exits, the display dialog command that follows does not get executed. The loop is then terminated because the validNumber in now true.

When the loop exits, program execution continues to the section of the program that calculates the requested triangular number. The result is then displayed with a display dialog command as in the previous version of this program.

A Final Look at the Triangular Number Program

What if the user keeps entering an invalid number? It may be a test of patience to see who gives up first! One wise approach might be to limit the number of chances you give the user to get it right. For example, you could let her try three times; if she doesn't get it right by the third time, you can give up.

In the following Try It Out, you modify your triangular number program to allow three attempts before giving up. I also introduce you to the concatenation operator as a way to combine one or more strings into a single string.

Try It Out   **Limiting the Number of Attempts**

These steps enable you to limit the number of times a user can attempt to provide a valid number.

1.   Type the following program into Script Editor:

```
-- Calculate a triangular number specified by the user - Version 3

set sum to 0 -- the sum so far
set validNumber to false
set tries to 1

repeat while tries    3 and not validNumber
    display dialog "Enter your integer" default answer ""
    try
        set triangularNumber to text returned of result as integer

        -- if this statement is reached, an integer was entered
        set validNumber to true
    end try

    if not validNumber then
        display dialog "You didn't enter an integer" with icon note
        set tries to tries + 1
    end if
end repeat

if not validNumber then
    display dialog "I give up!" with icon note buttons {"OK"} default button 1
else
    -- now calculate the requested triangular number
```

```
    repeat with n from 1 to triangularNumber
        set sum to sum + n
    end repeat

    -- display the result
    display dialog "The triangular number is " & (sum as string)
 end if
```

2. Compile and run the program.

3. When prompted to enter an integer, type abc and click OK. The dialog shown in Figure 4-9 is displayed.

4. Click OK.

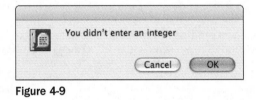

You didn't enter an integer

Cancel   OK

Figure 4-9

5. When prompted to enter an integer, type abc and click OK. You should get the dialog shown in Figure 4-9 again.

6. Click OK.

7. When prompted to enter an integer, type abc and click OK. Once again, this gives you the dialog shown in Figure 4-9.

8. Click OK. This was your third attempt to enter a valid number, so you should now see the dialog shown in Figure 4-10.

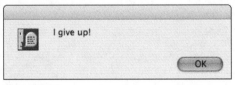

I give up!

OK

Figure 4-10

9. Rerun the program and enter the integer 10 this time.

10. Click OK, and you see the answer in a dialog, as shown in Figure 4-11.

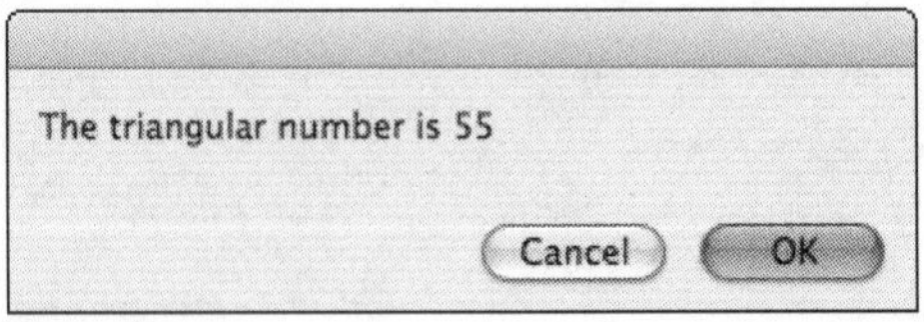

The triangular number is 55

Cancel   OK

Figure 4-11

How It Works

You can use the variable `tries` to keep track of how many times the user has attempted to key in an integer. Its value is initially set to 1.

The `repeat while` loop is encountered next in the program. It executes as long as the following is `true`:

```
tries ≤ 3 and not validNumber
```

This says that the body of the loop is to be executed as long as the value of `tries` is less than or equal to 3 *and* as long as `validNumber` is `false`. In other words, the loop will terminate if the user has failed on three attempts to enter an integer or if a valid integer has, in fact, been entered. If the reason for exiting the loop is the former condition, a dialog tells the user that the program has given up. If the reason is the latter condition, the triangular number is calculated in the variable `sum`.

A Quick Look at the Concatenation Operator

The `display dialog` command allows you to display a string, as you've seen many times. If you want to display more than one string in the same dialog, you have to combine them into a single string. This is done with the concatenation operator, which is the ampersand symbol `&`. When you write

```
"The triangular number is " & (sum as string)
```

the string to the right of the `&` operator is joined to the end of the string on the left, creating a single string. So if you execute this statement and `sum` has the value 55, the result of the concatenation is the following string:

```
"The triangular number is 55"
```

You can join more than two strings together at once using multiple concatenation operators. For example, the statement

```
"This is "  & "an example " & "of string concatenation."
```

produces the following string as its result:

```
"This is an example of string concatenation."
```

You learn more about the concatenation operator in Chapter 5. I introduce it at this point so that you can make your output messages more meaningful. In fact, go back to the previous program and change the last `display dialog` command to the following:

```
display dialog "Triangular number " & (triangularNumber as string) & ¬
        " is " & (sum as string)
```

When you run your program and enter 10 for the triangular number to calculate, you get the following message displayed in your dialog:

```
Triangular number 10 is 55
```

That's certainly a lot more meaningful than just displaying the result of 55!

The repeat until Statement

This form of the `repeat` statement is actually quite similar to the `repeat while`. Whereas the `repeat while` statement repeats execution of a set of statements while a condition is `true`, the `repeat until` repeats execution of a set of statements while a condition is `false`, or in other words, *until* it becomes `true`.

The general format of the `repeat until` statement is

```
repeat until Boolean-expression
    statement
    statement
    ...
end repeat
```

You could replace the `repeat while` from the second version of the triangular number program with the following equivalent:

```
repeat until validNumber
    ...
end repeat
```

And taking note of the inverted logic here, you could replace the `repeat while` from the final version of the triangular number program with the following:

```
repeat until tries > 3 or validNumber
    ...
end repeat
```

You've seen three different uses of the `repeat` statement to count to 10. Here's another example using the `repeat until`:

```
set n to 1
repeat until n > 10
    log n
    set n to n + 1
end repeat
```

As previously noted, you often have a choice of which form of the `repeat` statement to use to accomplish a given task. If you're going to execute a set of statements a specified number of times, the `repeat...times` is a logical choice. And if you need access to a variable that counts the repetition number along the way, the `repeat with-from-to` statement usually fits the bill.

In the following Try It Out, you write a simple guessing program and learn about a special command for generating random numbers.

Try It Out   A Simple Guessing Game

Follow these steps to use the `repeat until` to write a simple guessing program.

1.   Type the following program into Script Editor:

```
-- Simple guessing game

-- Pick a number

set myNumber to random number from 1 to 10

set tries to 0 -- Number of tries so far
set guess to missing value -- Not a valid guess

-- Introductory dialog

display dialog "I'm thinking of a number from 1 to 10"

repeat until guess = myNumber
    set guess to missing value

    display dialog "Enter your guess" default answer ""

    try
        set guess to text returned of result as integer
    end try

    -- Now see if a valid number was entered

    if guess = missing value or guess < 1 or guess > 10 then
        display dialog "I asked for a number from 1 to 10!" with icon note
    else
        set tries to tries + 1
    end if
end repeat

display dialog "Great!  You got it in " & (tries as string) & " guesses!" ¬
    with icon note buttons {"OK"}
```

2.   Save the program as an application called `guessing game`.

3.   In the Finder, locate your `guessing game` application and double-click it to run. The dialog shown in Figure 4-12 is displayed.

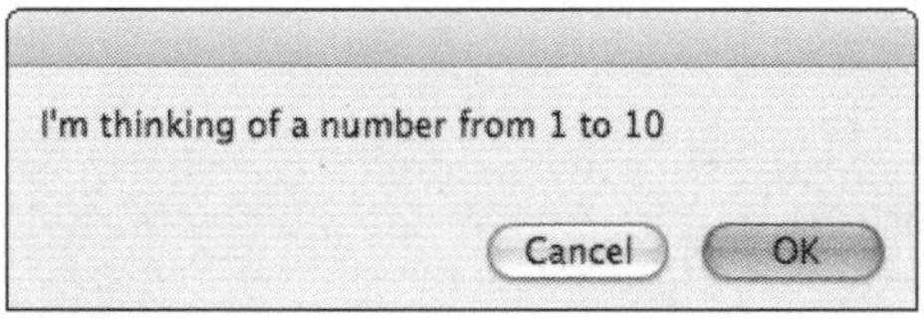

I'm thinking of a number from 1 to 10

Cancel   OK

Figure 4-12

4. Click OK. You see the dialog shown in Figure 4-13.

Enter your guess

Cancel   OK

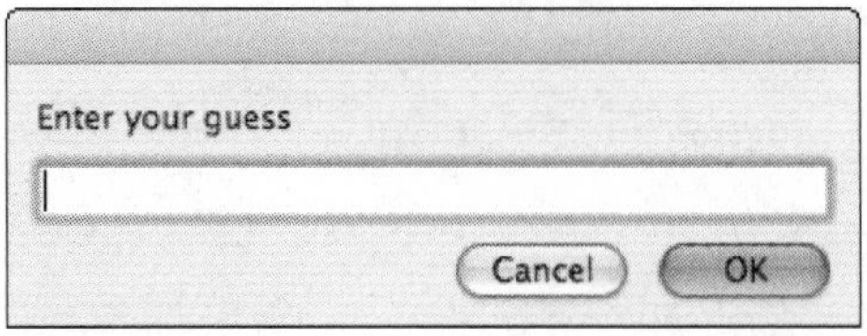

Figure 4-13

5. Enter 100. This is an invalid number, so you get the dialog shown in Figure 4-14.

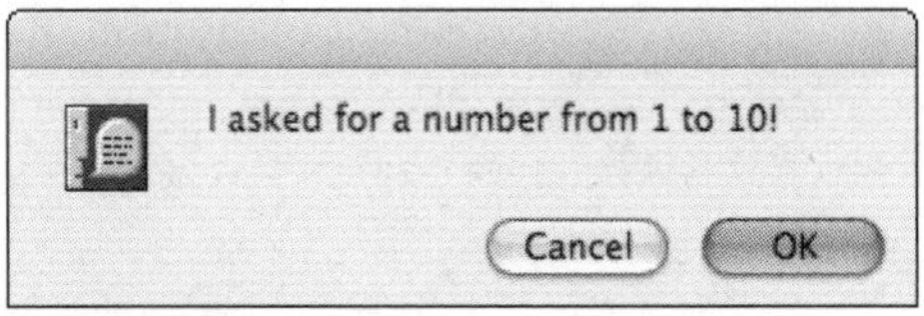

I asked for a number from 1 to 10!

Cancel   OK

Figure 4-14

6. Click OK. You should see the same dialog shown in Figure 4-13. Now enter a valid guess. Continue entering guesses until you get it right. In my case, it took me five tries; then the dialog shown in Figure 4-15 was displayed. You get a similar display with your number of guesses shown.

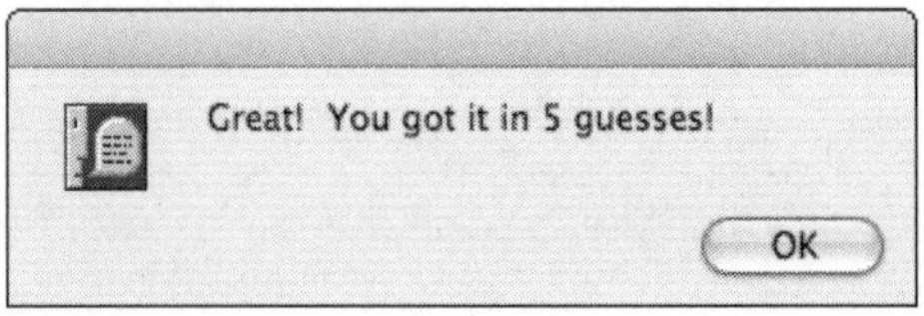

Great! You got it in 5 guesses!

OK

Figure 4-15

How It Works

Most of the program is straightforward. However, some points are worth noting. First, you need to understand how the program randomly selects the number for you to guess.

The `random number` command gives you a random number. In the program, it is used as follows:

```
random number from 1 to 10
```

This form of the command says to give you a random integer between 1 and 10, inclusive. You can specify any range you like. If the from and to numbers are integers (including negative integers), the random numbers are integral. If you write instead

```
random number from 1.0 to 10.0
```

you get random real numbers, like 1.57857759401 and 4.625096725708, that are in the specified range.

If you omit the `from` parameter, as in

```
random number to 10
```

you get random numbers from zero to the specified value. If you don't specify any range at all, as in

```
random number
```

you get a real random number between 0 and 1.0, inclusive.

To get the same sequence of random numbers each time you run a program (useful for repeatability), use the `with seed` parameter followed by a nonzero number. For example, the statements

```
random number with seed 1
random number from 1 to 10
```

produce the same results each time they are executed. The first statement seeds the random number generator, whereas the second statement asks for a random number from 1 to 10. Normally, you would seed the generator once at the start of your program, as in the first statement. Then, you would generate random numbers by repeatedly using the second `random number` statement.

After the program generates a random number from 1 to 10 and stores it in the variable `myGuess`, the program sets the number of tries to zero and the guess entered by the user to `missing value`. The program then displays an introductory dialog and enters a `repeat until` loop. This loop continues to execute until either the correct number is guessed or the user clicks Cancel on the dialog to terminate the program.

After prompting the user to enter a guess, the program executes the following `if` statement:

```
if guess = missing value or guess < 1 or guess > 10 then
    display dialog "I asked for a number from 1 to 10!" with icon note
else
    set tries to tries + 1
end if
```

This statement checks to ensure that the integer coercion succeeded and that a number between 1 and 10 was entered. The user is alerted if an invalid entry was made; otherwise, the number of guesses is incremented by 1. In either case, the loop continues execution until the guess entered by the user matches the number picked by the program. In that case, execution of the loop is terminated and the following `display dialog` command is executed:

```
display dialog "Great!  You got it in " & (tries as string) & " guesses!" ¬
    with icon note buttons {"OK"}
```

Here the user is told how many attempts he made before correctly guessing the number. The concatenation operator `&` is used to form a single string from the message and this value.

The repeat with Statement for Lists

The last form of the `repeat` statement is `repeat with`. It is used to sequence through the elements in a list. You've only had minimal exposure to lists so far. In Chapter 6, this topic is covered in depth.

If you wanted to set up a simple list that contained the names of four colors, you could write a statement like this:

```
set myColors to { "aqua", "silver", "brown", "olive" }
```

As you see in the following Try It Out, the `repeat with` statement lets you sequence through the elements in a list and assign each one in turn to a variable.

Try It Out   Sequencing through the Elements in a List

You can use `repeat with` to sequence through list elements.

1. Type the following program into Script Editor:

```
set myColors to { "aqua", "silver", "brown", "olive" }

repeat with theColor in myColors
    log theColor
end repeat
```

2. Click the `Event Log` tab and run the program. You should see the following in the log:

```
(*aqua*)
(*silver*)
(*brown*)
(*olive*)
```

How It Works

The `repeat with` statement lets you sequence through the elements in a list and assign each one to a variable, in turn. The general format of this statement is

```
repeat with loopvar in list
    statement
    statement
    ...
end repeat
```

Execution of the `repeat with` proceeds as follows: The first element in `list`, is assigned to the variable `loopvar`. The body of the loop, the statements that immediately follow up to the `end repeat`, are then executed. This process is repeated, with each element in `list` being assigned, in turn, to `loopvar` and the body of the loop being executed. After the last element in `list` has been assigned to `loopvar` and the body of the loop executed, the loop terminates.

You see this form of the `repeat` in action throughout this book. For now, a basic understanding of how it works will suffice.

Setting Up an Infinite Loop with repeat

If you simply write `repeat`, as in the following, you set up an infinite loop:

```
repeat
    statement
    statement
    ...
end repeat
```

Theoretically, this loop will execute forever, which of course, you don't want to happen. Therefore, you need some way to terminate the loop. Termination is usually based on some criteria, such as reaching the end of data or encountering some error condition. You can terminate execution of a `repeat` statement at any time by executing the following command:

```
exit repeat
```

When this command is executed, the loop is immediately terminated and execution continues with whatever follows the `end repeat` statement. If you execute this command within nested `repeat` statements, only the loop in which the command appears is terminated.

Incidentally, you have other ways to set up an infinite loop. For example, the following program counts to 10, as you saw with several other programs in this chapter:

```
set n to 1

repeat while true
    log n
    set n to n + 1
    if n > 10 then exit repeat
end repeat
```

Because `true` will always be, well, true, this `repeat` statement will theoretically execute forever, unless some action is taken to terminate the loop. After the value of n exceeds 10, the `exit repeat` is executed to exit from the loop. Certainly, this is not a very elegant way of doing things; I included it here for illustrative purposes only.

Summary

In this chapter, I showed you how easy it is to write program loops in AppleScript using the `repeat` statement. This statement enables you to repeatedly execute a set of statements. You learned the following:

❑ The `repeat...times` statement is used to repeat a set of statements a predetermined number of times.

❑ The `repeat with` statement is used to repeat a set of statements given a starting number, an ending number, and an optional increment.

❑ The second form of the `repeat with` is used to sequence through the elements in a list.

❑ The `repeat while` statement causes a set of statements to be executed as long as a particular condition is true, whereas the `repeat until` statement causes a set of statements to be executed until a particular condition is satisfied.

I show you many more examples of `repeat` statements throughout this book.

In the next chapter, you learn to work with strings, including how to reference elements of a string. Before proceeding, however, try the exercises that follow to test your understanding of the material covered in this chapter. You can find the solutions to these exercises in Appendix A.

Exercises

1. Triangular number n can also be calculated by the formula

    $$\frac{n(n+1)}{2}$$

    Modify the first triangular number program from this chapter to calculate the triangular number using this formula instead of the `repeat with` loop.

2. Rewrite the first triangular number program from this chapter to use the `repeat...times` form of the `repeat` statement instead of the `repeat with` used in the program.

3. Modify the final version of the triangular number program so that the invalid text entered by the user is displayed. So if the user enters `abc` in a dialog, you should display the following:

```
abc is not a valid integer.
```

4. Write a program to find the sum of the squares of the numbers from 1 to n, where the value of n is entered by the user. That is,

    $$\sum_{1}^{n} x^2 = 1^2 + 2^2 + \ldots + n^2$$

5. Modify the `guessing game` program to tell the user for each incorrect guess if his guess is too high or too low.

6. Modify the `guessing game` program to make some comments based on the number of guesses. For example, you might display "Wow! You got it in only 2 guesses!" or "8 guesses? Better luck next time!"

7. Modify the guessing game program to let the player play five times. Keep track of the number of guesses taken for each turn. At the end, display the average number of guesses.

8. Modify the program from the previous exercise to let the user specify how many times he wants to play. Combine the results from Exercises 5 and 6 into a single integrated program.

9. Using Script Editor, look up the `display dialog` command in the Standard Additions dictionary. Write a statement that tests the `giving up after` parameter for this command.

Working with Strings

In this chapter, you learn how to work with strings in more depth. You need to know how to manipulate strings to write more advanced programs. For example, you may want to add a suffix onto the end of every filename in a folder. Or you may want to see if each line in a document begins with a particular word.

I show you more about how special `considering` and `ignoring` statements can be used for string comparisons. You also learn how to test whether strings begin with, contain, or end with a specified string.

In this chapter, I also show you how to reference *elements* of a string, where an element can be a character, a word, or an entire paragraph. Understanding how to work with elements is critical to becoming proficient with AppleScript. The use of elements extends far beyond working with strings; you can apply elements to lists and to classes defined by other applications.

Strings, Text, and Unicode Text

Recall that a character string is simply one or more characters contained within a pair of double quotes. The quotes define the beginning and end of the string, but they do not actually get stored as part of the string. So when you write a statement like this:

```
set message to "Good afternoon!"
```

just the 15 characters between the quotes get stored inside `message`, and not the quotes themselves.

You can make your strings as long as you like. When entering long character strings, you can let Script Editor wrap the string to the next line for you. If you break the string by entering the line continuation character Option-L (or Option-Return in Script Editor) or by simply pressing the Return key, that character becomes part of the string, which may not be your intention.

You can have different types of strings in AppleScript, and they are summarized in the following list:

❑   `string`: A sequence of zero or more characters.

❑   `text`: For all intents and purposes, the same as `string`, even though it exists as a distinct class from `string`. You can coerce a value to `string` or to `text`; it makes no difference, the result is a string.

❑   `styled text`: Refers to a string that may contain font and style information. For example, it might be a string of text that is in 10 point Times Roman. The style information is stored as part of the text. This type is not used much in AppleScript programs.

❑   `nicode text`: A string that can represent characters from international character sets. Normally, each character in a string takes up 8-bits. For a Unicode text string, characters take up twice as much space, or 16-bits. For the most part, you can treat a Unicode text string like a normal string in your program. You've already done this based on the fact that the `display dialog` command actually returns the text entered into the dialog box as `Unicode text`.

The Null String

You can specify a character string containing a single space character by typing a space enclosed inside a pair of double quotes, as in

```
set spaceChar to " "
```

If you write a pair of adjacent quotes, you specify a string containing *no* characters. Such a string is called the *null* string. So when you write

```
set nullString to ""
```

you define a string containing zero characters that you store in the variable `nullString`.

Review of Concatenation

You may recall that using the operator & between two strings has the effect of joining (or concatenating) the two strings together. So if you write

```
set message to "Hello, " & "Greg!"
```

you end up with the string `"Hello, "` followed by the string `"Greg!"` being assigned to `message`, just as if you had written

```
set message to "Hello, Greg!"
```

If a user's name is stored inside a variable called `firstName`, you could write the statement

```
set message to "Hello, " & firstName
```

to join the string `"Hello, "` with the string stored in `firstName`, and then assign the result to `message`.

You can perform multiple concatenation operations in a single statement. If the variable `firstName` contains the string `"Allan"`, and the string `lastName` contains the string `"Fiber"`, writing the following statement

```
set message to "Hello, " & firstName & " " & lastName & "!"
```

has the effect of concatenating the five indicated strings in succession and storing the result of `"Hello, Allan Fiber!"` in the variable `message`.

If you concatenate a string with something that's not a string...

Getting the Size of a String

Sometimes you want to know the number of characters in a string. You can easily find this out by using the `count` command, followed by the string. For example, writing

```
count "Hello"
```

gives a result of 5, because that's the number of characters in the string. The pair of double quotes doesn't count; they're just there to delimit the characters in the string.

Obviously, you can use the `count` command to get the number of characters in a string stored inside a variable. So given the following statement:

```
set message to "AppleScript rocks!"
```

the statement

```
log count message
```

puts the value 18 into the log because that's the number of characters in the string stored in the variable `message`.

You learned that the null string is a string that contains no characters. That means you can predict that the expression

```
count ""
```

returns zero, which is, in fact, the case.

Later in this chapter, you see how to use the `count` command to count the number of elements in a list.

Using Special String Characters

Unlike many other programming languages, AppleScript does not distinguish single characters from character strings. So when you read about a character in this section, understand that it's a character string containing just a single character.

Special Properties Used Outside Strings

The following table shows some special *properties* in AppleScript that you can use when working with strings. A property is like a variable, with some unique differences that you learn about in Chapter 8. For now, just assume that you can use a property like other variables in your program.

Property	Meaning	Examples
return	end of line character	`"Line one" & return & "Line two"`
space	space character	`"one" & space & "two"`
tab	tab character	`if inChar = tab then ...`

In the first example from the table

```
"Line one" & return & "Line two"
```

the return character is inserted between the two strings "Line one" and "Line two", forming a single string that consists of the string "Line one" followed immediately by a return character. That character is, in turn, followed immediately by the string "Line two".

Assuming that the variable `firstName` is a string that stores someone's first name and `lastName` is a string that stores that person's last name, you can write the following:

```
set fullName to firstName & space & lastName
```

With this line, you assign the person's first and last name, delimited by a space, to `fullName`. Of course, this is equivalent to writing

```
set fullName to firstName & space & lastName
```

Escape Characters Used inside Strings

You can use other special character sequences *inside* a string. These characters each begin with the backslash character and are followed by a single character. The backslash character in the string tells AppleScript that a special character is to be inserted. These characters are referred to as *escape* characters. The two-character sequence gets removed and replaced with its corresponding ASCII equivalent by AppleScript.

The special AppleScript escape characters are summarized in the following table.

Escape character	Meaning	Examples
\r	end of line character	"Line one\rLine two"
\n	line feed character, often also referred to as the *newline* character	"Line one\nLine two"

Escape character	Meaning	Examples
\t	tab character	"ID\tName\tSalary"
\"	double quote character	"\"Hello,\" he said"
\\	backslash character	"A \\ introduces an escape character"

The linefeed character is used on UNIX systems (including Mac OS X) to mark the end of the line. However, Mac systems have historically used the return character. If you're searching some text from a file for the end of the line, make sure you recognize either the return or the linefeed character.

After you compile your program, Script Editor replaces any \r, \t, and \n characters with space characters in your window, but they're still there inside the string. So for example, if you enter this into Script Editor:

```
set threeLines to "line1\rline2\rline3"
```

it gets changed to the following after you compile your program:

```
set threeLines to "line1
line2
line3"
```

If you want, you can write this instead

```
set threeLines to "line1" & return & "line2" & return "line3"
```

which won't go through a similar type of conversion when it gets compiled.

More on Unicode Text

If you want to enter Unicode characters into your program, you can use this special notation:

```
«data utxtc1c2...»
```

The character « is a left guillemot (entered from the keyboard by typing Option-\). The Unicode characters c_1, c_2, ... are specified as four hexadecimal digits each, and » is the right guillemot character (entered from the keyboard by typing Shift-Option-\). The result of this expression is a string of type Unicode text.

The special notation «data type...» is used in AppleScript programs to enter data of all different types that cannot be directly keyed into the program.

For example, the following display dialog command:

```
display dialog («data utxt2661266226642667» as Unicode text)
```

passes a Unicode text string to display dialog and produces the dialog shown in Figure 5-1.

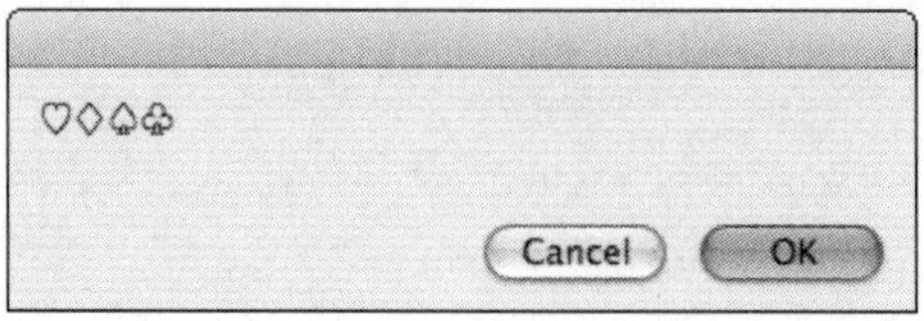

Figure 5-1

The heart symbol is hexadecimal 2661, the diamond is hexadecimal 2662, the spades symbol is hexadecimal 2664, and the clubs symbol is hexadecimal 2667. This works because the `display dialog` command accepts a Unicode text string as its argument. Other commands may accept only strings, so the previous code notation wouldn't work. You must check the documentation for the command before using `Unicode text` to make sure it is accepted.

The considering and ignoring Statements

You can use two special statements to control the way strings are compared: `considering` and `ignoring`. The `considering` statement enables you to specify an attribute to consider when comparing strings. The general format of the `considering` statement is the following:

```
considering attribute
    statement
    statement
    ...
end considering
```

Any of the statements included within the `considering` block, up to the `end considering`, ignore the specified *attribute* when string comparisons or containment operations (explained shortly) are performed. When you exit the block, the previous considering/ignoring status of *attribute* is restored.

As a simple example, you can use the attribute `case` to specify that the program distinguishes between uppercase and lowercase letters when comparing two strings. Normally, case is not taken into consideration. That means, if you write the statement

```
log "yes" = "YES"
```

`true` is entered into the log because these two strings are normally considered equal. That is, the case of the letters is normally ignored. If you, instead, write the following

```
considering case
    log "yes" = "YES"
end considering
```

`false` is entered into the log because the string `"yes"` is not equal to the string `"YES"` when uppercase and lowercase letters are considered as distinct letters.

The `ignoring` statement is the inverse of the `considering` statement: It enables you to specify an attribute to be ignored when comparing or searching strings. The general format of the `ignoring` statement is as follows:

```
ignorimg attribute
    statement
    statement
    ...
end ignoring
```

The statements in the `ignoring` block that perform string comparisons ignore the specified `attribute` when making the comparisons. When you exit the block, the previous considering/ignoring status of `attribute` is restored.

The following table summarizes all the attributes you can use in a `considering` or `ignoring` statement:

Attribute	Meaning	Default	Example and result
case	Upper- and lowercase letters	Ignored: Upper- and lowercase characters are considered equivalent	`"My ABCs" = "my abcs"` -- *true*
diacriticals	diacritical (accent) marks	Considered: An accented character is not equal to an unaccented one	`"première" = "premiere"` -- *false*
expansion	ligatures (æ, Æ, œ, Œ,)	Considered: A ligature is not equal to its two-character equivalent	`"bœuf" = "boeuf"` -- *false*
hyphens	A hyphen (dash) character	Considered: A hyphenated string is not equal to an unhyphenated one	`"re-animate" = "reanimate"` -- *false*
punctuation	The characters .,?:;!\'"`	Considered: Punctuation characters are used in the comparison	`"Yo, Bob! " = "Yo Bob"` -- *false*
white space	space, tab, return and newline character	Considered: White space characters are used in the comparison	`" one  two" = "onetwo"` -- *false*

As you can see, all attributes except `case` are considered by default. The examples show the result when the default condition is used. If you invert the default, the result is also inverted. For instance, the second example from the table, which assumes that diacriticals are considered, logs `true` if you write

```
ignoring diacriticals
    log "première" = "premiere"
end ignoring
```

Combining Attributes

Ignoring or considering an attribute is relatively straightforward. However, it starts to get more interesting if you nest these blocks or if you specify more than one attribute. The latter is achieved by listing multiple attributes to the `considering` or `ignoring` statement, separating attributes from each other by a comma. The last attribute in the list is delimited by the word `and`. In this case, the general format of the `considering` statement becomes

```
considering attribute1, attribute2, ..., and attributen
    statement
    statement
    ...
end
```

and the general format of the `ignoring` statement becomes

```
ignoring attribute1, attribute2, ..., and attributen
    statement
    statement
    ...
end
```

In the first case, *attribute1, attribute2, ...,* and *attributen* are all to be considered when performing string comparisons in the statements that follow in the block. In the second case, all the listed attributes are to be ignored when strings are compared.

As an example, the following `ignoring` statement says to ignore punctuation and white-space characters when comparing two strings (recall that case is ignored by default):

```
ignoring punctuation and white space
    statement
    statement
    ...
end ignoring
```

The following comparisons would each produce a true result if they occurred within the preceding `ignoring` block:

```
"Hello." = "hello"
"1., 2., 3." = "123"
"It's as easy as A, B, C" = "its as easy as abc."
```

You're not off the hook yet! The format for these two statements is even more general than that shown. You can add `but` clauses that let you specify attributes to ignore and consider in the same statement. In such a case, the general format of this clause is either

```
but ignoring attribute
```

to have *attribute* ignored in a `consider` statement or

```
but considering attribute
```

to have *attribute* considered in an `ignore` statement.

For example, you can modify the previous `ignoring` statement, which ignored punctuation and white space and implicitly ignored case, to consider case by writing the following:

```
ignoring punctuation and white space but considering case
    statement
    statement
    ...
end ignoring
```

Now any of the comparisons that follow up to the `end ignoring` will ignore punctuation characters but consider case when comparing strings. That means that the previous test

```
"Hello." = "hello"
```

that produced a `true` result will now produce a `false` result.

The `but` clause can list multiple attributes, as you might expect. However, you don't normally get this sophisticated in your comparisons. Most attributes are considered by default, so you typically use an `ignoring` statement to list those attributes you want to ignore. If your code gets deeply nested, you might need a `considering` or `ignoring` statement to override the outer `considering` or `ignoring` statement. You see how this works in the following Try It Out.

Try It Out   Using considering and ignoring Statements

You can use the following method to include `considering` and `ignoring` statements in nested blocks.

1. Type the following program into Script Editor:

```
-- Illustrate the use of considering and ignoring

set s1 to "Hello!"
set s2 to "hello"
set s3 to "\"bœuf\" is French for beef"
set s4 to "boeuf is French for beef"

log s1 = s2

ignoring punctuation
    log s1 = s2
end ignoring

-- ignoring ... but

considering case but ignoring punctuation
    log s1 = s2
end considering

log s3

-- ignoring ... and

ignoring punctuation and expansion
    log s3 = s4
end ignoring
```

```
-- nested statements

ignoring punctuation
    ignoring expansion
        log s3 = s4
    end ignoring
    log s3 = s4
end ignoring
```

2. Click the Event Log tab and run the program. You see the following results in the Event Log pane:

```
(*false*)
(*true*)
(*false*)
(*"bœuf" is French for beef*)
(*true*)
(*true*)
(*false*)
```

How It Works

The program begins with the following four assignments:

```
set s1 to "Hello!"
set s2 to "hello"
set s3 to "\"bœuf\" is French for beef"
set s4 to "boeuf is French for beef"
```

In the third line of your program, the ligature *œ* appears in the word *bœuf*, which is French for *beef*. You can enter this special character by pressing Option-q.

To see what other key combinations you can use in System Preferences, select International. Then click the Input Menu tab and turn on the Keyboard Viewer. Also enable Show Input Menu in the menu bar. This puts a locale flag in your menu bar (on my system, it's an American flag). You can then select Show Keyboard Viewer from the menu to get a keyboard displayed on your screen. Press the Shift, Option, or Shift-Option keys to see the characters that can be entered directly from the keyboard. Press the key on the keyboard for the desired symbol to enter that symbol at the insertion point in Script Editor.

Returning to your program, after the four strings have been assigned, the program performs a series of tests to see the effects of `considering` and `ignoring` statements. First, a test is made to see if `s1` is equal to `s2`, and the result is logged. You can see that `s1` contains the string `"Hello!"` and `s2` contains the string `"hello"`, so these two strings are not equal. The first string contains an exclamation point, whereas the second does not. The fact that the first string begins with a capital letter *H* and the second starts with a lowercase letter *h* does not cause the two strings to test unequal. Case is ignored by default.

In the first `ignoring` block

```
ignoring punctuation
    log s1 = s2
end ignoring
```

the same comparison is made, this time with punctuation ignored. Because an exclamation point is a punctuation character, it is ignored for purposes of the comparison. So the strings `"Hello!"` and `"hello"` are considered equal this time.

As noted, case is ignored by default when you subsequently test s1 against s2 in the following block:

```
considering case but ignoring punctuation
    log s1 = s2
end considering
```

So the two strings test as not equal this time. In this instance, the capital and lowercase letter *H* are the reason for the equality test to fail.

After logging the string s3, which contains the ligature character *æ*, the program tests s3 against s4 in the following block:

```
ignoring punctuation and expansion
    log s3 = s4
end ignoring
```

By ignoring punctuation, the double quote characters stored inside s3 are not used for the comparison. By ignoring expansion, the ligature character *æ* is considered equal to the two-character sequence *oe*. Therefore, the result of this test is `true`.

The last section of the program shows how these blocks work when they're nested:

```
ignoring punctuation
    ignoring expansion
        log s3 = s4
    end ignoring
    log s3 = s4
end ignoring
```

The first equality test of s3 against s4 is done with *both* punctuation and expansion ignored. The second test is done with punctuation ignored. Expansion is not ignored because that block was terminated in the previous line. When a considering or ignoring statement ends, the consideration attributes are restored to the state they had before the statement was entered. In this case, expansion was considered before the innermost `ignoring` statement was entered (that is its default value). So when that statement ends, expansion is no longer ignored and is again considered (or reconsidered). That explains why the second equality test of s3 against s4 in this block proves `false`.

Words, Characters, and Paragraphs

You saw that a character string is simply a sequence of characters. AppleScript allows you to perform some basic operations with strings. For example, you've already seen how to concatenate two strings and how to count the number of characters in a string. In this section, you see how you can extract *characters, words,* and *paragraphs* from character strings. First, examine the following table to see how AppleScript defines these terms.

Class	Meaning	Examples
character	A single character from a string	`"a"` `"!"` `"="` `"9"`
word	A contiguous sequence of letters, numbers, commas (between digits), periods (before digits), currency symbols, percent signs, apostrophes (within sequences of letter or numbers) and hyphens	`AppleScript` `3.14159` `$318,000` `re-animated` `1.34e+10`
paragraph	A sequence of characters up to the end of the string or a return or linefeed character, whichever occurs first	`"para1\rpara2\rpara3"`
text item	A sequence of characters delimited by the characters specified by `text item delimiters`; using the default setting, a text item is a single character from a string	`last text item of` `fileName`

You can see from the table that a word is not just a sequence of letters. It includes numbers, currency amounts, and in general, any sequence of characters that would be logically grouped together.

A paragraph is a sequence of characters ending in a return or linefeed character. If you're used to working with a word processing application like MS Word, this definition is familiar to you. To end one paragraph and begin a new one in Word, you press the Return key.

In the table, you see that the string

```
"para1\rpara2\rpara3"
```

contains three paragraphs. The first two are delimited by a return character. The last paragraph is delimited by the end of the string.

A text item is normally just a single character from a string. However, as you see later in the chapter, by using the special `text item delimiters` property, you can change this meaning. This property is useful for parsing a string into its components where a particular delimiter character like a slash or a colon is used in the string to delimit each component.

Working with Elements

Technically, an element is an object contained inside another object. Elements of a string include those listed in the preceding table. A character is an element of a string; it is also an element of a word or a paragraph. As you see in the next chapter, lists have elements, too.

The following table summarizes the various ways of specifying elements in a string.

Item Specifer	Meaning	Example
first, second, third, ..., tenth	Specified item	first word of myName
1st, 2nd, 3rd, ...	A specific item by number	2nd word of myName
item 1, item 2, item 3...	A specific *item* by number	word 1 of myName
-1, -2, -3	An item relative to the last item; where –1 references the last item	word -1 of myName
last *or* end	Last item	last word of myName
some	A random item	some word of theText
every	All items	every word of theText
plural form of *item*	Same as every *item*	words of theText
items m through n	Items *m* through *n*; beginning can be used for *m*, and end can be used for *n*	words 1 through 4 of theText

Whenever you reference elements from a string, whether they're characters, words, or paragraphs, the result is either a string or a list of strings. A list of strings is the result of getting every element or a range of elements from a string.

The following points are worth noting if you are writing expressions to reference elements:

❑ You can substitute the word in for of, as in

```
first word in myName
```

❑ You can use the implied get command like this:

```
get first word of myName
```

❑ You can insert the superfluous word the if you like as well, as in the following:

```
get the first word of myName
```

❑ If you try to get an element that doesn't exist, you get an AppleScript error. So if you write

```
character 4 of "ABC"
```

the error message Can't get character 4 of "ABC" appears when you run your program.

In the next several Try It Out examples, you write some programs to see how to work with string elements. You'll carry through these important concepts to the next chapter on lists. You learn in Chapter 6 that these same element specifiers are also used with lists.

Try It Out   **Working with Character Elements**

You can practice working with character elements by following these steps.

1. Type the following program into Script Editor:

```
-- Working with elements - characters

set s to "The AppleScript language rocks!"

-- these all get the first character of s

log first character of s
log 1st character of s
log character 1 of s

-- these all get the last character of s

log last character of s
log character -1 of s
log character (count s) of s

-- these get specific characters

log 5th character of s
log tenth character of s
log character -6 of s
```

2. Click the Event Log tab, run the program, and look at the log. You see the following:

```
(*T*)
(*T*)
(*T*)
(*!*)
(*!*)
(*!*)
(*A*)
(*S*)
(*r*)
```

How It Works

The program begins by assigning a string to the variable s with the statement

```
set s to "The AppleScript language rocks!"
```

Here are the first three log statements in the program:

```
log first character of s
log 1st character of s
log character 1 of s
```

Each has the effect of getting the first character from the string stored in s, which is a capital letter T. As you can see, three different references to the first character of the string are used. You can usually use several different methods to get elements from a string. As you learn later, you can even write a statement like this:

```
s's first character
```

or even this:

```
tell s to get its first character
```

You probably want to stick to just one method. However, if you want to look at scripts written by others or if you must maintain such scripts, you need to be familiar with these different methods of referencing elements.

Returning to the program, here are the next three log statements:

```
log last character of s
log character -1 of s
log character (count s) of s
```

Each has the effect of getting the last character of the string stored in s, which is the exclamation point. The first two log statements are straightforward, recalling from the table that –1 references the last character in a string, –2 the next to last character, and so on. The last log statement from this set also requires some explanation. You saw in the earlier section, "Getting the Size of a String," that the count command gives you the number of characters in a string. So writing

```
count s
```

gives you the number of characters in s. If you count the number of character in The AppleScript Language rocks!, you find that this number is 31. So the log statement reduces to

```
log character 31 of s
```

after the length of s has been calculated. This results in the last character of s.

The last three statements in the program look like this:

```
log 5th character of s
log tenth character of s
log character -6 of s
```

The first statement produces the fifth character of s, which is the A in AppleScript, whereas the second statement produces the tenth character of s, which is the S in the same word. The last log statement says to get the sixth character from the end from s. This is the character r in rocks.

In the next Try It Out, you learn how to get words from a string. You use *range specifiers* to obtain multiple elements from a string. A range specifier allows you to specify a series of elements to extract from a string, whether they're characters, words, or paragraphs.

Try It Out   Working with Word Elements

To practice working with word elements, follow these steps:

1. Type the following program into Script Editor:

```
-- Working with elements - words

set s to "The AppleScript language rocks!"

-- get a specific word

log first word of s
log last word of s
log word 2 of s

-- get every word

log words of s
log every word of s
log words 1 through -1 of s
log words 1 thru -1 of s

-- get a specific range of words

log words 1 through 3 of s

-- get a character from a word

log first character of second word of s
```

2. Click the Event Log tab, run the program, and then examine the output in the log. You should get the following results:

```
(*The*)
(*rocks*)
(*AppleScript*)
(*The, AppleScript, language, rocks*)
(*The, AppleScript, language, rocks*)
(*The, AppleScript, language, rocks*)
(*The, AppleScript, language, rocks*)
(*The, AppleScript, language*)
(*A*)
```

How It Works

The program begins by setting the variable s to the same string as in the previous program, namely `"The AppleScript Language rocks!"` The program is then divided into four sections of log statements. The first section contains the following statements:

```
log first word of s
log last word of s
log word 2 of s
```

The first statement logs the first word from s, which is the word The. You know about the different possible permutations, like 1st word and word 1, so they weren't used this time.

The second log statement logs the last word in s, which is the word rocks (and note that the exclamation point is not included). The third log statement gets the second word from s, which is AppleScript.

The next four log statements in the program show how you can get all the words from a string. You use the same technique to get every character or paragraph from a string. As noted in the table, using the plural of an item references *every* item. So when you write

```
words of s
```

(or words from s or words in s), you get a list containing every word from the string. Writing

```
every word of s
```

has the same effect, as does writing either

```
words 1 through -1 of s
```

or

```
words 1 thru -1 of s
```

The last case shows how the word thru can be used as a synonym for through.

You have to supply numbers when using a range. So you can't write

```
words first through third of s
```

However, you are allowed to use the word beginning to reference the first element and end to reference the last element, meaning that writing

```
words beginning through end of s
```

works. It is admittedly confusing, which is why you'll want to adopt one method and stick to it.

The last statement in the program is perhaps the most intriguing:

```
log first character of second word of s
```

This works just as you read it. The first character of the second word of s is obtained. Because the second word is AppleScript, and its first character is A, that's what is logged by the program.

If myDoc contains several different lines of text, a statement like this would be valid:

```
first character of first word of second paragraph of myDoc
```

To get the first two words of the third paragraph, a sentence like this would work:

```
words 1 thru 2 of third paragraph of myDoc
```

To get the characters from the first word of the third paragraph, you could write

```
characters of first word of third paragraph of myDoc
```

Just to test your understanding of this concept, consider why the following could not be used to get every character from the first two words of the third paragraph of myDoc.

```
characters of words 1 thru 2 of third paragraph of myDoc   -- no good!
```

The reason this doesn't work is because a range returns a list, not a string. So the expression

```
words 1 thru 2 of third paragraph of myDoc
```

gives a list of two words. And you can't apply the characters specifier to a list, just to a string. It is possible to get what you want, but you have to use the type of range discussed later in this chapter or else you must reconstitute the list back into a string.

In the next Try It Out, you select a random quotation from a string containing several different quotations. The strategy you use is to separate one quotation from the next inside the string by a return character and then select a random paragraph from the string using some paragraph.

Try It Out   Picking a Random Element

You can choose a random element from a string by following these steps:

1.   Type the following program into Script Editor. Make sure you press the Return key after each quote stored inside the string.

```
-- Display a funny random quote

set quotes to "I've had a wonderful time, but this wasn't it.
Time flies like the wind. Fruit flies like bananas.
I find television very educating. Every time somebody turns on the set,
I go into the other room and read a book.
Quote me as saying I was mis-quoted.
I was married by a judge. I should have asked for a jury.
What do you call people who are afraid of Santa Claus? Claustrophobic.
The shortest distance between two points is under construction.
The fact that no one understands you doesn't make you an artist.
A low voter turnout is an indication of fewer people going to the polls. "

-- Now pick a random quote and put it in the dialog box

set quoteoftheday to some paragraph of quotes

display dialog "Quote of the day: " & return & return & quoteoftheday buttons
        {"OK"} default button {"OK"}
```

Notice in the quotation starting "I find television. . . ." that the string as shown here was continued by Script Editor onto the next line. That's why it's shown as indented. The indentation is automatic by Script Editor, but it is not part of the string.

2. Run the program. Figure 5-2 shows the dialog box I got when I ran the program. You'll likely get a different quotation because, after all, the quote is randomly selected.

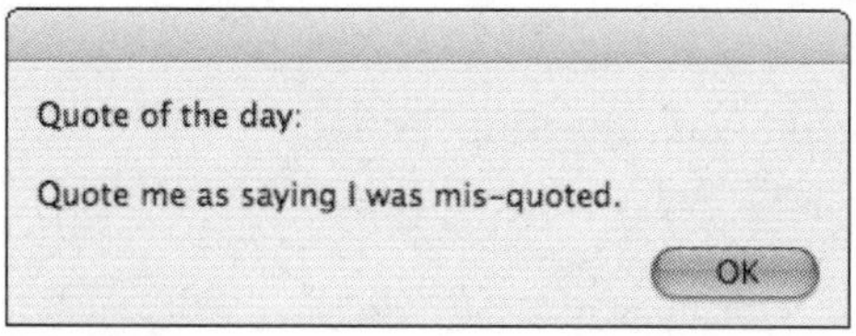

> Quote of the day:
>
> Quote me as saying I was mis-quoted.
>
> OK

Figure 5-2

3. Run the program several more times to verify that you get different quotes displayed by the program.

How It Works

Recall that a paragraph is a sequence of characters delimited by a return character. Each quote in the string is delimited by such a character (it's the end of line character entered into the string each time you pressed Return when keying it in).

After storing a series of quotations in the variable `quotes`, the program selects a random paragraph from the string using the following statement:

```
set quoteoftheday to some paragraph of quotes
```

The string to display is built from the string `"Quote of the day: "` concatenated with two return characters, followed by the selected quotation. This is displayed with the following `display dialog` command, which specifies a single default button labeled OK:

```
display dialog "Quote of the day: " & return & return & quoteoftheday buttons
    {"OK"} default button {"OK"}
```

You can use another approach for representing your quotes in a way that is more manageable. This involves representing each quote as an item in a list. You see how that's done in Chapter 6.

Understanding Text Item Delimiters

Sometimes you have to work with data that is delimited by special characters. For example, you may be reading data from a file where each field of data is separated from the next by a tab character. Or you may be working with a Mac file name path, where each component in the file name is separated from the next by a colon character. Finally, you might be working with a so-called POSIX file name path, where directories in the path are delimited by slash (/) characters. These types of paths are more precisely described in Chapter 7.

The `text item delimiters` property provides a convenient way to separate data that is delimited by a specific character into its components. You do this by setting this property to the particular delimiter character and then retrieving `text item` elements from the string. The following Try It Out shows how this is done.

Try It Out   **Working with text item delimiters**

In this program, you change the value of text item delimiters. In the following steps, you change the delimiter to a colon character so that you can easily parse (or extract) each component in a path name.

1. Type the following program into Script Editor:

```
-- Using text item delimiters

set myPath to "Macintosh HD:Users:steve:"

-- save the old delimiters and change to a :

set saveTextItemDelimiters to text item delimiters
set text item delimiters to ":"

-- sequence through each path component

repeat with component in (text items in myPath)
    log component
end repeat

-- restore text item delimiters

set text item delimiters to saveTextItemDelimiters
```

2. Click the Event Log tab, run the program, and look in the lower window. You see the following displayed:

```
(*Macintosh HD*)
(*Users*)
(*steve*)
(**)
```

How It Works

The program stores a path to my home folder in the variable myPath.

The current value of text item delimiters is then retrieved and stored in the variable saveTextItemDelimiters for safe-keeping with the following statement:

```
set saveTextItemDelimiters to text item delimiters
```

This is a matter of good programming style. Later in the program, the original value will be restored from this variable. If you don't restore the original value of text item delimiters, the modified value remains in effect for the remainder of your Script Editor session, even if you're working on another program in a different window! This could produce unexpected results and even cause a program to stop working.

After the value of text item delimiters is saved, its value is set to a colon character using the statement

```
set text item delimiters to ":"
```

Notice that components of the path name stored in `myPath` are delimited by colon characters. So you set `text item delimiters` to a colon so that you can now easily extract these components.

The `repeat` statement that follows is used to sequence through each component in the path:

```
repeat with component in (text items in myPath)
    log component
end repeat
```

Each component in the path is retrieved by writing `text items` (or, equivalently, `every text item`).

When you specify a `text item` element, the value of `text item delimiters` comes into play. Normally, the default value for `text item delimiters` is the null string, so a `text item` is just a single character. By changing it to a colon character, a `text item` is now defined as a sequence of characters up to the next colon character, or the end of the string, whichever comes first.

In your program example, the first text item from `myPath` is the character string `"Macintosh HD"`, as is verified from the first logged entry. Note here that if you had asked for the words from `myPath` instead of the text items, the first component of your path would have been considered two separate words: `Macintosh` and `HD`. This explains the motivation for working with text items instead of words.

The second text item from `myPath` is whatever characters follow the first colon, up to (but not including) the second colon. This is the string `"Users"`. Similarly, the third text item is the string `"steve"`. Notice that `myPath` ends with a colon character. So AppleScript actually produces a *fourth* text item from the string. In this case, there aren't any characters from the last colon to the end of the string. As a result, a null string is produced. Note that if `myPath` did not end in a colon character, only three text items would have been retrieved, not four.

> `text item delimiters` *can take a list of characters to be used as delimiters. In theory, each of the characters in the list is supposed to be used to delimit items in a string. However, the current AppleScript implementation uses just the first item in the list and ignores the remaining items.*

The `text item delimiters` property also comes into play when converting a list into a string. You learn about that in the next chapter.

Locating Strings inside Strings

Sometimes you want to see if a string contains another string. For example, you might want to see if a file contains a JPEG image by testing if the file name ends with the characters `.jpg`. Or you might want to see if a POSIX path specifies a *full* path by testing if it begins with a `/` character. Finally, you might want to locate the occurrence of a particular string inside some text, perhaps to delete or change it to something else.

You saw in Chapter 3 how you could use the operators `comes before` (or `<`) and `comes after` (or `>`) to test how two strings are ordered. AppleScript also provides operators, called *containment operators*, that let you test whether one string begins with another string, ends with another string, or contains another string. The `offset` command lets you determine precisely where within one string another string occurs.

The containment operators and the `offset` command are summarized in the following table.

Operator or Command	Meaning	Example
`s1 begins with s2`	Does string *s1* begin with string *s2*?	`"iTunes Library" begins with "iTunes"`
`s1 ends with s2`	Does string *s1* end with string *s2*?	`"Macintosh HD:Users:" ends with ":"`
`s1 contains s2`	Does string *s2* occur in string *s1*?	`theText contains "AppleScript"`
`s1 does not contain s2`	Does string *s2* not occur is string *s1*?	`theText does not contain "Cocoa"`
`s1 is in s2`	Does string *s1* occur in string *s2*?	`"AppleScript" is in theText`
`s1 is not in s2`	Does string *s1* *not* occur in string *s2*?	`"Cocoa" is not in theText`
`offset of s1 in s2`	Returns offset of first occurrence of string *s1* in string *s2*, or 0 if not present	`offset of space in theText`

These operators are fairly self-explanatory. The containment operators produce a true/false result. The `offset` command produces an integer representing the offset of the first string inside the second string. If the first string is not in the second string, the command returns `0`.

Note that considerations do come into play here. For example, if white space is currently being ignored, the following test is `true`

```
"     Hello"  begins with "H"
```

The next Try It Out shows how to use these operators and the `offset` command when working with strings.

Try It Out   Using Containment Operators and the offset Command

Follow these steps to see how these containment operators and the `offset` command work.

1. Type the following program into Script Editor:

```
-- Containment operator and offset command

set s1 to "bœuf is French for beef"
set fileName to "myHouse.jpg"

-- offset of

offset of "French" in s1
offset of "b" in s1
```

```
-- begins with

log s1 begins with "bœuf"

-- ends with

if fileName ends with ".JPG" then
    log fileName & " is a JPEG file"
end if

-- is in and contains

log "boeuf" is in s1

ignoring expansion
    log "boeuf" is in s1
end ignoring

log "oignon" is not in s1
log s1 contains "french"
log s1 does not contain "latin"
```

2. Click the Event Log tab and run the program. Examine the Event Log, and you should see the following output:

```
tell current application
    offset of "French" in "bœuf is French for beef"
        9
    offset of "b" in "bœuf is French for beef"
        1
    (*true*)
    (*myHouse.jpg is a JPEG file*)
    (*false*)
    (*true*)
    (*true*)
    (*true*)
    (*true*)
end tell
```

How It Works

For now, just ignore the `tell current application` and `end tell` that appear in the Event Log. The `offset` command is actually a Standard Additions command (like the `display dialog` command that you learned about in Chapter 4). You get more information logged in the Event Log when you use the `offset` command than you do when you use a built-in AppleScript command. For that reason, a separate `log` command is not needed in a program using the `offset` command.

The program starts by setting two variables like the following:

```
set s1 to "bœuf is French for beef"
set fileName to "myHouse.jpg"
```

The first assignment to `s1` uses the ligature character œ that you learned how to enter earlier in this chapter. The second assignment stores an arbitrary file name into the variable `fileName`.

A ligature is a single character, so when you ask for the offset of the string `"French"` in the string s1, with the statement

```
offset of "French" in s1
```

the Event Log records the offset as 9, meaning the string begins at the ninth character in s1 (count it out to verify this is the case).

The statement

```
offset of "b" in s1
```

produces a value of 1 because the string begins with the character *b*, and the offset of the first character is 1.

The statement

```
log s1 begins with "bœuf"
```

enters `true` into the Event Log because the string stored in s1 does, in fact, begin with the string `"bœuf"`.

The next `if` statement in the program might appear in a sequence of code that tests the extension of a file name to see if it specifies a JPEG image:

```
if fileName ends with ".JPG" then
    log fileName & " is a JPEG file"
end if
```

Note that the string stored in `fileName` actually ends in the characters `".jpg"`, and yet the test succeeds. That's because, as you will recall, case is normally ignored by default.

The next test in the program

```
log "boeuf" is in s1
```

logs `false` because the string `"boeuf"` does not appear inside s1. If you intend for this type of test to succeed, you must ignore expansion, as you do in the following statements:

```
ignoring expansion
    log "boeuf" is in s1
end ignoring
```

Ignoring expansion causes single character ligatures to match their two-character counterparts. This explains why the `"œ"` in `"bœuf"` matches the `"oe"` in `"boeuf"`.

Here are the remaining three tests in the program:

```
log "oignon" is not in s1
log s1 contains "french"
log s1 does not contain "latin"
```

Each causes `true` to be logged because `"oignon"` is not in `s1`, `s1` does contain `"french"` (recall that case is ignored by default), and `s1` does not contain the string `"latin"`.

Specifying a Range to Get a Substring

You have not yet encountered yet another form of element specifier that takes the following general format:

```
from  item m to item n
```

Here, `item` (when talking about strings) is either a `character`, `word`, or `paragraph`. This range can be used to extract a substring from a string by placing the word `text` in front of the range. For example, the following statement gets the first two words from the string stored in `myText`:

```
text from word 1 to word 2 of myText
```

This statement gets the fifth through tenth characters from the same string:

```
text from character 5 to character 10 of myText
```

> *Be sure not to confuse this range specifier that uses the `from...to` notation with the range specifier that uses the `through` (or `thru`) format. They are not interchangeable.*

You can use `beginning` to refer to the first item in the range and `end` to refer to the last item. So writing the following simply gives you back the string stored in `myText`

```
text from beginning to end of myText
```

Recognize that this form of specifying a range produces a single string and not a list of characters, words, or paragraphs. Thus, you are extracting a substring from the target string, which is why this format is useful.

As an example, if the variable `filePath` contains the string `"Macintosh HD:Users:GregKochan:"`, the following statements

```
set driveOffset to offset of ":" in filePath
set driveName to text from beginning to character (driveOffset - 1) of filePath
```

set the variable `driveName` to the first component of the path or to the string `"Macintosh HD"`.

More on the Count Command

You have seen how you can count the number of characters in a string with a statement like

```
count theText
```

You can also use the `count` command to count the number of elements in a list. Combine this fact with the knowledge that enumerating a range of elements produces a list. You can now see how writing a statement like

```
count words in theText
```

can be used to count the number of words in a string.

As you see in the next Try It Out, the count command comes in handy when you want to count the number of items of a particular type in a string.

Try It Out   **Count the Number of Words in Some Text**

In the following steps, you use the count command to count the number of elements of different types in a string.

1. Type the following program into Script Editor:

```
-- Using count

set s to "The AppleScript Language rocks!"

-- the length of s
log (count s)

-- the number of words in s
log (count words in s)

-- the number of characters in the first word
log (count characters in the first word of s)
```

2. Click the Event Log tab, run the program, and examine the log. You get the following results:

```
(*31*)
(*4*)
(*3*)
```

How It Works

The output of this program is straightforward. First, the characters in s are counted. Next, the number of words in s are counted. Finally, the number of characters in the first word of s are counted.

Using length instead of count

Incidentally, before leaving this topic you should note that the length property can also be used to obtain counts. So you can write

```
length of s
```

to get the number of characters in the string stored in s. You can also write

```
length of words in theText
```

to get the number of words stored in theText.

The next Try It Out combines several of the techniques you learned in this chapter. You sequence through each word in a string and log each word and its length. At the end, you log the total number of characters and words in the string. Obviously, this all goes to a log pane. In a real-world application, you might show the results in a dialog or write them to a file. You learn how to do those things in Chapters 6 and 7.

Try It Out   Enumerating the Words in a String

In the following steps, you see how to provide a simple summary about a string.

1. Type the following program into Script Editor:

```
-- Counting words and summarizing text

set theText to "AppleScript is a flexible language that allows you to
     easily work with elements in strings and lists."

-- sequence through each word in the string

repeat with theWord in (every word in theText)
    log theWord & ": " & (count theWord) as string
end repeat

-- summary statistics

log "Number of words: " & (count words in theText) as string
log "Number of characters: " & (count theText) as string
```

2. Click the Event Log tab, run the program, and examine the Event Log. You get the following results:

```
(*AppleScript: 11*)
(*is: 2*)
(*a: 1*)
(*flexible: 8*)
(*language: 8*)
(*that: 4*)
(*allows: 6*)
(*you: 3*)
(*to: 2*)
(*easily: 6*)
(*work: 4*)
(*with: 4*)
(*elements: 8*)
(*in: 2*)
(*strings: 7*)
(*and: 3*)
(*lists: 5*)
(*Number of words: 17*)
(*Number of characters: 102*)
```

How It Works

The program begins by storing some text in the variable `theText`:

```
set theText to "AppleScript is a flexible language that allows you to
    easily work with elements in strings and lists."
```

Recall that because this was a long line, it was just entered into the window; Script Editor wrapped and indented the continuation of the character string onto the following line. Remember that the leading white space at the start of the continuation line is *not* stored as part of the string.

After the assignment is made, the program enters the following `repeat` loop:

```
repeat with theWord in (every word in theText)
    log theWord & ": " & (count theWord) as string
end repeat
```

The expression `every word in the theText` produces a list of every word contained in the specified string. The `repeat` statement assigns each word from that list, in turn, to the variable `theWord` and executes the body of the loop, which is a `log` statement that enters the current word and its length into the log.

After the `repeat` statement finishes, the program logs the total number of words stored inside `theText` as well as the total number of characters by using the following two statements:

```
log "Number of words: " & (count words in theText) as string
log "Number of characters: " & (count theText) as string
```

Execution of the program is then complete.

A Quick Note on References

When you write a `repeat with` loop that uses a list, as you did in the previous program example, each element from the list that is assigned to the looping variable is actually a *reference* to the element in the list and not the element itself. Certainly, this sounds confusing, but you learn more about it in later chapters. For now, just recognize that if you want to access the element itself, you apply the `contents of` operator to the reference. This process in known as *dereferencing*. So to write a loop to count the number of times the word "AppleScript" appears in some text, you can't write

```
repeat with theWord in (every word in theText)
    if theWord = "AppleScript" then
        set hits to hits +1
    end if
end repeat
```

because the `if` statement compares a reference to the word in the list — and not the string itself — to the string `"AppleScript"`. Therefore, the two values can never compare as equal.

Instead, you have to write your loop this way for it to work correctly:

```
repeat with theWord in (every word in theText)
    if contents of theWord = "AppleScript" then
        set hits to hits +1
    end if
end repeat
```

What makes this a little confusing is that you *are* able to directly apply the count command to each element to gets its length, just as you did in the previous program example. That's because, in some cases, AppleScript automatically dereferences an object for you; but it other cases it does not! Again, don't worry about this now as it is covered in detail in Chapter 6.

Enhancing the Alarm Clock Program

Exercise 7 from Chapter 3 asked you to write a simple alarm clock program that would pause your application for a specified number of seconds before displaying a message. This exercise took advantage of the delay command, which pauses execution of your program for a specified number of seconds. Here's what your answer to that exercise might look like:

```
-- Simple alarm clock program
-- sets an alarm a specified number of seconds in the future

display dialog "Enter sleep time in seconds" default answer "60"
set delayTime to text returned of result as number

display dialog "Enter Message to Display" default answer "Your time is up!"
set message to text returned of result

-- pause execution for the specified number of seconds

delay delayTime

-- time is up; display the message

display dialog message with icon note buttons {"Thanks!"} default button 1
```

This program works fairly well. However, the following points show you a couple of annoying things about it:

❑   If the application isn't frontmost when the alarm goes off, it waits for you to click it before the dialog box is displayed

❑   You have to specify the delay time in seconds. This is a nuisance if the amount of time you specify is lengthy, say, 90 minutes, or if you want to set the alarm for 6:45 PM for example, and it's now 3:03 PM

You are going to make some enhancements to the program. In particular, you can extend this application so that it does the following:

❑ Allows you to specify a time in seconds, minutes, or hours, by entering a values such as 60 seconds, 10 minutes, or 2 hours

❑ Sets a particular time for the alarm to go off, such as 5:30 PM

When you're finished reading this book, you may want to add other enhancements of your own. For example, maybe you'd like to play a song from iTunes when the alarm goes off. By the time you're done reading Chapter 11, you'll know how to do that.

In the first case, you want to allow the user to specify some time relative to the current time, for example, 10 minutes or 2 hours. You can get the first word from the text entered by the user and treat it as a number. You can get the second word of text entered and treat it as a unit of time, either "seconds", "minutes", or "hours". You can then covert the number to the number of seconds to give to the delay command as the length of time to pause the program's execution.

The second case is a little trickier. You want the user to be able to type a time such as 5:30 PM. You're going to let AppleScript do the work for you in this case. If the text entered by the user ends in either AM or PM, you're going to convert it to a date by using the date command. This command converts it to a date relative to the current time. After you have the date, you can get the number of seconds it represents by getting the time property, which gives the number of seconds since midnight (you may recall that this procedure was reviewed in detail in Chapter 3). By subtracting the number of seconds represented by the current time from the number of seconds represented by the time entered by the user, you get the number of seconds in the future that the alarm time represents. Reread that if you don't get it, or just figure it out from the program in the following Try It Out.

Try It Out   Enhancing the Alarm Clock Program

To begin the enhancements to the alarm clock program, follow these steps:

1. Type the following program into Script Editor:

```
-- Simple alarm clock program
-- sets an alarm to sound at a specified time

-- Version 2:  accepts more time formats

display dialog "Enter sleep time" default answer ""

set textEntered to text returned of result
set units to missing value
set delayTime to missing value

-- see if a relative time was entered

if textEntered ends with "seconds" then
    set units to 1
else if textEntered ends with "minutes" then
    set units to minutes
else if textEntered ends with "hours" then
    set units to hours
end if
```

```
-- if no units entered, try for AM or PM

if units = missing value then
    if textEntered ends with "AM" or textEntered ends with "PM" then
        try
            set alarmDate to date textEntered

            -- adjust time if it means tomorrow

            if alarmDate < (current date) then
                set alarmDate to alarmDate + 1 * days
            end if

            set delayTime to alarmDate - (current date)
        end try
    end if
else -- units entered, get number of seconds
    try
        set delayTime to first word of textEntered as number
        set delayTime to delayTime * units -- delay in seconds
    end try
end if

-- now see if we have a valid delay time

if delayTime = missing value then
    display dialog textEntered & " is not a valid time!" with icon stop ¬
        buttons {"OK"} default button {"OK"}
else
    display dialog "Enter Message to Display" default answer "Your time is up!"
    set message to text returned of result

    delay delayTime

    display dialog message with icon note buttons {"Thanks!"} default button 1
end if
```

2.   Save the program as an application called Alarm Clock.

3.   Run your Alarm Clock program, trying out different times and messages to make sure it works properly. In order to test that it parses your times correctly without having to wait for the alarm to go off each time, you can change the `delay` command to a `log` command and just check the value that gets logged.

How It Works

This is your longest program so far, so it requires a detailed explanation. After prompting the user to enter an alarm time, the program sets some variables with the following statements:

```
set textEntered to text returned of result
set units to missing value
set delayTime to missing value
```

The variable `textEntered` is set to the text entered in the dialog box by the user. Presumably, it's in either of these two formats:

```
60 seconds
```

or

```
6:45 PM
```

In the first case, minutes or hours can also be entered. In the second case, AM can be typed as well.

The variables `units` and `delayTime` are set to `missing value` so you can test later to see if they get assigned a value.

The program next checks the text typed by the user to see which format was used and whether it ends with the string `"seconds"`, `"minutes"`, or `"hours"`. This is done with the following `if` statement:

```
if textEntered ends with "seconds" then
    set units to 1
else if textEntered ends with "minutes" then
    set units to minutes
else if textEntered ends with "hours" then
    set units to hours
end if
```

If the user keys in a value expressed in seconds, the variable `units` is set to 1. If the user entered a value in minutes, this variable is set to `minutes`, which is a predefined constant for working with dates that you may recall from Chapter 2. Finally, if the user entered a value in hours, the `units` variable is set to `hours`, another predefined constant that was covered in Chapter 2. This variable stores the multiplier that is used to convert the time entered by the user into seconds. This has to be done because the `delay` command takes a value expressed in seconds as the delay time.

The program next checks to see if `units` was assigned a value in the preceding `if` statement. If it's equal to `missing value`, it wasn't assigned a value, so you assume the user entered a time using AM or PM notation. In that case, the following `try` statement is executed:

```
try
    set alarmDate to date textEntered

    -- adjust time if it means tomorrow

    if alarmDate < (current date) then
        set alarmDate to alarmDate + 1 * days
    end if

    set delayTime to alarmDate - (current date)
end try
```

The `try` statement is used to capture any errors that might occur when converting the time entered by the user into a valid date. The statement

```
set alarmDate to date textEntered
```

converts the time entered into a time for the current date. So if the current date is May 18, 2005 and the user enters the time 5:15 PM, AppleScript stores a date representing Wednesday, May 18, 2005, 5:15 PM inside the variable `alarmDate`. If an invalid time is entered by the user, the conversion fails. The failure is caught by the `try` statement. In such a case, the variable `alarmDate` is not assigned a value (its value remains `missing value`), and the `if` statement that follows is not executed.

If a valid time is specified by the user, the `if` statement is executed to test if the current time represents a time that is *later* than the specified alarm time. This can happen if the user types in an alarm time in the past. For example, if it's 3:45 PM and the user enters 1:00 AM for the alarm time, AppleScript sets `currentDate` to 1:00 AM of the current day when converting the time to a date. Most likely, the user meant to set the alarm to 1:00 AM of the following day. The `if` statement checks this and adjusts accordingly by adding one day to the date.

The last statement in the `try` block,

```
set delayTime to alarmDate - (current date)
```

calculates the number of seconds to set the `delayTime` to by simply subtracting the `current date` from the `alarmDate`. Doing so, you will recall, results in a value expressed in seconds.

If a unit of time expressed in seconds, minutes, or hours is specified by the user, the value of `units` is not equal to `missing value`, in which case the second `try` block contained in the `else` clause is executed:

```
try
    set delayTime to first word of textEntered as number
    set delayTime to delayTime * units -- delay in seconds
end try
```

The first `set` statement gets the first word of the text typed by the user and converts it to a number. So if the user typed

```
10 minutes
```

executing this statement stores 10 into `delayTime` as a numeric value. If this conversion fails (if the user didn't enter a valid number), it is caught by the `try` statement and the variable `delayTIme` retains its value of `missing value`.

The second statement in the `try` block won't fail; you just want it to be skipped if the preceding statement fails. That's why it was included inside the block. This statement simply converts the number stored in `delayTime` to a value expressed in seconds by multiplying it by the value of `units`.

The last part of the program contains the following `if else` statement:

```
if delayTime = missing value then
    display dialog textEntered & " is not a valid time!" with icon stop
        buttons {"OK"} default button {"OK"}
else
    display dialog "Enter Message to Display" default answer "Your time is up!"
    set message to text returned of result
```

```
        delay delayTime

        display dialog message with icon note buttons {"Thanks!"} default button 1
    end if
```

If an error occurred earlier in the program, `delayTime` still has the value `missing value`. In that case, a dialog box is displayed to inform the user of the error, together with the improperly entered input text. Otherwise, the program asks the user to enter the message to display in the dialog box when the alarm goes off. The program then executes the `delay` command for the specified number of seconds. When the `delay` command is completed, meaning the desired number of seconds have elapsed, the message is displayed in a dialog box. At that point, the alarm clock program's execution is complete.

Summary

Manipulating character strings is an important skill if you want to become proficient at AppleScript programming. You learned the following concepts in this chapter:

❑   A review of how to concatenate two or more character strings using the concatenation operator &

❑   The difference between strings, text, and Unicode text

❑   How to count the number of characters, words, and paragraphs in a string

❑   How to compare character strings using the special `considering` and `ignoring` statements

❑   How to specify elements to extract characters, words, and paragraphs from a string

❑   How to enumerate every character, word, and paragraph from a string

❑   How to test if one character string contains another string

❑   How to find the location of one character string inside another string, and how to see if one string begins or ends with another string

❑   How to extract a substring from a string

❑   How to change the delimiter characters that define a text item using `text item delimiters`

In the next chapter, you learn to work with the two data structures available in AppleScript that enable you to collectively store and manipulate groups of data: lists and records. Before proceeding, however, try the exercises that follow to test your understanding of the material covered in this chapter. You can find the solutions to these exercises in Appendix A.

Exercises

1.   Modify the program from this chapter that enumerated words to log the number of special characters in the text. For purposes of this program, consider any characters that are not part of a word as a special character. (*Hint:* You can subtract the numbers of characters used by all the words in the text from the total number of characters in the text to get your answer.)

2.   Extend the quotation program from this chapter by adding some quotes of your own.

3. Write an AppleScript program to take a path represented as a string and log the last component. If the path ends in a : character , display the component before the colon. So for, example, the path

```
Macintosh HD:Users:stevekochan:mysrc:scripts:ch05:enum1.scpt
```

should cause the program to log the string `"enum1.scpt"`, and the path

```
Macintosh HD:Users:stevekochan:mysrc:
```

should cause it to log `"mysrc"`.

4. Predict the output logged from the following program. Then type and run the program to verify your answers.

```
set myText to "Don't get from-to mixed up with thru!"

log text from word 1 to word 2 of myText
log text from character 5 to character 10 of myText
log text from character ((count myText) - 4) to end of myText

set n to offset of "from" in myText
log text from character 1 to character (n - 1) of myText
log characters 1 through (n - 1) of myText
```

5. Write a program to count the number of occurrences of the word *the* in some text. Be sure to ignore case.

6. Extend the alarm clock program to accept abbreviations `"secs"`, for seconds, `"min"`, `"minute"`, and `"mins"` for minutes, and `"hr"`, `"hour"`, and `"hrs"` for hours.

7. Write a program that effectively removes a string from inside another string. For example, if the variable `myText` is defined as follows:

```
set myText to "There's got to be some way out of here!"
```

and the variable `removeString` is defined like this:

```
set removeString to "got to be "
```

you want to produce a string that contains the contents of `myText` with `removeString` effectively removed from it, that is, the following string:

```
"There's some way out of here!"
```

8. Predict the output logged by the following program:

```
considering case and hyphens
    log "ye-s" = "YES"
end considering

ignoring diacriticals
    log "première" = "premiere"
end ignoring

considering case but ignoring punctuation and white space
    log "1., 2., 3." = "123"
    log "It's as easy as A, B, C" = "its as easy as abc."
end ignoring
```

Working with Lists and Records

AppleScript gives you the capability to collectively store and manipulate groups of data. This chapter covers the two data structures you have available to work with: lists and records. You know something about lists from using the `display dialog` command in earlier chapters. As you also learned early in the book, the `buttons` parameter takes a list of up to three labels that specify the names of your dialog buttons. You also saw how getting a range of elements—including getting every element—from a string produces a list.

You know something about records from the `display dialog` command. This command returns its result in the form of a record. You saw how to get the text entered by the user (as well as the button the user clicked) from this record.

This chapter covers lists and records in detail.

Working with Lists

A list is simply an ordered set of data, much like an array in other programming languages. You refer to each value in the list as an *item*. To write a list in your program, you simply write your items, separating each by a comma. The entire list of items is enclosed in a pair of curly braces. For example, the following defines a list containing three integer items:

```
{12, 17, 1989}
```

The first item of the list is the integer 12, the second item is the integer 17, and the third item is the integer 1989. Naturally, you can assign a list to a variable in your program like so:

```
set lindasBD to {12, 17, 1989}
```

This simply stores the three-item list in the variable `lindasBD`.

Here's another example of a list containing integer and real values:

```
set someConstants to {3.14159, 2.718282, 344, 299792458}
```

The first constant in this list is presumably the value of π, which you know is already defined in AppleScript with the predefined constant pi. So you can rewrite your list as follows:

```
set someConstants to {pi, 2.718282, 344, 299792458}
```

If you have the following variable definitions in your program:

```
set e to 2.718282
set speedOfSound to 344
set speedOfLight to 299792458
```

you can write the same list this way:

```
set someConstants to {pi, e, speedOfSound, speedOfLight}
```

You can also use expressions when writing list items. For example, here's a list containing the values π, π/2, and π/4:

```
set piValues to {pi, pi/2, pi/4}
```

The expressions are evaluated, and the results become the values stored in the list. You can make lists of strings; for example, the following is a list containing the names of my kids:

```
set kidsNames to {"Gregory", "Linda", "Julia"}
```

You can even have lists of lists. So, recalling the first list shown in this section:

```
set lindasBD to {12, 17, 1989}
```

and the following additional lists:

```
set juliasBD to {8, 8, 1986}
set gregsBD to {2, 22, 1996}
```

you could write the following list to store all three birthdays:

```
set kidsBDs to {gregsBD, lindasBD, juliasBD}
```

This would be the same as writing the three-item list like this:

```
set kidsBDs to { {2, 22, 1996}, {12, 17, 1989}, {8, 8, 1986} }
```

Of course, you may choose to represent your dates using the date class instead of as a list of three integers. In such a case, you might store the three birthdays in your list like this:

```
set kidsBDs to {date "2/22/1996", date "12/17/1989", date "8/8/1986"}
```

After you compile this statement, Script Editor does its normal transformation and changes this statement to read as follows:

```
set kidsBDs to {date "Thursday, February 22, 1996 12:00:00 AM", date "Sunday, ¬
        December 17, 1989 12:00:00 AM", date "Friday, August 8, 1986 12:00:00 AM"}
```

Here's a list called myKids that has two items. The first item is a list of my kids' names; the second is a list of their birthdays:

```
set myKids to {kidsNames, kidsBDs}
```

So, you can see that your lists can contain any type of data, not necessarily homogenous. Your list might contain a number, another list, a date, and so on, like this:

```
set mixedList to { 100, pi / 2, kidsBDs, current date}
```

This is a list containing four items, each of a different type.

Empty Lists

Just as you can have a string containing zero characters (the null string), you can also have a list containing no items. The empty list is denoted simply by a pair of curly braces:

```
{ }
```

Empty lists are useful when you want to build a list by adding items to it, as you see in a later section of this chapter. In such a case, you typically start your list off as an empty list, like so:

```
set fileNameList to {}
```

This sets the variable fileNameList to an empty list, which presumably precedes code that adds items to this list.

Counting the Number of Items in a List

You recall that you used the count command in Chapter 5 to get the size of a string. You can also use it to count the number of items in a list, like so:

```
count mixedList
```

Given the previous definition from mixedList, this produces the result of 4 because that's how many items are in the list.

Recall that writing the expression

```
words in theText
```

produces a *list* of words. You can now understand why writing the expression

```
count words in theText
```

produces a count of the number of words in `theText`.

If you count the number of items in an empty list like this:

```
count {}
```

you get zero, which is what you expect.

As you see later in this section, you can also use the `count` command to count the number of items in a particular class in a list.

Accessing the Items in a List

The items in a list are ordered, as noted previously. Just as you can reference the characters in a string, you can also reference particular items from a list by number, starting with the first item, which is numbered 1.

The following table summarizes the various ways of specifying items in a list.

Item Specifier	Meaning	Example
`first item, second item, third item, ..., tenth item`	A specific item by number	`first item of kidsBDs`
`1st item, 2nd item, 3rd item, ...`	A specific item by number	`3rd item of mixedList`
`item 1, item 2, item 3...`	A specific item by number	`item 1 of myKids`
`item -1, item -2, item -3`	An item relative to the last item; where −1 references the last item	`item -2 of words in theText`
`beginning`	First item	`beginning of theText`
`last item` *or* `end`	Last item	`last item of words in theText`
`some item`	A random item	`some item in cardList`
`middle item`	The middle item; item $(n+1)\text{div }2$, where n is the size of the list	`middle item of orderedGrades`
`every item`	All items	`every item in theGrades`
`items`	Same as `every item`	`items in theGrades`
`items` *m* `through` *n*	Items *m* through *n*	`items 1 through 4 of fileList`

These should be familiar to you from the previous chapter, which dealt with string elements. Here, instead of using element names like `word`, `character`, or `paragraph`, you use the word `item`, or you use a class name, as you see shortly. You can also use `beginning` to refer to the first item in a list and `end` to refer to the last item. You can't do that with strings.

> *With strings, you can't write* `beginning of theText` *or* `end of theText`, *but you can use these two words in a range, as in* `words from beginning to end of theText`.

Recall that you can you use the words `of` and `in` interchangeably (as I do in this chapter), and you can supply the word `get` and use the word `the` accordingly. Thus, the statement

```
item 1 of myKids
```

can be expressed in several different ways, including the following:

```
get item 1 in myKids
```

Recall also that you can use the word `thru` in place of `through`:

```
items 1 thru 4 of fileList
```

The following Try It Out gives you some more practice with list items.

Try It Out   Working with List Items

In the following steps, you see how to identify list items in different ways.

1. Type the following program into Script Editor:

```
-- Working with lists

set theGrades to {100, 93, 94, 84, 88, 83, 80, 75}

-- first item in the list

log first item in theGrades
log 1st item in theGrades
log item 1 in theGrades

-- last item in the list

log last item in theGrades
log item -1 in theGrades

-- arbitrary item in the list

log some item in theGrades

-- middle item

log middle item in theGrades
```

```
-- range of items

log items 2 thru 4 in theGrades

-- all items

log items in theGrades
log every item in the theGrades
log items 1 thru -1 in theGrades

-- expressions

log (item 1 in theGrades) + (item 2 in theGrades)
log item 3 in theGrades < item 4 in theGrades
```

   2.   Click the Event Log tab and run the program. (Note that the `log` command does not show lists inside curly braces; it just lists their elements.) Your output should look like what's shown here:

```
(*100*)
(*100*)
(*100*)
(*75*)
(*75*)
(*94*)
(*84*)
(*93, 94, 84*)
(*100, 93, 94, 84, 88, 83, 80, 75*)
(*100, 93, 94, 84, 88, 83, 80, 75*)
(*100, 93, 94, 84, 88, 83, 80, 75*)
(*193*)
(*false*)
```

How It Works

The program starts by setting up a list of eight integers — presumably representing grade scores — and assigning the list to the variable theGrades, like so:

```
set theGrades to {100, 93, 94, 84, 88, 83, 80, 75}
```

The next three statements in the program show different ways to access the first item in the list:

```
log first item in theGrades
log 1st item in theGrades
log item 1 in theGrades
```

In each case, the first item from the list, which is the integer 100, is retrieved from the list and logged.

The statements that follow next in the program

```
log last item in theGrades
log item -1 in theGrades
```

show two different ways to retrieve the last item in the list, which is 75.

The statement

```
log some item in theGrades
```

retrieves a random item from the list. According to the output shown, this had the effect of fetching the third item in the list, which is 94. You will likely get a different result when you run the program.

The list theGrades has eight items. So when you ask for the middle item, you get item four, which is the integer 84. (You would also get item four if the list had seven items.) This is consistent with the description of the middle item in the previous table.

In order to get the second through fourth items in the list, you write the following in the program:

```
log items 2 thru 4 in theGrades
```

This results in a list of three items containing the integers 93, 94, and 84.

The three statements that follow next in the program

```
log items in theGrades
log every item in the theGrades
log items 1 thru -1 in theGrades
```

show different ways to enumerate every item in the list. Of course, in most cases you can just specify the list itself, as in the following:

```
log theGrades
```

The last two statements in the program illustrate that items from lists can be used in expressions. In the first case, the statement

```
log (item 1 in theGrades) + (item 2 in theGrades)
```

adds the first item in the list (100) to the second item in the list (93), giving the result of 193.

If you don't put in the parentheses, they are added by Script Editor when you compile this statement.

In the second case, the statement

```
log item 3 in theGrades < item 4 in theGrades
```

tests if the third item in the list (94) is less than the fourth item in the list (84). It isn't, so the result is false.

In the following Try It Out, you learn to sequentially process the items in a list. You learned how to do that in Chapter 5 when you wrote the program to sequence through the words in a string and count the length of each word. Here the task is to calculate the average of the grades stored in your theGrades list. You just add up all the grades and, at the end, divide the resulting sum by the number of grades.

Try It Out   **Sequencing through the Items in a List**

In the following steps, you practice sequencing through the items in a list.

1.   Type the following program into Script Editor:

```
-- Sum and average the integers in a list

set theGrades to {100, 93, 94, 84, 88, 83, 80, 75}
set sum to 0
set n to count theGrades

repeat with i from 1 to n
    set sum to sum + (item i of theGrades)
end repeat

log "The sum is: " & sum as string
log "The average is: " & (sum / n) as string
```

2.   Click the Event Log tab and run the program. You see the following output in the log:

```
(*The sum is: 697*)
(*The average is: 87.125*)
```

How It Works

The program sets up the same list called theGrades as used in the preceding Try It Out. It then initializes two variables:

```
set sum to 0
set n to count theGrades
```

The sum variable is used to keep a running total of the sum of the grades in the list. The variable n is set to the number of items in theGrades or to the number of grades in the list. The program then enters a repeat loop to add up the integers in the list:

```
repeat with i from 1 to n
    set sum to sum + (item i of theGrades)
end repeat
```

When the loop exits, the variable sum contains the sum total of all the numbers in the list. This value is logged; and the average value is then calculated, converted to a string, and logged:

```
log "The sum is: " & sum as string
log "The average is: " & (sum / n) as string
```

To become more familiar with working with lists, you write a program in the following Try It Out that enables the user to enter the name of a city in the United States. The program then reports back to the user the population of that city (as of 1990). For practical purposes, you start with a small list of cities; you can always extend the program if you like.

You can represent the information about a city and its population in several different ways in your program. The next several Try It Out examples look at a few different methods.

Try It Out   A Program to Display Populations of U.S. Cities

In this first example, you maintain two separate lists. The first list contains the names of the cities; the second list contains the corresponding populations for those cities.

1. Type the following program into Script Editor:

```
-- Show the population of a given city

set USCityNames to {"Boston", "Chicago", "Dallas", "Houston", "Los Angeles", ¬
    "Philadelphia", "San Diego", "San Francisco", "New York"}
set populations to {574000, 2784000, 1007000, 1631000, 3485000, 1586000, ¬
    1111000, 724000, 7323000}

display dialog "Enter your city: " default answer ""
set cityEntered to text returned of result

-- now look for the city in the list

set found to false
set n to 1

repeat while not found and n ≤ (count USCityNames)
    if item n of USCityNames = cityEntered then
        set found to true
    else
        set n to n + 1
    end if
end repeat

-- either show the population or give a message that the city wasn't found

if not found then
    display dialog "Sorry, I don't know the population of " & cityEntered with ¬
        icon note buttons {"OK"} default button 1
else
    set cityPopulation to item n of populations
    display dialog "The population of " & cityEntered & " is " & (cityPopulation ¬
        as string) buttons {"OK"} default button 1
end if
```

2. Run the program. You see the dialog shown in Figure 6-1.

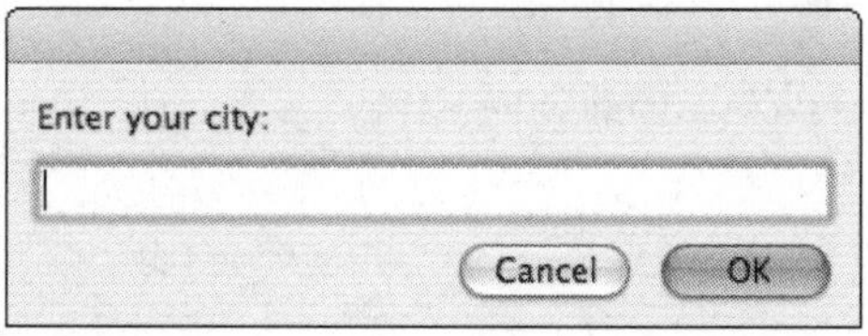

Figure 6-1

3. Type new york in the dialog and click OK. You get the dialog shown in Figure 6-2.

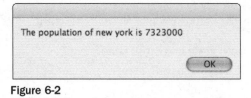

Figure 6-2

4. Run the program again. This time enter Seattle into the dialog and click OK. You get the dialog shown in Figure 6-3.

> Sorry, I don't know the population of Seattle
>
> OK

Figure 6-3

How It Works

The program begins by defining two lists, like so:

```
set USCityNames to {"Boston", "Chicago", "Dallas", "Houston", "Los Angeles", ¬
    "Philadelphia", "San Diego", "San Francisco", "New York"}
set populations to {574000, 2784000, 1007000, 1631000, 3485000, 1586000, ¬
    1111000, 724000, 7323000}
```

The first list, USCityNames, contains the names of nine arbitrarily chosen cities in the United States. The second list, populations, contains the corresponding populations of those cities. Boston is the first item in the USCityNames list, so 574000 is its population because that's the first item in the populations list. In general, the population of city *i* in the USCityNames list is given by item *i* in the populations list.

The program prompts you to enter the name of a city and stores the text entered into the variable cityEntered. This is done with the following lines of code:

```
display dialog "Enter your city: " default answer ""
set cityEntered to text returned of result
```

Next the program initializes two variables like so:

```
set found to false
set n to 1
```

The variable found is a flag that is used to keep track of finding a match for the city name in the USCityNames list. The variable n is used as a counter as you sequence through each item in the list.

When you type new york, as directed in the example, the program takes the text you entered and stores it in the variable cityEntered. The program next enters a repeat loop to see if the city typed by the user is in the USCityNames list. The first line of the loop reads as follows:

```
repeat while not found and n ≤ (count USCityNames)
```

This says to execute the loop as long as you haven't found a match (not found) and you haven't tested all items in the list (n ≤ (count USCityNames)). If either condition occurs, the loop terminates without a match being found.

Inside the loop a test is made to see if there's a match. This is done with the following if-else statement:

```
if item n of USCityNames = cityEntered then
    set found to true
else
    set n to n + 1
end if
```

This statement compares the city name stored in item n in the list with the city entered by the user. If the two match (and recall here that case is ignored by default) the variable found is set true. If they don't match, the counter variable n is incremented by 1 and the loop continues.

When the loop exits, one of two conditions is true:

1. A match was found, in which case the variable found is true. The variable n, in such a case, is equal to the value it had when the loop exited. That is, its value is set to the index number of the matching item in the USCityNames list.

2. A match was not found, in which case the variable found is still false.

If found is false, the program displays a dialog telling the user that the city entered was not found. If the value of found is true, the program uses the value of n to retrieve the population from the populations list that corresponds to the matching city found in the USCityNames list.

Working with Lists of Lists

The problem with maintaining two separate lists, as you did in the previous population program, is that it becomes easy to make a mistake. For example, if you remove or add a city from the USCityNames list, you have to be careful that the corresponding item from the populations list is also removed or added.

Another approach is to store all the information in a single list. Each item of the list can contain both the name of the city and its population. But how do you do that? It's easy. Each item of your list can be itself a list that contains two items: the name of the city and its population. So instead of the two lists that you previously defined in this way:

```
set USCityNames to {"Boston", "Chicago", "Dallas", "Houston", "Los Angeles", ¬
    "Philadelphia", "San Diego", "San Francisco", "New York"}
set populations to {574000, 2784000, 1007000, 1631000, 3485000, 1586000, ¬
    1111000, 724000, 7323000}
```

you create a single list that looks like this:

```
set USCities to {{"Boston", 574000}, {"Chicago", 2784000}, {"Dallas", 1007000}, ¬
    {"Houston", 1631000}, {"Los Angeles", 3485000}, {"Philadelphia", 1586000}, ¬
    {"San Diego", 1111000}, {"San Francisco", 724000}, {"New York", 7323000}}
```

Study this list carefully. It contains nine items. The first item in the list is itself a list:

```
{"Boston", 574000}
```

This item can be retrieved using the expression

```
first item in USCities
```

The last item in the list contains information about New York:

```
{"New York", 7323000}
```

which you can get using the expression

```
last item in USCities
```

The name of the city stored in the second item of the list is retrieved by this expression:

```
item 1 of (item 2 of USCities)
```

The result is the string `"Chicago"`.

The parentheses are not required here, but are added for readability.

To get the corresponding population for the second city in the list, write the following:

```
item 2 of (item 2 of USCities)
```

This produces the result `2784000`, which is the population of Chicago.

You've learned the foundation for a modified version of your population program that works with a list of lists. You use this modification in the following Try It Out.

Try It Out   A Modified Version of the Population Program

In the following steps you create a modified form of the population program.

1. Type the following program into Script Editor:

```
-- Show the population of a given city
-- Version 2

set USCities to {{"Boston", 574000}, {"Chicago", 2784000}, {"Dallas", 1007000}, ¬
    {"Houston", 1631000}, {"Los Angeles", 3485000}, {"Philadelphia", 1586000}, ¬
    {"San Diego", 1111000}, {"San Francisco", 724000}, {"New York", 7323000}}
```

```
display dialog "Enter your city: " default answer ""
set cityEntered to text returned of result

-- now look for the city in the list

set found to false
set n to 1

repeat while not found and n ≤ (count USCities)
    if item 1 of (item n of USCities) = cityEntered then
        set found to true
    else
        set n to n + 1
    end if
end repeat

-- either show the population or give a message that the city wasn't found

if not found then
    display dialog "Sorry, I don't know the population of " & cityEntered with ¬
        icon note buttons {"OK"} default button 1
else
    set cityPopulation to item 2 of (item n of USCities)
    display dialog "The population of " & cityEntered & " is " & (cityPopulation ¬
        as string) buttons {"OK"} default button 1
end if
```

2. Run the program. Enter some valid and invalid city names as you did with the previous program to verify proper operation of this version of the program.

How It Works

After defining your list of lists — USCities — and allowing the user to key in her chosen city, the program searches the list in a way that is similar to the search in the preceding version of the population program. Recall that each item in the USCities list is a two-item list. The first item of each two-item list is the name of the city, and the second item is the population of that city. So in the if statement in the program

```
if item 1 of (item n of USCities) = cityEntered then
    set found to true
else
    set n to n + 1
end if
```

the nth item from the USCities list is retrieved, giving the two-item list for a particular city. The first item of that list, which represents the name of the city, is then compared to the city entered. If they match, the variable found is set to true. Otherwise, they don't match and the index variable is incremented by 1 and the execution of the loop continues.

As in the previous version of this program, the value of found is tested after the loop is finished to determine whether a match was made in the list. If found is false, the city was not found and an appropriate message is displayed. If found is true, then n contains the index into the USCities list where the match was made. In that case, after retrieving that two-item list, the second item of that list gives the corresponding population for the matched city. This value is assigned to the variable `cityPopulation` with the statement

```
set cityPopulation to item 2 of (item n of USCities)
```

and the resulting value is displayed with an appropriate message to the user.

The choose from list Command

Unfortunately, one big flaw with the population program is that the user has no idea what cities you have stored in your list. It's hit or miss. A better approach involves using a convenient AppleScript command called `choose from list`. With this command, you can present a list of choices to the user and have her select from the list. This is convenient if you want to present a list of files to choose from, for example. Or you might present a list of songs or URLs. In just a minute, you're going to go back and modify the first version of the population program to give the user a list of cities from which to choose. Based on the selection, you then display the corresponding population.

But before you can write your new version of the program, you need to learn how to use the `choose from list` command. Given that this command is a Standard Additions command, I show you how to use the command by first looking it up in the Standard Additions dictionary. You learned how to do that in Chapter 3 when you looked up the `display dialog` command. The following Try It Out helps refresh your memory about this task.

Try It Out   Looking Up the choose from list Command in the Dictionary

To look up the `choose from list` command from the Standard Additions dictionary, follow these steps:

1. Start up Script Editor and choose File ⇨ Open Dictionary. A dialog appears (refer to Figure 4-5 and subsequent screen shots from Chapter 4 to recall what these dialogs look like).

2. Scroll down in the window until you see `Standard Additions`. Click this line.

3. Click Open.

4. Scroll down the right frame of this window until you find the `choose from list` command. Your window should look like Figure 6-4. The information displayed here describes the syntax of the `choose from list` command and its parameters.

You see that the basic form of the command is `choose from list` followed by a list of plaintext, which means a list of strings. You want to display the list containing the names of cities. Using the `USCityNames` list from a previous Try It Out, you can write this:

```
choose from list USCityNames
```

The second version of your population program does not have this list of names readily available. (They're stored inside your list of lists structure.) You can create the list dynamically from the `USCities` list and supply it to the `choose from list` command. You see how to do that later in this chapter.

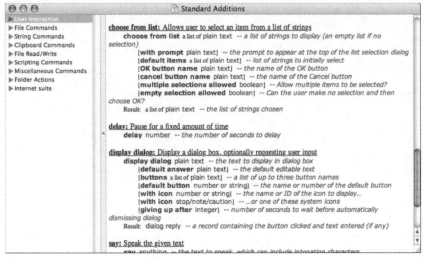

Figure 6-4

You also see from the description of this command that it supports a bunch of optional parameters. One of these is the `with prompt` parameter, which enables you to tell the users what it is you want them to select:

```
choose from list USCityNames with prompt "Pick a city to find its population:"
```

You should note that the description of the command says that it returns a "list of strings chosen." You only want to deal with a single city at a time here, so you won't allow multiple selections.

Although you can't tell from the documentation, the `choose from list` *command does not allow multiple selections by default. You can find out things like this by experimentation with the command. This is often necessary because the documentation of a command in the dictionary is often incomplete.*

You also want to require the user to pick a city, so you won't allow for an empty selection, which is an option you can set with the `choose from list` command. This means that you should expect to get a list returned containing the name of the selected city as its first and only item. The following Try It Out lets you add the `choose from list` command to the program you created earlier.

Try It Out   Using the choose from list Command

In these steps, you incorporate the `choose from list` command into your population program.

1. Type the following program into Script Editor:

```
-- Show the population of a given city
-- Version 3

set USCityNames to {"Boston", "Chicago", "Dallas", "Houston", "Los Angeles", ¬
    "Philadelphia", "San Diego", "San Francisco", "New York"}
```

```
set populations to {574000, 2784000, 1007000, 1631000, 3485000, 1586000, ¬
    1111000, 724000, 7323000}

choose from list USCityNames with prompt "Pick a city to find its population:"
set cityEntered to item 1 of result

-- now look for the city in the list

set found to false
set n to 1

repeat while not found and n ≤ (count USCityNames)
    if item n of USCityNames = cityEntered then
        set found to true
    else
        set n to n + 1
    end if
end repeat

-- either show the population or give a message that an error occurred

if not found then
    display dialog "Some sort of error occurred; I couldn't find " & cityEntered ¬
        with icon caution buttons {"OK"} default button 1
else
    set cityPopulation to item n of populations
    display dialog "The population of " & cityEntered & " is " & (cityPopulation ¬
        as string) buttons {"OK"} default button 1
end if
```

2. Run the program. You see the dialog shown in Figure 6-5.

Pick a city to find its population:

Boston
Chicago
Dallas
Houston
Los Angeles
Philadelphia
San Diego
San Francisco
New York

Cancel   OK

Figure 6-5

3. Highlight one of the cities in the list and click OK. You get the population for the selected city in a dialog similar to that shown in Figure 6-2.

4. Run the program again. After getting the dialog shown in Figure 6-5, click Cancel. You see the error shown in Figure 6-6.

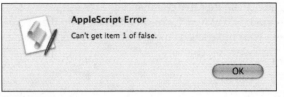

Figure 6-6

How It Works

After defining your list of city names and populations as you did before, the program displays a dialog with a list of city names to choose from, using the `choose from list` command:

```
choose from list USCityNames with prompt "Pick a city to find its population:"
```

Because you don't allow multiple selections, the single choice is returned as a single-item list in `result`. You get the name selected by the user and assign it to `cityEntered` using the following statement:

```
set cityEntered to item 1 of result
```

The rest of the program remains as before. Unfortunately, the `choose from list` command tells you the choice that was made, but not its relative position in the list. So you have to search your list to find the match.

You should always find the city in your list because it's the same list you presented to the user. However, the program checks just to make sure. If for some reason a match is not made (and, therefore, the value of `found` is `false`), the program executes the following `display dialog` command:

```
display dialog "Some sort of error occurred; I couldn't find " & cityEntered ¬
        with icon caution buttons {"OK"} default button 1
```

Again, this should never occur, but you handle it just in case something bizarre happens.

After the city is found in the `USCityNames` list, the corresponding population from the `populations` list is retrieved and displayed to the user.

Handling the Cancel Button and the return Command

Note what happens when you click the Cancel button instead of selecting a city. Your program terminates with an error. But why did that happen? The error message says that you "Can't get item 1 of false." That seems to imply that when you click Cancel the command returns false, even though that fact wasn't mentioned when you looked up the command in the dictionary. This is different behavior from the `display dialog` command, which stops execution of your program when Cancel is clicked.

As noted earlier in this section, inadequate or incomplete documentation is something you have to get used to when working with AppleScript. Only experience (which often means taking a trial-and-error approach) teaches you the correct behavior of many commands.

Some good tools allow you to more easily experiment with commands to determine their behavior. One is Smile, and the other is Script Debugger. See Appendix C for more information about AppleScript resources.

It seems like a good guess, then, that this command does in fact return `false` when Cancel is clicked. So go back to your program and assign the result returned from the `choose from list` command to a variable; then test it in your program. You can accomplish this by basing your code on the following template:

```
choose from list USCityNames with prompt "Pick a city to find its population:"
set theSelection to result

if theSelection = false then
    -- statements to handle the cancel button
else
    set cityEntered to item 1 of theSelection
    -- statements to process the city entered
end if
```

If all you want to do is terminate the program when Cancel is clicked and avoid another level of nested code, you can use the `return` command, which causes your program to stop executing.

> *The `return` command is also used to return from handlers and scripts, as you see in Chapters 8 and 12.*

Here's what your restructured code would look like using this new command:

```
choose from list USCityNames with prompt "Pick a city to find its population:"
set theSelection to result

if theSelection = false then
    return    -- stops the program's execution
end if

set cityEntered to item 1 of theSelection

-- now look up the selected city
```

> *The `return` command is distinct from the predefined value `return`, which is the return character you used in Chapter 5. AppleScript figures out the meaning of `return` based on its context.*

Accessing Items by Class

When you retrieved particular items from your lists, you used the keyword `item`. For example, to get the first item of the list, you write

```
item 1 of theGrades
```

To get every item from the list `mixedList`, you write

```
every item in mixedList
```

If you just want to get items of a particular class, for example `integer`, `string`, `date`, and so on, you simply use the name of the class in place of the keyword `item`. This is useful when the items in your list are not of a homogenous type.

You can use the name of the class in place of the keyword item *(or* items*) for each entry in the table of item specifiers earlier in the chapter.*

As an example, if you want the fifth number from the list theGrades, you can write any of the following expressions:

```
number 5 of theGrades
```

or

```
fifth number of theGrades
```

or

```
5th number of theGrades
```

If you want to get every number from the list mixedList, you could write the following:

```
every number in mixedList
```

This is convenient when you want to process just the items of a particular class in a list that contains different types of data.

Counting the Number of Class Items

You know how to use the count command to find the number of items in a list. You can use this to count the number of items of a particular class as well. For example, the following shows how you can count the number of integers in the list numList:

```
set numList to {100, 75, 3, -5, 12, 12.5, 0.0, -18, 44.4}
count integers in numList
```

This last statement gives the value 6 because that's how many integers are in the list (100, 75, 3, -5, 12, and -18). Given the same list, the following statement

```
count reals in numList
```

counts the number of reals in numList, producing the result 3 (12.5, 0.0, and 44.4). Finally, the statement

```
count numbers in numList
```

counts all the numbers in numList and produces the result of 9 because each item in the list is a number. This handy fact can be used to check if a list contains a homogenous data type. For example, you could write the following test to see if every item in numList is a number:

```
(count numbers in numList) = (count numList)
```

If the answer is true, the list consists entirely of numbers.

Enumerating Lists: A Quick Review

You may recall that the following special form of the `repeat` statement enables you to easily sequence through each item in a list:

```
repeat with loopvar in list
    statement
    statement
    ...
end
```

Based on this, you can rewrite the earlier example that summed and averaged the integers in a list as follows:

```
-- Sum and average the integers in a list
-- Version 2

set theGrades to {100, 93, 94, 84, 88, 83, 80, 75}
set sum to 0
set n to count theGrades

repeat with aGrade in theGrades
    set sum to sum + aGrade
end repeat

log "The sum is: " & sum as string
log "The average is: " & (sum / n) as string
```

The rest and reverse Properties

Every list has three properties associated with it: `length`, `rest`, and `reverse`:

❑   `length`: Provides the number of items in the list, which you can also get using the `count` command.

❑   `reverse`: Gives you a list with its items reversed.

❑   `rest`: Gives you all the items in the list *except* the first item.

In the following Try It Out, you can test out these three list properties.

Try It Out   **Exercising List Properties**

In the following steps, you practice using the three list properties.

1.   Type the following program into Script Editor:

```
-- List properties

set someWords to words of "The meaning of life"

log length of someWords
log reverse of someWords
```

```
log rest of someWords

log rest of (rest of someWords)
```

2. Click the Event Log tab and run the program. You should get the following output:

```
(*4*)
(*life, of, meaning, The*)
(*meaning, of, life*)
(*of, life*)
```

How It Works

Most of the program is straightforward. Here you're dealing with a list of words generated by the statement

```
set someWords to words of "The meaning of life"
```

The `length` property reports four items (words) in the list. The `reverse` property creates a list with the four words reversed. The `rest` property gives the last three items (words) in the list.

The last statement in the program, which reads

```
log rest of (rest of someWords)
```

gets the "rest of the rest" from the list. The second use of `rest` on the line (which gets evaluated first) gives the second through last items from the list `someWords`. That produces this intermediate result:

```
{"meaning", "of", "life"}
```

Applying the `rest` property to this list gives the second through last items, or the following:

```
{"of", "life"}
```

So the net effect of applying the two consecutive `rest` properties is to get the third through last items in the list.

Modifying Lists

AppleScripts allows you to make certain types of changes to your lists. You can change a particular item in the list, insert new items to the front of the list, and add new items to the end of the list. You can't directly insert a new item into the middle of a list, nor can you directly delete an item from a list. However, you can accomplish these tasks using a combination of the available commands.

Changing Items in a List

You can change a single item in a list using the `set` command. You simply reference the item you want to change and the value you want to change it to, according to the following general format:

```
set list-item to value
```

So to change the fifth item in a list called `bookScripts` to the string `"population.scpt"`, you write the following:

```
set fifth item in bookScripts to "population.scpt"
```

Inserting an Item at the Beginning of a List

You can insert an item at the beginning of a list by setting the `beginning` item of the list to a value. So, given the following list

```
set myKids to {"Linda", "Gregory"}
```

writing this statement:

```
set beginning of myKids to "Julia"
```

results in this list:

```
{"Julia", "Linda", "Gregory"}
```

Note that setting the `beginning` *item this way is not the same as setting the* `first` `item` *or* `item 1` *in the list, which replaces the first item in the list with the specified value.*

Appending an Item to the End of a List

You can add an item to the end of a list by setting the `end` item of the list to a value. So, given the following list:

```
set myKids to {"Julia", "Linda"}
```

writing this statement:

```
set end of myKids to "Gregory"
```

results in this list:

```
{"Julia", "Linda", "Gregory"}
```

Note that setting the `end` *item this way is not the same as setting the* `last` `item` *or* `item -1` *in the list, which replaces the last item in the list with the specified value.*

To append an item to the list `Fibonacci` consisting of the sum of the previous two items in the same list, you could write the following:

```
set end of Fibonacci to item -2 of Fibonacci + item -1 of Fibonacci
```

See Exercise 1 at the end of this chapter to see how you can put this statement to good use.

In the following Try It Out, you experiment with inserting and replacing items in a list.

Modifying List Items

In the following steps, you modify items in a list.

1. Type the following program into Script Editor:

```
-- Modifying list items

set L to {100, 2, 3, 400, 500, 6, 7, 8, 9, 10}

-- setting single items

set 1st item of L to 1
set item 4 of L to 4
set item 5 of L to last item of L div 2

-- insertion at the beginning

set beginning of L to 0

-- appending at the end

set end of L to 11

log L
```

2. Click the Event Log tab and run the program. You get the following result logged by the program:

```
(*0, 1, 2, 3, 4, 5, 6, 7, 8, 9, 10, 11*)
```

How It Works

The first line of the program defines a 10-item list of numbers like so:

```
set L to {100, 2, 3, 400, 500, 6, 7, 8, 9, 10}
```

The statement

```
set 1st item of L to 1
```

sets the first item in the list to the value 1, replacing the value 100 that was stored there. This statement is followed in the program by the statement

```
set item 4 of L to 4
```

which sets the fourth item in the list to the value 4, replacing the value 400 that was stored there. The next statement in the program

```
set item 5 of L to last item of L div 2
```

sets item 5 in the list to the result of dividing the last item in the list by 2. Because the last item in the list is 10, the result of dividing 10 by 2, or 5, is stored in the fifth item in the list, replacing the value 500 that was previously stored there.

The next two program statements illustrate inserting at the beginning of a list and appending to the end of a list. The statement

```
set beginning of L to 0
```

inserts the value 0 at the start of the list, whereas the statement

```
set end of L to 11
```

appends the value 11 to the end of the list. Once again, these are not replacements operations; they insert or append items to the start or the end of the list, respectively.

The program's last statement logs the value of the list L. As you can see from the log, the resulting list contains the integers 0 through 11 in sequential order (what a coincidence!).

Concatenating Lists

Often when writing AppleScript programs, you need to join one or more lists. Sometimes you want to do this iteratively inside a loop to build up a list. Each time through the loop you may want to add a new item to the end of the list.

The concatenation operator & that you use to join two strings together can also be used to join two lists together. So if L1 is a list of m items and L2 is a list of n items, writing

```
L1 & L2
```

produces a list of $m + n$ items. The resulting list consists of the m items in L1 followed by the n items in L2. So if you write

```
{1, 2, 3} & {4, 5}
```

you end up with the following five-item list:

```
{1, 2, 3, 4, 5}
```

Of course, you can concatenate more than one list at a time, like so:

```
{1, 2, 3} & {4, 5} & {6, 7, 8, 9, 10}
```

This produces the following 10-item list:

```
{1, 2, 3, 4, 5, 6, 7, 8, 9, 10}
```

Often you'll want to concatenate a value that's not a list to the end of an existing list. For example, you know you can write

```
set end of L to 5
```

to add 5 to the end of the list L, but can you also write the following to achieve the same result?

```
set L to L & 5
```

The answer is "Yes." If you concatenate two items, and one is a list and the other is a number, the number is coerced into a list, if possible. That means that writing this

```
{100, 200, 300} & 400
```

produces this

```
{100, 200, 300, 400}
```

and so does writing this:

```
100 & {200, 300, 400}
```

The rules are quite involved for different types of items. Sometimes concatenating two items, neither of which is a list, will produce a list! For example writing this

```
100 & 200
```

gives you this

```
{100, 200}
```

And if the first operand is a string and the second is a list, the second is converted to a string. That means that writing this

```
"Script Editor  " & {2.0}
```

gives this

```
"Script Editor 2.0"
```

but writing this

```
{"Script Editor "} & 2.0
```

gives this two-element list

```
{"Script Editor", 2.0}
```

because the first operand is a list.

Rather than learning all the rules, you're better off knowing what you're concatenating. You can always use explicit coercions rather than rely on the implicit coercion rules, which can make your programs harder to read and debug.

Deleting an Item from a List

Unfortunately, AppleScript does not provide a direct way to delete an item from a list. However, you can programmatically delete an item based on what you know about setting items in a list and list concatenation. So if you wanted to delete item n from a list, you could retrieve items 1 through $n - 1$ from the list and concatenate the result to retrieve items $n + 1$ through the end of the list. The next section shows an example of this method.

You can use the `rest` property to delete the first item in a list, if that's your goal. This can be accomplished like so:

```
set L to rest of L
```

Here the second item through the last item in the list L is stored in L. This has the net result of deleting the first item. Of course, you can also do it this way:

```
set L to items 2 through -1 of L
```

Inserting an Item in a List

As with item deletion, AppleScript provides no direct way to insert an item at an arbitrary spot into a list. However, you can also accomplish this task programmatically. So if you wanted to insert an item before item n in your list, you could retrieve items 1 through $n-1$ from the list and concatenate that with the item you want to insert followed by retrieval of items n through the end of the list.

In Chapter 8, you see how to write general-purpose list insertion and deletion routines. For now, try deleting and inserting list items in the following Try It Out.

Try It Out   **Deleting and Inserting items in a List**

The following steps provide a small example of inserting and deleting list items.

1. Type the following program into Script Editor:

```
-- Inserting and deleting list items

set L to {1, 2, 3, 4, 5, 6, 7, 8, 9, 10}

set L to rest of L -- delete first item
set L to items 1 thru -2 of L -- delete last item

log L

-- delete item 4

set L to (items 1 thru 3 of L) & (items 5 thru -1 of L)
log L

-- delete arbitrary item n
-- n ≠ 1 and n ≠ last item in list

set n to 2

set L to (items 1 thru (n - 1) of L) & (items (n + 1) thru -1 of L)
log L

-- list insertion
```

```
set L to {1, 2, 3, 4, 5, 6, 7, 8, 9, 10}

-- insertion at beginning and end

set beginning of L to 0
set end of L to 11
log L

-- insertion before arbitrary item n
-- n ≠ 1

set n to 5
set insertItem to {500}

set L to (items 1 thru (n - 1) of L) & insertItem & (items n thru -1 of L)
log L
```

2. Click the Event Log tab and run the program. You get the following results logged:

```
(*2, 3, 4, 5, 6, 7, 8, 9*)
(*2, 3, 4, 6, 7, 8, 9*)
(*2, 4, 6, 7, 8, 9*)
(*0, 1, 2, 3, 4, 5, 6, 7, 8, 9, 10, 11*)
(*0, 1, 2, 3, 500, 4, 5, 6, 7, 8, 9, 10, 11*)
```

How It Works

After setting the list L to the consecutive integers 1 through 10, the program deletes the first and last items from the list using the statements

```
set L to rest of L -- delete first item
set L to items 1 thru -2 of L -- delete last item
```

The program then proceeds to delete the fourth item in the list using this statement:

```
set L to (items 1 thru 3 of L) & (items 5 thru -1 of L)
```

This concatenates a list consisting of the first three items of L with a list consisting of the fifth through last items of L, effectively "squeezing out" the fourth item from the list. At this point, the fourth item is the number 5 (recall that you previously deleted the first item), so it gets effectively deleted from the list.

After setting the variable n to the number 2, the program next shows how an arbitrary item can be removed from the list. The statement

```
set L to (items 1 thru (n - 1) of L) & (items (n + 1) thru -1 of L
```

sets L to a list consisting of the first n - 1 items from the list concatenated with a list consisting of items n + 1 through the end of the list. Because n is set equal to 2, this effectively removes the second item from the list.

When identifying items in a list using an expression with more than one term, like n + 1, you must insert parentheses around the expression.

Be aware that n cannot have the value 1. If it did, the previous statement would generate the following AppleScript error when you run your program:

```
Can't get items 1 thru 0 of {2, 3, 4, 6, 7, 8, 9}.
```

Item n – 1 in this case is 0, and there is no item 0 in the list. The fact that the range is in decreasing order does not upset AppleScript. In fact, it lets you write expressions such as items 5 thru 2 of L and silently reorders the range for you.

For the same reason, the value of n can't be equal to the number of items in the list. In this case, the list has seven items, so setting n to 7 would also cause an AppleScript error because no item n + 1 (or 8) is in the list.

In the general case, if n is equal to any valid item number in a list, the following code removes that item from the list:

```
-- remove item n from list L

if n > 0 and n ≤ (count L)  -- make sure n is valid
    if n = 1 then
        set L to rest of L -- remove first item
    else if n = (count L) then
        set L to items 1 thru -2 of L  -- remove last item
    else
        set L to (items 1 thru (n - 1) of L) & (items (n + 1) thru -1) of L
    end if
end if
```

Returning to your program, list insertion is illustrated next. The list L is set once again to the integers 1 through 10. The two statements that follow next are familiar to you from a previous program example:

```
set beginning of L to 0
set end of L to 11
```

The first statement inserts 0 at the front of the list. The second statement appends 11 to the end of the list.

The next sequence of code shows how to insert an arbitrary item into the list:

```
set n to 5
set insertItem to {500}

set L to (items 1 thru (n - 1) of L) & insertItem & (items n thru -1 of L)
```

The value of n is set to 5, meaning you want to insert an item in front of item 5 in the list. The variable insertItem is then set to the value you want to insert. In this case, it's a single-item list containing the value 500. The list can contain multiple items if you want to insert more than one item into the list at once.

The third statement shown previously sets L to concatenation of the first n – 1 items in the list, followed by the item to be inserted, followed by items n through the end of the list. This effectively inserts the item into the list.

As in the previous discussion on item deletion, in this case, n cannot have the value 1 because there is not an n - 1, or 0th item in the list.

Similar to what was previously shown, the following code inserts an item insertItem into a list L before an arbitrary item number n, where the value of n can range from 1 to the number of items in the list. To handle the special case of inserting at the end of the list (appending), you interpret the value of n equal to −1 to have this special meaning:

```
-- add item insertItem in front of item n in list L
-- special case of n = -1 for insertion at end of list

if n = -1 or (n ≥ 1 and n ≤ (count L))   -- make sure n is valid
    if n = 1 then
        set beginning of L to insertItem   -- insert at front of list
    else if n = -1 then
        set end of L to insertItem   -- add to end of list
    else
        set L to (items 1 thru (n - 1) of L) & insertItem & (items n thru -1 of L)
    end if
end if
```

Exercise 4 at the end of this chapter has you write a program to test the code for list item insertion and also the code for list item deletion (shown previously).

Copying Lists

Take a look at the following four statements and predict the output from the log command:

```
set x to 100
set y to x
set x to 200
log y
```

What do you think gets logged for the value of y? Well, x is first assigned the value 100 and then its value is assigned to y. Subsequently setting the value of x to 200 has no effect on the value of y, just on the value of x. So the answer is that the value of 100 gets logged by the previous four-statement sequence.

Now look at these four statements and predict the output from the log command:

```
set x to {1, 2, 3, 4, 5}
set y to x
set first item of x to 100
log y
```

This time you'd be wrong if you thought that the list logged would be

```
{1, 2, 3, 4, 5}
```

The output from the log shows that the first item in y has the value of 100. When you set a list to another list, AppleScript does not create a new copy of the list. Instead, it refers to the same list in memory. So when you write the statements

```
set x to {1, 2, 3, 4, 5}
set y to x
```

the variables x and y *both refer to the same list*. This has important implications because, as you saw in the example, changing an item in the list through any reference to the list changes that item where it is stored in memory. So when you set the first item in x to 100 with the statement

```
set first item of x to 100
```

it also has the effect of setting the first item of y to 100 because x and y both reference the same list.

Here's another example. Predict the values of x and y after executing these statements:

```
set x to {1, 2, 3}
set y to x
set beginning of y to 0
set end of x to 4
```

You are correct if you predicted that both x and y would contain the following list after these statements are executed:

```
{0, 1, 2, 3, 4}
```

What if your list is not made by direct assignment but is created from a range of items? For example, what do you think happens to the value of the third item of y after you execute these statements:

```
set x to {"a", "b", "c", "d", "e"}
set y to items 1 thru -1 of x
set item 3 of x to "XXX"
```

Unlike assigning the entire list with the set command like this:

```
set y to x
```

The effect of assigning all the statements to the list this way is to create a new list with all the items contained in x.

```
set y to items 1 thru -1 of x
```

In this case, x and y reference two different lists. Changing an item in one list does not affect the corresponding item in the other list. Therefore, setting the third item of x does not affect the third item of y, whose value remains "c".

The copy Command

When assigning one list to another, a way to guarantee that the lists are independent is to use the copy command. The general format of this command is as follows:

```
copy value to variable
```

Here *value* is copied to the specified *variable*. You can use this command to set the value of variables in the ordinary way. For example, instead of writing

```
set n to 0
```

you can write

```
copy 0 to n
```

But the copy command is never used this way. When you use it for a list, however, as in

```
set x to {1, 2, 3, 4, 5}
copy x to y
```

its use becomes more significant because, in this case, a distinct copy of the list is made.

To witness the effects of the copy command, change the previously shown sequence of statements

```
set x to {1, 2, 3, 4, 5}
set y to x
set first item of x to 100
log y
```

to use copy instead of set. The sequence now becomes

```
set x to {1, 2, 3, 4, 5}
copy x to y
set first item of x to 100
log y
```

When you run this sequence of statements again, you see that changing the value of the first item of x has no effect on the first item of y. Its value remains 1.

Copying Lists of Lists

What happens when you use the copy command for a list that itself contains lists as its items? In other words, what happens when you run the following sequence of statements:

```
set x to {{1, 2, 3}, {4, 5, 6}}
copy x to y
set item 1 of y to {7, 8, 9}
```

The question here is whether the first item of x is changed when the first item of y gets changed. That is, if a list contains one or more lists as items, do copies of those get made as well? If you look at the value of x after executing these statements, you can see it has the following value:

```
{{1, 2, 3}, {4, 5, 6}}
```

Therefore, the answer is that lists inside lists are themselves copied when the copy command is used.

Using Containment Operators with Lists

In Chapter 5, you learned how to use containment operators such as `contains` and `is in` when working with strings. You can also use these operators when working with lists. They are summarized in the following table.

Operator	Meaning	Example
`l1 begins with l2`	Does list `l1` begin consecutively with the items in list `l2`?	`L1 begins with {1, 2, 3}`
`l1 ends with l2`	Does list `l1` end consecutively with the items in list `l2`?	`L1 ends with {8, 9, 10}`
`l1 contains l2`	Do the items in list `l2` occur consecutively in list `l1`?	`favoriteTeams contains {"Yankees"}`
`l1 does not contain l2`	Do the items in list `l2` not occur consecutively in list `l1`?	`theGrades does not contain {100}`
`l1 is in l2`	Do the items in `l1` occur consecutively in list `l2`?	`{"New York"} is in USCityNames`
`l1 is not in l2`	Do the items in `l1` not occur consecutively in list `l2`?	`{"Hey Jude"} is not in myFavorites`

When you're querying a list to see if it starts with, ends with, or contains another *list*, recognize that both operands are lists. So you write

```
USCityNames contains {"New York"}
```

to see if the string `"New York"` is an item in the list `USCityNames`. As you might expect, AppleScript tries to makes things easier for you when it can, so if you write this:

```
USCityNames contains "New York"
```

it still works because AppleScript coerces the string `"New York"` into a single-item list for you. This paradigm is used so often that I will use it throughout the rest of this text.

As noted in the table, when you query for more than one item in a list, order matters. So given your list `theGrades` used earlier:

```
set theGrades to {100, 93, 94, 84, 88, 83, 80, 75}
```

this test is `true`

```
theGrades contains {93, 94, 84}   -- true
```

whereas this test is `false` because the listed items do not appear consecutively in `theGrades`:

```
theGrades contains {93, 94, 80}   -- false
```

As another example, the following statement tests whether the variable `theAnswer` contains a number:

```
class of theAnswer is in {real, integer}
```

This is equivalent to writing the following test:

```
class of theAnswer is real or class of theAnswer is integer
```

Recall that you can't write the following test

```
class of theAnswer is number
```

because a numeric value never exists as a `number`; it's either an `integer` or a `real`.

All containment operators return a true/false value. Unfortunately, they don't tell you the *location* of the match in the list. So using your population program (any version), you could write the following

```
if cityEntered is in USCityNames then
 ...
 end if
```

to easily test whether the city entered was in your list, but you would still have to search the list sequentially to get its index number in the list.

Recall that like string containment, considerations are taken into account when these operators are applied to lists containing string items. So using the `USCityNames` list shown earlier, the following code produces a `true` result even though the list contains the string `"New York"`:

```
USCityNames contains "new york"
```

This matches because, as you recall, case is ignored by default.

Multiple Assignments with Lists

Included here for the sake of completeness is a shorthand notation supported by AppleScript. This notation enables you to assign multiple variables in a single statement. If you write the following in your program

```
set {a, b, c} to {100, 200, 300}
```

the first variable in the first list, which is `a`, is assigned the first value from the second list, which is `100`. The second variable in the first list, which is `b`, is assigned the second value from the second list, which is `200`, and so on. It's as if you wrote the following three statements:

```
set a to 100
set b to 200
set c to 300
```

You can initialize any types of variables this way, including strings and lists. Here's an example:

```
set {found, kidsNames, n} to {false, {"Julia, "Linda", "Gregory"}, 0}
```

This is equivalent to the following three statements:

```
set found to false
set kidsNames to {"Julia", "Linda", "Gregory"}
set n to 0
```

List Coercions

You can coerce other data types into lists and lists into other data types as well, as I describe in this section.

If you coerce a basic data type value like an integer, boolean, real, string, or date into a list, you get a single-item list containing that value. For example

```
100 as list
```

produces

```
{100}
```

You can coerce a single-item list containing a particular value into any data type that a single item can be coerced into. For example

```
{100} as integer
```

produces

```
100
```

and

```
{100} as string
```

gives

```
"100"
```

This works because an integer can be coerced into a string.

You can coerce a list of multiple items into a string if each item in the list can be coerced into a string. The result is a concatenation of all the items. For example, when you write this

```
{1, 2, 3} as string
```

you get this:

```
"123"
```

And if you write the following:

```
{"I am ", "n", "o", "t", " behaving like a ", 5, " year old!"} as string
```

you get this:

```
"I am not behaving like a 5 year old!
```

The special `text item delimiters` property is used by AppleScript when converting a list to a string. Its value is inserted between each item in the list when the list is coerced into a string. As you may recall, its value is null by default. However, setting the value to something else can have interesting effects. If you have a list of words, setting `text item delimiters` to a space character is an easy way to make a string with a space delimiting each word, like so:

```
set text item delimiters to " "
{"This", "is", "an", "exciting", "topic!"} as string
```

This produces the following string:

```
"This is an exciting topic!"
```

Of course, you should always remember to subsequently restore `text item delimiters` to its previous null value, as I pointed out in Chapter 5.

If you have a list of path components, setting `text item delimiters` to a colon character is an easy way to reconstruct those components back into a path, like so:

```
set text item delimiters to ":"
set pathParts to {"Macintosh HD", "Users", "steve", "Documents", ""}
pathParts as string
```

The result from executing these three statements is the following string:

```
"Macintosh HD:Users:steve:Documents:"
```

A Quick Note about Efficiency and Large Lists

I want to mention an important point about program efficiency here, if only because in certain cases it can have a dramatic impact on the speed of your program. It has to do with referencing items in a list, typically inside a loop that repeats a large number of times. You saw in an earlier program how the following code was used to sum the numbers in your list of grades called `theGrades`:

```
set theGrades to {100, 93, 94, 84, 88, 83, 80, 75}
set sum to 0

repeat with aGrade in theGrades
    set sum to sum + aGrade
end repeat
```

This example only uses eight grades, so execution speed is of no concern here. However, if you had 8,000 grades, for example, execution time would become significant, taking 30 seconds or more to sum the grades. You have several ways to optimize this code. One method has to do with creating a *reference* to the list, and you learn how to do that in Chapter 13. Another way is by inserting the keyword my in front of the list wherever you reference it inside the loop. Without explaining what's going on, here's a modified version of the repeat statement that produces significant improvements in the execution time of your code (reducing the execution time down to less than a second!):

```
repeat with aGrade in my theGrades
    set sum to sum + aGrade
end repeat
```

If you are referencing the items individually by item number inside a loop, here's how you can take advantage of this speed improvement:

```
repeat with i from 1 to count theGrades
    set sum to sum + (item i of my theGrades)
end repeat
```

Again, don't worry about how or why this works. Take it on faith for now and remember to come back to this section if you find your programs are taking a long time to execute when you are working with large lists.

Working with Records

You know that a list contains an ordered series of items. You can reference items in a list by number or by a range of numbers. So you can ask for the first item in the list, the 25th item in the list, or the 10th through 15th items in the list. You can also ask for every item in the list.

A record is, in some ways, similar to a list in that it enables you to collectively refer to a set of values. Whereas a list is a collection of items, a record is a collection of *properties*. A property consists of a name (or label) and a value that is associated with that name. Unlike a list, the properties of a record are not ordered and can only be referenced by name. These properties cannot be referenced by number or by beginning or end. You also cannot directly enumerate all the properties in a record.

Defining a Record

The general format of a record looks like this:

```
{ label1: value1, label2: value2, ..., labeln: valuen }
```

The properties in this record are named *label1, label2, . . ., labeln* and have corresponding values *value1, value2, . . . valuen*. Property names are formed by following the same rules for forming variable names that you learned about in Chapter 2. You can have a property with the same name as a variable in your program. AppleScript figures out your intentions based on the context in which the name is used.

As a simple example, the following defines a record that contains two properties called name and email with the corresponding values "Greg Kochan" and "greg222@techfitness.com":

```
{ name: "Greg Kochan", email: "greg222@techfitness.com" }
```

In your program, your records are presumably assigned to a variable, like so:

```
set userInfo to { name: "Greg Kochan", email: "greg222@techfitness.com" }
```

After this assignment, `userInfo` contains a record with two properties: `name` and `email`.

> *If you enter this record into Script Editor, you may notice after you compile that the property* `name`
> *appears in blue (indicating it's an application keyword) whereas the property* `email` *appears in green
> (indicating it is a variable name). That's because* `name` *is built into AppleScript, and it can be used to
> reference the name of the current application. As noted earlier, AppleScript can handle this without con-
> flict based on the context of using the word* `name` *in your program.*

To get a property from a record, you specify the name of the property, followed by `of` (or `in`), followed
by the record, like so:

```
name of userInfo
```

This gives you the value of the `name` property in the record `userInfo`, which is the string `"Greg Kochan"`.

Of course, you can optionally precede this expression with the implied `get` command, as in:

```
get name of userInfo
```

To get the `email` record from `userInfo`, you can write the following expression:

```
get email of userInfo
```

As you would expect, each property can have a value that can be of any data type. Here's a record that
stores my son's name, his date of birth, his height (in inches), and his weight (in pounds):

```
set greg to { name: "Gregory", DOB: date "2/22/96", height: 52, weight: 55 }
```

The record `greg`, as defined here, contains four properties. The first property is `name` and is assigned a
string value; the second property is `DOB` and is assigned a `date` value; the last two properties are `height`
and `weight`, respectively, and are assigned `integer` values.

Like list items, record properties can have values specified by expressions. AppleScript evaluates the
expressions and stores the resulting values in the record.

To get Greg's height from the previously defined record, you write

```
height of greg
```

Other properties are retrieved from the record in a similar fashion.

> *Remember that the properties are not stored in the record in any particular order. So you can't ask for
> the first property, or the last, or the seventh. You also can't ask for a range of properties. Finally, you
> can't enumerate all the properties in a record using* `every` *or a* `repeat` *statement. This last point is
> particularly irritating, because you'll often want to do this.*

The result Record from the display dialog Command

Some commands return a record as their result. You're familiar with the display dialog command. This command returns a record containing the property button returned, whose value is the name of the button clicked by the user. If the default answer parameter is supplied, the record also contains the property text returned, whose value is the data entered by the user.

So when you wrote this statement in your alarm clock program

```
set textEntered to text returned of result
```

you were fetching the value of the text returned property from the result record and storing it into the variable textEntered.

Realize that for the record returned by display dialog, button returned and text returned are the property names. That is, these property names are each composed of two words. You'll find that many applications use records containing multiword property names. You can't easily do this yourself with your records; you'd have to use the | . . . | syntax discussed in Chapter 2, which hardly makes it worth the effort.

Working with Lists of Records

Records are useful when you start dealing with lists of them. For example, suppose you have a record called track1 that stores the name, artist, and album for a particular song (or *track* as it's often called):

```
set track1 to {name: "By Your Side", artist: "Sade", album: "Lovers Rock"}
```

Further, suppose you have a bunch of other tracks as well:

```
set track2 to {name: "Lose Yourself", artist: "Eminem", album: "8 Mile"}
set track3 to {name: "Riders on the Storm", artist: "The Doors", album: ¬
    "The Best of the Doors"}
set track4 to {name: "Someday", artist: "Sugar Ray", album: "14:59"}
```

You can group all your tracks together into a list like this:

```
set playList to {track1, track2, track3, track4}
```

If you recall that lists are ordered (unlike records), the variable playList, as defined here, might also indicate the order of playing for the songs in your playList.

Of course, you might have a lot more tracks, and the tracks might come from other sources, such as from a file or directly from an application like iTunes.

To get the first track in your playList, you write the following:

```
first item of playList
```

This gives you track1, which is a record containing three properties.

To get the name of the first track in your `playList`, you write

```
name of first item of playList
```

This gives you the string `"By Your Side"`, which is the name of the first song in your `playList`.

To get the artist for the last song in your `playList`, you could write

```
artist of last item of playList
```

This gives you the string `"Sugar Ray"`.

In Chapter 11, you see how you can tell an application like iTunes to give you the names of its songs and also how you can tell it to play each song in your `playList` for you.

Lists from Records

You've heard it mentioned enough times by now: The properties in a record are not ordered and cannot be referenced by number. That means that *none of the following expressions work*, even though you may be tempted is to write these types of expressions (and here we are referencing the record `track1` and the list of records `playList` as defined in the previous section):

```
item 1 in track1   -- NO!
every name in playList -- NO!
every artist of every item in playList   -- NO!
```

You can coerce a record into a list, but you lose all the property labels. For example, given the previous definition for `track1`, writing the following

```
track1 as list
```

produces this three-item list:

```
{"By Your Side", "Sade", "Lovers Rock"}
```

Because records are not ordered, it's not guaranteed that the items in the list are in the same order as the properties in the record are defined. In this example, it just happens to work out that way.

You can also convert a record into a list by asking for its items. So writing the expression

```
every item in track1
```

or

```
items in track1
```

produces the same list as shown when the record was explicitly coerced into a list. AppleScript knows that items apply to lists and, therefore, converts the record `track1` to a list to carry out the operation.

Because this sort of enumeration is allowed, you can retrieve all the values in a record. However, because the property labels are discarded in the process and the order is not defined, this fact is of limited applicability.

Using a method that is similar to converting a record to a list, you can extract all the values of a particular class from a record. Just as you can write

```
numbers in theGrades
```

to get every number from the list theGrades, you can likewise write the following to get every string from the record track1:

```
strings in track1
```

Because track1, *as you previously defined it, contains only strings as values, the preceding code produces the same list as if you wrote* items in track1.

To count the number of integers in a record called fileStats, you could write the following:

```
count integers in fileStats
```

You should recognize that this works only because AppleScript converts fileStats from a record to a list before extracting the integers from that list.

In the following Try It Out, you return to the population program you developed earlier in this chapter to see how you can use a list of records to store your data.

Try It Out   A Version of the Population Program Using Records

The three versions of the previously shown population program each used one or more lists to store information about several US cities and their populations. In the first and third versions, two separate lists were maintained. The second version used a single list:

```
set USCities to {{"Boston", 574000}, {"Chicago", 2784000}, {"Dallas", 1007000},
    {"Houston", 1631000}, {"Los Angeles", 3485000}, {"Philadelphia", 1586000},
    {"San Diego", 1111000}, {"San Francisco", 724000}, {"New York", 7323000}}
```

Each item of the list is itself a two-item list that contains the city's name and its population. A minor disadvantage of this unified list approach is that you can't readily give the list of city names to the choose from list command to display.

It's a natural extension to this example to use records to store the city populations. Each record can be defined to have two properties. The first property you can call name, and you can use it to hold the name of the city as a string. The second property can be named population, and you can use it to store the corresponding population for the city. Here's what the record for Boston looks like:

```
{name:"Boston", population:574000},
```

If you make a list of these records, you have a convenient way to work with your population data. That's what you do in the following program, which is the fourth version of your population program.

1. Type the following program into Script Editor:

```
-- Show the population of a given city
-- Version 4

set USCities to {¬
    {name:"Boston", population:574000}, ¬
    {name:"Chicago", population:2784000}, ¬
    {name:"Dallas", population:1007000}, ¬
    {name:"Houston", population:1631000}, ¬
    {name:"Los Angeles", population:3485000}, ¬
    {name:"Philadelphia", population:1586000}, ¬
    {name:"San Diego", population:1111000}, ¬
    {name:"San Francisco", population:724000}, ¬
    {name:"New York", population:7323000}}

-- Now build a list of city names to give to the
-- choose from list command

set USCityNames to {}

repeat with cityRecord in USCities
    set end of USCityNames to name of cityRecord
end repeat

choose from list USCityNames with prompt "Pick a city to find its population:"

set theSelection to result

-- see if Cancel was clicked

if theSelection = false then
    return -- stops the program's execution
end if

set cityEntered to item 1 of theSelection

-- now look for the city in the list of records

set found to false
set n to 1

repeat while not found and n ≤ (count USCities)
    if name of (item n of USCities) = cityEntered then
        set found to true
    else
        set n to n + 1
    end if
end repeat

-- either show the population or give a message that the city wasn't found
```

```
    if not found then
        display dialog "Sorry, I don't know the population of " & cityEntered ¬
                with icon note buttons {"OK"} default button 1
    else
        set cityPopulation to population of (item n of USCities)
        display dialog "The population of " & cityEntered & " is " & (cityPopulation ¬
                as string) buttons {"OK"} default button 1
    end if
```

2.   Run the program. Select a city from the list and verify that the program displays the correct population for the selected city.

3.   Run the program again. This time click Cancel to verify that processing stops if the user clicks the Cancel button.

How It Works

The program starts by defining a list of records like this:

```
set USCities to {¬
        {name:"Boston", population:574000}, ¬
        {name:"Chicago", population:2784000}, ¬
        {name:"Dallas", population:1007000}, ¬
        {name:"Houston", population:1631000}, ¬
        {name:"Los Angeles", population:3485000}, ¬
        {name:"Philadelphia", population:1586000}, ¬
        {name:"San Diego", population:1111000}, ¬
        {name:"San Francisco", population:724000}, ¬
        {name:"New York", population:7323000}}
```

In this example, you explicitly continued each line to visually align your records. Recall that you can do this in Script Editor by typing Option-Return at the end of the line. The line continuation is denoted by the ¬ character at the end of the line.

The first item in the USCities list contains the record for Boston. The name property has as its value the string "Boston", and the population property has the value 574000.

The program next builds a list of city names to give to the choose from list command. You do this with the following statements:

```
set USCityNames to {}

repeat with cityRecord in USCities
        set end of USCityNames to name of cityRecord
end repeat
```

The list USCityNames is first set to an empty list. The repeat loop then sequences through each item in the USCities list and tacks the name of the city from each record onto the end of the USCityNames list. Make sure you fully understand the operation of the statement

```
    set end of USCityNames to name of cityRecord
```

and how the list is built through each iteration of the loop.

You can insert a `log USCityNames` *statement into the loop to see how the list gets built through each iteration.*

When the loop is complete, the list of names is given to the `choose from list` command to be presented to the user, as in previous versions of the population program.

The `if` statement that appears in the program after the `choose from list` command

```
if theSelection = false then
    return -- stops the program's execution
end if
```

tests to see if the user clicked Cancel. If that's the case, the program simply executes a `return` command to stop the program's execution.

Now the program searches through the `USCities` list looking for a match. The test for a match is done with the following `if` statement:

```
if name of (item n of USCities) = cityEntered then
    set found to true
else
    set n to n + 1
end if
```

If the `name` property for a particular record in the `USCities` list matches the city selected by the user, the variable `found` is set to `true` and the loop is subsequently exited. If the city names don't match, the index variable `n` is incremented by `1` and the search continues.

When the loop exits with a successful match (which, as you will recall, should always be the case), the following statement is executed:

```
set cityPopulation to population of (item n of USCities)
```

Since `n` is set to the index of the matching record from the `USCities` list, the `population` property from the same record is accessed to get the corresponding population value. This value is reported to the user in a dialog as before. The program's execution is then complete.

Modifying Records

In this section, you learn how to modify the values stored in a record. You also see how you can use concatenation to add new properties to a record and how to copy a record.

Changing Property Values in a Record

To change the value of a property in a record, you can use the `set` command. Consider the following record called `editFileInfo`:

```
set editFileInfo to {fileName: "ch6.doc", fileSize: 189150, creationDate: date ¬
        "6/1/04",  modificationDate: date "6/5/04"}
```

To set the modification date to the current date, you write the following:

```
set modificationDate of editFileInfo to current date
```

That seems straightforward enough.

Concatenating Records

You can concatenate records using the concatenation operator &. When you do this, the records are combined according to the following two rules:

1. The resulting record consists of all properties from both records.

2. If a property exists in both records, the value of the property from the first record is used.

The first rule allows you to add properties to a record. So when you write the following

```
set mergedRecord to {name: "Greg Kochan", age: 8} & {height: 52 weight: 55}
```

you get the following record assigned to mergedRecord:

```
{name: "Greg Kochan", age: 8, height: 52 weight: 55}
```

When you write the following

```
set mergedRecord to {name: "Greg Kochan", age: 8} & {name: "Julia Kochan", ¬
        weight: 55}
```

you get this record as the result (because rule 2 comes into play):

```
{name: "Greg Kochan", age: 8, weight: 55}
```

Because the name property exists in both records, the value from the first record is used. This fact can be used to update a record by listing the updated value *first*. For example, returning to the editFileInfo record from the previous section

```
set editFileInfo to {fileName: "ch6.doc", fileSize: 189150, creationDate: date ¬
        "6/1/04", modificationDate: date "6/5/04"}
```

you can use the following statement to update the modification date to the current date:

```
set editFileInfo to {modificationDate: current date} & editFileInfo
```

In this case, because the modificationDate property exists in both records, the value from the first record is used, effectively replacing or updating the value in the second record. This does not work if you write the statement this way:

```
set editFileInfo to editFileInfo & {modificationDate: current date}
```

In this case, the property modificationDate exists in both records, so the value from the first record gets used; therefore, the date is not updated.

You can also update the modification date directly, like this:

```
set modificationDate of editFileInfo to current date
```

The subtle difference here is that in this last case the property `modificationDate` must exist in `editFileInfo` or an AppleScript error occurs. In the case of using the concatenation operator, you won't get an error. In fact, as noted, the property is added even if it doesn't exist. This works here because you know in advance that `editFileInfo` does in fact contain a property named `modificationDate`.

Copying Records

The discussion about copying lists applies equally to copying records: If you assign a record to another variable using the `set` command, you simply create another reference to the same record and not a distinct copy of the record. So if you want to make two records for Greg Kochan and set the `email` property to two different e-mail addresses, like this

```
set user1 to { name: "Greg Kochan", email: "greg222@techfitness.com" }
set user2 to user1
set email of user2 to "support@techfitness.com"
```

you are foiled in your efforts. Because `user1` and `user2` reference the same record, setting the `email` property in `user2` effectively sets the `email` property in `user1` to the same value.

You can use the `copy` command to make a distinct copy of a record, like this:

```
copy user1 to user2
```

Subsequently changing the `email` property of `user2` has no effect on the `email` property of `user1`, and vice versa. The same applies to the `name` property: Both records hold distinct values, so changing the value in one record has no effect on the corresponding property in the other record.

Retrieving Multiple Properties

It's possible to retrieve multiple properties from a record in a single statement. When you do that, you get a list of values returned. As an example, consider the `editFileInfo` record from an earlier section:

```
set editFileInfo to {fileName: "ch6.doc", fileSize: 189150, creationDate: ¬
        date "6/1/04", modificationDate: date "6/5/04"}
```

Here is how you can get both the file name and size from this record and store them in a variable called `fileInfo`:

```
set fileInfo to {fileName, fileSize} of editFileInfo
```

The result stored in `fileInfo` is a two-item list of the values of the two properties:

```
{"ch6.doc", 199150}
```

Using the Containment Operators with Records

Earlier in this chapter, you saw how to use the containment operators with lists. You can also use them with records. Because properties in a record are unordered, however, it makes sense that the `begins with` and `end with` operators cannot be used with records. The containment operators that you can use with records are summarized in the following table.

Operator	Meaning	Example
`r1 contains r2`	Do the properties and their values in record *r2* all occur in record *r1*?	`currentTrack contains {name: "My Love"}`
`r1 does not contain r2`	Do the properties and their values in record *r2 not* all occur in record *r2*?	`currentTrack does not contain {artist: "Paul McCartney"}`
`r1 is in r2`	Do the properties and their values in record *r1* all occur in record *r2*?	`{font: "Geneva", size: 10} is in currentTextStyle`
`r1 is not in r2`	Do the properties and their values in record *r1* not all occur in record *r2*?	`{folder: false, hidden: true} is not in fileInfo`

Note that these queries seek to match properties both in name and value. So in the first example from the table

```
currentTrack contains {name: "My Love"}
```

the record `currentTrack` must have a property called `name`, and its value must be equal to the string `"My Love"` (based on current considerations) for the result to be `true`.

When you query a record to see if it contains more than one property, you can list the properties in any order. This makes sense because the properties in a record aren't ordered anyway. So given this record

```
set editFileInfo to {fileName: "ch6.doc", fileSize: 189150, creationDate: date ¬
    "6/1/04", modificationDate: date "6/5/04"}
```

the following line tests to see if the name of the file in the record is `ch6.doc` and if its size is `189150`:

```
editFileInto contains {fileSize: 189150, fileName: "ch6.doc"}
```

Recall that like string containment, considerations are taken into account when these operators are applied to lists containing string elements. So using the `USCityNames` list used earlier, the following line produces a `true` result even though the list contains the string `"New York"`:

```
USCityNames contains "new york"
```

As you may recall, case is ignored by default. So this produces a true result.

Summary

A lot has been covered in this chapter. Lists and records are the two fundamental data structures for collecting data that are built into AppleScript. Knowing how to define and manipulate these data structures is a key component of becoming proficient with the AppleScript language.

In particular, you learned the following in this chapter:

❑ That a list is an ordered collection of values called items.

❑ How to access single and multiple items in a list and how to insert items into and delete items from a list.

❑ How you can use the concatenation operator (&) to merge two lists together.

❑ How to work with lists of lists and how you can use the `choose from list` command to present the user with a list of choices from which to choose.

❑ How to use containment operators to see if one or more items are contained in a list.

❑ That a record is an unordered collection of values, called properties. A property consists of a name and a corresponding value.

❑ That unlike lists, you cannot refer to the properties in a record by number, nor can you enumerate their names.

❑ How to retrieve and modify a property's value and how you can use the concatenation operator to effectively add new properties to a record or to update existing ones.

❑ That containment operators enable you to test if a record contains one or more properties with particular values.

❑ How working with lists of records can be a powerful technique.

❑ How to use the `copy` command to make distinct copies of a list or record. This is in contrast to using the `set` command, which simply creates a new reference to a list or record.

In the next chapter, you learn to use AppleScript's built-in commands to work with files and folders. Before proceeding, however, try the exercises that follow to test your understanding of the material covered in this chapter. You can find the solutions to these exercises in Appendix A.

Exercises

1. *Fibonacci* numbers have many applications in the field of mathematics and in the study of computer algorithms. The first two Fibonacci numbers, which we will call *F1* and *F2*, are defined to be 0 and 1, respectively. Thereafter, each successive Fibonacci number *Fi* is defined to be the sum of the two preceding Fibonacci numbers *Fi-2* and *Fi-1*. So *F3* is calculated by adding together the values of *F1* and *F2*. Write a program to calculate the first 20 Fibonacci numbers, storing each number as it is calculated into a list. (Hint: Each new Fibonacci number can be appended to the end of the list as the sum of the last two items in the list.)

2. Based on the population program used in this chapter, write a program to display the city with the smallest population as well as the city with the largest population.

```
set USCities to {{"Boston", 574000}, {"Chicago", 2784000}, {"Dallas", 1007000},  ¬
    {"Houston", 1631000}, {"Los Angeles", 3485000}, {"Philadelphia", 1586000}, ¬
    {"San Diego", 1111000}, {"San Francisco", 724000}, {"New York", 7323000}}
```

3. Repeat the preceding exercise (#2), substituting the following list for USCities:

```
set USCities to {¬
    {name:"Boston", population:574000}, ¬
    {name:"Chicago", population:2784000}, ¬
    {name:"Dallas", population:1007000}, ¬
    {name:"Houston", population:1631000}, ¬
    {name:"Los Angeles", population:3485000}, ¬
    {name:"Philadelphia", population:1586000}, ¬
    {name:"San Diego", population:1111000}, ¬
    {name:"San Francisco", population:724000}, ¬
    {name:"New York", population:7323000}}
```

4. In the section on deleting items from a list, a general method is given to remove any item from a non-empty list given its index number. The same is true for the section on inserting items in a list: A general method was shown to insert an item anywhere in a list. Write a program that verifies that these two methods work as presented. Be sure to verify that they work for the end cases, that is for the first and last items in a list.

5. Here are some more cities and their populations in 1990:

City	Population
Baltimore	736000
Columbus	633000
Detroit	1028000
Memphis	610000
Phoenix	983000

Incorporate these cities and their respective populations into any version of the population program presented in this chapter.

6. Given the following list from the second version of the population program:

```
set USCities to {{"Boston", 574000}, {"Chicago", 2784000}, {"Dallas", 1007000},¬
    {"Houston", 1631000}, {"Los Angeles", 3485000}, {"Philadelphia", 1586000}, ¬
    {"San Diego", 1111000}, {"San Francisco", 724000}, {"New York", 7323000}}
```

rewrite the program to work with the list structured like this:

```
set USCities to {"Boston", 574000, "Chicago", 2784000, "Dallas", 1007000, ¬
    "Houston", 1631000, "Los Angeles", 3485000, "Philadelphia", 1586000, ¬
    "San Diego", 1111000, "San Francisco", 724000, "New York", 7323000}
```

7. The land areas for the cities used in the population program are shown in the following table.

City	Land Area (Square Miles)
Boston	48
Chicago	227
Dallas	342
Houston	540
Los Angeles	469
Philadelphia	135
San Diego	324
San Francisco	47
New York	309

Based on the information in this table, extend the last version of the population program presented in this chapter to display both the population and the land area for a given city. Add a new property to your list of records for land area.

8. Using the record format defined in the chapter for storing information about a song, add some more records for your favorite songs in the same format. Then add those songs to the `playList` record defined in the chapter. Finally, add a `playTime` property to your song records and set the value as appropriate to store the playing time in seconds for each song.

9. Based on the result from the preceding exercise (#8), calculate the total playing time for all songs in the `playList` record.

10. Given the result from the preceding exercise (#9), write a program that presents the user with a list of songs stored in the `playList`. After the user selects a song from the list, display the song's artist, album, and playing time in the format `m mins. n secs.`.

11. The following gives the sequence of steps that you can use to sort all the items in a list in ascending order. This is a simple *exchange sort* algorithm. The assumption is made here that the list L contains n items, each of the same type, such as numbers or strings, which can be compared:

Step 1:	Set i to 1.
Step 2:	Set j to $i + 1$.
Step 3:	If item i of L > item j of L, exchange their values.
Step 4:	Set j to $j + 1$. If $j < n$, go to Step 3.
Step 5:	Set i to $i + 1$. If $i < n - 1$, go to Step 2.
Step 6:	L is now sorted in ascending order.

Write a program based on this algorithm and test it out. (*Hint:* Use two nested `repeat` statements to implement the loops in Steps 2 through 5.) Can you think of a way to change the sort so that the items in the list are sorted in *descending* order?

12. Incorporate your exchange sort algorithm into your program from exercise #10. Have it sort the names of the songs before presenting them to the user.

Working with Files

Now it starts to get interesting. Up to this point, you haven't known how to access files on your system from your AppleScript programs. This chapter teaches you how to use AppleScript's built-in commands for working with files and folders. Each of these commands is in AppleScript's Standard Additions dictionary.

You may want to get a list of the files in your home directory. Or you might want to back up (in your Documents folder) all the files that have changed in the past 10 days. Perhaps you want to determine the space taken up by all the images you are using for a web page. Each of these tasks can be programmed in AppleScript after you know how to work with files.

Unfortunately, AppleScript's built-in commands do not give you all the power and flexibility you may need for your application. Luckily, the Finder can be used to fill in the gaps. In Chapter 10, you see how you tell the Finder to do these sorts of things for you.

Path Names: Traditional Mac and POSIX-style

You probably know that Mac OS X is based on the UNIX operating system. UNIX uses a different notation to identify files from what is traditionally used to identify files on the Mac. For example, the traditional Mac path to a file called `resume.doc` in your `Documents` folder might be expressed as follows:

```
Macintosh HD:Users:chris:Documents:resume.doc
```

When expressed as a POSIX path name, it looks like this:

```
/Users/chris/Documents/resume.doc
```

POSIX is the name of a UNIX standard that emerged in the 1980s from the IEEE committee. It was created in an effort to standardize the different versions of UNIX that existed at the time.

If the last component of a path is a folder, a trailing : character is used when writing the traditional path to the folder, like so:

```
Macintosh HD:Users:chris:Documents:
```

In the case of a POSIX path name, you can put a trailing slash at the end of the path, but it's optional to do so:

```
/Users/chris/Documents/
```

Path names are typically expressed as strings in AppleScript. For example, the path to Chris's Documents folder might be written like this:

```
set docsPath to "Macintosh HD:Users:chris:Documents:"
```

You can ask AppleScript to give you the POSIX-equivalent path name for a traditional path name by asking for the POSIX path property of the path name like this:

```
set docsPath to POSIX path of "Macintosh HD:Users:chris:Documents:"
```

This sets the variable docsPath to the string

```
/Users/chris/Documents/
```

because on my system, Macintosh HD is the name of the startup disk. Note that the leading / in the POSIX path name replaces the name of the startup disk in the path. Also note you must distinguish case when you write path names. That means that you must use uppercase characters as appropriate when writing Macintosh HD in the preceding example.

Full Path Names

A path name that starts with a slash represents a *full* path to a directory or file. Such a path name starts at the top of the file system hierarchy, or at what's often referred to as the *root* directory.

> *When dealing with POSIX path names, you normally use the term* directory *instead of* folder. *For all intents and purposes, the two terms are synonymous and are used interchangeably throughout the rest of this book.*

Full path names provide a complete and unambiguous description for the location of a particular file on your system. For that reason, it is the preferred way to identify a file.

Relative Path Names

If a path name does not begin with a slash, it is a *relative* path name, meaning that the specification is relative to the *current directory*.

> *The current directory is set by the application when it starts running. Script Editor sets the current directory to the root directory when it starts. Even if you save your script as an application, the current directory is set to the root directory when the application is launched. It's best not to make any assumption about what the current directory is set to when you or someone else runs your scripts.*

When you write the path name

```
chapter5.doc
```

you specify the file `chapter5.doc` relative to the current directory. Similarly, the traditional path name

```
books:AppleScript:chapter5.doc
```

and the equivalent POSIX path name

```
books/AppleScript/chapter5.doc
```

both identify a file `chapter5.doc` contained in the AppleScript directory, which itself is contained in the books directory.

A few special characters used in POSIX path names are worth mentioning. They are summarized in the following table.

Characters	Meaning	Example
..	The parent directory	../books
.	The current directory	./AppleScript/books/chapter5.doc
~	The home directory of the user running the program	~/Documents
~user	The specified user's home directory	~greg/games

Even though Mac OS X is based on UNIX, in many respects AppleScript remains entrenched in traditional Mac path names. In fact, it's a little schizophrenic. For example, the Finder's Go⇨Go to Folder command accepts only a POSIX-style path. However, if you do a File⇨Get Info on a file, the Finder reports the location of the file using traditional path names!

File Name Extensions

As you know, the Finder associates files on your system with applications. So when you are in the Finder and you double-click one of your script files, the application associated with that file is automatically launched. The association is based on the file's *extension*. This extension is a sequence of characters appended to the file's name, separated by a period. For example, the file named `population.scpt` has the extension `.scpt`. The Finder associates (by default) this extension with the Script Editor application. So whenever you open a file whose extension is `.scpt`, Script Editor is launched by the Finder.

When you are browsing in the Finder, the extension for a file is not normally shown. However, you can display these extensions by going to Finder⇨Preferences⇨Advanced and placing a check mark in the Show All File Extensions box. The extension for all files may still not be shown, however. This might happen if an individual file has its Extension Hidden property set to `true`. You can get the extension for such a file by doing a Get Info on the file (that is, by selecting the file in the Finder and choosing File⇨Get Info).

When you identify a file by name in AppleScript, you must also use its extension. So the following would be a valid path to a script stored on my system:

```
Macintosh HD:Users:steve:MySrc:scripts:ch6:population.scpt
```

This, however, is not a valid path:

```
Macintosh HD:Users:steve:MySrc:scripts:ch6:population
```

What's in a Name?

One of the contributions that UNIX made to the world of operating systems was the simple notion that everything is just a *file*. Under UNIX, a Word document is obviously a file. But the folder it's stored in is also a file, as is the hard disk that contains the folder. Finally, and less intuitively, even devices like DVD drives, monitors, and printers are considered files under UNIX. This simple yet elegant approach greatly simplifies the way programmers work with devices, directories, and ordinary files.

As you see in the following descriptions, AppleScript still distinguishes files from folders in many cases.

The file Class

AppleScript has a `file` class that you use with certain commands to reference a file or folder. You can create a `file` object for a file or directory simply by inserting the specifier `file` in front of a traditional path name like this:

```
file "Macintosh HD:Users:chris:Documents:resume.doc"
```

The class of the result produced by this expression is identified by AppleScript as a *file specification*.

You can also specify a file using a POSIX path name by placing `POSIX file` in front of the path name:

```
POSIX file "/Users/chris/Documents/resume.doc"
```

When you compile this line, Script Editor changes it to look like the previous command:

```
file "Macintosh HD:Users:chris:Documents:resume.doc"
```

The way AppleScript deals with files can be confusing. In the case of the first `file`... example, AppleScript creates a file specification from the specified file name. In the case of the `POSIX file` example, a file URL is created, even though after the line is compiled it appears identical to the first example. You don't need to concern yourself with this difference.

File Name Aliases

If you make an alias for a file in the Finder (by choosing File⇨Make Alias), you don't create a new copy of the file; rather you create a *reference* to the original file. The alias identifies the file by its name and its location. If you rename the original file or move it somewhere else, the alias to the file still tracks the original file.

Mac OS X knows whether an alias refers to a file on another volume. For example, if you create an alias on your desktop to a file on a removable drive and then unmount that drive, the system tells you to mount the volume that contains the file if you try to access the file through its alias.

You can create an alias to a file in AppleScript as well. You do this by writing the following:

```
alias filename
```

Unlike making an alias in the Finder, this doesn't actually create a file; instead it creates a reference to the specified file. In a sense, the alias to the file becomes part of the program because it is created when the program gets compiled (or saved); therefore, the file must exist at compile time.

An alias is particularly useful when you want to create an application that relies on a particular file. By creating an alias to that file (using a literal path name), AppleScript stores the reference to the file inside your application and can find the file if it subsequently gets moved or renamed after the application is built.

So if your program contains

```
set myPrefs to alias "Macintosh HD:Users:greg:prefFile"
```

and you create an application from this program, the alias to the specified file is stored as part of the application. Then, if prefFile gets renamed or moved, your program can still find it.

If you make changes to the script file that contains the previous alias, you'll get an error from Script Editor when you compile the file if prefFile is no longer at the specified path. That's because recompiling or saving the script causes Script Editor to create a new alias for the specified file.

Reading and Writing Files

Now that you know all about path names, POSIX path names, and aliases, it's time to learn how to perform some basic operations with files. You start by learning how you create a file, write some data to it, and subsequently read it back to verify its contents.

To perform I/O operations on a file in AppleScript, you can follow these three steps:

1. Open the file using the open for access command. This command returns a number that you use to subsequently identify the file for any I/O operations you perform on the file.

2. Read data from the open file using the read command. You write data to the open file using the write command.

3. Close the file using the close access command.

The next Try It Out helps you begin manipulating files in AppleScript. You create a sample text file called TextFile101 in your Documents directory and use this file in examples throughout this chapter.

You may want to ensure that you don't already have a file by that name in your Documents *folder. If you have one, you may want to rename it so that it isn't overwritten by the file you create next.*

Try It Out **Creating a File in AppleScript**

In the following steps, you type a program that creates a new file in AppleScript.

1. Type the following program into Script Editor:

```
-- Create a sample file in the user's Document folder

-- create the file name

set fileName to (path to documents folder as string) & "TextFile101.txt"

-- open the file for write access

set fileID to open for access file fileName with write permission

-- write some lines of data to the file

write "ABCDEFGHIJKLMNOPQRSTUVWXYZ\rline 2\rline 3\rline 4" to fileID

-- close the file now that you're done with it

close access fileID

-- get information about the file

info for file fileName
```

2. Run the program. You should get output similar to the following in the Result pane:

```
{name:"TextFile101.txt", creation date:date "Wednesday, June 23, 2004 12:47:42 PM",
modification date:date "Wednesday, June 23, 2004 12:47:42 PM", icon position:{0,
0},
size:47.0, folder:false, alias:false, name extension:"txt", extension hidden:false,
visible:true, package folder:false, file type:"TEXT", file creator:"ttxt",
displayed
name:"TextFile101.txt", default application:alias "Macintosh
HD:Applications:TextEdit
.app:", kind:"Plain text document", locked:false, busy status:false, short version:
"", long version:""}
```

3. Go to the Finder and locate a file called TextFile101 in your Documents folder. (If you have your preferences set to show file name extensions, the file will appear as TextFile101.txt.)

4. Double-click the file. This should launch Text Edit (unless you've changed your default association for text files), and you should get a window like that shown in Figure 7-1. Verify the contents of your file with what's shown in the figure.

5. Quit the Text Edit Application.

Figure 7-1

How It Works

The program begins by creating a file name and storing it in the variable `fileName`:

```
set fileName to file ((path to documents folder as string) & "TextFile101.txt")
```

The special `path to` command is followed by one or more words that indicate the particular path you're interested in obtaining. So if you want to know where your `Documents` folder is located, you write

```
path to documents folder
```

On my system, this produces the following:

```
alias "Macintosh HD:Users:steve:Documents:"
```

Note that the value returned by the `path to` command is an *alias* and that the path is expressed as a traditional path. Also note that case isn't important here (it seldom is in AppleScript), so you can write `path to documents folder` or `path to Documents folder`.

You can get the POSIX-equivalent path for a path returned by the `path to` command like this:

```
POSIX path of (path to documents folder)
```

The following table summarizes some of the more commonly used arguments for the `path to` command. For a complete list, consult Appendix B. In this table, *user* is the user name of the person running this command (your user name if you're the one running it). Also, Macintosh HD: is shown here as the name of the disk containing these folders and files; your disk name may be different.

Path To	Typical alias result
`application "appName"`	`"Macintosh HD:Applications:appName.app:"` *or wherever the application is located*
`applications folder`	`"Macintosh HD:Applications:"`
`current application`	`"Macintosh HD:Applications:AppleScript:Script Editor.app:"` *or whatever application is running the script*
`desktop`	`"Macintosh HD:Users:user:Desktop:"`
`documents folder`	`"Macintosh HD:Users:user:Documents:"`
`frontmost application`	*depends on frontmost application*
`home folder`	`"Macintosh HD:Users:user:"`
`library folder`	`"Macintosh HD:Library:"`
`me`	*Same as* `path to current application`
`movies folder`	`"Macintosh HD:Users:user:Movies:"`
`music folder`	`"Macintosh HD:Users:user:Music:"`
`pictures folder`	`"Macintosh HD:Users:user:Pictures:"`
`public folder`	`"Macintosh HD:Users:user:Public:"`
`scripts folder`	`"Macintosh HD:Users:user:Library:Scripts:"`
`shared documents`	`"Macintosh HD:Shared:"`
`startup disk`	`"Macintosh HD:"`
`system folder`	`"Macintosh HD:System:"`
`temporary items folder`	`"Macintosh HD:private:tmp:501:TemporaryItems:"`
`trash`	`"Macintosh HD:Users:user:Trash:"`
`users folder`	`"Macintosh HD:Users:"`
`utilities folder`	`"Macintosh HD:Applications:Utilities:"`

The nice thing about using the `path to` command is that the paths relate to *you*, the person running the program. So in the program example, when you write `path to documents folder`, you get a path to *your* Documents folder. When Greg runs the same program containing this command, he gets the path to *his* Documents folder. As noted earlier, you want to avoid hard coding path names into your programs whenever possible. The `path to` command provides an easy way to avoid doing so.

You can also refer to folders from other domains, *such as from the System domain or the Mac Classic domain by using the* from *parameter with the* path to *command. For more information, consult the description of the* path to *command in Appendix B.*

The `temporary items folder` gives a path to a folder that you can use to create temporary files. It's convenient because the system periodically removes the files in that folder (on system restarts), so you don't have to worry about files accumulating on your system. However, it's still good programming practice to remove a file after you're done working with it. In Chapter 10, you see how to do that.

If you want to tack on another file name or part of a path to the alias returned by the `path to` command, you first convert the value it returns to a string. In the program example, you want to create a file called `TextFile101.txt` in your `Documents` folder, so you concatenate the string `"TextFile101.txt"` to the end of the path returned by the `path to` command after it has been converted to a string. The result of the concatenation is then stored in the variable `fileName`. The extension `txt` is used to indicate that the file is a text file, which is associated with the Text Edit application by default.

The open for access Command

By using the `open for access` command, you can tell AppleScript to open the file specified by `fileName` and that you want to write data to the file:

```
set fileID to open for access file fileName with write permission
```

If the file name is a POSIX path, you write the following instead:

```
set fileID to open for access POSIX file fileName with write permission
```

You can simply specify a string (as either a variable or a literal characters string) directly as the file name when using `open for access`, like so:

```
open for access "Macintosh HD:Users:greg:Documents:TextFile101" with write
permission
```

Of course, this naturally leads you to assume that the following works as well:

```
open for access "/Users/greg/Documents/TextFile101" with write permission -- nope!
```

This doesn't work because the `open for access` command assumes if a string is used to specify a file name, it is a traditional path name. So, in this case, the command creates the file `/Users/greg/Documents/TextFile101`, slashes and all, in the current directory where the script is running! If you run this from Script Editor, the current directory is the root directory (on my system that's Macintosh HD:). If you have administrator privileges, the command ends up creating a file called `/Users/greg/Documents/TextFile101` in your root directory. If you don't have permission to create a file in the root directory, the operation fails and you get an error message. In either case, it's not what you intended.

The parameter `with write permission` tells AppleScript that you want to write data to the file you are opening. You can also read data from a file opened this way; however, the inverse is not true. If you don't specify the `with write permission` parameter and you try to write to the file, you will get a `File not open with write permission` error from AppleScript.

If you open a file for either reading or writing, AppleScript creates the file for you if it doesn't exist. However, all the directories leading to the file do need to exist. That is, in the following example

```
open for access "Macintosh HD:Users:fred:temp:filelist.txt" with write permission
```

the directories Macintosh HD, Users, fred, and temp must all exist. AppleScript creates the filelist.txt file if it doesn't exist in the specified place.

The open for access command returns a reference number that you assign to a variable. Because AppleScript allows you to have more than one file open at a time, you tell it to which file you want your read or write operations directed. You use this number returned by open for access to subsequently identify the open file when performing I/O operations on the file.

> *The AppleScript file I/O commands always allow you to reference a file directly by its name. However, in this and the following examples, I always reference a file by the reference number returned by the* open for access *command.*

I/O operations can often fail for one reason or another (your file system is full, you don't have the proper permissions to access the file, an invalid path name is specified, and so on), so you may want to encapsulate your operations in a try block.

Another good reason for doing I/O operations inside a try block is that if your script gets an error, you can still close any files you opened in your program. Otherwise, your program will be terminated without your having a chance to close any open files. This can lead to errors when you try to run your program again. Script Editor will tell you that the file is still open and will not allow you to reopen it in your program.

For the sake of simplicity, many of the program examples in this chapter do not use try blocks. See the answers to Exercises 6 and 8 at the end of this chapter for examples of performing I/O operations in a try block.

Writing Data with the write Command

Your program opened the file TextFile101.txt in your Documents folder and returned a file reference number that you stored in the variable fileID. Now you can use the write command to write some data to this file. In your program, you write four lines of data to the file. You type in the following line, recalling that the special character sequence \r is used to insert a return character in a string:

```
write "ABCDEFGHIJKLMNOPQRSTUVWXYZ\rline 2\rline 3\rline 4" to fileID
```

After compilation, notice that the Script Editor changes this line to the following:

```
write "ABCDEFGHIJKLMNOPQRSTUVWXYZ
line 2
line 3
line 4" to fileID
```

If you need a refresher on why this happens, see Chapter 5.

Closing a File with the close Command

When you finish your I/O operations on a file, you should close it. To do this, use the `close access` command, followed by the file's reference number. In the program, the following line accomplishes this task:

```
close access fileID
```

After a file is closed, you have to reopen it if you want to perform any more I/O operations on the file. The reference number previously used to identify the file is no longer valid. It's a good idea to close a file as soon as you're done using it. Doing so frees up system resources that may be allocated to the file and, in general, helps ensure the file's integrity (any data not yet written out to the file normally gets flushed when the file is closed).

Getting Information about a File or Folder Using the info for Command

After you wrote your four lines to the file `TextFile101` and closed the file, you executed the following command:

```
info for file fileName
```

Remember that writing an expression like this at the end of the program causes the result to appear in the Result pane.

The `info for` command gives you detailed information about a file. It doesn't take a file reference number, but rather a file specification. That means you don't have to first open a file before you can get information about it.

The result is returned by this command as a record:

```
{name:"TextFile101.txt", creation date:date "Wednesday, June 23, 2004 12:47:42 PM",
modification date:date "Wednesday, June 23, 2004 12:47:42 PM", icon position:{0, 0},
size:47.0, folder:false, alias:false, name extension:"txt", extension hidden:false,
visible:true, package folder:false, file type:"TEXT", file creator:"ttxt", displayed
name:"TextFile101.txt", default application:alias "Macintosh
HD:Applications:TextEdit
.app:", kind:"Plain text document", locked:false, busy status:false, short version:
"", long version:""}
```

You can see from the output that you get all sorts of useful information about the file, including its creation and modification dates, its size (in bytes—yes, as a real number), its extension, type, and the default application associated with the file.

The information in this record provides the basis for performing more sophisticated tasks in AppleScript. For example, the following sequence gives you the modification date for the file `fileName`:

```
set fileInfo to (info for file fileName)
set modDate to modification date of fileInfo
```

Of course, you can do this in a single line:

```
set modDate to modification date of (info for file fileName)
```

Given that `modDate` now contains the modification date of the file, you can test to see if it has been modified in the last 10 days like this:

```
modDate > current date - 10  * days
```

You may recall from Chapter 2 that to specify 10 days, you write 10 * days. *You are actually specifying a time in seconds, and* days *is a constant that represents the number of seconds in a day.*

This test can form the basis for writing a backup utility, a program that tests each file to see if it has been modified within the last *n* days (or the date since a backup was last made) and archives the file if it has been modified.

You can get information about a folder as well as a file using the same `info for` command. The following gives the total size of the files stored in your `Documents` folder:

```
size of (info for file (path to documents folder))
```

This uses the fact that the size of a folder is the size of all the files contained in that folder. Be forewarned: executing an `info for` command on a folder like this can take a considerable amount of time because the folder's size has to be calculated by adding up the sizes of all the files in the folder. Consider, also, that the folder itself may contain subfolders.

Reading Data with the read Command

Now that you've created a simple text file in your `Documents` folder, you learn how to use the `read` command to read the data from the file into your program. In its simplest form, the `read` command looks like this:

```
read fileID
```

Here `fileID` is an identifier that has been previously returned from the `open for access` command. When this command is executed, the entire contents of the file specified by `fileID` are read and returned. This result is normally stored in a variable in your program.

In the following Try It Out, you learn how to read data from a file by using the file you created in the preceding Try It Out.

Try It Out   Reading Data from a File

In the following steps, the program reads all the data from the file you just created and displays the results.

1.   Type the following program into Script Editor:

```
-- Read back the sample file

set fileName to (path to documents folder as string) & "TextFile101.txt"

-- open the file to read

set fileID to open for access file fileName

-- read the data

set dataFromFile to read fileID as string

-- display the data you read

display dialog "Here's what I read: " & dataFromFile buttons {"Great!"} default ¬
    button 1

-- close the file now that you're done with it

close access fileID
```

2. Run the program. You should get the dialog box shown in Figure 7-2.

Here's what I read:
ABCDEFGHIJKLMNOPQRSTUVWXYZ
line 2
line 3
line 4

Great!

Figure 7-2

How It Works

The variable `fileName` is used as in the previous program to store the path to the `TextFile101.txt` file:

```
set fileName to (path to documents folder as string) & "TextFile101.txt"
```

The file is then opened using the `open for access` command. Because you only want to read from the file, the format of the command is as shown:

```
set fileID to open for access file fileName
```

The `read` command is used next in the program to read all the data from the file. This command is followed by the file's reference number. The data that is read can be interpreted in different ways, typically based on how the data was written to the file in the first place. Because you wrote four lines of text as a string to the file in the first example, you read it back as a string as well. This is done with the following command:

```
set dataFromFile to read fileID as string
```

After the entire contents of the file have been read and stored in the variable dataFromFile, a dialog is put up to show the contents of the file using the standard display dialog command:

```
display dialog "Here's what I read: " & dataFromFile buttons {"Great!"} default ¬
        button 1
```

Finally, because you're finished with the file, it is closed using the close access command:

```
close access fileID
```

Additional Parameters to the read Command

The read command supports a number of different parameters. They're summarized in the following table.

Parameter	Meaning	Example
for *length*	read *length* bytes from the file	read fileID for 128
from *offset*	read from file starting at byte *offset*	read fileID from fileOffset
to *offset*	read from file up to byte *offset*	read fileID to 128
before *char*	read bytes from the file up to but not including the character *char*	read fileID before '\n'
until *char*	read bytes from the file up to and including the character *char*	read fileID until '\n'
using delimiter *char*	Use the character *char* as the delimiter character read	read fileID using delimiter ":"
using delimiters *list*	Use any character in *list* as a delimiter character	read fileID using delimiters {tab, space}
as *type*	convert the data that is read to *type*	read fileID as integer

These parameters are often combined. For example, to read 50 bytes from the file inFile starting at offset 100, you write

```
read inFile from 100 for 50
```

Alternatively, you could write

```
read inFile from 100 to 150
```

The following Try It Out illustrates the use of some of the parameters listed in the preceding table.

Try It Out   Using Various read Command Parameters

In the following steps, you use the TextFile101 file you created at the beginning of this chapter.

1. Type the following program into Script Editor:

```
-- Using read parameters

set fileName to (path to documents folder as string) & "TextFile101.txt"

-- open the file to read

set fileID to open for access file fileName

-- read for

read fileID for 5 as string -- read 5 chars
read fileID for 5 as string -- read another 5 chars

-- read from...to

read fileID from 12 to 20 as string -- read from..to

-- read until and before

read fileID from 1 until return as string -- read first line
read fileID before return as string       -- read next line
read fileID before return as string       -- read next line

-- read using delimiter

read fileID using delimiter "S" from 1 to 26

-- read all lines

read fileID using delimiter return from 1

-- close the file now that you're done with it

close access fileID
```

2. Click the Event Log tab and run the program. The output in the Event Log should look like the following, although you may have a different number than the 385 used in this example:

```
tell current application
    path to documents folder as string
        "Macintosh HD:Users:steve:Documents:"
    open for access file "Macintosh HD:Users:steve:Documents:TextFile101"
        385
    read 385 for 5 as string
        "ABCDE"
    read 385 for 5 as string
        "FGHIJ"
```

```
         read 385 from 12 to 20 as string
              "LMNOPQRST"
         read 385 from 1 until "
" as string
              "ABCDEFGHIJKLMNOPQRSTUVWXYZ
"
         read 385 before "
" as string
              "line 2"
         read 385 before "
" as string
              "line 3"
         read 385 using delimiter "S" from 1 to 26
              {"ABCDEFGHIJKLMNOPQR", "TUVWXYZ"}
         read 385 using delimiter "
" from 1
              {"ABCDEFGHIJKLMNOPQRSTUVWXYZ", "line 2", "line 3", "line 4"}
         close access 385
   end tell
```

How It Works

You don't need to use any log commands here because the I/O commands and their results automatically get recorded in the Event Log, as you can see from the output.

The program begins by opening the file TextFile101.txt for reading, using these statements:

```
set fileName to (path to documents folder as string) & "TextFile101"

-- open the file to read

set fileID to open for access file fileName
```

Remember, if the file doesn't exist, it is created for you by the system. In this case, TextFile101.txt *does* exist, so it gets opened for read access and the resulting reference number gets stored in the variable fileID. As you can see from the corresponding entries in the Event Log output, the number returned to subsequently reference this file is 385. The actual number should be of no concern to you and will likely be different from the one shown when you run this program on your computer.

After the file has been opened, the program uses the for parameter of the read command to read five characters from the file and then uses another similar read command to read an additional five characters. This is done with the following two statements:

```
read fileID for 5 as string -- read 5 chars
read fileID for 5 as string -- read another 5 chars
```

Recall the contents of TextFile101.txt from Figure 7-2. The first 26 characters in the file are the uppercase letters of the alphabet. So the first read statement reads the characters ABCDE from the file, and the second reads the characters FGHIJ. Note that, unless you specify an offset to begin your reads using the from parameter, successive reads are made sequentially through the file, each one picking up where the previous read left off.

The next `read` statement in the program shows the use of the `from` and `to` parameters:

```
read fileID from 12 to 20 as string -- read from..to
```

This statement reads nine characters starting at character number 12, or the characters LMNOPQRST. Note that this `read` statement is equivalent to the one just shown:

```
read fileID from 12 for 9 as string -- read from..for
```

Realize that using only the `from` parameter causes AppleScript to read from that character to the end of the file. That means if you write the following:

```
read fileID from 12 as string
```

the statement reads characters 12 through the end of the file.

The program next shows how you can read entire lines of data from a file. The lines in the text file that you created are terminated by return characters. So you use this as your delimiter character to read entire lines.

> *Standard UNIX utilities normally recognize the newline character (`"\n"`) as the line terminator. If you are reading a file and you don't know what character is used as the line terminator, you may need to examine the contents of the file using a file dumping utility. For example, using the Terminal application, you can use the `od` command with the `-c` option on the file to see what character is at the end of each line.*

These statements from the program read three lines of data:

```
read fileID from 1 until return as string -- read first line
read fileID before return as string       -- read next line
read fileID before return as string       -- read next line
```

The first statement reads the first line from the file. This is done by reading from character 1 until a return character is encountered. By examining the corresponding output from the log, you can see that the return character is also read and returned by this statement.

The second and third statements show how successive lines can be read from the file. In the case of the second statement, the string `"line 2"`, which represents the second line from the file, is read. From the output you can see that in this case, the return character is *not* returned. It does get read, it just doesn't get returned as part of the result. In a similar manner, the third statement reads and returns the third line from the file, excluding the terminating return character.

The last two `read` statements in the program show the use of the `using delimiter` parameter. The first `read` statement arbitrarily uses the character `"S"` as the delimiter. The effect of executing the statement

```
read fileID using delimiter "S" from 1 to 26
```

is to read the first 26 characters from the file using the specified delimiter character. The result returned is a list of two strings. The first string contains the characters up to the delimiter character, and the second string contains the characters after the delimiter character up to character 26. Note that the delimiter character itself is *not* included in either of these strings.

The last read statement shows how you can easily read all the lines in a file into a list of strings. The statement

```
read fileID using delimiter return from 1
```

says to read all the characters from the file using the return character as a delimiter. As you can see from the log output, this has the effect of returning the following list of strings:

```
{"ABCDEFGHIJKLMNOPQRSTUVWXYZ", "line 2", "line 3", "line 4"}
```

After the last read operation on the file has been performed, the program closes the file and execution of the program is complete.

You should bear in mind that if you try to read from a file that has no data (is of zero length), or you try to read data after you've already read all the data from a file, you get an error. The error message is End of file error; *it terminates your program, unless, of course, you execute the* read *command inside a* try *block.*

More on Using the write Command

In its simplest form, the write command looks like this:

```
write data to fileID
```

Here *fileID* is an identifier that has been previously returned from an open for access command. The various parameters accepted by the write command are summarized in the following table.

Parameter	Meaning	Example
starting at *offset*	write to file starting at *offset*	write dataRec to fileID starting at nextRecOffset
for *length*	write *length* bytes of data to the file	write dataRec to fileID for 128
as *type*	convert the data to *type* for writing	write USCityNames as string to fileID

Reading and Writing Data Structures

The capability to read and write lists and records from and to files in AppleScript is a useful feature. It enables you to write small database applications and record data in a file for later retrieval and possible update.

If you write a list or record to a file, AppleScript preserves the integrity of the data structure. When you read the data structure back in, just be sure to coerce the data back into the appropriate type using the read command's as *type* parameter.

Recall the list of records you defined in the last version of the population program from Chapter 6:

```
set USCities to {¬
    {name:"Boston", population:574000}, ¬
    {name:"Chicago", population:2784000}, ¬
    {name:"Dallas", population:1007000}, ¬
    {name:"Houston", population:1631000}, ¬
    {name:"Los Angeles", population:3485000}, ¬
    {name:"Philadelphia", population:1586000}, ¬
    {name:"San Diego", population:1111000}, ¬
    {name:"San Francisco", population:724000}, ¬
    {name:"New York", population:7323000}}
```

You can write this entire data structure to a file with a single `write` command. When you read it back from the file, make sure that you specify the data is to be read as a list. This technique is shown in the following Try It Out.

Try It Out   **Writing and Reading a List of Records**

In the following steps, you practice writing and reading records.

1.   Type the following program into Script Editor:

```
-- Reading and Writing Lists

-- the USCities list from before

set USCities to {¬
    {name:"Boston", population:574000}, ¬
    {name:"Chicago", population:2784000}, ¬
    {name:"Dallas", population:1007000}, ¬
    {name:"Houston", population:1631000}, ¬
    {name:"Los Angeles", population:3485000}, ¬
    {name:"Philadelphia", population:1586000}, ¬
    {name:"San Diego", population:1111000}, ¬
    {name:"San Francisco", population:724000}, ¬
    {name:"New York", population:7323000}}

-- first write the list to a file

set fileName to (path to documents folder as string) & "ListFile101"
set outFile to open for access file fileName with write permission
write USCities to outFile as list
close access outFile

-- now read the list back in

set inFile to open for access file fileName
set USCitiesFromFile to read inFile as list
close access inFile

-- now compare the two lists
```

```
if USCities = USCitiesFromFile then
    display dialog "The two lists are equal!" buttons "Great!" default button 1
else
    display dialog "The lists don't match!" buttons "Darn!" default button 1 ¬
            with icon stop
end if
```

2. Run the program. If all goes well, you should get a dialog telling you that the list in your program matches the list you wrote and subsequently read back from the file ListFile101.

How It Works

After the USCities list has been defined, the program writes it out to the file ListFile101 in the Documents folder with the following four statements:

```
set fileName to (path to documents folder as string) & "ListFile101"
set outFile to open for access file fileName with write permission
write USCities to outFile as list
close access outFile
```

Notice that you didn't give an extension for this file. You don't need one here because you don't want to associate any default application with this file, anyway.

The USCities list is written to the file outFile using the following write command:

```
write USCities as list to outFile
```

The as list parameter is not really needed here, but it's good programming practice to use it.

After writing the file and closing it, the program reopens the file and reads the list back in, storing it in the variable USCitiesFromFile. This is done with the following three statements:

```
set inFile to open for access file fileName
set USCitiesFromFile to read inFile as list
close access inFile
```

Note the use of the as list parameter to read. Here it is required. If you omit it, your data will be read in as binary data and stored as a string in the specified variable.

After the list has been read back in and the file closed, the original list and the one read from the file are compared. This is done with the following if statement:

```
if USCities = USCitiesFromFile then
    display dialog "The two lists are equal!" buttons "Great!" default button 1
else
    display dialog "The lists don't match!" buttons "Darn!" default button 1 ¬
            with icon stop
end if
```

If the two lists match (which they should), the first display dialog command is executed. If they don't match, something unexpected obviously occurred. In that case, a message to that effect is displayed to the user.

Truncating a File Using the set eof Command

An important point to remember when writing to files is that if you open an existing file with write permission, AppleScript does not truncate the file for you. That is, you can write to the file and the previous contents will be overwritten. If you write less data than existed in the file before you opened it, the excess data from the original file will still be there.

A solution to this problem is to open a file with write permission and then *truncate* the file using the set eof command, which has this general format:

```
set eof fileID to n
```

The effect of executing this command is to set the length of the file identified by `fileID` to a length of *n* bytes. So, for example, you can wipe out the previous contents of the file referenced by inFile by setting its length to zero, like so:

```
set eof inFile to 0
```

Getting the Size of a File Using the get eof Command

Sometimes you want to know how much data is in a file. The size property of the info for command readily gives you the number of bytes in the file. Alternatively, after a file has been opened for access, you can also get this information using the get eof command, like this:

```
get eof  fileID
```

This command, like the size property of the record returned by the info for command, returns the size as a real number.

Appending Data to the End of a File

If you open a file that contains some data and you want to add some more data to the end of it, you can do so by first getting the file's size and then doing your write operations based on that result. For example, the following two commands could be used to write the data stored in the variable newRec to the file name specified by dbFileName:

```
set newRecID to open for access file dbFileName with write permission
write newRec to newRecID  starting at (get eof newRecID)
close access newRecID
```

Enumerating Disks and Folders

It's easy to get a list of all the disks on your system or all the files in a folder using the list disks and list folder commands. The former command doesn't take any parameters, so simply writing

```
list disks
```

gives you a list of the disks on your system. On my PowerBook, when I have a DVD in my drive and my iPod plugged in, I get the following list returned:

```
{"Macintosh HD", "Network", "Steve Kochan's iPod", "DVD_VIDEO"}
```

The list folder command takes as its argument the folder whose contents you want to list. The result returned is a list of files. The optional parameter invisibles is followed by either true or false to indicate whether to list files that are normally hidden. The default is that hidden files are listed if the parameter is not supplied.

> The documentation for the list folder command shows a parameter called invisibles followed by a boolean value. Script Editor changes the invisibles true parameter to with invisibles and the invisibles false parameter to without invisibles after compilation.

As an example of the list folder command, the following command assigns to docList a list of the files in your Documents folder:

```
set docList to list folder (path to documents folder)
```

The following command does the same thing except that hidden files are not part of the list:

```
set docList to list folder (path to documents folder) invisibles false
```

As noted, after compiling, this command gets changed to read like this:

```
set docList to list folder (path to documents folder) without invisibles
```

Note that the list folders command returns a list of strings, not a list of aliases or file specifications. Also, the files in the list are relative path names, not full path names. To form a full path to the file, you have to concatenate the name of the folder you are listing to the front of each individual file name in the list.

The following Try It Out lists the files in your Documents folder that have been modified within the last 10 days. This program could form the basis for a backup utility.

Try It Out   Using the list folder Command

In the following program, notice the use of the choose from list command; it's used here in an atypical way.

1. Type the following program into Script Editor:

```
-- Find all files in your Documents folder newer than a specified number of days

set folderName to (path to documents folder as string)
set modDays to 10

set fileList to list folder folderName with invisibles
set newFiles to {}
set modDate to (current date) - modDays * days
```

```
repeat with fileItem in fileList
    set theFile to contents of fileItem
    set infoFile to info for file (folderName & theFile)

    if modification date of infoFile > modDate then
        set end of newFiles to theFile
    end if
end repeat

choose from list newFiles with prompt "The following files in the folder " &
        folderName & " have been modified within the last " & (modDays as string) & ¬
        " days:"
```

2. Run the program. You should see a dialog similar to that shown in Figure 7-3 (your folder name and the files listed will be different, of course). If your list is empty, try increasing the value of modDays in the program or adding some files to your Documents folder and rerunning the program.

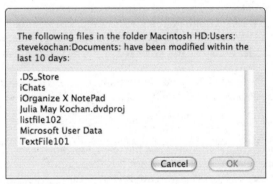

Figure 7-3

How It Works

The program starts by setting the variable folderName to the path to the Documents folder:

```
set folderName to (path to documents folder as string)
```

Next, the variable modDays is set to the number of days you want to test for:

```
set modDays to 10
```

The list of files in the folder folderName is then obtained using the list folders command and the result is assigned to the variable fileList:.

```
set fileList to list folder folderName
```

Next, the program sets the variable newFiles to an empty list:

```
set newFiles to {}
```

This variable is used to build the list of newly modified files inside the `repeat` loop that follows.

You want to test for files that have been modified within the last `modDays` days, so the variable `modDate` is set to the date that is `modDays` earlier than the current date, like this:

```
set modDate to (current date) - modDays * days
```

The `repeatwith` statement that follows next is used to process each file stored in `fileList`:

```
repeat with fileItem in fileList
    set theFile to contents of fileItem
    set infoFile to info for file (folderName & theFile)

    if modification date of infoFile > modDate then
        set end of newFiles to theFile
    end if
end repeat
```

The content of each item in the list is assigned in turn to the variable `theFile` (that's so you don't get `Item 1 of...` added to the list you're building.) The `info for` command is then executed to get information about the file. The file in question is identified by the name of the folder (`folderName`) followed by the name of the particular file in the folder tacked on to the end (`folderName & theFile`).

If the modification date of the file whose info is stored in `infoFile` is greater than `modDate`, it has been modified within the last `modDays` days. In that case, it gets added to the end of the `newFiles` list, and the loop continues.

After the list of files that have changed has been compiled, the program uses the `choose from list` command to display the results:

```
choose from list newFiles with prompt "The following files in the folder " &
        folderName & " have been modified within the last " & (modDays as string) & ¬
        " days:"
```

Of course, you don't want the user to select a file here, but you can use the `choose from list` command as a convenient way to present a list of strings, one per line, to the user.

You should note that the list produced by the `list folder` command includes the names of subfolders as well. If you were writing a backup utility, you might not want to back up an entire subfolder, but only the files within that folder that have changed within the last 10 days. Of course, the files in that folder might themselves be folders, so you'd have to descend the hierarchy of folders until you got to a file that was not a folder. You can write an AppleScript program to do this. However, if the nesting of your files is deep, this is not a very efficient approach.

A folder's modification date doesn't necessarily reflect whether files inside the folder have been modified. The modification date is updated on a folder if a file gets added to or removed from the folder, not if the content of one of the files in the folder is modified or if a file is renamed.

Although you can easily get information about files by using AppleScript commands, in general, the Finder can do this more efficiently than AppleScript can. In fact, as you see in Chapter 10, you can ask the Finder to give you a list of files that have been modified within the last 10 days. This is much faster than having to individually examine the modification date of each file returned by the list folder *command. Nevertheless, I continue with this example because it illustrates some key points about working with files in AppleScript.*

Using the choose file Command to Pick a File

Sometimes, you want to allow the user to choose a file on the system. That's because your program may perform some operation with that file, such as sending it as an attachment to an e-mail you're composing. Or perhaps you want to print the particular file or upload it to your website. The choose file command provides an easy and convenient way for you to allow the user to select a file. Here's what the entry for the command looks like in the Standard Additions dictionary:

```
choose file: Choose a file on a disk or server
    choose file
        [with prompt plain text]  -- a prompt to be displayed in the file chooser
        [of type a list of plain text]  -- restrict the files shown to only these
                file types
        [default location alias]  -- the default file location
        [invisibles boolean]  -- Show invisible files and folders? (default is
            true)
        [multiple selections allowed boolean]  -- Allow multiple items to be
                selected? (default is false)
    Result: alias  -- to the chosen file
```

You can see that all the parameters are optional, meaning you can simply write the following:

```
set theFile to choose file
```

To set the starting folder to your Documents folder with the prompt Choose a File and without showing hidden files, you write the following:

```
set theFile to choose file with prompt "Choose a File" default location (path to
        documents folder) invisibles false
```

The choose file command returns an alias for the chosen file and terminates the program if the user clicks Cancel. Therefore, you may want to execute this command inside a try block if you don't want your program to be terminated on Cancel.

In the following Try It Out, you write your own version of Get Info. That is, you have the user pick a file and then you display some useful information about the file.

Try It Out   **Using the choose file Command**

In the following steps, you use the choose file command to have the user select a file.

1.   Enter the following program into Script Editor:

```
-- Implement a "Get info" command

set theFile to choose file default location (path to home folder)

set infoRec to info for theFile
```

235

```
set theResult to "Info for " & (theFile as string) & return & return
set theResult to theResult & "Size (bytes):  " & (size of infoRec as integer) & ¬
        return
set theResult to theResult & "Created:  " & (creation date of infoRec as string) ¬
        & return
set theResult to theResult & "Last Modified: " & (modification date of infoRec as ¬
        string) & return

display dialog theResult buttons {"OK"} default button 1
```

2. Run the program. When the Choose a File dialog appears, select the file TextFile101.txt that
    you created in your Documents folder earlier in this chapter. Before you click Choose, your dia-
    log should look like the one shown in Figure 7-4.

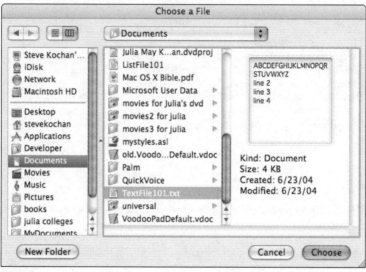

Figure 7-4

3. Click Choose. You should get a dialog similar to that shown in Figure 7-5. Your dates will be dif-
    ferent from those shown.

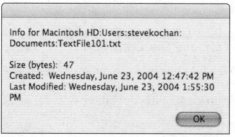

Figure 7-5

How It Works

The program asks the user to select a file using the `choose file` command. The starting point is the user's home directory, like so:

```
set theFile to choose file default location (path to home folder)
```

The resulting file alias returned by `choose file` is stored in the variable `theFile`; then the `info for` command is executed to get information about the file:

```
set infoRec to info for theFile
```

Because you know that the `choose file` command returns an alias, it would be incorrect to write the previous statement like this:

```
set infoRec to info for file theFile
```

Make sure you understand this. The variable `theFile` already contains a reference to a file as an alias and not a string. Therefore, you don't want to write `file theFile`; you get an error when you run the program if you try it.

The next four statements in the program show a way to use the concatenation operator to build the output string. Each statement builds one more line of output, adding some information about the file and a return character at the end of each line (except the first line, which adds two return characters):

```
set theResult to "Info for " & (theFile as string) & return & return
set theResult to theResult & "Size (bytes):  " & (size of infoRec as integer) & ¬
        return
set theResult to theResult & "Created:  " & (creation date of infoRec as string) ¬
        & return
set theResult to theResult & "Last Modified: " & (modification date of infoRec as ¬
        string) & return
```

The `size` property of the `info for` record is a real number. In order to display the file size in a more aesthetically pleasing way, it gets coerced to an integer in the second statement of the previous set. It's likely that an integer will be large enough to store the file's size, especially when you use the `choose file` command. This command doesn't let you pick entire folders.

After the output message has been built, the `display dialog` command displays information about the selected file:

```
display dialog theResult buttons {"OK"} default button 1
```

Using the choose folder Command to Pick a Folder

The `choose folder` command is similar to `choose file`, except that `choose folder` allows you to pick a folder. In fact, here's the description of the command from the Standard Additions dictionary:

```
choose folder: Choose a folder on a disk or server
    choose folder
        [with prompt plain text]   -- a prompt to be displayed in the folder chooser
        [default location alias]   -- the default folder location
```

```
        [invisibles boolean]   -- Show invisible files and folders? (default is
    false)
        [multiple selections allowed  boolean]   -- Allow multiple items to be
            selected? (default is false)
    Result: alias  -- chosen folder
```

Like the `choose file` command, in its simplest form you can write it as follows:

```
choose folder
```

This command puts up a dialog to allow the user to pick a folder. Also like the `choose file` command, an alias for the selected folder is returned.

In the next section, you see this command used to select a folder that will be examined for recently modified files.

Using the choose file name Command to Pick a File Name

The last command to be discussed in this chapter is the `choose file name` command. This command allows the user to select a file name. Unlike the `choose file` command, which requires that the file already exist, the `choose file name` command lets you enter the name of a file that may not already exist. This command doesn't create the file for you; that's up to you. However, if the file does exist, the command asks you if you want to replace the file or cancel the operation. Even if you opt to replace the file, it's up to you to do so in the program.

The file may not already exist, so `choose file` returns a file specification and not an alias. However, note that it's not returning a string.

In the following Try It Out, you modify the program that identifies files newer than a specified date to do the following things:

❑   To ask the user for the number of days to be used as the criterion, with a default of 7.

❑   To ask the user to select the folder to be used for the search. .

❑   To skip any subfolders inside the selected folder.

❑   To write each file that matches your criteria to a file specified by the user. If the file already exists, the program first truncates its contents.

Try It Out   **Generating a List of Files for Backup**

In the following steps, you generate a list of files for backup.

1.   Type the following program into Script Editor:

```
-- Find all files in a folder newer than a specified number of days

-- Get the folder to check
```

```
set folderName to (choose folder with prompt "Select your folder for backup") ¬
    as string

-- Get the number of days for the list

set modDays to missing value

display dialog "List files modified within this number of days:" default answer "7"

try
    set modDays to text returned of result as integer
end try

if modDays = missing value or modDays < 1 then
    display dialog "You didn't enter a valid integer, exiting" buttons {"OK"} ¬
            default button 1 with icon stop
    return
end if

set modDate to (current date) - modDays * days

-- Get the file name for storing the final list

set outFile to choose file name with prompt "Specify the file name for the list:" ¬
    default location (path to home folder)

-- Open the file for writing and truncate its length

set fileID to open for access outFile with write permission
set eof fileID to 0

-- Now list the folder's contents and compare the modification times

set fileList to list folder folderName

repeat with fileItem in fileList
    set theFile to contents of fileItem
    set infoFile to info for file (folderName & theFile)

    -- see if it's not a folder and newer then modDate

    if (folder of infoFile ≠ true) and (modification date of infoFile > modDate)
then
        write theFile & return to fileID
    end if
end repeat

close access fileID

display dialog "Your list of files has been written to the file " & outFile ¬
        buttons {"Thanks!"} default button 1
```

2. Run the program. Experiment with different values for the modification days and the folder you select. Examine the resulting backup list that gets created by the program and verify its contents.

How It Works

The program is fairly straightforward. It begins by prompting the user to select a folder using the `choose folder` command:

```
set folderName to (choose folder with prompt "Select your folder for backup") ¬
    as string
```

The folder name gets returned as an alias. Here you coerce it into a string so you can later concatenate file names to the end of it.

After the folder has been selected, the program uses the familiar `display dialog` command to prompt the user to enter the number of days with 7 as the default. The program checks to make sure that a valid integer number greater than zero is entered. It displays a message if this is not the case:

```
set modDays to missing value

display dialog "List files modified within this number of days:" default answer "7"

try
    set modDays to text returned of result as integer
end try

if modDays = missing value or modDays < 1 then
    display dialog "You didn't enter a valid integer, exiting" buttons {"OK"} ¬
        default button 1 with icon stop
    return
end if

set modDate to (current date) - modDays * days
```

After getting the folder and the number of days, the program uses the `choose file name` command to let the user select a file in which to store the resulting file list. The file is then opened for writing, and any previous content is erased by setting the eof on the file to 0. These steps are accomplished with the following code:

```
-- Get the file name for storing the final list

set outFile to choose file name with prompt "Specify the file name for the list:" ¬
        default location (path to home folder)

-- Open the file for writing and truncate its length

set fileID to open for access outFile with write permission
set eof fileID to 0
```

Now the program needs to list the contents of the specified folder and check whether each file is newer than the specified number of days. This is accomplished with the following code sequence:

```
-- Now list the folder's contents and compare the modification times

set fileList to list folder folderName
```

```
repeat with fileItem in fileList
    set theFile to contents of fileItem
    set infoFile to info for file (folderName & theFile)

    -- see if it's not a folder and newer then modDate

    if (folder of infoFile ≠ true) and (modification date of infoFile > modDate)
then
        write theFile & return to fileID
    end if
end repeat
```

The folder property of the record returned by the `info for` command is `true` if the file is a folder and `false` if it is not. If the file isn't a folder and it's newer than `modDate` days, the name of the file, followed by a return, is written to the file identified by `fileID`. The `return` is added so that each file name appears as a separate line in the output file.

When the `repeat` loop is done and all files have been examined, the program closes the output file and puts up a dialog to tell the user that the file has been created. The program's execution is then complete.

Summary

This chapter taught you how to work with files in AppleScript. In particular, you learned the following:

❑ A path name describes the location of a file or folder on your system.

❑ You can create a file object by placing a `file` specifier in front of a traditional path name or a `POSIX file` specifier in front of a POSIX path name.

❑ An alias to a file allows you to create a reference to a file that continues to track the file even if it gets renamed or moved to some other place.

❑ AppleScript has several built-in commands that allow you to work easily with files. These commands are in the Standards Additions dictionary. Using them you can create, write data to, and read data from files. The commands `open for access`, `read`, `write`, and `close access` are the basic commands for performing these I/O operations.

❑ Other Standard Addition commands allow you to list the contents of a folder or the disks you have mounted and enable the user to choose a file, a folder, or a file name.

In the next chapter, you learn to use AppleScript handlers, which let you to develop your programs in a modular fashion for easier writing, reading, and maintenance. Before proceeding, however, try the exercises that follow to test your understanding of the material covered in this chapter. You can find the solutions to these exercises in Appendix A.

Exercises

1. Using the `info for` and `path to` commands, write a program to get information about your `Documents` folder.

2. Using the `info for`, `path to application` commands, and the fact that `short version` is a property contained in the record returned by the `info for` command, write a program to find the version of Script Editor you are running.

3. Modify the `Get Info` program presented in this chapter to also display the `file extension` and whether the selected file is an alias.

4. Using the `list folder` and the `path to` commands, write a program to add up the size of all the files in your `Documents` folder.

5. Using the `list folder` and the `path to` commands, write a program to find the file with the oldest creation date in your `Applications` folder (ignore any subfolders).

6. Write a program that allows the user to update the list in the `ListFile101` file you created in this chapter. First, have the program read the list in from the file; then prompt the user to enter information for a new city and its respective population (use two display dialog commands for this). Add the new city to the end of your list and write the updated list out to the file. Write a separate program to read the list back in to verify that it was updated with the new city.

7. Modify the last version (version 4) of the population program from Chapter 6 so that the population data is read from a file when the program begins execution. As before, have the user enter a city; then look up the city in the list and display its population.

8. Write a simple file copying program. Let the user pick the file to be copied. Then allow her to choose a name for the new file. After that, copy the contents of the selected file.

8

Handlers

If you have any programming experience, you know about the benefits of writing code that can easily be reused for other applications. You also know about the advantages of writing functions that allow your programs to be developed in a modular fashion, thereby making them easier to write, read, and maintain.

In AppleScript, functions go under the name *handlers*, but they provide the same type of flexibility and offer the same advantages as functions in other languages. In this chapter, you learn how to write your own handlers.

Writing a Handler

Some notable differences exist between AppleScript handlers and the functions you may be used to writing in other programming languages. I point out these differences as you work through this chapter.

The purpose of the handler in the following Try It Out is simply to write a message to the Event Log.

Try It Out   **Writing Your First Handler**

In this program, you get your feet wet by writing a simple handler.

1.   Type the following program into Script Editor:

```
-- Simple handler to log a message

on logMsg()
    log "This is from the logMsg handler"
end logMsg

-- Test out the handler

logMsg()

-- Call the handler five more times
```

```
repeat 5 times
    logMsg()
end repeat
```

2. Click the Event Log tab and run the program. You see the following recorded in the Event Log:

```
(*This is from the logMsg handler*)
(*This is from the logMsg handler*)
(*This is from the logMsg handler*)
(*This is from the logMsg handler*)
(*This is from the logMsg handler*)
(*This is from the logMsg handler*)
```

How It Works

You *define* a handler in AppleScript by writing the keyword on followed by the handler's name. This, in turn, is followed by a comma-separated list of *parameters* or *arguments* that the handler takes, enclosed in a set of parentheses. If the handler takes no arguments, as is the case with your first handler, it uses just empty parentheses.

The statements that are part of the handler then follow on subsequent lines, up to the end statement, which closes the handler's definition.

> *As with typing any* end *statement in Script Editor, it suffices to just type the keyword* end. *Script Editor fills in the handler's name when you compile your program.*

In your program, you define a handler called logMsg like this:

```
on logMsg()
    log "This is from the logMsg handler"
end logMsg
```

This handler takes no arguments (as indicated by the empty set of parentheses) and consists of a single statement, which executes a log command.

The statements inside a handler are not executed until you explicitly call the handler. You do this by listing the handler's name, followed by a parenthesized list of arguments to be passed to the handler. Again, if the handler takes no arguments, an empty set of parentheses must be specified. So when you write

```
logMsg()
```

the effect is for execution to be transferred directly to the logMsg handler. The statements in the handler are then executed in turn. This has the effect of executing the log statement, which places the string "This is from the logMsg handler" into the Event Log. After the last statement in a handler is executed, control is returned to the point in your program where the handler is called.

The program next executes a loop five times:

```
repeat 5 times
    logMsg()
end repeat
```

Inside the loop is a call to the logMsg handler. The net effect is that the handler gets called five times. Each time it is called, control is transferred to the handler, the log statement is executed, and then control returns to the point in the program where the call initiated. The result of calling the logMsg handler five times is that the message "This is from the logMsg handler" gets logged five times.

Passing Parameters to Handlers

The logMsg handler is not very flexible. Each time it is called, it writes the same string to the Event Log. You may want to have handlers that perform very specialized tasks like this. More often, you'll want to write handlers that perform different actions based on values supplied as arguments or parameters.

The terms argument and parameter are used interchangeably when speaking about handlers in this chapter.

The next Try It Out program extends the usefulness of the logMsg handler by allowing the caller to specify precisely what message he wants added to the Event Log.

Try It Out   **Passing Parameters to Handlers**

In the following program, you see how to pass a parameter to a handler.

1.   Type the following program into Script Editor:

```
-- Handler to log a message given as its parameter

on logMsg(theMsg)
    log theMsg
end logMsg

-- Test out the handler

logMsg("Log this message")

-- Call the handler five more times

repeat with i from 1 to 5
    set theArg to "Message Number " & (i as string)
    logMsg(theArg)
end repeat
```

2.   Click the Event Log tab and run the program. You should see the following in the Event Log pane:

```
(*Log this message*)
(*Message Number 1*)
(*Message Number 2*)
(*Message Number 3*)
(*Message Number 4*)
(*Message Number 5*)
```

How It Works

This time you want to pass a value to the logMsg handler, so you define your handler like this:

```
on logMsg(theMsg)
    log theMsg
end logMsg
```

Inside the parentheses, you list the parameter to be passed to the handler. This variable name is the name you use to reference the parameter by statements inside the handler. Here, you call the parameter theMsg, which can be used like any other variable in your logMsg handler. In this case, you use it to specify the value to be logged by the log command.

Unlike most other programming languages, you don't specify the type of the arguments to your handlers.

The first call to logMsg that appears in the program looks like this:

```
logMsg("Log this message")
```

The logMsg handler is called, and the literal string "Log this message" is passed as the argument. Inside the handler, this value is assigned to the variable theMsg. The log statement is then executed to log the value stored inside that variable, and control is returned to the point in the program where the call was initiated.

Next, the program enters a loop that is repeated five times:

```
repeat with i from 1 to 5
    set theArg to "Message Number" & (i as string)
    logMsg(theArg)
end repeat
```

Inside the loop the variable theArg is set to the concatenation of the string "Message Number" and the value of the loop counter i. The result is then passed as the argument to the logMsg handler where, as before, it is assigned to the variable theMsg during the handler's execution. The handler logs the message and returns. The net result is that these five lines are added to the Event Log:

```
(*Message Number 1*)
(*Message Number 2*)
(*Message Number 3*)
(*Message Number 4*)
(*Message Number 5*)
```

Incidentally, you didn't need the intermediate theArg variable in the program. That means the following loop is perfectly valid and produces the same results:

```
repeat with i from 1 to 5
    logMsg("Message Number " & (i as string))
end repeat
```

The expression inside the parentheses is evaluated before the handler is called. This gives you the flexibility to write expressions as arguments to your handlers.

Returning Handler Results

Suppose you wanted to write a handler that simply adds two numbers for you. Okay, that's not very practical. Let's assume, however, that you wanted to do it anyway. If you don't want the handler to display or log the result, how can you get that sum as calculated by the handler back to you, the caller? The answer is by using the `return` command, as you see in the next Try It Out.

Try It Out   **Returning Values from Handlers**

This program defines a handler called `sum` that adds two numbers. These two numbers are passed as parameters to the handler. After the numbers have been added together, the handler returns the result.

1. Type the following program into Script Editor:

```
-- Illustrate a simple handler to add two numbers and return a value

on sum(x, y)
    return x + y
end sum

-- test out the handler

log sum(100, 200)
log sum(100, 200) + sum(300, 400)

set i1 to 100
set i2 to 50
log sum(i1, i2/2)
```

2. Click the Event Log tab and run the program. The following appears in the log:

```
(*300*)
(*1000*)
(*125*)
```

How It Works

The program begins by defining the `sum` handler as follows:

```
on sum(x, y)
    return x + y
end sum
```

The definition for a handler can appear anywhere in the program, even after it is called. Common programming practice is to place your handler definitions at the beginning of the program where they can be located easily.

The `sum` handler takes two parameters that you name `x` and `y`. Inside the handler, only a single statement appears. This statement adds the values of `x` and `y` together and then executes a `return` command. This has the effect of returning the result of the expression to the caller, where it can be assigned to a variable or used in another expression.

In your program, your first call to sum passes the values of 100 and 200 as arguments and gives the result that is returned to the log command to be recorded into the Event Log:

```
log sum(100, 200)
```

The next statement in the program shows how the results of a handler call can be used in an expression. Here, the sum of 100 and 200 is added to the sum of 300 and 400, and the result of 1000 is logged.

```
log sum(100, 200) + sum(300, 400)
```

The final call uses the values of variables and expressions as the arguments to sum:

```
set i1 to 100
set i2 to 50
log sum(i1, i2 / 2)
```

The value of i1, which is 100, is passed as the first argument, whereas the value of i2 / 2, which is 50 / 2, or 25, is passed as the second argument. The result that is returned by the handler, namely 125, is then logged.

You saw the return command used in program examples in earlier chapters to stop your program's execution. This is its effect when it is executed outside a handler (in a sense, you are *returning* from your program). When you execute a return command from inside a handler, it does not stop your program's execution, but it immediately returns to the caller. If you don't specify a value after the return command, no value is returned.

If the last statement executed in a handler is not a return command, the value returned is the value (if any) of that last statement. That means that the following handler always returns the value 5 because that's the value of the set command:

```
on test ()
     set x to 5
end test
```

However, this version of test returns no value because the return command without a following expression does not have a value:

```
on test ()
     set x to 5
     return
end test
```

In general, if your program is supposed to return a value, don't rely on the value of the last statement in the handler. You may later add statements after that one that can affect the returned value. Always use an explicit return command followed by the value you want returned. That makes it clearer to anyone reading the handler's code that it is, in fact, returning a value.

Unlike most other programming languages, you don't specify the type of value your handler returns.

Argument Types

If you've programmed before, you may have noticed that when you define your handler in AppleScript, you don't declare the *types* of the arguments it takes. Nor does AppleScript do any checking on the types of arguments you supply when you call the handler. AppleScript just makes sure that you supply the correct *number* of arguments to the handler. That means if you write this call

```
sum(100)
```

AppleScript comes back with the following error message when you compile the script:

```
{100} doesn't match the parameters {x, y} for sum.
```

This is an indication that you have not supplied the correct number of arguments. (It actually means that you haven't matched the *pattern* of the arguments. I explain this later in this chapter).

If you try to call the sum handler with an argument that can't be coerced into a number, like this

```
sum("abc", 10)
```

you get an AppleScript error when you run the program because AppleScript can't add the string "abc" with the number 10. However, the following works

```
sum ("5", "10")
```

because both strings can be coerced into numbers when the addition is performed.

You can check the type of your arguments inside your handler and take appropriate action if they aren't the types you expect. For example, you can rewrite your sum handler to make sure both arguments are numbers. If either is not a number, you can return some arbitrary value as the result (for example, zero or missing value). Alternatively, you could generate an error; but you don't know how to do that yet. You learn how to do that in Chapter 9.

Here's a version of the sum handler that checks to make sure both arguments are numbers:

```
on sum(x, y)
    if class of x is in {real, integer} and class of y is in {real, integer} then
        return x + y
    else
        return 0
    end if
end sum
```

If x or y is not a number (that is, if the class of either x or y is not contained in the list of classes {integer, real}), the handler returns the value 0. Otherwise, the handler returns the sum of the two arguments as before.

Now that you are testing the types of the arguments, a call like the following:

```
sum ("5", "10")
```

no longer works because you are requiring numbers to be passed as arguments and not as values that can possibly be coerced into numbers. This is a design decision that seems to make sense; it's not a big stretch to expect a handler that adds two numbers to get two numbers as its arguments. Of course, this would always work:

```
sum ("5" as integer, "10" as integer)
```

In this case, the burden is placed on the caller to ensure the argument types are correct, and that's the right place for that burden.

Local Variables

So far, you have not set the values of any variables from inside your handlers. However, as you start to write your own handlers, you'll certainly want to do this. Unless specified otherwise, variables to which you assign values inside a handler are called *local* variables. That means that such variables can only be accessed directly from within the handler in which they appear; their use is local to the handler.

The next Try It Out program is an extension of the preceding Try It Out, "Returning Values from Handlers."

Try It Out   Local Variables

In this program, instead of adding just two numbers, the program takes a list of numbers as its argument, adds them up, and returns the result.

1.   Type the following program into Script Editor:

```
-- sum all the numbers in a list

on listSum(L)
    set theSum to 0

    if class of L is list then
        repeat with num in L
            set theSum to theSum + num
        end repeat
    end

    return theSum
end listSum

-- test out the handler

set myNums to {1, 2, 3, 4, 5}

log listSum(myNums)                     -- 1 + 2 + 3 + 4 + 5
log listSum(rest of myNums)             -- 2 + 3 + 4 + 5
log listSum({100, 200, 300, 400, 500}) -- literal list

-- Demonstrate local variable
```

```
set theSum to 999
listSum (myNums)
log theSum
```

2. Click the Event Log tab and run the program. You see the following results in the log:

```
(*15*)
(*14*)
(*1500*)
(*999*)
```

How It Works

The definition of the listSum handler is straightforward enough:

```
on listSum(L)
    set theSum to 0

    if class of L is list then
        repeat with num in L
            set theSum to theSum + num
        end repeat
    end if

    return theSum
end listSum
```

The handler begins by setting the value of the variable theSum to 0. This variable is used to accumulate the running total of the values in the list L.

Take note of the test of the argument L that is passed to the handler. If it is not a list, an error is avoided and the handler simply returns the value of 0. Otherwise, the handler enters a repeat loop to sum all the items in the list. When the loop has finished executing, the resulting sum — as stored in the variable theSum — is returned to the caller.

> *It would be reasonable to ensure that each item is a number before it is added into the sum. This is left as an exercise for you at the end of this chapter.*

After the handler has been defined, the program sets up a small five-item list of numbers:

```
set myNums to {1, 2, 3, 4, 5}
```

This list is then passed as the argument to the first call to listSum:

```
log listSum(myNums)                -- 1 + 2 + 3 + 4 + 5
```

The result of adding the five integers in the list is 15, which is recorded in the Event Log after the call to the handler returns.

The next call to the handler simply passes the last four items in the list to the listSum handler, recalling the use of the rest list property:

```
log listSum(rest of myNums)            -- 2 + 3 + 4 + 5
```

The next call to listSum shows how a literal list can be supplied as the argument:

```
log listSum({100, 200, 300, 400, 500}) -- literal list
```

Before the final call to listSum, a variable called theSum is assigned the value 999. The handler is then called, and the value of theSum is logged after the handler returns:

```
set theSum to 999
listSum (myNums)
log theSum
```

Notice that the value 999 is the last entry in the log. This illustrates an important point. It's no coincidence here that the variable theSum shares the same name with a variable used in the listSum handler to accumulate the total. Notice that even though the value of the variable theSum was changed inside the handler, this had no effect on the value of the variable defined outside the handler. That's because the variable theSum inside the listSum handler is distinct from the variable theSum used outside the handler. The variable inside the handler is *local*. Its use is restricted to the handler in which it is defined. Changing its value has no effect on any other variables called theSum defined outside the handler or in other handlers. That's why the variable theSum that was set outside the handler to 999 retained that value even after the listSum handler was called and returned.

The same discussion applies to parameters of a handler. For example, return to the first version of the sum handler:

```
on sum(x, y)
    return x + y
end sum
```

The parameter names x and y are used to reference the first and second arguments passed to the handler, respectively. However, they are also local to the handler. That is, if you change the value of x or y inside the handler, it has no effect on the values of other variables called x or y that are defined outside the handler or in other handlers. In fact, changing these values brings up another important point, which is the subject of the following section.

Call by Value

You may be wondering what happens to a parameter passed to a handler if you assign a value to it inside the handler. (Okay, so you're probably not wondering what happens, but follow along anyway!) The next Try It Out defines two simple handlers to illustrate some important points.

Try It Out   **Understanding Call by Value**

In this program, you see how to call a parameter by value.

1. Type the following program into Script Editor:

```
-- Illustrating Call by Value

on testHandler(x)
    set x to 100
end testHandler

on testHandler2(L1, L2)
    set end of L1 to 4
    set L2 to {100, 200, 300}
end testHandler2

set y to 50
testHandler(y)
log y

set list1 to {1, 2, 3}
set list2 to {4, 5, 6}
testHandler2(list1, list2)
log list1
log list2
```

2. Click the Event Log tab and run the program. Here's what should be logged:

```
(*50*)
(*1, 2, 3, 4*)
(*4, 5, 6*)
```

How It Works

As mentioned, these handlers are very simple. The first one simply sets the value of its argument to `100`:

```
on testHandler(x)
    set x to 100
end testHandler
```

Of course, the question is what happens to the value of a variable passed to this handler. Will its value get changed as well? This question is easily answered by assigning a value to a variable, calling the handler, and then examining the variable's value after the handler returns:

```
set y to 50
testHandler(y)
log y
```

If you look at the log, you see that the value of y did not change. Its value remains at 50 after the handler returns. That's because arguments are passed to handlers by *value*. That is, the value of the variable y, which is 50, is what gets passed as the argument to `testHandler`. Inside the handler, that value is stored in the variable x. Changing the value of x only affects the value of that local variable and has no effect whatsoever on the variable that was passed as the argument. In fact, in general, it's not possible for a handler to directly modify the value of an argument that is passed to it.

In Chapter 13, you learn that you can change the value of a variable by passing to a handler a reference to the variable.

The second handler called in the program seems to contradict this rule. This handler, called testHandler2, takes two arguments, which are lists:

```
on testHandler2(L1, L2)
    set end of L1 to 4
    set L2 to {100, 200, 300}
end testHandler2
```

The handler sets the end of the list passed as the first argument to 4. It then sets the second list to the literal list {100, 200, 300}. The question is what effect, if any, does this have on the arguments passed to the handler. The five lines of the program that follow are designed to answer this question:

```
set list1 to {1, 2, 3}
set list2 to {4, 5, 6}
testHandler2(list1, list2)
log list1
log list2
```

After setting the lists list1 and list2 to two literal lists, testHandler2 is called with the two lists as arguments. When the handler returns the two lists, list1 and list2 are logged. Notice what happens. The log indicates that list1 after the call contains the following items:

```
{1, 2, 3, 4}
```

So it appears that the handler was able to change the value of list1. This seems to contradict the definition of call by value, doesn't it? Well, not really. When a list (or a record, a date, or a script, which you learn about in Chapter 12) is passed as an argument, what gets passed is a reference to the list. That is, a pointer to where the list is actually located is what is passed. (This is the *value* when you write the name of a list.) That means that the actual items in the list are not copied into the corresponding parameter variable in the handler, only a reference to where the list is located. That further implies that making changes to the list does have an effect on the original list passed as the argument because only one copy of the list exists. This is an important point that you must understand.

Notice what happens to list2. The value logged is that of the original list:

```
{4, 5, 6}
```

Now this is confusing! Why didn't list2 get changed to the list {100, 200, 300} because that was assigned to the parameter L2 in the handler? The explanation is as follows: It's true that a reference to list2 was passed as the argument to the handler and stored in the variable L2 inside the handler. Before going any further, let's review this process with some diagrams.

Figure 8-1 depicts the lists list1 and list2 before the handler is called.

When testHandler is called, the references to these two lists are copied into the parameter variables L1 and L2, respectively. This is depicted in Figure 8-2.

As you can see from Figure 8-2, both L1 and list1 point to the same three-item list when the handler is entered. This is also true for L2 and list2.

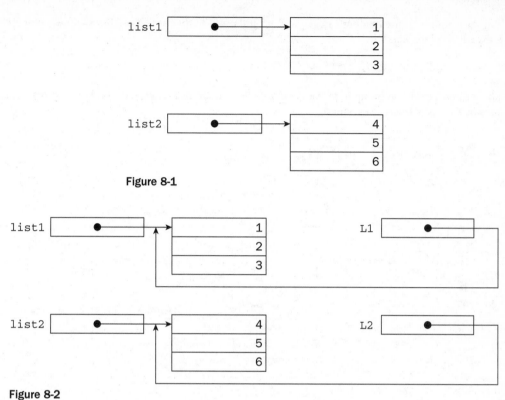

Figure 8-1

Figure 8-2

Now, when the following statement is executed inside testHandler2

```
set end of L1 to 4
```

the value 4 is tacked onto the end of the list pointed to by L1. The lists now appear as shown in Figure 8-3.

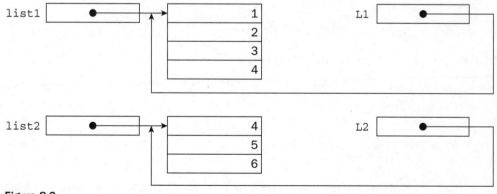

Figure 8-3

You see from the figure that both `list1` and `L1` still point to the same list. After the following statement is executed by the handler:

```
set L2 to {100, 200, 300}
```

a new three-item list is set up in memory, and `L2` is set to point to it. Figure 8-4 depicts how the lists look after this `set` statement is executed.

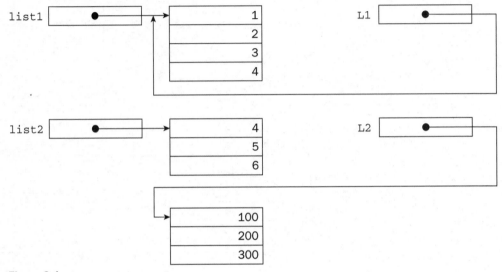

Figure 8-4

You can clearly see from Figure 8-4 that `list2` and `L2` point to different lists after the assignment. The rule to remember is that if you change an item in a list, you are modifying the original list. However, if you set the variable to a different list, or to even a subset of the same list, you won't modify the original list. Here are some examples of statements that will affect the original list:

```
set last item of L1 to 100
set item 2 of L1 to 100
set beginning of L1 to 100
```

Here are examples of statements that do not alter the original list:

```
set L1 to items 1 through 3 of L1
set L1 to rest of L1
set L1 to L1 & {600}
```

In each of the preceding cases, `L1` is set to point to a different list, so the original list passed as the argument is not modified by the handler.

The discussion about lists applies equally to records and dates. For example, the following handler *does not* change the value of the date passed as its argument and, therefore, must return the result:

```
on previousDay(d)
    set d to d - 1 * days
    return d
end previousDay
```

The following modifies one of the properties of the date variable passed as its argument without reassigning it to another date; so it *does* change its argument and, therefore, does not have to return the result:

```
on startOfMonth(d)
    set day of d to 1
end startOfMonth
```

You may want to review this section if any of the concepts remain unclear. Understanding how this works is important to your understanding of how to write handlers.

Recursive Handlers

Not only can a handler call other handlers, but it can also call itself! When a handler does that, it is called a *recursive* handler. Recursion is often a suitable choice for problems that can be solved by applying the same solution to subsets of the problem. Examples might be in the evaluation of parenthesized expressions, processing the elements of a list, or enumerating the contents of a folder, which itself might contain subfolders.

Perhaps the most commonly used illustration of recursion is in the calculation of factorials. The factorial of a positive integer n, written $n!$, is the product of the integers from 1 through n, inclusive. So the factorial of 5, or $5!$, is calculated like this:

```
5! = 5 ( 4 ( 3 ( 2 ( 1 = 120
```

And the calculation of $6!$ is done like this:

```
6! = 6 ( 5 ( 4 ( 3 ( 2 ( 1 = 720
```

If you compare the calculation of $6!$ to that of $5!$, you may notice that $6!$ is equal to 6 ($5!$. In general, the factorial of any positive integer n can be expressed as the product of n and the factorial of $n - 1$:

```
n! = n ( (n - 1)!
```

Defining the factorial of $n!$ like this is a recursive definition because the calculation of the factorial is based on the calculation of another factorial. The following Try It Out gives you some practice with writing a recursive handler.

Try It Out   **Recursive Factorial Handler**

In the following program, you write a recursive handler called `factorial` that calculates the factorial of an integer given as its argument.

1.   Type the following program into Script Editor:

```
-- Find the factorial of integer n

on factorial(n)
    if n = 1 then
        return 1
    else
        return n * (factorial(n - 1))
    end if
end factorial

log factorial(3)
log factorial(10)
```

2. Click the Event Log tab and run the program. You get the following output:

```
(*6*)
(*3628800*)
```

How It Works

The fact that the `factorial` handler calls itself makes it a recursive handler. This handler takes an argument that is called n. We presume it's a positive integer, and you could test for that if you so desired. Any recursive handler needs some way to know when to stop recursing. In this case, if the value of n is equal to 1, the handler simply returns the value 1 (1! is defined as 1). Otherwise, the handler returns the product of n and the factorial of n - 1.

When the handler is called the first time to calculate the factorial of 3, this value gets stored inside the parameter variable n. Because this value is not equal to 1, the handler executes the `else` clause, which executes this statement:

```
return n * (factorial(n - 1))
```

Since n is equal to 3, the statement is executed with these values:

```
return 3 * (factorial(2))
```

The `return` statement is left pending while the factorial of 2 is calculated. The `factorial` handler is then called again, this time with the argument of 2. This value is stored inside n, *which is distinct from the parameter n that is still pending from the previous call to the `factorial` handler*. In fact, each time a function is called, it gets a new and distinct set of parameter and local variables to work with.

Because the value of n, which is 2, is still not equal to 1, the `else` clause is executed again. After substituting the value of n, the statement that is executed looks like this:

```
return 2 * (factorial(1))
```

This `return` statement is again left pending, whereas the `factorial` handler is called once again, this time with the argument 1. Inside the handler, this value is assigned to n and the `if` statement is executed. Now, the value of n is equal to 1, so the statement

```
return 1
```

is executed. This initiates the chain of returns. The value of 1 is returned as the factorial of 1, where it is substituted into the pending statement

```
return 2 * (factorial(1))
```

This then becomes

```
return 2 * 1
```

or simply

```
return 2
```

This value of 2 is then returned to the preceding call to the handler that was left pending:

```
return 3 * (factorial(2))
```

After the value of `factorial(2)` is substituted, the statement looks like this:

```
return 3 * 2
```

or simply

```
return 6
```

This value of 6 is returned as the final result of the calculation of the factorial of 3, at which point it is added to the log:

```
log factorial(3)
```

The following summarizes the sequence of evaluations that occurs when calculating 3!:

```
factorial(3) = 3 * factorial(2) = 3 * 2 * factorial(1) = 3 * 2 * 1 = 3 * 2 = 6
```

In the following Try It Out, you write a more practical recursive handler: one to sort a list.

Try It Out   A Recursive List Sort Handler

In this program, don't try to understand the method or *algorithm* used to sort the list; it's very complicated! It does what's known as a *quick sort* and is a very fast sorting method.

1. Type the following program into Script Editor:

```
-- Recursive quick sort handler

on listSort(L)
    return quickSort(L, 1, count L)
end listSort

on quickSort(L, leftIndex, rightIndex)
    if L = {} then
```

```
            return L
     end if

    set lHold to leftIndex
    set rHold to rightIndex

    set pivot to item leftIndex of L

    repeat while leftIndex < rightIndex
        repeat while item rightIndex of L ≥ pivot and leftIndex < rightIndex
            set rightIndex to rightIndex - 1
        end repeat

        if leftIndex ≠ rightIndex then
            set item leftIndex of L to item rightIndex of L
            set leftIndex to leftIndex + 1
        end if

        repeat while item leftIndex of L ≤ pivot and leftIndex < rightIndex
            set leftIndex to leftIndex + 1
        end repeat

        if leftIndex ≠ rightIndex then
            set item rightIndex of L to item leftIndex of L
            set rightIndex to rightIndex - 1
        end if
    end repeat

    set item leftIndex of L to pivot
    set oldLeft to leftIndex
    set leftIndex to lHold
    set rightIndex to rHold

    if leftIndex < oldLeft then
        quickSort(L, leftIndex, oldLeft - 1)
    end if
    if rightIndex > oldLeft then
        quickSort(L, oldLeft + 1, rightIndex)
    end if

    return L
end quickSort

-- generate a list of 200 random numbers

set numList to {}

repeat 200 times
    set end of numList to random number from 1 to 500
end repeat

listSort(numList)
```

2. Click the Result tab and run the program. You should see a sorted list of 200 numbers in the Result pane. Your numbers will differ from those shown because they're randomly generated:

```
{1, 2, 3, 3, 6, 9, 12, 13, 17, 19, 23, 24, 26, 26, 31, 36, 42, 47, 49, 49, 50, 51,
51, 53, 53, 55, 60, 60, 60, 64, 64, 64, 65, 69, 69, 75, 76, 76, 79, 81, 83, 85, 88,
92, 92, 105, 106, 108, 109, 114, 116, 119, 124, 136, 137, 139, 143, 145, 146, 151,
155, 162, 168, 169, 178, 181, 184, 185, 188, 191, 191, 199, 201, 206, 209, 212,
214, 214, 217, 223, 223, 226, 227, 229, 231, 232, 233, 233, 240, 245, 246, 250,
251, 256, 256, 259, 262, 263, 264, 266, 269, 270, 274, 275, 280, 282, 283, 284,
284, 285, 285, 286, 287, 287, 292, 293, 294, 295, 302, 310, 311, 313, 315, 318,
319, 325, 329, 331, 332, 333, 336, 337, 337, 339, 339, 340, 343, 343, 345, 345,
346, 350, 351, 360, 363, 368, 370, 371, 379, 379, 382, 383, 383, 385, 386, 388,
388, 388, 389, 390, 393, 394, 397, 401, 401, 402, 406, 407, 408, 409, 412, 412,
414, 414, 428, 432, 432, 434, 434, 434, 435, 439, 444, 444, 447, 449, 456, 460,
461, 467, 472, 473, 476, 481, 484, 491, 494, 495, 495, 498}
```

How It Works

As noted, I don't provide a detailed explanation of the quick sort algorithm here. Notice that a handler called `listSort` is defined that simply calls the `quickSort` handler, passing the list to be sorted, the number 1, and the count of number of items in the list. This is a convenience for the user; the user can simply call `listSort` with a single argument (the list to be sorted) instead of three.

The recursive part of the `quickSort` handler is in this code:

```
if leftIndex < oldLeft then
    quickSort(L, leftIndex, oldLeft - 1)
end if
if rightIndex > oldLeft then
    quickSort(L, oldLeft + 1, rightIndex)
end if
```

This code sorts "pieces" of the list, based on the tested criteria.

To test the handler, the program generates a list of 200 random numbers using the following code:

```
set numList to {}

repeat 200 times
    set end of numList to random number from 1 to 500
end repeat
```

Recall the `random number` command from the guessing game program you developed in Chapter 4. Here you use it to generate 200 numbers in the range of 1 to 500.

After generating the random numbers, the program calls the `listSort` handler to sort the list. Notice that the handler sorts the list in place (that is, it modifies individual items in the list and never assigns the entire list). The handler also returns the sorted list as the result, in case you want to use it in an expression. It is important to know whether a handler modifies a list, record, or date that is given as its argument. If that poses a problem, you can always make a copy of the object (using the `copy` command and not the `set` command) to preserve its original values.

Local/Global Variables and Variable Scope

In this section, I show you the difference between local and *global* variables. It's important that you fully understand the nature of a variable's scope. The scope is the extent to which a variable is known within a program. For example, you already know that the scope of a local variable is the handler within which it is defined. That is, the variable cannot be accessed from outside the handler.

A local variable can be explicitly declared as such by placing the keyword `local` in front of the variable name, like so:

```
local sortList
```

Note that variable declared to be local in this manner does not have a value assigned to it. You still have to do that before you use it in an expression.

If you intend to use a variable only within a handler, it is good programming practice to declare it
`local` *in this fashion. Why? Because if you do this, you avoid the possibility of overwriting the value of a global variable that might be defined outside the handler with the same name. You learn more about global variables later in this section. As you might surmise, the scope of a global variable is, well, global. That is, its value can be accessed from anywhere within the source file. You can declare more than one variable to be local on the same line by separating each variable with a comma.*

Suppose you have a variable named x in your program and you want to access its value from inside a script. The following `test` handler shows the simplest way to do this:

```
set x to 5

on test()
    x       -- this causes an error!
end test

test()
```

If you run this program, you get an AppleScript error, complaining `The variable x is not defined`. Why does this happen? It happens because when a handler runs it does not have access to variables defined outside the handler — unless those variables have been declared *global*. A variable can be declared as a global variable by placing the keyword `global` before the variable's name, like so:

```
global x
```

If you add a global declaration to the previous program, the program looks like this:

```
global x
set x to 5

on test()
    x
end test

test()
```

When this program runs, the value 5 will be the result. By declaring a variable to be global, any handlers that subsequently appear in the program gain access to that variable. Not only can they access the value, but they can change it as well.

Any variable that you define outside a handler, as in the previous example, is global by default. The catch, however, is that its value can only be accessed inside handlers if an explicit global declaration for that variable is made. In fact, such a declaration can occur either inside or outside the handler. That means that the last example shown can also be written like this to achieve the same result:

```
set x to 5

on test()
    global x
    x
end test

test()
```

The variable x is first assigned a value outside any handler, so it is implicitly global. By declaring the variable global inside the test handler, the handler can access and optionally modify the value of the global variable. You type a program example shortly that illustrates this point.

As with local variables, you can declare more than one variable to be global at the same time by separating each variable from the next with a comma, like this:

```
global dbFileName, dbFileID, userName
```

In the next Try It Out, you define a global variable and then a local variable inside a handler.

Try It Out   Local versus Global Variables

In this program, you call the handler several times. This should help you understand the difference between local and global variables.

1.   Type the following program into Script Editor:

```
-- Understanding global variables

global gCounter
set gCounter to 50

on testHandler()
    local lCounter
    set lCounter to 50

    set lCounter to lCounter + 1
    set gCounter to gCounter + 1
    log ("local = " & lCounter as string) & ", global = " & gCounter as string
end testHandler

repeat 5 times
    testHandler()
```

```
repeat

log gCounter
```

2. Click the Event Log tab and run the program. The following appears in the Event Log pane:

```
(*local = 51, global = 51*)
(*local = 51, global = 52*)
(*local = 51, global = 53*)
(*local = 51, global = 54*)
(*local = 51, global = 55*)
(*55*)
```

How It Works

The program begins by declaring a global variable gCounter and setting its value to 50:

```
global gCounter
set gCounter to 50
```

Because gCounter is explicitly declared as a global variable, its value can be accessed by any handler defined in the program.

The program next defines a handler called testHandler. In that handler, a local variable called lCounter is declared and its value is set to 50, like so:

```
local lCounter
set lCounter to 50
```

The testHandler next adds 1 to both the local and global variable and then logs their values:

```
set lCounter to lCounter + 1
set gCounter to gCounter + 1
log ("local = " & lCounter as string) & ", global = " & gCounter as string
```

You can see that, because the program doesn't generate any errors, AppleScript allows you to access and change the value of the global variable gCounter from inside the handler.

After the handler is defined, the program calls testHandler() five times to see its effect on the values of the local and global variables. The first five lines of the log file are shown:

```
(*local = 51, global = 51*)
(*local = 51, global = 52*)
(*local = 51, global = 53*)
(*local = 51, global = 54*)
(*local = 51, global = 55*)
```

As you see, the local variable lCounter gets reinitialized to 50 each time the handler is called. Inside the handler, its value is incremented to 51, and that is the value it attains each and every time it is called.

On the other hand, the global variable gCounter is incremented and retains its incremented value through successive handler calls. Unlike a local variable, whose value is created and destroyed when a handler is entered and exited respectively, global variables *live* outside the handler and, therefore, retain their values through successive handler calls. For that reason, the value of gCounter changes from 51 to 55 as a result of the handler being called five times.

After the loop finishes executing, the program logs the value of gCounter to verify that its value persists outside the handler. The last line of the log's output verifies that its value is 55.

The next several Try It Out examples should give you greater understanding of how to work with variable scope.

Try It Out   Understanding Variable Scope: Protecting a Global Variable

This program illustrates what happens when you have a global variable defined at the top level and a local variable of the same name defined in a handler.

1. Type the following program into Script Editor:

```
global x
set x to 5

on test()
    local x

    x    -- this will cause an error!
end test

test()
```

2. Run the program. You should get an AppleScript Error dialog with the following error message:

```
The variable x is not defined.
```

How It Works

The variable x is declared as a global variable and its value is set to 5. In the test handler, a variable of the same name is declared as a local variable. When you do this, you create a new variable that is local and distinct from the corresponding global variable. Because you never assign a value to this local variable, AppleScript complains that the variable is not defined.

Try It Out   Understanding Variable Scope: Local and Global Variables with the Same Name (Part 1)

The following program illustrates what happens when you have both local and global variables, and you assign values to both.

1. Type the following program into Script Editor:

```
global x
set x to 5

on test()
    local x
```

```
        set x to 10
    end test

test()
x
```

2. Click the Result tab and run the program. You get the following result:

```
5
```

How It Works

The only difference between this program and the preceding one is the assignment of the value `10` to the local variable `x` inside the `test` handler. When the handler is executed, as noted, the local variable `x` is distinct from the corresponding global variable with the same name. Therefore, assigning `10` to the local variable has no effect on the global variable `x`. This fact is verified by the result of `5`.

Try It Out   **Understanding Variable Scope: Local and Global Variables with the Same Name (Part 2)**

What do you think happens if you switch the `local` and `global` keywords in the previous program? Try it out and see.

1. Type the following program into Script Editor:

```
local x
set x to 5

on test()
    global x

    set x to 10
end test

test()
x
```

2. Click the Result tab and run the program. You should see the following result:

```
5
```

How It Works

The variable `x` is declared as a local variable at the outer level. Another variable `x` is declared as a global variable inside the handler. Once again, two distinct variables are declared. This may seem a little confusing, but whenever `x` is subsequently referenced outside any handler, it is the local variable `x` that is referenced. However, if you add the following handler to the previous program:

```
on test2()
    global x

    log x
end test2
```

and then call it after you call `test`, the `test2` handler accesses the value of the *global* variable x that you declared inside `test`. The result is that the value 10 is logged by `test2`.

Don't worry too much about this. It's not the typical scenario. More often, you declare global variables at the start of your program, outside any handlers, because you want their values to be accessible to the handlers you define. And inside your handlers, you declare variables to be local if you want to guarantee they don't interfere with global variables having the same name.

Better yet, it's generally a good idea to avoid overusing global variables. Their use reduces the generalization of a handler because it requires the existence of a particular variable having a particular name. A wiser strategy is to write your handlers so that any values from the outside that they need to access are passed in as parameters. If you do this, it will be clear, when you look at the first line of your handler's definition, what parameters the handler expects as its arguments.

> *As you learn in Chapter 12, using script properties that are defined outside your handlers is another technique that's often used to work with global values.*

Okay, so the next Try It Out is the last program example in this chapter that is likely to add to the confusion. You might want to earmark this section so you can come back and look at a simple program example that illustrates these points whenever the need arises.

Try It Out   Understanding Variable Scope: Accessing a Global Variable Declared Outside a Handler

The following program shows how you can use the keyword `my` to access a variable that is otherwise outside the scope of a handler.

1. Type the following program into Script Editor:

```
set x to 5

on test()
    set my x to 10
end test

test()
x
```

2. Click the Result tab and run the program. You get the following result:

```
10
```

How It Works

If you have a global variable and a local variable of the same name and you want to access the global variable from within a handler, you can do so by preceding the variable's name with `my`. How and why this works is described in more detail in the next chapter. Incidentally, you can also use the keyword `its` instead of `my`.

As I pointed out earlier, one of the great advantages of handlers is their reusability. A well-designed handler can be used in different applications without your having to write the same or similar code from scratch.

You've seen that a list is one of the fundamental data types in AppleScript. It makes perfect sense, then, to develop a set of handlers that you can use to more easily work with lists. The previous sort routine is one such example. In an earlier chapter, you saw the usefulness of generalized code for inserting and deleting items from a list. In the following Try It Out, you develop handlers for these two purposes: to add and remove items from a list.

Try It Out   **Writing General Purpose Handlers**

The following program gives you more practice in writing handlers.

1.   Type the following program into Script Editor:

```
-- Arbitrary list item deletion and insertion handlers

-- remove item n from list L

on removeItem(L, n)
    if n > 0 and n ≤ (count L) then -- make sure n is valid
        if n = 1 then
            set L to rest of L -- remove first item
        else if n = (count L) then
            set L to items 1 thru -2 of L -- remove last item
        else
            set L to (items 1 thru (n - 1) of L) & (items (n + 1) thru -1) of L
        end if
    end if

    return L
end removeItem

-- add item lItem in front of item n in list L
-- special case of n = -1 for insertion at end of list

on insertItem(L, n, lItem)
    if n = -1 or (n ≥ 1 and n ≤ (count L)) then -- make sure  n is valid
        if n = 1 then
            set beginning of L to lItem -- insert at front of list
        else if n = -1 then
            set end of L to lItem -- add to end of list
        else
            set L to (items 1 thru (n - 1) of L) & lItem & (items n thru -1 of L)
        end if
    end if

    return L
end insertItem

set list1 to {1, 2, 3, 4, 5}
set list2 to {"a", "b", "c", "d"}

set list1 to removeItem(list1, 2)
log list1

set list2 to insertItem(list2, 2, "x")
log list2
```

2. Click the Event Log tab and run the program. You get the following output:

```
(*1, 3, 4, 5*)
(*a, x, b, c, d*)
```

How It Works

`On...end` wrappers were placed around the code to remove an item from a list and also to insert an item into a list to turn them into handlers. At the very end of both handlers, the resulting list is also returned. Otherwise, the code remains unaltered from Chapter 6.

Note that these lines from the `removeItem` handler

```
set L to rest of L -- remove first item

set L to items 1 thru -2 of L -- remove last item

set L to (items 1 thru (n - 1) of L) & (items (n + 1) thru -1) of L
```

and this one from the `insertItem` handler

```
set L to (items 1 thru (n - 1) of L) & lItem & (items n thru -1 of L)
```

dictate that the modified list must be returned because, as previously described in detail, these statements have the effect of setting `L` to point to a different list in memory. Therefore, they do not always modify the list passed as the argument in place.

Saving and Loading Handlers

With your general purpose list handling routines, you can go ahead and use them in any program that needs to work with lists. One way to do that is simply to copy the code into any program that needs access to these handlers.

As you see in the following Try It Out, another alternative is to save your collection of handlers in a file in the normal way and then load it, using the `load script` command, into any program that needs to use it. The advantage of this approach is that you don't have to copy the code into each program. And if you ever find a bug in one of your handlers or want to make improvements, you only have to do it in the original file and not hunt down every file that contains the copied code.

Try It Out   **Saving and Loading the List Handlers**

Now you see how you can load your handlers into another program.

1. Type the list handlers `listSum`, `listSort`, `removeItem`, and `insertItem` from previous examples. Just type the handlers, not the code at the end of each program that tested them out. For space considerations, I don't show the code again here, just the structure of the program.

```
-- General purpose list handlers

-- Insert the code for the listSum handler here
```

```
on listSum(L)
    ...
end listSum

-- Insert the code for the listSort and quickSort handlers here
on listSort(L)
    ...
end listSort

on quickSort (L, leftIndex, rightIndex)
    ...
end quickSort

-- Insert the code the insertItem and removeItem handlers here
on insertItem (L, N, lItem)
    ...
end insertItem

on removeItem (L, N)
    ...
end removeItem
```

2. Choose File⇨Save As and then navigate to your Home folder⇨Library⇨Scripts. If the `Scripts` folder doesn't exist there, click the New Folder button and create a `Scripts` folder in your `Library` folder. In the Save As box type `List Handlers`. In the File Format box, select Script. Your dialog should resemble Figure 8-5. Finally, click Save.

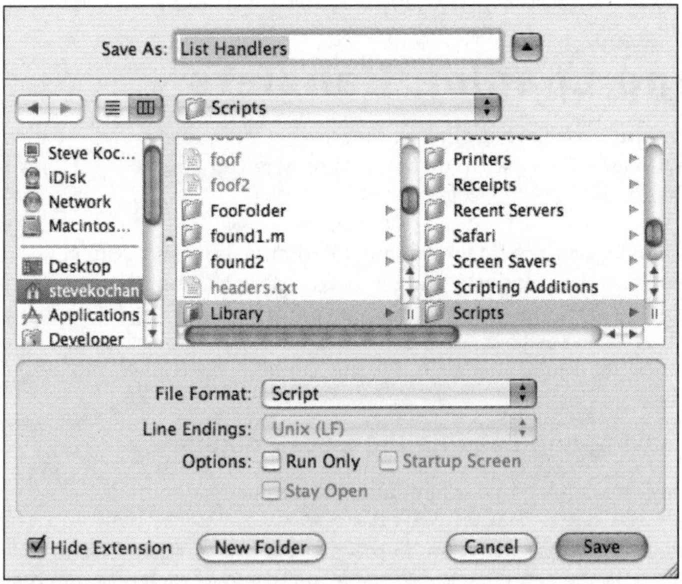

Figure 8-5

3. Notice that the file name in your Script Editor window changed to `List Handlers.scpt`. Close this window.

4.   Choose File⇨New and type the following program:

```
-- Test list handlers

set listHandlers to load script file ((path to scripts folder as string) &
      "List Handlers.scpt")

set L1 to {300, 7, 24, 6, 17}

log L1
log listSort(L1) of listHandlers
log listSum(L1) of listHandlers
set L1 to insertItem(L1, 1, "Hello!") of listHandlers
set L1 to removeItem(L1, 5) of listHandlers
log L1
```

5.   Click the Event Log tab and run the program. You see the following four lines toward the end of the Event Log pane:

```
(*300, 7, 24, 6, 17*)
(*6, 7, 17, 24, 300*)
(*354*)
(*Hello!, 6, 7, 17, 300*)
```

How It Works

Scripts that can be used by other programs are normally kept in the Scripts folder, which is a subfolder of the Library folder, which itself is a subfolder of your home folder.

> *There is also a system-wide Library/Scripts folder where you can place your scripts if you want to grant access to your scripts to all users of your system. To store your scripts in the Scripts folder there, you need administrator privileges.*

> *If you want to give a library of handlers to someone else to use, but you don't want to allow them to edit your code, you can check the Run Only option when you save your script. However, be careful; be sure to first make a copy for yourself because you won't be able to subsequently edit the file.*

To load your handlers into your program, you use the load script command, followed by an alias or file specification that indicates the location of the script file:

```
set listHandlers to load script file ((path to scripts folder as string) &
      "List Handlers.scpt")
```

When the resulting script file is read and its contents returned, it can be stored in a variable in your program. In this case, you select a variable called listHandlers.

After the handlers have been loaded, you can call them in your program. However, because their definitions are stored *inside* the variable listHandlers, you have to inform AppleScript of that fact when you make your calls. So when the listSort handler is called in your program, you make the call like so:

```
listSort(L1) of listHandlers
```

This tells AppleScript to look in the listHandlers variable for a handler called listSort.

The Apostrophe-s notation

In the last program example, you used the `of` keyword to access the handlers stored in your `listHandlers` variable. You can also specify an object that belongs to another object by using the *apostrophe-s* notation. For example, you can write

```
listSort(L1) of listHandlers
```

as

```
listHandlers's listSort(L1)
```

In general, any expression in AppleScript that you can write in the form

```
x of y
```

can be equivalently written as

```
y's x
```

Here are some more examples of this notation:

```
set L1 to {1, 2, 3}
L1's first item

{1, 2, 3}'s last item    -- not practical at all but it works!

L1's items 1 thru 2

set theText to "Illustrate the apostrophe-s notation"
theText's words

set fileRec to info for file (path to documents folder as string)
fileRec's size

-- The following does the same as the previous two lines, but it's too cryptic!

(info for (file (path to documents folder as string)))'s size
```

This notation hasn't been used up to this point because it's better to get used to doing things one way first. However, if you are required to look at other people's scripts, which will inevitably happen, you need to understand this notation. You may want to use the notation in your own scripts as well.

Labeled Parameters

When you call any of the handlers you defined so far, you have to make sure that you list all the arguments to the handler in the same order that they were listed when you defined the handler. This list of arguments is enclosed within a pair of parentheses and each argument is delimited from the next by a comma. Parameters specified this way are known as *positional* parameters because their position in the list matters and determines how the arguments are assigned to the corresponding parameters inside the handler.

AppleScript allows you to define and call handlers using a different format that is more like English. It also allows you to specify your arguments in any order. In one form of these so-called *labeled* parameters, you precede each argument by a chosen label, followed by a colon, followed by the argument. In another form, you precede each argument by a word chosen from a list of prepositions reserved for this purpose. These two forms can be used together, but the syntax starts to get confusing, so you may want to avoid doing that at first.

The next two Try It Out examples show you how to work with the two forms of labeled parameters.

Try It Out   Writing a Handler with Labeled Parameters–Form 1

In this program, you modify your `insertItem` handler so you can easily remember how to call it. This introduces the first form of labeled parameters.

1. Type the following program into Script Editor:

```
on insertItem given theList:L, beforeItem:N, theItem:lItem
    if N = -1 or (N ≥ 1 and N ≤ (count L)) then -- make sure  n is valid
        if N = 1 then
            set beginning of L to lItem -- insert at front of list
        else if N = -1 then
            set end of L to lItem -- add to end of list
        else
            set L to (items 1 thru (N - 1) of L) & lItem & (items N thru -1 of L)
        end if
    end if

    return L
end insertItem

set superHeroes to {"Superman", "Batman", "Thor", "Daredevil"}

insertItem given theList:superHeroes, beforeItem:3, theItem:"Spiderman"
```

2. Click the Result tab and run the program. You get the following result:

```
{"Superman", "Batman", "Spiderman", "Thor", "Daredevil"}
```

How It Works

When a handler is defined using labeled parameters, you write the keyword `given` and follow it by your labeled parameters. The label is an identifier, which is followed by a colon, which in turn is followed by the name of the parameter. That parameter name is the name you use to refer to the corresponding argument inside the handler. You can use the same name for the label and the parameter if you like.

In your program, you start the definition of your `insertItem` handler like so:

```
on insertItem given theList:L, beforeItem:N, theItem:lItem
```

Here the labels are `theList`, `beforeItem`, and `theItem`. Each colon is followed by the corresponding parameter name. Other than this change to the first line of the handler's definition, the remainder of the handler's code is identical to the version presented earlier in this chapter.

In the first version of the insertItem handler, if you want to insert the item "Spiderman" into the list superHeroes before the third item, your call would look like this:

```
insertItem (superHeroes, 3, "Spiderman")
```

The arguments to your insertItem handler must appear in the order shown to correspond with the parameter names that you listed in the handler's definition. So, the first argument is the list, the second argument is the item number in the list, and the third argument is the value to insert into the list.

In the second version of that handler, which is written using labeled parameters, you accomplish the same task with a call to the insertItem handler that looks like this:

```
insertItem given theList: superheroes, beforeItem: 3, theItem: "SpiderMan"
```

Instead of enclosing the arguments in a set of parentheses, the keyword given follows the handler's name, followed by each labeled argument.

As previously noted, one advantage of using labeled parameters is that the order of the arguments doesn't matter. So you can write your call like this:

```
insertItem given beforeItem: 3, theItem: "SpiderMan", theList: superHeroes
```

or this:

```
insertItem given theItem: "SpiderMan", theList: superHeroes, beforeItem: 3
```

and achieve the same result as you did in the first call to the insertItem handler.

Identifying Parameters with Prepositions

As noted at the beginning of this section on labeled parameters, you have another way to specify the parameters to your handlers. Instead of preceding each parameter by a label and a colon, you precede each parameter with a word selected from the following table.

about	beneath	on
above	beside	onto
against	between	out of
apart from	by	over
around	for	since
aside from	from	through
at	instead of	thru
below	into	under

Writing a Handler with Labeled Parameters–Form 2

Now you see how to write a handler using the second form of labeled parameter. In this program, you modify your `removeItem` handler.

1. Type the following program into Script Editor:

```
on removeItem at N from L
    if N > 0 and N ≤ (count L) then -- make sure n is valid
        if N = 1 then
            set L to rest of L -- remove first item
        else if N = (count L) then
            set L to items 1 thru -2 of L -- remove last item
        else
            set L to (items 1 thru (N - 1) of L) & (items (N + 1) thru -1) of L
        end if
    end if

    return L
end removeItem

set superHeroes to {"Superman", "Batman", "Thor", "Daredevil"}

removeItem at 3 from superHeroes
```

2. Click the Result tab and run the program. You should get the following output:

```
{"Superman", "Batman", "Daredevil"}
```

How It Works

For this form of writing a handler, you proceed as follows: You start with the keyword `on`, followed by the handler's name. Then you select a preposition from the previous table and follow it with the parameter's name (note that you don't use the keyword `given` here). You repeat this process for each of your handler's parameters. You can use a preposition only once in a handler's definition. Obviously, you want to choose words from the table that correspond to the purpose of the parameter. You can't pick your own words; they have to be chosen from the table.

To call the handler, you write the handler's name followed by the appropriate prepositions and corresponding arguments. These can be listed in any order, and commas are not used to separate arguments.

In this program, the call to the `removeItem` handler was written as

```
removeItem at 3 from superHeroes
```

but you could also have written it like this:

```
removeItem from superHeroes at 3
```

Combining Labeled Parameter Formats

The two forms of labeled parameters can be used together. If you do this, the list of prepositional parameters must appear *before* the list of *label:* parameters.

Here is another way you could define your `insertItem` handler:

```
on insertItem into L given theItem:lItem, beforeItem:L
```

Not only do the prepositional parameters have to appear first when defining the handler, but this rule also applies when you call the handler. So this call works as you would expect:

```
insertItem into superHeroes given theItem:"Spiderman", beforeItem:3
```

but this does not:

```
insertItem given theItem:"Spiderman", beforeItem:3 into superheroes   -- Nope!
```

Make sure you master the syntax if you're going to use this combined format. The prepositional parameters come first and they can appear in any order. They are not comma-delimited. The *label:* parameters are listed next, again in any order. They are comma-delimited and preceded by the keyword `given`.

Specifying a Direct Parameter

When you define your handler, you are allowed to use the keyword `of` followed by a parameter name. However, the stipulations are that it must be the *first* parameter listed when the handler is defined, it must appear first when the handler is called, and it must be used in combination with other labeled parameters. This last point means that you can't use it for a handler that takes just a single argument or uses positional parameters.

You can substitute the keyword `in` for the keyword `of` in the direct parameter format. However, its use in both the handler's definition and the call are changed to `of` when your program is compiled.

For an example using prepositional parameters, recall the second version of your `removeItem` handler:

```
on removeItem at N from L
    ...
end removeItem
```

You can rewrite the handler as

```
on removeItem of L at N
    ...
end removeItem
```

and then call it like this:

```
removeItem of superHeroes  at 2
```

The point worth remembering here is that using the keyword `of` requires that the parameter be listed first. That means you can't write this:

```
removeItem at 2 of superHeroes   -- Not valid!!
```

For an example using the *label:* form of labeled parameters, recall this version of your `insertItem` handler:

```
on insertItem given theList:L, beforeItem:N, theItem:lItem
   ...
end insertItem
```

You can rewrite the handler this way

```
on insertItem of L given beforeItem:N, theItem:lItem
   ...
end insertItem
```

and then call it like this

```
insertItem of superHeroes given beforeItem: 2, theItem: "SpiderMan"
```

or like this.

```
insertItem of superHeroes given  theItem: "SpiderMan", beforeItem: 2
```

But you can't call it like this

```
insertItem given theItem: "SpiderMan", beforeItem: 2 of theList: superHeroes –
No!!!
```

because using the keyword of dictates that the parameter always appears first.

Using with and without for Boolean Parameters

If you use the *label:* form for specifying your parameters, you can take advantage of another shortcut when calling the handler. AppleScript allows you to specify the keyword with followed by a list of one or more parameters whose value is to be set true. Alternatively, you can specify the keyword without, followed by a list of one or more parameters whose value is to be set false.

If you extend your listSort handler to take an optional parameter that specifies whether the sort should consider case, you might define it like this

```
on listSort of L given consideringCase:caseFlag
   ...
end listSort
```

and you might call it like this:

```
listSort of wordList given consideringCase:true
```

Using the with keyword, you could equivalently call it like this:

```
listSort of wordList with consideringCase
```

In a similar manner, this call to listSort

```
listSort of wordList given consideringCase:false
```

can be written like this:

```
listSort of wordList without consideringCase
```

If your listSort routine also takes an optional ascendingOrder flag and is defined like so:

```
on listSort of L given consideringCase:caseFlag, ascendingOrder:orderFlag
    ...
end listSort
```

You could call it like this:

```
listSort of wordList given consideringCase:true, ascendingOrder:true
```

or, equivalently, like this:

```
listSort of wordList with consideringCase and ascendingOrder
```

or this:

```
listSort of wordList with consideringCase, ascendingOrder
```

In this last case, the statement is changed to look like the previous statement (using the keyword and) after it gets compiled.

A call to wordList that sets the consideringCase parameter to true and the ascendingOrder to false can be made this way:

```
listSort of wordList given consideringCase:true, ascendingOrder:false
```

or this way:

```
listSort of wordList with consideringCase without ascendingOrder
```

If you specify a true or false value for a prepositional parameter, be aware that it is automatically changed to a with or without format after it's compiled. This means that a handler call like this

```
funnyHandler from true
```

looks like this after compilation:

```
funnyHandler with from
```

Specifying Patterns for Parameters

The last topic in this chapter illustrates the idea of specifying patterns for the parameters to your handlers. A pattern can be a list, a record, or even a more complicated combination of the two. For example, suppose you want to define a handler called makeDate that takes a list of three integer items representing the month, day, and year, respectively. You also want to return a date object for that specified date. Here's one way to do it:

```
on makeDate(D)
    set theMonth to item 1 of D as string
    set theDay to item 2 of D as string
    set theYear to item 3 of D as string
    return date  (theMonth & "/" & theDay & "/" & theYear)
end makeDate
```

A call to this handler might appear like so:

```
makeDate({7, 16, 2005})
```

The handler extracts each item from the list, converting each to a string in the process. A string of the form *mm/dd/yyyy* is then created, converted to a date, and returned.

If you were writing this handler for use in your programs, you would probably want to make sure that each of the integers passed to the handler is in the proper range.

Of course, your handler could have been written to take three separate integer arguments, but here you decide to have it take a list instead (otherwise, you would defeat the purpose of this example!).

You can tell AppleScript that the handler is expecting a three-item list as its argument by specifying a three-item list as the parameter when the handler is defined. It's done like this:

```
on makeDate({MM, DD, YYYY})
    set theMonth to MM as string
    set theDay to DD as string
    set theYear to YYYY as string
    return date  (theMonth & "/" & theDay & "/" & theYear)
end makeDate
```

AppleScript won't complain if a list containing more than three items is passed whenever the handler is called (just the first three items are assigned to the variables MM, DD, and YYYY). It will complain if the list contains fewer than three items. One of the nice things about using this format is that the second version of makeDate is more self-documenting. After reading the first line of that handler's definition, you can see that a three-item list is expected as the handler's argument. That's not at all clear from the first handler's definition.

If your makeDate handler instead takes a record as its argument and the record contains properties labeled theMonth, theDay, and theYear, you could define your handler like this:

```
on makeDate({theMonth:MM, theDay:DD, theYear:YYYY})
    set theMonth to MM as string
    set theDay to DD as string
    set theYear to YYYY as string
    return date  (theMonth & "/" & theDay & "/" & theYear)
end makeDate
```

To call this handler, you obviously need to pass a record as the argument. The record must contain at least the three properties listed in the handler's definition (it can contain more properties) or AppleScript will generate an error.

Here's a highly-manufactured call to this version of the handler:

```
makeDate({theYear: 2005, theMonth:7, theDay:16})
```

The patterns you specify for your parameters can be even more complex. As a last example, here's a version of makeDate that takes two lists as arguments. The list is a record that contains the date information. The second list is a record specifying the time:

```
on makeDate ({theMonth:MM, theDay:DD, theYear:YYYY}, {theHour: hrs, theMins: ¬
    mins, theSecs: secs})
    ...
end makeDate
```

This might be a call to this version of makeDate:

```
-- make the date 2/22/1996, 10:12 AM
makeDate({theMonth:2, theDay:22, theYear:1996}, {theHour:10, theMins:12,
theSecs:00})
```

Of course, with all the sample calls in this section, variables would normally be used as arguments instead of hard-coded values.

Summary

A handler provides a way of writing code that you can reuse for other applications. It also provides a way for you to divide your programming tasks into smaller, modularized pieces. In this chapter, you learned the following points about working with handlers:

❑ Handlers can be written to take one or more parameters or arguments.

❑ You can provide a simple, comma-separated list of parameters (known as positional parameters); or you can define your handlers to use labeled parameters, in which case the arguments can be specified in any order when the handler is called.

❑ Arguments are passed to a handler by value. The handler cannot modify these arguments, unless a list, record, date, or script object is passed as the argument. The handler can change individual elements of a list or record, as well as properties of a date object.

❑ You can declare local and global variables. How they are declared influences the scope of the variables in your program.

❑ Handlers can be loaded into the program using the load script command.

You learn more about special handlers that are automatically called when certain events occur — such as running your program, quitting your program, or dragging a file on top of your program's icon — in Chapter 10, which deals with applications.

In the next chapter, you learn how to predict the types of program errors you may encounter and how to handle them. Before proceeding, however, try the exercises that follow to test your understanding of the material covered in this chapter. You can find the solutions to these exercises in Appendix A.

Exercises

1. Based on the `sum` handler from this chapter, write a handler called `sum3` that returns the sum of its three numeric arguments.

2. Modify the `listSum` handler to sum only the numbers in the list given as its argument. So the call

```
listSum ({"Hello", 100, 200, current date, 300})
```

should return a result of 600 (= 100 + 200 + 300).

3. Based on the `removeItem` handler you developed in this chapter, write a handler called `removeItems` that takes three arguments: the list as the first item, the starting index as the second, and the number of items to remove as the third. So the call

```
removeItems ({1, 2, 3, 4, 5}, 2, 3)
```

removes three items from the list {1,2,3,4,5} starting with the second item, returning the list {1,5}.

4. Given the `listSort` handler defined in this chapter and a list of numbers stored in the variable L, what would be the effect of the following call?

```
reverse of listSort(L)
```

5. Based on the result of the last exercise, modify the `listSort` handler so that this call

```
listSort of numList with ascendingSort
```

gives an ascending sort of the list `numList`, whereas the call

```
listSort of numList without ascendingSort
```

produces a descending sort of the list `numList`. Bonus: This is not the most efficient way to produce a descending sort because the list is first sorted in ascending order and then reversed. Modify the `quickSort` handler to take an argument that specifies the direction of the sort and handles this directly within the code.

6. Can you explain (or guess!) why the following program generates an error?

```
local x
set x to 5

on test()
    set my x to 10
end test

test()
x
```

7. Load the collection of list handlers you developed in this chapter. Prompt the user to select a file. Generate a sorted list of the words in the file. *Note:* Make sure you perform this operation on text files smaller than 32KB in size.

8. Write a handler called `removeDuplicateItems` that takes a sorted list as its argument and removes all duplicates from the list. Using the results from the previous exercise, verify the program's operation with the contents of a text file. Add your new handler to the collection of list handlers that you stored in your Library:Scripts folder.

9. Write a handler called `itemCounts` that takes a list as its argument and returns a list of records. Each record should have two properties called `sItem` and `sCount` that represent an item from the list and the number of times it occurs in the list. Be sure to use the `listSort` handler you previously developed and add your new handler to the collection of list handlers that you stored in your Library:Scripts folder. *Note:* Refer to your solution to the previous exercise.

10. Load the list handlers you developed in this chapter and log the result of the load. Can you explain the output?

Error Handling

In an ideal world, you write a program and it runs perfectly on every computer for every user and in every situation. The real world is different, however, and throws curve balls at every opportunity. Your programs are afflicted with errors you never even dreamed of. Perhaps the user types in an unexpected answer. Or you get back an empty list (which, of course, is never supposed to be empty), and then you try to access items from the list. Or maybe you try to write to a file, and you don't have the correct permissions to do so. These types of events often generate errors that cause your program to terminate. Predicting these types of errors and handling them gracefully is one of the keys to being a good programmer. It is also the subject of this chapter.

Beeps and Dialogs

Sometimes when an error occurs you just want to get the user's attention. You know about the beep command, which takes an optional integer indicating the number of beeps to give the user:

```
beep 3
```

This generates three beeps. You can combine it with a display dialog command and an icon to really get your point across:

```
beep 3

display dialog "You entered a file name and now I can't open it!" with icon
stop ¬
        buttons {"OK"} default button 1
```

The stop icon usually means the program can't continue. Typically, the note icon is used to provide some information to the user, whereas the caution icon is used to give a more serious message about a situation that must be acknowledged or corrected before the program can continue.

You can supply an optional giving up after parameter to specify the maximum number of seconds you're willing to wait before the user acknowledges a dialog by clicking a button. If the user does not click a button before the specified time has elapsed, the dialog is dismissed. In the following statement information is provided to the user about the success of the operation:

```
display dialog "The files were successfully copied" with icon note ¬
        buttons {"OK"} default button 1 giving up after 5
```

However, if the user doesn't click OK within five seconds, the dialog is automatically dismissed.

When you use the `giving up after` parameter, AppleScript returns a boolean property named `gave up` in the result record. If the value of this property is `true`, the dialog was dismissed because the specified time elapsed. If the `gave up` property is `false`, the dialog was dismissed because the user clicked a button.

As noted, you can take advantage of this parameter to display informative messages that don't require interaction on the part of the user. This is particularly helpful if you're running a time-consuming script and you step away from your computer. It's frustrating to return only to find out that the program has stopped waiting for you to acknowledge some silly message.

The try...on error Statement

You are familiar with the `try` statement, which was first introduced in Chapter 3. You use it according to this general format:

```
try
    statement
    statement
    ...
end try
```

A statement in the `try` block that generates an error causes execution of the statements that follow, up to the `end try`, to be skipped. Execution of the program otherwise continues with whatever statement follows the `try` block.

One technique you learned to determine whether a statement in a `try` block fails is illustrated by the following code fragment from Chapter 4:

```
set validNumber to false
try
    set triangularNumber to text returned of result as integer
    set validNumber to true
end try

if not validNumber then
    display dialog "You didn't enter an integer" with icon note
end if
```

Here you set a flag to `false` before entering the `try` block and then set the flag to `true` after the last statement inside the `try` block is executed. This statement is reached only if none of the preceding statements — and here, you have only one such statement — in the `try` block generated an error. Outside the `try` block, you test the value of the flag to see if any errors occurred.

An easier way to accomplish this same logic involves using this form of the try statement:

```
try
    statement
    statement
    ...
on error
    statement
    statement
    ...
end try
```

If any of the statements between try and on error generates an error, the statements that follow the on error, up to the end try, get executed. If no errors are generated by the statements between the try and the on error, the statements between the on error and end try are skipped.

Taking this new format into account, you can write the example shown previously like this:

```
try
    set triangularNumber to text returned of result as integer
on error
    display dialog "You didn't enter an integer" with icon note
end try
```

If the set statement generates an error because the user did not key in a valid integer, the display dialog command gets executed to display an error. If a valid integer is entered and assigned to triangularNumber, the display dialog command gets skipped.

Even with an on error *clause, statements that follow the* try *block are executed whether or not an error occurs. If you want to terminate your program's execution after reporting an error to the user, you can always execute a* return *command.*

If any statement between the on error *and* end try *generates an error, the program is terminated in the normal manner, unless an outer* try *block encloses its execution.*

More on the on error Clause

The on error clause *catches* an error that occurs anywhere previously in the try block. As noted, this might result from several different statements. For example, consider the following code:

```
try
    display dialog "Enter a number" default answer ""
    set theNumber to text returned of result as integer
end try
```

Inside this try statement, two possible errors can occur (at least two that can occur under normal conditions — someone could always spill coffee on your keyboard, which might also cause weird things to happen). First, the user can click Cancel, which normally causes your program to terminate. Here, your program won't be terminated because the display dialog command is executed in a try block. The second error might occur in the set statement if an invalid integer is keyed in by the user.

It's often useful to determine the cause of a particular error inside a `try` statement. When the `on error` clause is executed, AppleScript makes two important pieces of information available to you: a description of the error and a number that uniquely identifies the error. You can get these two bits of information by using this form of the `on error` clause:

```
on error eMessage number eNumber
```

When you use this form, a string describing the cause of the error is stored in the variable *eMessage*. The number associated with that error is stored inside the variable *eNumber*.

In the following Try It Out, you test out this new form of the `try` statement so that you understand how errors can be caught and identified in your programs.

Try It Out   Experimenting with Errors

Following these steps, you can intentionally generate some errors and see their effects.

1. Type the following program into Script Editor:

```
-- The try statement with the on error clause

try
    display dialog "Enter a number" default answer "0"
    set theNumber to text returned of result as integer
on error errorMsg number errorNum
    display dialog ("Error number " & errorNum as string) & ": " & errorMsg
end try
```

2. Run the program and click Cancel. You should see the dialog shown in Figure 9-1.

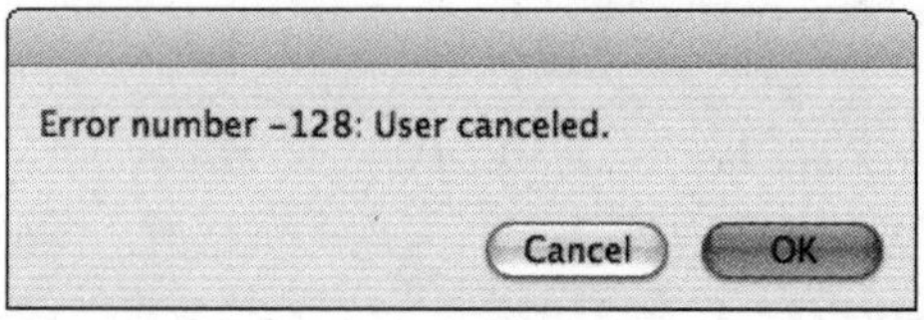

Error number –128: User canceled.

Cancel   OK

Figure 9-1

3. Rerun the program. This time, type abc into the dialog box and click OK. You should see the dialog shown in Figure 9-2.

Error number –1700: Can't make "abc" into a integer.

Cancel   OK

Figure 9-2

4. Rerun the program. This time, type 100 into the dialog box and click OK. You don't get a dialog this time because no error was generated.

How It Works

The `try` statement consists of two statements followed by an `on error` clause:

```
try
    display dialog "Enter a number" default answer ""
    set theNumber to text returned of result as integer
on error errorMsg number errorNum
    display dialog ("Error number " & errorNum as string) & ": " & errorMsg
end try
```

If an error occurs while your program is executing the first `display dialog` or the following `set` statement, the statements in the `on error` clause are executed. Before that occurs, the error message is stored in the variable `errorMsg`, and the error number is stored in the variable `errorNum`. Then the second `display dialog` command is executed to display the error number and the error message.

The first time the program was run, you clicked Cancel. This caused an error to be generated in the program. This, in turn, caused the `set` statement that followed to be skipped and the `display dialog` command in the `on error` clause to be executed. As you can see from the output shown in Figure 9-1, the string `"User canceled."` was assigned to the variable `errorMsg`, and the number –128 (yes, it's a negative number!) was assigned to the variable `errorNum`.

The second time the program was run, you entered the characters abc. This is not a valid integer, so when an attempt was made to coerce the text returned to an integer, an error was generated. This time, the string `"Can't make "abc" into a integer."` got stored in the variable `errorMsg`, and the error number stored in `errorNum` was –1700.

The final time the program was run, a valid integer was entered. Because no error was generated, the `display dialog` that is part of the `on error` clause was not executed.

Each error has a unique number associated with it, so you can take advantage of this in your error-handling code. In the following Try It Out, you modify the program from the preceding Try It Out to test for the particular cause of your error.

Try It Out   Identifying Errors by Number

In the following steps, you acknowledge if the user clicks Cancel. If the user enters an invalid number, you tell him that a bad number was entered and urge him to try again.

1. Type the following program into Script Editor:

```
set eCancel to -128
set eBadNumber to -1700

try
    display dialog "Enter a number" default answer "0"
    set theNumber to text returned of result as integer
on error errorMsg number errorNum
    if errorNum is eCancel then
        display dialog "Sorry you don't want to continue!" buttons {"OK"} default ¬
            button 1
```

```
      else if errorNum is eBadNumber then
          display dialog "You entered a bad number, try running the program again!" ¬
              buttons {"OK"} with icon stop
      else
          display dialog "Error: " & errorMsg
      end if
  end try
```

2. Run the program. Click Cancel. You should get the dialog box in Figure 9-3.

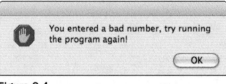

Sorry you don't want to continue!

OK

Figure 9-3

3. Rerun the program. Enter abc and click OK. You should get the dialog box shown in Figure 9-4.

You entered a bad number, try running the program again!

OK

Figure 9-4

How It Works

The program sets two variables, eCancel and eBadNumber, to –128 and –1700, respectively, when the program begins execution. This is just to make the program more readable. For example, when a subsequent test against eCancel is made, you understand clearly what error you're testing for, rather than explicitly testing against the number –128. An alternative is to add a comment when you create the text, like so:

```
if errorNum is -128 then    -- Cancel button clicked?
    ...
```

After assigning values to the two variables, the program enters a try block. This time, if an error occurs inside the try block, an if statement that is part of the on error clause is executed to identify the cause of the error:

```
if errorNum is eCancel then
    display dialog "Sorry you don't want to continue!" buttons {"OK"} default
        button 1
else if errorNum is eBadNumber then
    display dialog "You entered a bad number, try running the program again!"
        buttons {"OK"} with icon stop
```

```
    else
        display dialog "Error: " & errorMsg
    end if
```

If the user clicks Cancel, you put up a dialog expressing your regrets (see Figure 9-3). At that point, to honor the user's request, you can execute a `return` command to terminate the script. Another option is to ask users if they're sure they want to cancel. This is a good strategy if you're running a script where canceling could have some serious consequences (see Exercise 1 at the end of this chapter).

If the user enters an invalid integer (based on the fact that the error number is equal to –1700), you put up a dialog to that effect (see Figure 9-4). Although not shown here, you could have the user re-enter the number at this point (see Exercise 2 at the end of this chapter).

If `errorNum` doesn't match either of the two error numbers `eCancel` or `eBadNumber`, some other unforeseen error must have occurred. This situation is handled by the `else` clause in the `if` statement. In this case, a dialog is presented using just the system-supplied error message. Using this fall-through alternative is good programming practice because you can't always be sure that you have identified all possible errors.

Catching a Specific Error by Number

You have the option to catch a specific error by number with the `on error` clause. You do this according to the following general format:

```
on error number number
```

Here `number` is a literal number and not a variable. The following code snippet asks for an integer to be entered and just checks for the Cancel button getting clicked:

```
set eCancel to -128

try
    display dialog "Enter a number" default answer "0"
    set theNumber to text returned of result as integer
on error number eCancel
    display dialog "Sorry you don't want to continue" buttons {"OK"} default button 1
    return
end try
```

The `display dialog` command is executed to display a message and exit only if the user clicks Cancel, which is error number –128. You can also get the error message string if you want to display it, using this format for the `on error` clause:

```
on error eMessage number number
```

Here, as before, `eMessage` is a variable in which AppleScript stores the error message string.

This next code snippet asks for an integer and catches and displays a message if a bad number is entered:

```
set eBadNumber to -1700
display dialog "Enter a number" default answer "0"

try
    set theNumber to text returned of result as integer
on error eMessage number -eBadNumber
    display dialog eMessage buttons {"OK"} default button 1
end try
```

In this case, if the user clicks Cancel, the normal error handling (program termination) occurs because the `display dialog` command is not executed inside the `try` block. If the user enters an invalid integer, error number –1700 is generated. The `display dialog` command in the `on error` clause then executes to display the system's error message.

More on Error Numbers and Error-Handling Strategy

You can find the error number generated by a particular error by experimentation, as you did in the second Try It Out in this chapter. Here's a template you can use for finding an error number:

```
try
    -- insert a statement that causes an error here
on error number N
    display dialog N as string
end try
```

As an example, the error –1728 is generated if you try to access an invalid element from a list. You can determine this error number by looking in a table (such as the one shown shortly) or by making the invalid access in the previous template like so:

```
try
    item 1 of {}
on error number N
    display dialog N as string
end try
```

The following table summarizes some of the errors you may want to catch in your program.

A complete list of error codes (not all of which you can catch in your program) is stored on your system in the following file:

```
/System/Library/Frameworks/CoreServices.framework/Versions/A/Frameworks/
    CarbonCore.framework/Versions/A/Headers/MacErrors.h
```

Error Number	Meaning
–34	Disk <name> is full.
–37	Bad name for file.
–39	End of file error.
–43	File <name> wasn't found.

Error Number	Meaning
–44	Disk <name> is write protected.
–47	File <name> is busy.
–48	Duplicate file name.
–49	File <name> is already open.
–61	File not open with write permission.
–120	Folder <name> wasn't found.
–128	User canceled.
–1700	Can't make <data> into a <type>.
–1708	<reference> doesn't understand the <commandName> message.
–1712	Apple event timed out.
–1728	Can't get the specified item.
–1730	Container specified was an empty list.
–2701	Can't divide <number> by zero.
–2702	The result of a numeric operation was too large.
–2703	<reference> can't be launched because it is not an application.
–2704	<reference> isn't scriptable.
–2705	The application has a corrupted dictionary.
–2708	Attempt to create a value larger than the allowable size.
–2721	Can't perform operation on text longer than 32K bytes.
–2753	The variable <name> is not defined.
–30720	Invalid date and time <date string>. (*Note this code is not listed in the* `MacErrors.h` *file.*)

Don't substitute error-catching for good programming practice. For example, as you've just seen, error number –1728 is generated if you try to reference an invalid item from a list. This number is also generated for other similar types of errors: trying to get a property that doesn't exist from a record, trying to get an item by number from a record, or attempting an invalid reference in a string.

Given an index number called i and a list called L, you can rely on the fact that an invalid reference into a list generates error number –1728:

```
try
    set theItem to item i of L
on error number -1728
    -- handle bad index number
    ...
end if
```

Alternatively, you can check whether i is a valid item number in the list *before* you access the item like so:

```
if i > 0 and i ≤ count L then
    set theItem to item i of L
else
    -- handle bad index number
    ...
end if
```

Personally, I prefer the latter approach. The first is an example of *reactive* programming, whereas the second approach is an example of *proactive* programming. I think it's better to prevent an error from occurring rather than allowing it to occur and then handling it.

In general, you want to try to protect your programs from abnormal termination. That doesn't mean you need to handle every possible error that can occur. Often, letting the system handle the error is just fine. However, if you are in the middle of your program's execution, and files and/or documents are open, you probably want to catch as many errors as is practical so that you can exit *cleanly*. A clean exit means closing any open files or documents and alerting the user that the program is exiting. Of course, you also have the option of continuing execution of the program, if that makes sense.

The error Command

You can use the AppleScript error command to explicitly generate an error yourself. You can use a built-in error message or one of your own creation. You can also assign error numbers in your programs.

The most general form of the error command is as follows:

```
error eMessage number eNumber partial result eList from eFrom to eTo
```

Here the error message string stored in *eMessage* is displayed to the user. The error number is indicated by *eNumber*. The remaining parameters are rarely used by programmers, but are typically passed along to AppleScript for further error processing.

Unless the error command is executed inside a try block, the program's execution is terminated after the error command is executed and the dialog is acknowledged.

All the error command's parameters are optional. If you just write the following:

```
error
```

AppleScript puts up a dialog saying that "An error has occurred." If you specify a message, as in

```
error "I couldn't open your database file!"
```

then the specified message is displayed to the user. If you omit the message, but just supply a number, as in

```
error 1001
```

a dialog is displayed with just the error number (which is not very helpful). Apple has reserved all integer numbers for possible error codes except the numbers 1,000 through 9,999 inclusive. This means that you can assign you own error codes for errors that occur in your program. This is often done inside a handler to indicate to the caller of the handler that an error occurred. If the caller chooses to call the handler inside a try block, the error can be caught and tested, and appropriate action can be taken.

The same five parameters shown for the error *command can also be specified for the* on error *clause in the* try *block (although I didn't show you that previously). As you'll see, these parameters are usually used to record the values and then passed to the system to handle by executing an* error *command.*

Many times when you want an integer value from the user, you follow this procedure: You display a prompt, you get the answer that is keyed in, you convert the answer to an integer, and then you check to make sure the conversion succeeded. Perhaps you recognize the Cancel key in your handler, or you let the system handle it for you.

In the following Try It Out, you write a handler called getInteger that does all the aforementioned work for you. The prompt displayed to the user is given as an argument to the getInteger handler. The value returned is the integer as keyed in by the user.

Try It Out   Catching Errors in Your Handlers

In the following steps, you use the error command to send back an indication that the user clicked Cancel because you don't necessarily want the handler to make assumptions on what to do in such situations.

1. Type the following program into Script Editor:

```
-- handler to get an integer from the user

global eCancel
global eBadNumber

set eCancel to -128
set eBadNumber to -1700

on getInteger(promptString)
    -- let the system handle Cancel here

    display dialog promptString default answer "0"

    try
        set theNumber to text returned of result as integer
    on error errorMsg number errorNum partial result eList from eFrom to eTo
        if errorNum is eBadNumber then
            return missing value
        else
            error errorMsg number errorNum partial result eList from eFrom to eTo
        end if
    end try

    return theNumber
end getInteger
```

```
set numEntered to getInteger("Enter your number")

display dialog "You entered " & numEntered as string buttons {"OK"} default
button 1
```

2. Run the program. When prompted for an integer, type `100` and click OK. You should get the dialog shown in Figure 9-5.

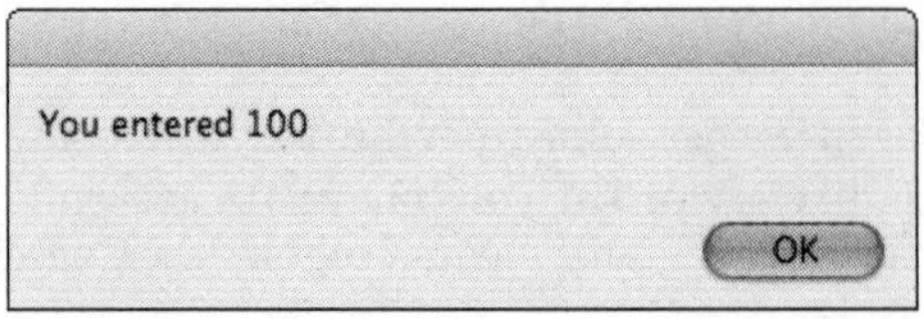

> You entered 100
>
> OK

Figure 9-5

3. Rerun the program. When prompted for an integer, type `abc`. You should get the dialog shown in Figure 9-6.

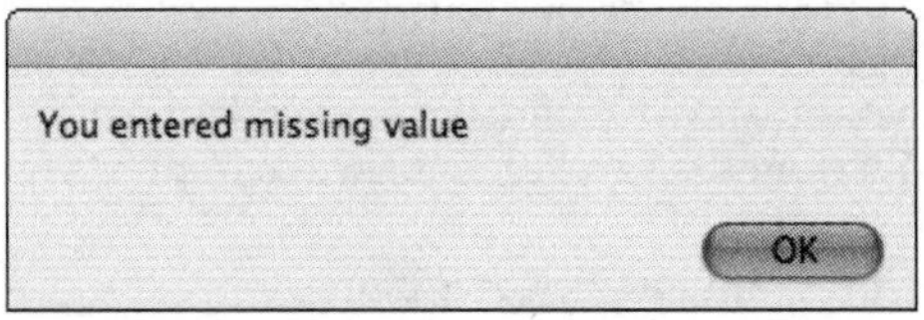

> You entered missing value
>
> OK

Figure 9-6

4. Rerun the program. When prompted for an integer, click Cancel. The program stops executing with no dialog displayed.

How It Works

The program starts by declaring two global variables, `eCancel` and `eBadNumber`, and assigning to them the corresponding error codes:

```
global eCancel
global eBadNumber

set eCancel to -128
set eBadNumber to -1700
```

The two variables are made global so that they can be accessed from inside the `getInteger` handler that follows in the program.

> *Even though the handler uses only* `eBadNumber`, `eCancel` *is defined for later use.*

The handler then executes a `display dialog` command outside a try block, using the prompt string supplied as the argument to the handler:

```
display dialog promptString default answer "0"
```

If the user clicks Cancel, the program is terminated. This was an arbitrary design decision for the handler. You could have placed the `display dialog` command inside the `try` block. In that case, it would be caught and handled inside the `on error` clause. (Can you predict its effect?)

After the dialog has been displayed and dismissed, the `getInteger` handler executes a `try` statement:

```
try
    set theNumber to text returned of result as integer
on error errorMsg number errorNum partial result eList from eFrom to eTo
    if errorNum is eBadNumber then
        return missing value
    else
        error errorMsg number errorNum partial result eList from eFrom to eTo
    end if
end try
```

If the user types a bad number, `missing value` is returned from the handler. Any other error causes the handler to pass the error along to the system for handling. This is done by executing the `error` command with the same five parameters from the `on error` clause.

If no error occurs, the `try` block finishes and the `return` command is executed to return the keyed-in integer back to the caller:

```
return theNumber
```

The program tests the `getInteger` handler with a sample prompt string and displays the result that is returned:

```
set numEntered to getInteger("Enter your number")

display dialog "You entered " & numEntered as string buttons {"OK"} default
button 1
```

You don't have to terminate execution of the program if the user clicks Cancel. But how can you prevent that from happening without modifying the code in the `getInteger` handler? The solution is to place the call to the `getInteger` handler inside its own `try` block, like this:

```
try
    set numEntered to getInteger("Enter your number")
on error eCancel
    display dialog "Sorry you canceled." buttons {"Me too!"} default button 1
    return
end try
```

Now if the user clicks Cancel, the program doesn't immediately terminate from inside the `getInteger` handler. Instead, it is caught by this `try` block and a dialog is displayed to the user. Then the program executes a `return` command to stop its execution. Obviously, you could take an alternative action at this point, such as closing any open files.

You can make the `getInteger` handler even more robust. For example, you can give the user another try if an invalid number is entered. You can also extend the handler to take a range of acceptable values. These are left as exercises for you at the end of the chapter.

In the following Try It Out, you take the file copy program that you developed for Exercise 8 at the end of Chapter 7 and modify it to handle errors intelligently. However, you don't want to overdo the error handling. As noted earlier, sometimes it's okay to let the system take care of things for you.

Try It Out   Error-Proofing Your Code

This program shows different forms of the `error` command.

1.   Type the following program into Script Editor:

```
-- A simple copy program for text files

set eCancel to -128
set eEof to -39

-- get the file to be copied

set fromFile to choose file with prompt "Select the file to be copied:"

try
    set fromFileID to open for access fromFile
on error eMsg
    error "I coulnd't open the file " & fromFile & return & "(" & eMsg & ")"
end

-- now get the destination file name

try
    set toFile to choose file name with prompt "Select a name for the copy"
on error number eCancel
    close access fromFileID
    error "You canceled!"
end try

try
    set toFileID to open for access toFile with write permission
    set eof toFileID to 0 -- truncate if it exists

    set theData to read fromFileID as string
    write theData as string to toFileID
on error eMsg number eNum partial result eList from eFrom to eTo
    if eNum is not eEof then
        close access fromFileID
        close access toFileID
        error eMsg number eNum partial result eList from eFrom to eTo
    end if
end try

-- close the files

close access fromFileID
close access toFileID
```

2. Run the program. Try to generate different errors and see the result on the program's execution. For example, pick a file in a directory you can't write to (try the root directory if you're not running as the administrator). Click Cancel when prompted for the file name for the copy. Try copying an empty file (that is, a file with no data in it).

How It Works

First, you take a look at this program and see where things can potentially go wrong. Then you see the error-handling strategy for each situation.

The program begins by assigning two error numbers to variables for later use and then prompts for the file to be copied:

```
set fromFile to choose file with prompt "Select the file to be copied:"
```

This command normally generates an error only if the user cancels the dialog. In that case, you can let the system handle this condition, which causes your program to terminate. You don't need to worry about cleaning up anything because you haven't done anything yet! Of course, you can handle the Cancel key if you want to do something other than terminate the program.

After getting the name of the file to be copied, the program opens the file for reading inside a `try` block:

```
try
    set fromFileID to open for access fromFile
on error eMsg
    error "I coulnd't open the file " & fromFile & return & "(" & eMsg & ")"
end
```

Why did you use a `try` block this time? You use it because if the open fails, you may get a cryptic message from the system. In the case of a file for which you don't have read permission, the error dialog simply states that a `Network file permission error` occurred. That's not very helpful, if not cryptic. You want to catch the error and display a more meaningful message together with the name of the file that can't be opened.

After successfully opening the file to be copied, you prompt the user to choose a file name for the resulting copy:

```
try
    set toFile to choose file name with prompt "Select a name for the copy"
on error number -128
    close access fromFileID
    error "You canceled!"
end try
```

One nice thing about the `choose file name` command is that it won't let you pick an existing file that you don't have permission to overwrite; it also won't let you specify a file name inside a directory that you can't write into. So those won't cause errors in your program. However, the user can simply click Cancel in the `choose file name` dialog, which would terminate your program. To prevent that from happening, you execute the `choose file name` command inside a `try` block and catch the error that occurs if the user clicks Cancel. If that happens, you close the file you opened earlier and use the `error` command to display a message conveying that the Cancel has been acknowledged.

After the output file name has been selected, the program proceeds with opening the file with write permission, reading the data from the original file, and writing it out to the copy. This is all done inside a single try block like so:

```
try
    set toFileID to open for access toFile with write permission
    set eof toFileID to 0 -- truncate if it exists

    set theData to read fromFileID
    write theData to toFileID
on error eMsg number eNum partial result eList from eFrom to eTo
    if eNum is not eEof then
        close access fromFileID
        close access toFileID
        error eMsg number eNum partial result eList from eFrom to eTo
    end if
end try
```

If the file to be copied is empty, you get an error if you try to read from it. That fact was noted in Chapter 7. The error number is –39, which is an end-of-file error. The program checks for this case inside the on error clause because you don't want to give an error message if an empty file is copied.

If an error other than end of file occurs, the program closes the open files and executes the error command, passing along all five parameters as specified on the on error line. This causes an error message to be displayed and the program to be terminated.

If no error is generated in the try block, the last two statements in the program are executed to close the open files:

```
close access fromFileID
close access toFileID
```

It's worth mentioning here that you can use the Finder's duplicate command to create a copy of a file, a folder, or even a disk! You learn how to do that in Chapter 10.

Summary

This program gave you information that enables you to intelligently anticipate and handle errors in your programs. You learned the following:

❑ You can use the on error clause in a try block to catch errors that would otherwise cause your program to terminate.

❑ You can use the error command to display a system error message or your own custom message before your program is terminated.

❑ You can catch the error number generated by a particular error using the on error command and then insert code in your program to handle that particular error.

Handling errors intelligently and cleaning up before your program terminates is part of good programming discipline. It's always a good strategy to run your program and intentionally try to create errors to see what can go wrong. If you're writing a script that others may use, it's particularly important that you *bullet-proof* your programs so that they terminate as gracefully as possible when an error occurs. I show you many more examples of error handling throughout the rest of this book.

In the next chapter, you learn how to talk to applications. Arguably, this is the single most important thing you need to learn to become an effective AppleScript programmer. Before proceeding, however, try the exercises that follow to test your understanding of the material covered in this chapter. You can find the solutions to these exercises in Appendix A.

Exercises

1. Using the program from the Try It Out labeled "Identifying Errors By Number" earlier in the chapter, modify the logic so that the user verifies that she really wants to Cancel.

2. After completing Exercise 1, give the user as many chances as needed to correctly type an integer value.

3. Modify the getInteger handler developed in this chapter to accept two additional arguments that specify the minimum and maximum allowable values for the user to enter. So the statement

```
set monthNumber to getInteger ("Enter a month number (1-12): ", 1, 12)
```

   calls the getInteger handler to prompt the user to enter a number between 1 and 12. The handler checks the value entered against the specified range, giving a message if the number falls outside the range.

   If the minimum value or maximum value is specified as a missing value, no minimum or maximum bound is desired. So the statement

```
set monthNumber to getInteger ("Enter a positive number: ", 0, missing value)
```

   can be used to allow any positive integer to be entered.

4. Instead of having the getInteger handler return missing value if a bad integer number is entered by the user, extend the answer from Exercise 3 to allow for an additional argument that specifies the maximum number of tries you give to the user before giving up.

5. Write a program that determines the error number generated when you divide by zero (no peeking at the table!).

Working with Applications

One of the key uses of AppleScript is for automating tasks. These can be simple tasks such as renaming the files in a folder or more sophisticated tasks such as extracting images from the Internet and creating a slide show from them. In both cases, AppleScript can be used to automate the task. This is particularly valuable when the task requires that you type the same sequence of commands over and over again.

When you can communicate with an application using a scripting language like AppleScript, the application is called *scriptable*. Unfortunately, not all applications that run on the Mac are scriptable. Some applications are more scriptable than others, meaning that some applications (such as the Finder) provide a rich assortment of commands that enable you to automate just about anything you could if you were sitting at the keyboard and typing commands.

This chapter teaches you how to work with other applications. AppleScript's `tell` command provides the mechanism that enables you to talk to another application in order to ask it to do something for you. Because the Finder is an application found on all Mac systems and because it is very scriptable, the focus of this chapter is talking to the Finder. The principles that underlie working with the Finder can be applied to working with other applications as well.

Talking to Other Applications: The tell Statement

The `tell` statement is perhaps the single most important command in your repertoire of AppleScript commands. It enables you to direct commands to a *target*, which in the simplest situation might be one of your variables. In more typical situations, the target is another application.

In the following Try It Out, you ask the Finder to open a new Finder window for you. You set that window to show the contents of your `Documents` folder.

Try It Out   Using the tell Statement

In the following program, you use the `tell` statement.

1. Type the following program into Script Editor:

```
tell application "Finder"
    make new Finder window to (path to documents folder)
end tell
```

2. Run the program. You get a new Finder window showing the contents of your `Documents` folder. These may be similar to what is shown in Figure 10-1.

Figure 10-1

Your window will differ based on the contents of your `Documents` *folder and the Finder's View settings.*

How It Works

The general format of the compound `tell` statement is as follows:

```
tell target
    statement
    statement
    ...
end tell
```

The *statements* that appear inside the compound `tell` statement (or as it's often referred to, the `tell` *block*) are ordinary AppleScript statements. The difference is the way they are interpreted. In the case of *telling* an application to do something, the statements are interpreted using the application's *vocabulary*. As you may surmise, this vocabulary consists of the classes and commands stored in the application's dictionary.

> *Notice that the terms from the application's dictionary are highlighted in blue when you compile your program in Script Editor. That's an indication that these terms are now interpreted in a special way.*

When you execute a command inside a `tell` block, AppleScript sends the command to the targeted application first. The application either handles it or tells AppleScript it can't handle it. In the latter case, AppleScript tries to handle the command itself. It does this using its built-in classes and commands.

> *Recall that we are considering the Standard Additions here as part of AppleScript's built-in classes and commands.*

If AppleScript doesn't know how to handle the command, you get an error.

> *If you have prior experience with object-oriented programming, it may help if you can think of a command executed in a `tell` block as a message sent to an object (the target). The target can be an AppleScript object, including another application.*

As noted, most often the *target* in a `tell` statement is an application object. In that case, the `tell` statement looks like this:

```
tell application "appname"
     statement
     statement
     ...
end tell
```

AppleScript tries to locate the specified application called *appname*, and launches it if it's not already running. You have to specify the application by the name of the file (but you don't need the `.app` extension) used to store the application. For example, `"Adobe Photoshop 7.0"`, `"AOL Instant Messenger (SM)"`, and `"QuickTime Player"` are the actual file names of the applications on my system. These are the names I would use for *appname*.

> *When typing a `tell` statement, you can abbreviate the word `application` as `app`. After your program is compiled, `app` gets expanded into the word `application`. This saves you a little typing.*

If AppleScript can't find the application you specify, it puts up a dialog and asks you to locate the application on the disk. After you identify the application, AppleScript inserts the correct name for you on the `tell` statement line.

Because the statement

```
make new Finder window to (path to documents folder)
```

appears inside a `tell` block, the `make` command is sent to the target of the `tell` — which is the Finder — to handle. The `new` parameter is followed by an object that you want to create. The program asks the Finder to make a new Finder window. The term `Finder window` is the name of a class defined in the Finder's dictionary. The `to` parameter specifies what you want to view in that new Finder window. In this example, you set it to view your `Documents` folder.

Note that if you tried to execute the previous `make` command outside a `tell` block, AppleScript is the target and would, therefore, try to handle the command itself. Because AppleScript doesn't know how to make a Finder Window, you would get an error.

You can also open a Finder window to view a folder using the Finder's `open` command. The following program does the same thing as the previous Try It Out program:

```
tell application "Finder"
    open (path to documents folder)
end tell
```

When you make a new object in the Finder with the `make` command, the command returns a reference to the newly created object. As you see in the following Try It Out, that reference can be used to subsequently identify the object in future operations.

Try It Out   References to Objects and More on the tell Statement

This program creates a new Finder window, sets the window to view the `Documents` folder, pauses the program for five seconds, and then closes the window using the `close` command.

1.   Type the following program into Script Editor:

```
-- Illustrate the tell statement - Part 2

tell application "Finder"
    set newWin to make new Finder window
    set target of newWin to (path to documents folder)
    delay 5
    close newWin
end tell
```

2.   Run the program. You see a new Finder window open on your screen. The window then changes to show the contents of your `Documents` folder. After five seconds, the window closes.

How It Works

The program starts by asking the Finder to make a new Finder window. The reference to the window returned by the `make` command is then stored in the variable `newWin`. In the previous program, you used the `to` parameter of the Finder's `make` command to set the window to your `Documents` folder. In this example, you create the Finder window first and then set it to view a particular folder.

After a window has been created, you need to set its `target` property to view a particular disk or folder. But how do you do that? You find out by looking at the Finder's dictionary. If you look at the description of the `Finder window` class in that dictionary, you discover that it has a `target` property. This is shown in Figure 10-2.

The description for the target property of a Finder window says that it takes a reference, which is a *container*. You learn about containers shortly. A folder is a container. The program sets the `target` property to this folder.

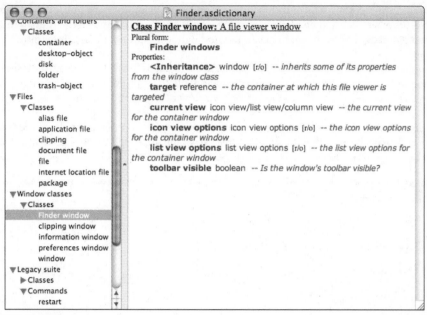

Figure 10-2

As previously noted, you can also use the open command to view a particular folder in the Finder. However, this command doesn't return a reference to the window that it opens. This creates a problem for you. How do you close the open window without having a reference to it? The answer involves understanding that the Finder orders it windows. The most recently accessed window is window 1, the next most recently accessed window is window 2, and so on. With this in mind, the previous program could have been written as follows:

```
-- Illustrate the tell statement - Part 2

tell application "Finder"
    open (path to documents folder)
    delay 5
    close Finder window 1
end tell
```

A potential drawback here is that if you open a new Finder window while this program is executing its five-second delay, the window you open is the one that gets closed (that will become Finder window 1) and not the one you opened in your script. To avoid this problem, you can ask the Window for a reference to the first Finder window before you execute the delay:

```
tell application "Finder"
    open (path to documents folder)
    set winRef to Finder window 1
    delay 5
    close winRef
end tell
```

Now `winRef` still references the window you opened, even if another one gets opened during the delay. Of course, there's a chance that a Finder window could be opened between the time of the `open` and the next statement that obtains the reference to the first window, but that possibility is small.

Many applications that you talk to from AppleScript — such as browsers, word processors, and spread-sheet programs — maintain windows and/or documents that you reference by number. Often, the term `window 1` or `document 1` refers to the current window of the application that you want to address.

The program shown in the next Try It Out changes the `position` property of your Finder window inside a repeat loop. The net effect is that the window *slides* from the upper-left corner diagonally down and to the right portion on your screen.

Try It Out   Sliding Windows

In this program, you work with sliding windows.

1. Type the following program into Script Editor:

```
-- Sliding windows

tell application "Finder"
    set newWin to make new Finder window

    repeat with i from 1 to 200
        set position of newWin to ({i * 4, i * 4} as point)
    end repeat

    close newWin
end tell
```

2. Run the program. You get a Finder window that marches from the upper-left corner of your screen diagonally down and to the right.

How It Works

Your screen is viewed as a two-dimensional grid of coordinates with (0,0) in the *upper-left corner*. If your screen is running at a resolution of 1280 × 854, for example, the coordinates of the corners of the screen look like the ones shown in Figure 10-3.

When you position a window on your screen, the top-left corner of the window is positioned at the specified location. Actually, the origin of a Finder window is below the top portion of the window that includes the toolbar.

The repeat loop from the program is shown here:

```
repeat with i from 1 to 200
    set position of newWin to ({i * 4, i * 4} as point)
end repeat
```

The `position` property of a `Finder window` (which is inherited from the `window` class) is set to a `point`. A `point` is a built-in AppleScript class that is simply a list of two numbers.

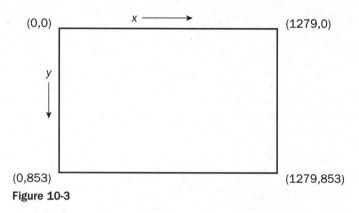

Figure 10-3

You can supply just a list of two numbers to the Finder when it expects a point, *and the program coerces the list into a* point *so that that Finder gets the class it expects according to the documentation of the* position *property in its dictionary.*

The loop runs 200 times. Each time through the loop, the Finder window's upper-left corner is set to the coordinate (i × 4, i × 4). Therefore, the window is first placed at (4, 4), next at (8, 8), and so on. The last location of the window is at (800, 800). The decision to move it by four points (or *pixels*) at a time on the screen is arbitrary. The smaller the increment, the smoother the window moves on the screen (and the longer it takes to run).

Many applications supply their objects to you as a list. In order to reference a particular object from that list, you reference items in a manner consistent with the techniques described in Chapter 6. For example, you saw in a previous example how to reference the current Finder window as Finder window 1. You could also reference it as first Finder window or as 1st Finder window. Similarly, the last Finder window can be identified as last Finder window or Finder window −1.

The following Try It Out shows how you can stack your open Finder windows.

Try It Out   Stacking Windows

In the following program, you stack the open Finder windows.

1. Type the following program into Script Editor:

```
-- Stack the Finder's windows

set topX to 0
set topY to 100

tell application "Finder"
    set n to count of every Finder window
    if (n > 0) then
        repeat with i from n to 1 by -1
            set position of Finder window i to {topX, topY} as point
```

```
            set topX to topX + 30
            set topY to topY + 30
        end repeat
    end if
end tell
```

2.   Open a few windows in the Finder, scatter them around your screen, and then run the program. Your open windows are stacked in the upper-left corner of your screen in a similar way to those shown in Figure 10-4.

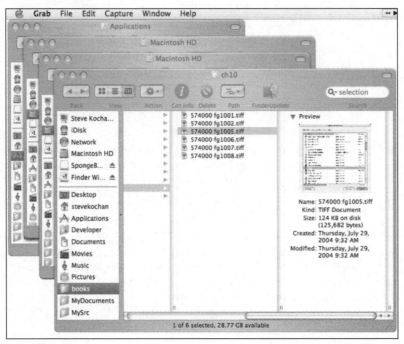

Figure 10-4

3.   Scatter your Finder windows around the screen again. Then click one of the Finder windows and choose Finder ⇨ Hide Finder from the Finder's menu. Your Finder windows should now be hidden from the screen.

4.   Rerun the program. Notice that your Finder windows do not appear.

5.   Click the Finder's icon in the Dock. Notice that your Finder windows appear, but they have not been stacked.

6.   Hide your Finder windows again, as you did in Step 3.

7.   Add the following line after the line `tell application "Finder"` in your program:

```
activate
```

8.   Rerun your program. You see your Finder windows displayed and stacked as shown in Figure 10-4.

How It Works

The Finder's windows are numbered. You can get a list of all Finder windows by asking the Finder for `every Finder window`. The program counts the number of windows in the list and, if it's greater than zero, proceeds to position each window on the screen. The repeat loop starts with the last window in the list, counting down to 1. This is done so that the most current Finder window (window 1) is stacked last on the screen (that is, is put on top). Each window is positioned on the screen with its top-left corner at coordinate (`topX`, `topY`). These two variables are initially set to 10 and 100, respectively, and are incremented by 30 each time through the repeat loop.

When you hide the Finder application, your Finder windows are hidden from view. In that case, asking for every Finder window returns an empty list; as a result, the windows don't get moved. When you send an `activate` command to an application, the application is brought to the front, causing its windows to be displayed.

The One-Liner tell Statement

You've seen how you can write an `if` statement on a single line. If you want to tell an object to do just one thing, you can also write your `tell` statement on a single line. The general format of this single-line `tell` statement is as follows:

```
tell target to command
```

Here's an example asking the Safari browser to set the URL of its first window to `http://www.yahoo.com`:

```
tell application "Safari" to set URL of document of first window to ¬
        "http://www.yahoo.com"
```

More on Targets

You can see from the next two Try It Out examples that wherever you can use `of` to access a property of an object, you can often use a `tell` statement to specify the same target.

Try It Out   Understanding Targets–Part 1

This program shows how you can use the `tell` statement to get an item from a list.

1. Type the following program into Script Editor:

```
-- More on targets

set myList to {100, 200, 300}

tell myList
    get first item
end tell
```

2. Click the Result tab and run the program. You get this output:

```
100
```

How It Works

Generally, when you write this:

```
get propertyOrElement of object
```

you can also write it like this:

```
tell object
    get propertyOrElement
end tell
```

Of course, the use of `get` is optional in both cases.

If you specify a property name for `propertyOrElement`, you should put the word `its` in front of the property name. In some cases, this is not required; but in other instances, you get an error if you don't use `its`. That's because AppleScript tries to resolve the name at compile time; if the name is not in the AppleScript dictionary or defined as a property or variable, you get an error. This doesn't apply when the object is an application; in that case, the application's dictionary is consulted first.

The program asks for the first item of the target of the `tell`, which is the list `myList`. This is equivalent to writing the following:

```
first item of myList
```

Direct Objects

When you write an AppleScript command, you often immediately follow it by an object that you want the command to act on. For example, you write `get` followed by the object you want to get, or `count` followed by the object you want to count. These objects that follow the command are known as *direct objects*. If the direct object does not completely identify an object (or, in some cases, is omitted), AppleScript tries to complete the specification by working its way outward from any nested `tell` blocks.

| Try It Out | Understanding Targets–Part 2 |

In the following program, you modify the sliding windows program you wrote earlier in this chapter to show how a `tell` statement can be directed to a Finder window. Then you can compare this version of the program with the previous program.

1. Type the following program into Script Editor:

```
-- Sliding windows -- version 2

tell application "Finder"
    set newWin to make new Finder window

    tell newWin
        repeat with i from 1 to 200
            set position to ({i * 4, i * 4} as point)
        end repeat
```

```
            close
        end tell
    end tell
```

2. Run the program. You see a Finder window open up and slide diagonally down your screen as it did before.

How It Works

The target of the innermost `tell` statement is a Finder window from the Finder application. When you set the position of this object, you write this statement inside the `tell` block:

```
set position to ({i * 4, i * 4} as point)
```

Because you don't specify a complete target here (you just write `position` and not `position of object`), AppleScript uses `newWin` as the target. Note that this statement is executed within an outer `tell` statement, so this is all being done within the context of the Finder application. If you structure your program like this, it doesn't work:

```
-- Sliding windows -- version 2

tell application "Finder"
    set newWin to make new Finder window
end tell

tell newWin
    repeat with i from 1 to 200
        set position to ({i * 4, i * 4} as point)
    end repeat

    close
end tell
```

The reason this does not work is because AppleScript does not look up the term `position` in the context of the Finder, and the net result is that you set (and repeatedly reset) an AppleScript variable called `position` to the specified point each time through the repeat.

When you compile the program, you see that the color of `position` is green, indicating that it is treated like an ordinary variable and not a special term.

Note that the `close` command at the end of the `tell` block also does not specify a target. In this case, AppleScript sends the command to the current target, which is the Finder window `newWin` from the Finder application. The result is that `newWin` gets closed.

Using my, me, and its inside tell Blocks

When trying to call a handler or access a property that's defined outside a `tell` block, you do something special.

You learn all about properties in Chapter 12.

In the next Try It Out, you see what happens when you try to reference a handler from inside a `tell` block.

Try It Out   Calling Handlers from within tell Blocks

In this program, you call a handler from inside a `tell` block.

1. Type the following program into Script Editor:

```
-- accessing Handlers from tell blocks

on displayMsg()
    display dialog "It worked!"
end displayMsg

tell application "Finder"
    displayMsg()
end tell
```

2. Run the program. You get the following error message from AppleScript: `Finder got an error: Can't continue displayMsg`.

3. Modify the handler call inside the `tell` block so that the `tell` block now reads as follows:

```
tell application "Finder"
    my displayMsg()
end tell
```

4. Rerun the program. You get a dialog containing the message `It worked!`

How It Works

When you call a handler from inside a `tell` statement, AppleScript sends the command to the target of the `tell`. In this example, that target is the Finder. The Finder doesn't know about `displayMsg`, so an error is generated.

The use of the special variable `my` tells AppleScript that you want to use the current script as the target, so the command is not sent to the Finder for execution.

Note that the `tell` block serves no useful purpose here other than to illustrate how to call a handler from inside the `tell` block. Incidentally, you can't define the `displayMsg` handler inside the `tell` block; handlers cannot be defined inside a `tell` block.

You can also call a handler from inside a `tell` block by following the handler call with `of me` instead of preceding it with `my`. Therefore, the call

```
my displayMsg()
```

can also be written as

```
displayMsg() of me
```

In the next couple of Try It Out examples, you see a few ways to access a property or variable.

Accessing Properties or Variables from within tell Blocks–Part 1

In addition to other properties, the Finder application (like most applications) has a version property, whose value is the application's version as a string. This is illustrated in the following program.

1. Type the following program into Script Editor:

```
-- accessing Properties and Variables  from tell blocks

tell application "Finder"
    get version
end tell
```

2. Click the Result tab and run the program. You see the following output in the Result pane:

```
"10.3.2"
```

3. Modify the get name statement inside the tell block so that the tell block reads as follows:

```
tell application "Finder"
    get its version
end tell
```

4. Rerun the program. You see the following displayed in the Result pane:

```
"10.3.2"
```

5. Modify the get name statement inside the tell block so that the tell block now reads as follows:

```
tell application "Finder"
    get my version
end tell
```

6. Rerun the program. The following is displayed in the Result pane:

```
"1.9.3"
```

How It Works

By default, AppleScript consults the target of the tell block first to interpret commands and words. In the first case, version is recognized by the Finder and, therefore, it is handled directly by that application. The value returned is the version property of the application or "10.3.2".

When you precede a term with its (or follow it with of it), AppleScript explicitly targets the default case. So, in the program, when you write

```
get its version
```

the Finder application returns its version, as it did when you wrote

```
get version
```

Sometimes the use of its is needed when a name is defined in an application's dictionary as both a class name and as the name of a property or element. In the Finder's dictionary, for example, disk, folder, container, and file are class names and also elements of other Finder objects. So if you write the following code sequence, you get the class name folder as the result written to the Result pane:

```
set fileName to (path to documents folder)

tell application "Finder"
    tell folder fileName
        get folder
    end tell
end tell
```

If you modify the get command by inserting the word its in front of the term folder, you get the folder element that contains your Documents folder:

```
set fileName to (path to documents folder)

tell application "Finder"
    tell folder fileName
        get its folder
    end tell
end tell
```

On my system, this gives the following result:

```
folder "steve" of folder "Users" of startup disk of application "Finder"
```

You'll understand how to interpret this output later in this chapter when you learn more about the Finder's containers.

When you preface the word version (which could be a property or a variable) with my, the current target (the Finder) is bypassed, and the word is handled directly by the current script. In the program example, the value of version is shown as "1.9.3", which is the version of AppleScript I was using when I ran the program.

Technically speaking, even though the current target does not evaluate the word, AppleScript still consults the target's dictionary, even when my is used. The word gets classified according to its definition in that dictionary, and this can sometimes lead to an unexpected error. That discussion is beyond the scope of this text.

Try It Out   Accessing Properties or Variables–Part 2

If a variable or property name cannot be resolved by the target of a tell block, the current script is given a chance to resolve it, even if the name is not preceded by my. This is shown in the next program example.

1.   Type the following program into Script Editor:

```
-- Accessing properties and variables from tell blocks - Part 2

set progName to "Using my with variables"

tell application "Finder"
    get progName
end tell
```

2. Click the Result tab and run the program. You get the following output displayed in the Result pane:

```
"Using my with variables"
```

How It Works

Because `progName` is not in the Finder's dictionary, it's given to the current script for resolution. In this case, the use of `my` (or `of me`) is not necessary. However, in general, it's always safer to use one of these terms to unambiguously identify a variable or property just in case the application defines a term you think it doesn't. Also, if a newer version of the application has the term in its dictionary, that could cause a running application to stop working.

Tell Me Some More

Just to give you more exposure to the `tell` statement, here are some additional examples of asking applications to do something. You don't have to understand how these examples work. Just read through to get a feel for what's going on. Of course, if curiosity gets the better of you, you can key in these programs, run them, and try to extend their functionality. Examining the dictionary for each application is another good way to learn more about what's going on.

❑ **Open a web page in a new window in Safari.** The following code shows how you can ask the Safari browser to open a new window with the URL http://macscripter.net:

```
-- Open a web page

tell application "Safari"
    activate
    make new document
    set URL of document of first window to "http://macscripter.net"
end tell
```

❑ **Open a web page in the current window of Safari, or make a new window if no window is open.**

```
-- Open a web page

tell application "Safari"
    activate
    if (not exists first window) then
        make new document
    end if

    set URL of document of first window to "http://macscripter.net"
end tell
```

❑ **Download a file from the Internet.** The next example shows how to use the URL Access Scripting addition to download a file (in this case, a web page). An `upload` command is also provided for uploading files.

```
-- Download a file

tell application "URL Access Scripting"
    download "http://www.kochan-wood.com/index,cfm" to file ¬
        ((path to desktop folder as string) & "myPage.html")
end tell
```

❑ **Play a song in iTunes.** The next example shows how to ask iTunes to play a song called "How Come" that you have in your Library:

```
-- Play a song

tell application "iTunes"
    play track "How Come" of first library playlist
end tell
```

❑ **Get the name of every running process on your system.** The System Events application lets you get information about the processes running on your system. It also handles folder actions. The following shows how to get a list containing the name of every active process on your system:

```
-- List all processes

tell application "System Events"
    get name of every process
end tell
```

❑ **Send an e-mail with Mail.** Here's a more involved example showing how to send a new e-mail message from the `Mail` application. Note the nested `tell` statements in this example. To send an e-mail, you create a new `outgoing message`. Then you ask that message to make a new `to recipient` object:

```
-- Send an email message

tell application "Mail"
    set newMsg to make new outgoing message
    tell newMsg to make new to recipient

    set sender of newMsg to "me@mac.com"
    set subject of newMsg to "AppleScript test!"
    set content of newMsg to "Testing out sending an email from AppleScript!"
    set address of first to recipient of newMsg to "steve@kochan-wood.com"

    send newMsg
end tell
```

You may remember that in the chapter on lists and records you learned about making multiple assignments with a single `set` command. This is often done when assigning or retrieving properties. For example, in the previous example, the three statements

```
set sender of newMsg to "me@mac.com"
set subject of newMsg to "AppleScript test!"
set content of newMsg to "Testing out sending an email from AppleScript!"
```

can be equivalently written like this:

```
set {sender, subject, content} of newMsg to {me@mac.com, "AppleScript test!", ¬
    "Testing out sending an email from AppleScript!"}
```

More on Working with the Finder

I noted at the start of this chapter that the Finder is a good starting point to learn how to work with applications in AppleScript. You'll want to use Finder to delete and rename files and to do other things that are not handled directly by AppleScript's built-in file commands.

Looking at the Finder's Dictionary in Greater Detail

Applications that you communicate with from AppleScript define their own classes and commands. The best way to learn how to use these is by looking at other AppleScript examples (see Appendix C, "Resources") and by examining the application's dictionary. Unfortunately, the dictionary is sometimes inaccurate or incomplete and doesn't tell you how the classes and commands work together. Nevertheless, it is sometimes the only information you have available, so it's well worth your time to become proficient at navigating these dictionaries.

You saw a portion of the Finder's dictionary in Figure 10-2. It listed the properties of the `Finder window` class. In the following Try It Out, you back up a bit and take a closer look the Finder's dictionary.

Try It Out   Examining the Finder's Dictionary

In this example, you open the Finder's dictionary, see how it's structured, and learn about the *Standard Suite* and the Finder's classes, including containers, disks, folders, and files:

1.   In Script Editor, choose File ➪ Open Dictionary. Locate the Finder application in the window that is displayed (see Figure 10-5).

2.   Click Open.

3.   Highlight Standard Suite in the left pane (see Figure 10-6). Click the disclosure triangle (▶) in front of Standard Suite and then click the disclosure triangle in front of Commands that is subsequently revealed. Take a look at some of the commands that are part of the Standard Suite. What parameter can you use to specify that a file you are duplicating is to replace a pre-existing file of the same name?

4.   In the left window pane, locate the line labeled ▶Containers and folders. Click the disclosure triangle; then click the disclosure triangle that appears on the line labeled ▶Classes. Finally, under the list of classes, click `disk`. Your window should look like Figure 10-7.

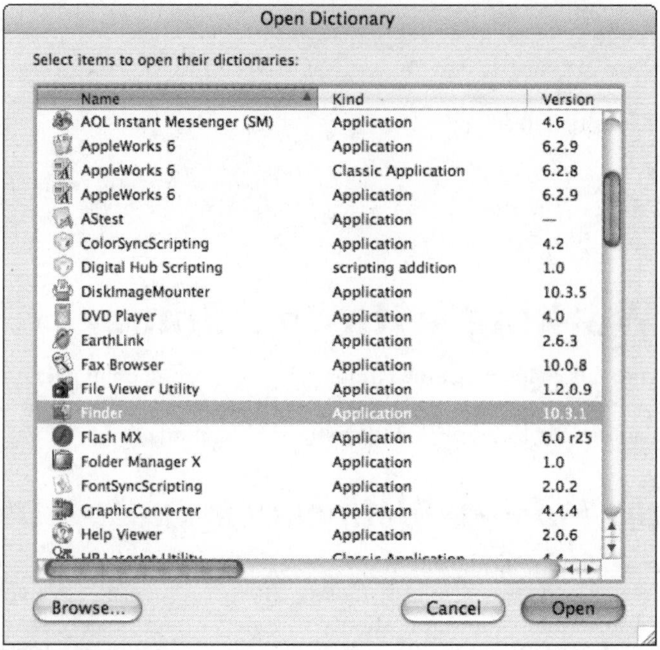

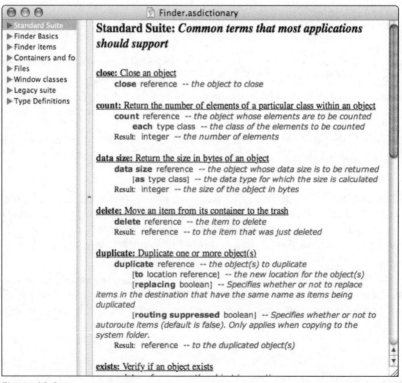

Figure 10-5

Figure 10-6

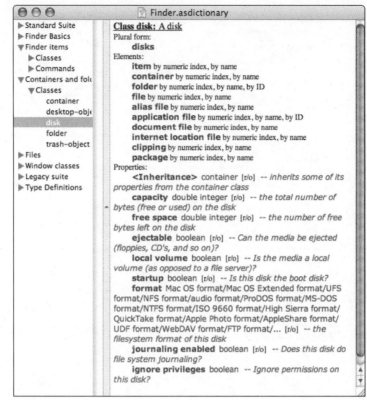

Figure 10-7

5. Notice that the sections are divided into the following: Plural form, Elements, and Properties. Look at some of the elements and properties of a disk.

6. Examine other items under the Classes of Containers and folders: `container`, `desktop-object`, `folder`, and `trash-object`. Look at the elements and properties of each class. Can a container contain another container? Can a file be an element of a desktop object? How do you think you can reference a file on the desktop? How do you think you can reference a file stored in a folder?

7. Look under Files in the dictionary. Notice the different types of file classes. Also notice that all the file classes — other than `file` itself — inherit from the file class.

8. Look up the `item` class, which is listed under Classes (under Finder items). Your window should resemble Figure 10-8. Look at each property. You see the key properties of files, folders, and disks; this is where you can get all sorts of useful information about a file, folder, or disk, such as its name, size, creation date, modification date, the container that holds it, and the disk it's stored on.

9. Spend some more time navigating the Finder's dictionary. Look at other commands and classes. Try to visualize how everything fits together.

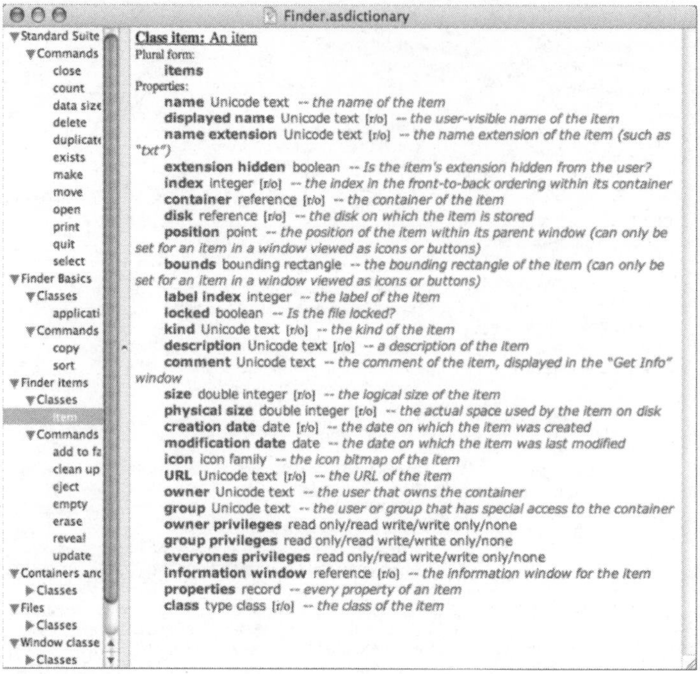

Figure 10-8

How It Works

The Standard Suite contains commands that an application is supposed to implement in order to provide a minimal level of scriptability. These include commands for closing, opening, deleting, counting, moving, duplicating, selecting, and printing objects, and for quitting the application. Some applications implement a subset of the Standard Suite. Another application may list a command or class in its dictionary, yet still not implement it or implement it only for specific types of objects. Sometimes (if you're lucky) the class or command is marked as not yet available (such as the Finder's sort command). Often, the best way to determine what's implemented and to what extent is by writing small test programs and by looking at other examples. An interactive script editing tool such as Smile (see Appendix C) is particularly handy for such purposes.

When you examine an application's classes, you see one of more of the following categories listed under each class name:

❑ **Plural form:** If a plural name for the class exists, this tells you how it's spelled. If a plural form exists, then elements from this class can be identified by the plural name. Examples: folders of startup disk, files of trash, disks, every disk. (Remember that the plural form can also be equivalently expressed as every followed by the singular form of the class.)

❑ **Inheritance:** This tells you if the class inherits some or all of its properties and elements from another class. If it does, look at that class to see what properties and/or elements it contains. For example, if you look at the file class, you see that it inherits from the item class. The file class inherits many properties listed under that class. They include name, size, creation date, kind, and properties.

❏ **Elements:** If this category is present, items can be accessed in one or more of the listed ways:

❏ *By numeric index:* A numerical index is 1, 2, 3, first, last, 1st, 2nd, and so on. Examples: `last disk`, `file 1 of 2nd folder of disk 3`

❏ *By name:* You can supply a name for the specified item. Example: `disk "Servers"`

❏ *By ID:* You can identify the item by its ID, if it has one.

❏ **Properties:** If this category is present, properties can be accessed using the `of` or apostrophe-s notation. A property marked as `[r/o]` is a read-only property. That means you can access its value, but you can't change it. Examples: `free space of startup disk`, `properties of disk 1`

The Finder's Classes

The following table contains a brief summary of many of the Finder's classes.

Class	Description
application	Contains information about the application itself, such as its `name` and `version`
Finder window	A window in the Finder for viewing files; inherits from the `window` class
item	This is a basic element; some of its properties are inherited by all the classes listed here. Its properties include `name`, `name extension`, `creation date`, `modification date`, and `size`.
container	An object that holds other objects, such as disks, folders, and files
file	A file object. Other file classes include `application file`, `document file`, and `internet location file`
alias file	A file alias on the disk, created with the Finder's `make alias` command. (*Not to be confused with AppleScript's alias class, which represents a reference to a file, and not an actual file stored on the disk*)
folder	Contains other objects like containers, folders, and files
disk	Contains other objects like containers, folders, and files. Includes disk-specific properties indicating its capacity, free space, format, whether it's a startup disk, and so on
desktop-object	Contains your desktop objects, which can include other containers, disks, folders, and files
trash-object	Contains objects that have been moved to the trash

The rest of this section teaches you how to work with most of these classes. As noted in the table, the item class properties are inherited by most of the other Finder classes. You will want to use these properties in many of your programming applications.

Containers

A `container` in the Finder is used to hold other Finder objects. It can exist as the property of an object and also as an element, which can be confusing. If you ask for the `container` of a Finder object, you find out what holds that object (you're referencing its property here). If you ask for `container 1` or `every container` of a Finder object, you get the containers that exists *inside* that Finder object. A container can refer to a folder, a disk, the trash, or the desktop. Think of it as a way to group all those objects together under a single name.

The next several Try It Outs give you some practice in working with containers.

Try It Out   Learning about Containers–Part 1

These steps show you more about containers:

1.   Type the following program into Script Editor:

```
path to documents folder
```

2.   Click the Result tab and run the program. You see output similar to the following:

```
alias "Macintosh HD:Users:steve:Documents:"
```

How It Works

You learned how the `path to` command gives you an alias to a particular folder on your system. Here it's used to give you an alias to your `Documents` folder. The alias lists three containers: the `Documents` folder, the folder `steve`, and the startup disk Macintosh HD.

Try It Out   Learning about Containers–Part 2

The Finder can work with path names and aliases. A path name must be identified to the Finder by its type, such as file, folder, disk, and so on. In the case of aliases, the alias can be used directly by the Finder.

1.   Type the following program into Script Editor.

```
-- Finder containers

set docPath to path to documents folder as string

tell application "Finder"
    get folder docPath
end tell
```

2.   Click the Result tab and run the program. You get a result similar to the following:

```
folder "Documents" of folder "steve" of folder "Users" of startup disk of
    application "Finder"
```

How It Works

The Finder references files, folders, and disks using a format that differs from what you've seen in previous AppleScript programs. Any time you ask the Finder for a file, a folder, or a disk, you get back a reference in this format. This reference fully identifies the file by its location on your system, using a series of container references. The full reference even includes the application that understands this format (`application "Finder"`). You learn more about this shortly.

Try It Out   **Learning about Containers–Part 3**

This program shows how you can ask the Finder to give you the container that holds another Finder object.

1. Type the following program into Script Editor:

```
-- Finder containers - Part 2

set docPath to path to documents folder as string

tell application "Finder"
    get container of folder docPath
end tell
```

2. Click the Result tab and run the program. You see a result similar to the following:

```
folder "steve" of folder "Users" of startup disk of application "Finder"
```

How It Works

A container holds another Finder object. In this case, the container that holds your Documents folder is another folder. In my case, it's stored in my home folder called steve, as you see from the output.

Try It Out   **Learning about Containers–Part 4**

This program continues the exploration by asking for the container of a container.

1. Type the following program into Script Editor:

```
-- Finder containers - Part 4

set docPath to path to documents folder as string

tell application "Finder"
    get container of container of folder docPath
end tell
```

2. Click the Result tab and run the program. You should see a result similar the following:

```
folder "Users" of startup disk of application "Finder"
```

How It Works

The container of the container of my Documents folder is the folder Users on my startup disk. If you haven't moved your Documents folder somewhere else, you get the same output.

What do you think you will get if you modify this program to ask for one more container, as in the following:

```
get container of container of container of folder docPath
```

You're correct if you predicted that a disk object is returned:

```
startup disk of application "Finder"
```

Learning about Containers–Part 5

This program shows how you can get AppleScript to convert a Finder reference to a path name.

1. Type the following program into Script Editor:

```
-- Finder containers - Part 5

set docPath to path to documents folder as string

tell application "Finder"
    get folder docPath as string
end tell
```

2. Click the Result tab and run the program. You get a result similar to the following:

```
"Macintosh HD:Users:steve:Documents:"
```

How It Works

You can convert a Finder's file container reference format to a traditional Mac path name by coercing it into a string. You can also convert it to a file alias (which is different from creating a Finder `file alias` object!) like this:

```
get folder docPath as alias
```

You can get a Finder reference converted to a POSIX path, but not directly. The following doesn't work:

```
get POSIX path of folder docPath    -- Sorry!!!
```

But because you can get a POSIX path from a string or alias, this will work:

```
get POSIX path of (folder docPath as string)    -- This is okay!!!
```

In the next section, a program is presented that demonstrates the difference between referencing the `container` property of a Finder object and referencing `container` elements of a Finder object. (Yes, it can be confusing!)

Common File Operations

The following table summarizes some common operations you may ask the Finder to do for you.

You are encouraged to write small programs to try each of these commands. You can base your programs on the examples shown in the table.

File Action	Finder Command	Example
Rename a file	`set name of fileRef to newName`	`set name of file "Macintosh HD:Users:greg:myPrefs" to "oldPrefs"`
Move a file	`move fileRef1 to fileRef2`	`move file ((path to home folder as string) & "chapter01.doc") to ((path to documents folder as string) & "Beginning AppleScript:"))`
Make a copy of a file	`duplicate fileRef1 to fileRef2` *-or-* `duplicate fileRef`	`duplicate file chapter1File to (path to documents folder)`
Open a file with its associated application	`open fileRef`	`open file "MacintoshHD:Users: steve:photo1.gif"`
See if a file exists	`fileRef exists`	`if file tempFile exists then delete file tempFile`
Delete a file	`delete fileRef` *-or-* `move fileRef to trash`	`delete file tempFile` *-or-* `move file tempFile to trash`
Show a file in the Finder	`reveal fileRef`	`reveal file tempFile`
Get a list of all the properties for a file	`properties of fileRef`	`properties of file tempFile`

Note that `fileRef` is a file reference. This can be an alias or file specification as you learned in Chapter 7, or it can be a Finder file reference. Also note that you cannot move a file to another file, only to another folder under the same name. The `duplicate` and `move` commands each take optional `replacing` parameters. If `replacing yes` is used, then a preexisting file is replaced by the operation.

Common Folder Operations

The following table shows common operations you can ask the Finder to perform on folders.

Once again, you are encouraged to try these commands on your own by writing small program examples.

Folder Action	Finder Command	Example
Create a new folder	`make new folder at fileRef with properties proprec`	`make new folder at (path to desktop folder) with properties {name: "NewImages"}`

Table continued on following page

Folder Action	Finder Command	Example
Move a folder	`move fileRef to path`	`move folder "ch1figs" to (path to documents folder as string)`
Rename a folder	`set name of fileRef to newName`	`set name of folder ((path to documents folder as string) & ASbook) to "Beginning AppleScript"`
Open a folder with its default application (normally, the Finder)	`open fileRef`	`open folder "Macintosh HD:Users:steve"`
Show a folder in the Finder	`reveal fileRef`	`reveal folder tempFolder`
See if a folder exists	`folder fileRef exists`	`set tempFolder to path to temporary items as string set imageFolder to "downloadedImages" if not (folder (tempFolder & imageFolder) exists) then make new folder at temp- Folder with properties {name: imageFolder}`
Copy all the files in a folder to another folder	`duplicate fileRef1 to path` -or- `duplicate fileRef1`	`duplicate folder tempImages to (path to documents folder as string)`
Get a list of files in a folder	`files of fileRef`	`files of (path to documents folder)`
Get a list of file *names* in a folder	`name of files of fileRef`	`name of files of (path to documents folder)`
Get a list of folders in a folder	`folders of fileRef`	`folders of home`
Get a list of folder *names* in a folder	`name of folders of fileRef`	`name of folders of startup disk`
Get a list of all files *and* folders in a folder	`items of fileRef`	`items of (path to documents folder)`
Get a list of all files and folders in a folder, including those contained in subfolders*	`entire contents of fileRef`	`entire contents of folder ((path to documents folder as string) & "Beginning AppleScript")`
Get a list of all the properties for a folder	`properties of fileRef`	`properties of home`

Note: Be careful when you use this command; it can take a considerable amount of time to run.

Note that many operations listed in this table are similar to the ones shown in the previous table, except here *fileRef* refers to a folder and not a file. In many cases, you can substitute other Finder references as well, such as `item`, `container`, or `disk`.

If *fileRef* is a string (and not an alias, file specification, or Finder file reference), you make the string into a file reference in the first table and a folder reference in the second table. For example, you can't write the following:

```
tell application "Finder" to get files of "Macintosh HD:Users"
```

because you're specifying a string here and not a folder reference. But you can write the following:

```
tell application "Finder" to get files of folder "Macintosh HD:Users"
```

The `path to` command you learned about in Chapter 7 returns an alias, so you can use its results directly with a Finder command. That means the following is valid:

```
tell application "Finder" to get files of (path to documents folder)
```

The Finder also recognizes these special file references (some of which were used in previous examples):

❑   `home`: Reference to your home folder

❑   `startup disk`: Reference to the disk your system boots from

❑   `trash`: Reference to the special folder containing your deleted Finder items

❑   `desktop`: Reference to the folder that contains your Desktop items

To get a list of the files in your home folder, you can write the following:

```
tell application "Finder" to get files of home
```

To get a list of the files and folders in the trash, you can write this:

```
tell application "Finder" to get items of trash
```

Finally, this gives you a list of folders on your desktop:

```
tell application "Finder" to get folders of desktop
```

The next program helps you understand the difference between accessing the `container` property of a Finder object and enumerating the `container` items of that object.

Try It Out   Getting a List of Containers

The following steps show you how to get a list of folders.

1. Type the following program into Script Editor:

```
-- Finder containers

tell application "Finder"
    get containers of startup disk
end tell
```

2. Click the Result tab and run the program. You get a result similar to the following (the output has been slightly reformatted for easier reading):

```
{folder "Applications" of startup disk of application "Finder",
 folder "Applications (Mac OS 9)" of startup disk of application "Finder",
 folder "Developer" of startup disk of application "Finder",
 folder "Documents" of startup disk of application "Finder",
 folder "hp LaserJet Folder" of startup disk of application "Finder",
 folder "Library" of startup disk of application "Finder",
 folder "System" of startup disk of application "Finder",
 folder "System Folder" of startup disk of application "Finder",
 folder "Temporary Items" of startup disk of application "Finder",
 folder "User Guides and Information" of startup disk of application "Finder",
 folder "Users" of startup disk of application "Finder"}
```

How It Works

When you write the statement

```
get containers of startup disk
```

you are asking the Finder to give you a list of all containers in the specified object, which in this case is the startup disk. Recall from the discussion about elements in Chapter 6 that you can also write the statement this way:

```
get every container of startup disk
```

Each item in the list returned by the Finder is in the Finder's file reference format, as you can see from the output.

In the next Try It Out, you see how to coerce the list of folders into aliases.

Try It Out   A List of Containers as Aliases

The next program shows how you can coerce a list of containers into a list of aliases.

1. Type the following program into Script Editor:

```
-- Finder containers

tell application "Finder"
```

```
        get folders of startup disk as alias list
    end tell
```

2. Click the Result tab and run the program. You get results similar to the following:

```
{alias "Macintosh HD:Applications:", alias "Macintosh HD:Applications (Mac OS 9):",
 alias "Macintosh HD:Developer:", alias "Macintosh HD:Documents:",
 alias "Macintosh HD:hp LaserJet Folder:", alias "Macintosh HD:Library:",
 alias "Macintosh HD:System:", alias "Macintosh HD:System Folder:",
 alias "Macintosh HD:Temporary Items:",
 alias "Macintosh HD:User Guides and Information:", alias "Macintosh HD:Users:"}
```

How It Works

You saw in the preceding Try It Out how to get a list of folders in the Finder's file reference format. In this Try It Out, you see how you can coerce the entire list into a list of aliases by appending as alias list to the end of the statement. This list of aliases has advantages as described in Chapter 7: If a file or folder gets moved or renamed, the alias will track it.

Just a word of caution here: If executing folders of startup disk *returns just one folder here (highly unlikely in this example), you get an AppleScript error. That's because the coercion to an alias list requires a list to convert. In the case of a single folder, the Finder returns a reference to that single folder, and not to a list containing one item. If you are going to use the* as alias list *coercion, first make sure you have a list to coerce.*

In the following Try It Out, you see how to add a prefix to each file in a folder.

Try It Out   Adding a Prefix to Each File in a Folder

This program prompts the user to choose a folder. Then the user is asked to enter a prefix. The program adds the prefix that is entered to the beginning of each file name in the selected folder.

1. Type the following program into Script Editor:

```
-- Add a prefix to all files in a selected folder

-- prompt for folder

set folderPath to (choose folder with prompt "Select a folder")

-- now get the prefix

display dialog "Please enter your prefix" default answer ""
set prefix to text returned of result

-- Rename each file in the folder

tell application "Finder"
    set fileList to files in folderPath -- list files in the folder
    repeat with aFile in fileList
        set newFileName to prefix & name of aFile
            try
                set name of aFile to newFileName
```

```
            on error
                display dialog "Can't rename " & name of aFile
            end try
        end repeat
    end tell
```

2. Create a folder on your disk and copy some files into it.

3. Run the program. When prompted, select the folder you created in the previous step.

4. When prompted for a prefix, key in the characters OLD.

5. When the program has completed execution, examine the contents of the folder you created. Each file in that folder should now begin with the characters OLD.

How It Works

You will recall that the choose folder command returns an alias for the selected folder (just as the choose file command returns an alias for a selected file). The Finder is used to list all the files in the selected folder, by issuing the following (implicit) get command:

```
files in folderPath
```

A file is an element of a folder (look at the Finder's dictionary to verify that), so you can ask the Finder to give you the files in a particular folder. When you ask the Finder to list the files in a folder, just the files are returned and not any subfolders (refer to the previous table to see how to get the folders listed as well).

The program executes a repeat loop to process each file in the selected folder. The new file name is created by prepending the chosen prefix to the front of each file name. This is accomplished with the following command:

```
set newFileName to prefix & name of aFile
```

You get just the base file name for the new file and eliminate all its containers. That's why the name property of the file is obtained. For example, if afile is set to the following:

```
document file "gdb.txt" of folder "Documents" of folder "steve" of
    folder "Users" of startup disk of application "Finder"
```

the name property of afile is "gdb.txt". Then, if prefix contains the string "OLD", newFileName is assigned the value "OLD" & "gdb.txt" or, simply, "OLDgdb.txt".

The program then asks the Finder to set the name property of the file to the new file name. That's done with this command:

```
set name of aFile to newFileName
```

Note that although aFile specifies a complete reference to the file, the new name is just the new base name of the file, excluding its containers. A full path cannot be supplied to specify the new file name.

The program does the renaming of each file inside a `try` block. If the renaming fails for some reason (the new file name is invalid, you don't have permission to rename the file, and so on), a dialog is displayed to that effect. The user can then click OK — in which case the program continues on to the next file in the list — or the user can click Cancel and the program terminates.

More on Understanding Finder File References

When the Finder returns a reference to an object such as a file, folder, or disk, its reference is based on the names of the components in the path to that file. If you change the name of any of those components, the reference to that item is no longer valid.

The following Try It Out helps you get a better understanding of file references.

Try It Out   Understanding File References

In the following steps, this program, which changes the name of a file and then tries to get its size, generates an error from AppleScript:

1. Make sure that the file `TextFile101.txt` still exists in your `Documents` folder. If it doesn't, create a file there under that name.

2. Type the following program into Script Editor:

```
tell application "Finder"
    set textFile to file ((path to documents folder as string) & "TextFile101.txt")
    set name of textFile to "TextFile102.txt"
    set fileSize to size of textFile
end tell
```

2. Run the program. You get the following AppleScript error (the actual message will differ slightly on your system): `Finder got an error: Can't get size of document file "TextFile102.txt" of folder "Documents" of folder "steve" of folder "Users" of startup disk.`

How It Works

When you ask the Finder to create a reference to your file `TextFile101.txt`, it creates a `file` object that looks like the following code (because you're dealing with a text file, the Finder actually creates a `document file` object):

```
document file "TextFile101.txt" of folder "Documents" of folder "steve" of folder
    "Users" of startup disk of application "Finder"
```

Your login name will appear where `"steve"` *is shown.*

The reference to the file that is stored inside the variable `textFile` maintains the names of the components of that file. So if you change the name of any of those components — which is what you did when you changed the file's name from `TextFile101.txt` to `TextFile102.txt` — the reference to the original file stored in `textFile` is no longer valid. That's why you get an error when you try to get the `size` property from that file.

You can use a couple of solutions. One is to get the size of the file before you change its name:

```
tell application "Finder"
    set textFile to file ((path to documents folder as string) & "TextFile101.txt")
    set fileSize to size of textFile
    set name of textFile to "TextFile102.txt"
end tell
```

Another solution is to work with an alias to the file that, as you recall from the discussions in Chapter 7, still tracks the file even if it's moved or renamed. This is what code using an alias might look like:

```
tell application "Finder"
    set textFile to ((path to documents folder as string) & "TextFile101.txt") ¬
        as alias
    set name of textFile to "TextFile102.txt"
    set fileSize to size of textFile
end tell
```

As noted earlier, the Finder is happy to work directly with aliases in addition to its own file reference format. That explains why this code works.

The next Try It Out shows how the Finder fully identifies a file reference.

Try It Out   Using Finder Filer References outside a tell Block

The following program assumes that you have the file TextFile101.txt still stored in your Documents folder. (If you renamed it in the last exercise to TextFile102.txt, change it back again!)

1.   Type the following program into Script Editor:

```
-- Accessing information outside of a tell block

tell application "Finder"
    set f to file ((path to documents folder as string) & "TextFile101.txt")
end tell

get size of f
```

2.   Click the Result tab and run the program. You get output similar to the following:

```
47.0
```

How It Works

When the Finder creates a reference to a file, it includes not only all the components of the file, but even the reference to the application itself. So if f gets set to the following by this program:

```
document file "TextFile101.txt" of folder "Documents" of folder "steve" of folder
        "Users" of startup disk of application "Finder"
```

and then you execute this statement:

```
get size of f
```

it's as if you typed this:

```
get size of document file "TextFile101.txt" of folder "Documents" of folder ¬
    "steve" of folder "Users" of startup disk of application "Finder"
```

As you can see, a `tell` block is not needed here because there's a full reference to the target, which is a file. In fact, based on the prior discussions about using `of` and `tell`, you could unfold this statement into the following code:

```
tell application "Finder"
    tell startup disk
        tell folder "Users"
            tell folder "steve"
                tell folder "Documents"
                    tell document file "TextFile101.txt"
                        get size
                    end tell
                end tell
            end tell
        end tell
    end tell
end tell
```

Or perhaps it's a little clearer when written like this:

```
tell application "Finder"
    get size of document file "TextFile101.txt" of folder "Documents" of folder ¬
        "steve" of folder "Users" of startup disk
end tell
```

Either code sequence works. Try them both and see!

Beware of the repeat-with Statement!

You have to be careful when you ask an application to enumerate items for you directly on the `repeat-with` statement line. The details are a little too complicated to explain in this text, so you just have to take my word for it. The problem arises when you write a code sequence like this:

```
tell application "Finder"
    repeat with aFile in files in (path to applications folder)
        -- some code to work with aFile
    end repeat
end tell
```

This code fragment looks harmless enough. You want to list all the files in your `applications` folder and then presumably do something with each file inside the loop. Yet, if you even write a seemingly harmless statement like this in the loop

```
set theName to name of aFile
```

you get this error from AppleScript: `Finder got an error: Can't get name of item 1 of every file of alias "Macintosh HD:Applications`. Again, the reason is not important, but it has to do with how the files get enumerated in the `repeat with` statement.

There are two easy solutions. One is to create the list before you enter the `repeat` loop, like so:

```
tell application "Finder"
    set fileList to files in (path to applications folder)

    repeat with aFile in fileList
        -- some code to work with aFile
    end repeat
end tell
```

Another easy solution is to explicitly use the `get` command with the `repeat` statement, like so:

```
tell application "Finder"
    repeat with aFile in (get files in (path to applications folder))
        -- some code to work with aFile
    end repeat
end tell
```

Here, unlike in the first example, the Finder returns the list of file references you need. In general, it's a good habit to use the `get` command with `repeat-with` loops so you avoid potential problems that can be difficult to track down.

AppleScript versus the Finder's File Class

As you learned in Chapter 7, AppleScript has a built-in file class. You used it to create a file specification when you were working with files. For example, here's how you learned to get the size of the file `TextFile101.txt` stored in your `Documents` folder:

```
set pathName to (path to documents folder as string) & "TextFile101.txt"
set fileInfo to info for file pathName
size of fileInfo
```

Using the term `file` inside a Finder `tell` block is not the same thing as using the term outside the block. That's because the Finder has its own definition for `file`. A Finder `file` object already contains all sorts of information about the file, including its name, size, and so on. You can readily see that by looking at the `file` class in the Finder's dictionary.

So, as you saw in the previous section, here's how you would ask the Finder to give you the size of your `TextFile101.txt` file:

```
set pathName to (path to documents folder as string) & "TextFile101.txt"
tell application "Finder"
    get size of file pathName
end tell
```

In the first case, `size` is a property of the record returned by the `info for` command for the specified file. In the second case, it's a property of a Finder file object. Make sure you understand this subtle but important difference.

Note that this works to give you the size of your `Documents` folder:

```
set pathName to path to documents folder as string
set fileInfo to info for file pathName
size of fileInfo
```

However, this does not work:

```
set pathName to path to documents folder as string
tell application "Finder"
    get size of file pathName    -- No! No! No!
end tell
```

It doesn't work because your `Documents` folder is a *folder* and not a *file*. And the Finder cares about the distinction. It has a `folder` class for working with folders. Given that information, this will work:

```
set pathName to path to documents folder as string
tell application "Finder"
    get size of folder pathName
end tell
```

If you don't know whether a path represents a file, a folder, or a disk, you can simply refer to it using the Finder's `item` class, like so:

```
set pathName to path to documents folder as string
tell application "Finder"
    get size of item pathName
end tell
```

Because the Finder accepts aliases and that's what `path to` produces, you can also get the size like this:

```
set pathName to path to documents folder
tell application "Finder"
    get size of pathName
end tell
```

Study these examples and try to understand their subtle yet critical differences. This understanding is paramount to working with files and folders in AppleScript and the Finder.

When you were reading through the explanation of the file renaming program, it may have dawned on you that you could have used the `list folder` command to enumerate the contents of the selected folder. In the example, the Finder was used instead. It's useful to consider the implications of using the `list folder` command.

Following is a modified `tell` block using the `list folder` approach. Statements that have been modified or added are highlighted in bold.

```
tell application "Finder"
    set fileList to list folder folderPath without invisibles
    repeat with aFile in fileList
        set newFileName to prefix & aFile
        try
            set name of file (folderPath as string) & aFile to newFileName
        on error
            display dialog "Can't rename " & aFile
        end try
    end repeat
end tell
```

When you ask the Finder to give you a list of files in a folder, the invisible files are not listed. However, AppleScript's built-in `list folder` command does just the opposite. That's why the `without invisibles` parameter is given to the `list folder` command. However, recall that the `list folder` command also lists subfolders, whereas the previous version of this program did not.

> *This version attempts to rename a folder, which causes an error. You can ignore the error, or you can add code to test whether the file is a folder and then skip the renaming step if it is.*

Because the `list folder` command returns a list of file name strings and not full paths, the new file name is calculated by simply prepending the prefix to the beginning of each file name. These file names returned by `list folder` are just strings. They're not Finder file objects. They don't have any file properties associated with them, so you can't directly get their names or their sizes, for example.

To rename a file, you identify the file by its full path name. You also must give the Finder a file object to be renamed and not a string. When you write the statement

```
set name of file (folderPath as string) & aFile to newFileName
```

you create a Finder file object, not an AppleScript file specification. As I previously explained, that's because your reference to the term `file` is done inside the `tell` block, meaning that the Finder gets first crack at its interpretation.

The change to the `display dialog` command from the previous version of the program should be self-explanatory.

Filters

You can ask an application to selectively *filter* the results it returns to you. A filter (potentially) reduces a list to a smaller list based on some criteria. This is generally a good thing because it makes the application do the work for you and often reduces the amount of data transferred from the application back to your program.

Try It Out   Using a Filter

Here's an example showing how you can ask the Finder to give you a list of files in your `Documents` folder that start with the letter *T*.

1. Type the following program into Script Editor:

```
tell application "Finder"
    get files of (path to documents folder) whose name begins with "T"
end tell
```

2. Click the Result tab and run the program. If you still have the file TextFile101.txt that you created in Chapter 7, you get output similar to the following, plus a list of any other files you have in your Documents folder that start with the letter T:

```
{document file "TextFile101.txt" of folder "Documents" of folder "steve" of folder
    "Users" of startup disk of application "Finder"}
```

How It Works

The list of files in your Documents folder is filtered *by the Finder* according to the following criteria:

```
whose name begins with "T"
```

Here name refers to the file's name property. The resulting list is returned by the Finder. Once again, the Finder is doing the filtering here, and not you.

Here are some more examples using filters. Notice the format in each case is the same: A list of items is followed by the word whose (or where) followed by a comparison. The comparison is usually a property that is tested using a comparison or containment operator, as described in earlier chapters:

❑ **Count the number of files in your home folder that end in .txt.**

```
tell application "Finder"
    count (files of home whose name ends with ".txt")
end tell
```

❑ **Find files in your Documents folder that have been modified within the last seven days.**

```
tell application "Finder"
    get files of (path to documents folder) whose modification date is ¬
        greater than ((current date) - 7 * days)
end tell
```

❑ **Locate a file in your Documents folder called "TextFile101.txt".**

```
tell application "Finder"
    get files of entire contents of (path to documents folder) whose name is ¬
        "TextFile101.txt"
end tell
```

❑ **Ask iTunes to give you a list of the names of all tracks that contain the word "Winter".**

```
tell application "iTunes"
    get name of tracks of first library playlist whose name contains "Winter"
end tell
```

❑   **Look up someone in Address Book and get her e-mail address.**

```
set firstName to "Julia"
set lastName to "Kochan"

tell application "Address Book"
    set matches to people whose first name is firstName and last name is lastName

    if (count matches)    0 then
        get value of first email of item 1 of matches
    else
        display dialog "I couldn't find " & firstName & " " & lastName
    end if
end tell
```

The preceding code looks up a person in Address Book given her first and last name. Note that you can join expressions together using the and and or operators. The logical negation not operator can also be used in a filter expression.

Because multiple matches can occur when performing a lookup in the Address Book, only the first match is used here. From that match, the first e-mail address is extracted (an entry can have multiple e-mail addresses). The value property of an Address Book e-mail object is the actual e-mail address. The label property, although not used here, tells you which kind of e-mail address it is (for example, home, work, and so on).

You can see how powerful these filter constructs are. Remember, the filtering is done by the application and not handled directly by AppleScript. Unfortunately, filtering is not supported by all applications and is not documented in the application's dictionary. The best way to find out if a filter works with a particular application is through experimentation.

More on Working with Applications

In this section, you learn additional details about working with applications. You start by examining a program in the next Try It Out that's a little more sophisticated than those you've encountered so far in this chapter.

| Try It Out | **Generating a List of Backup Files** |

This program shows how to use the Finder to create a list of files for backup that is then displayed as an HTML file in the Safari browser. The folder that is searched and the backup criteria used are hard-wired into the program. An exercise at the end of this chapter asks you to extend this program to increase its flexibility.

1.   Type the following program into Script Editor. Change the backupFolder variable to a folder on your system that contains some files you have modified within the last week.

```
(*
 Create an HTML file that shows the files from your
 Documents folder that have been modified within the last 7 days
*)
```

```
set modifiedDays to 7 * days

-- Change the following to a path to one of your folders
set backupFolder to (path to documents folder as string) & "books:AppleScript:"

set HTMLFile to (path to temporary items as string) & "backuplist.html"

-- open temporary file and write a header to it

set f to open for access file HTMLFile with write permission
set eof of f to 0  -- truncate the file if it already exists

-- write an HTNL header to the file

-- Note: The following lines were entered with \r inside each string. The following
-- shows how they appear after being compiled

write "<HTML>
<HEAD>
<TITLE>Document Files for Backup</TITLE>
</HEAD>
<BODY>
<H1>The Following Files are Ready for Backup</H1>" to f

-- get list of recently modified files

tell application "Finder"
    set fileList to files of entire contents of folder backupFolder whose ¬
        modification date is greater than ((current date) - modifiedDays)
end tell

-- write each file path to the HTML file as a string

if (count fileList) is 0 then
    write "No files to backup!" to f
else
    write "<UL>" to f

    repeat with aFile in fileList
        write "<LI>" & (aFile as string) & "</LI>" to f
    end repeat

    write "</UL>" to f
end if

write "</BODY></HTML>" to f
close access f

-- open the file in Safari

tell application "Safari" to open file HTMLFile
```

2.   Run the program. After a while, the Safari browser opens a window similar to the one depicted in Figure 10-9. Which files are actually listed depends on the files on your system and their modification times.

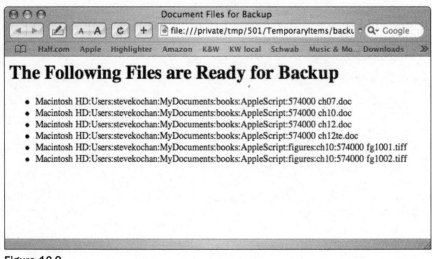

Figure 10-9

How It Works

This program demonstrates a combination of working with files directly in AppleScript and working with files in the Finder. A temporary file called `backuplist.html` is created, and an HTML header is written to the file. If you don't know HTML, don't worry about it. The lines that write the header to the file read like the following in the program listing:

```
write "<HTML>
<HEAD>
<TITLE>Document Files for Backup</TITLE>
</HEAD>
<BODY>
<H1>The Following Files are Ready for Backup</H1>" to f
```

These lines were keyed in like this:

```
write "<HTML>\r<HEAD>\r<TITLE>Document Files for
Backup</TITLE>\r</HEAD>\r<BODY>\r<H1>The
        Following Files are Ready for Backup</H1>" to f
```

Recall that the `\r` characters in a string signify a return character; Script Editor removes that character when you compile your script.

After writing the HTML header to the file, the program asks the Finder to give a list of files that have been modified within the last `modifedDays`. This is done with the following `tell` block:

```
tell application "Finder"
    set fileList to files of entire contents of folder backupFolder whose ¬
        modification date is greater than ((current date) - modifiedDays)
end tell
```

The list that is returned is stored in the variable `fileList`. The Finder is no longer needed because you now have a list of file references stored inside `fileList`, so the `tell` block is ended.

Depending on the depth of the folder you search, the Finder can take a long time to return the file list to you. If it takes more than a minute, you a timeout error. See the section later in this chapter about application timeouts.

The program checks to see if the file list is empty. If it is, a statement to that effect is written to the HTML file. If the list is not empty, an unnumbered list (which is a bullet list, by default) is started with the HTML code <UL>. Each file path is then written to the HTML file inside a `repeat` loop. Recall that converting a file reference to a string changes it from the Finder's container format to a normal Mac path name.

Note that each file reference is coerced by the `write` command into a string anyway (and thus to a Mac path name), even without the explicit coercion that's done in the program.

Each file name is listed as a bulleted item on the web page by prefacing the file name with the HTML code <LI> and following it with the code </LI>. After the repeat loop is finished, the list is closed off by writing the code </UL> to the HTML file.

Finally, the program writes the codes </BODY> and </HTML> to properly terminate the HTML code and then closes the file. The HTML file is then opened in Safari by sending it an `open` command:

```
tell application "Safari" to open file HTMLFile
```

The result is shown in Figure 10-9. You could have also asked the Finder to open the file using the default application associated with the file like this:

```
tell application "Finder" to open file HTMLFile
```

This will work as long as the Finder knows that `.html` files are to be opened by a browser.

You can also use the Standard Addition's `open location` command to open a web page in your default browser, given a URL. For example, this works to open Apple's home page:

```
open location "http://www.apple.com"
```

In the case of your program, a URL-equivalent for the file whose path is

```
Macintosh HD:private:tmp:501:TemporaryItems:backuplist.html
```

is the following:

```
file:///private/tmp/501/TemporaryItems/backuplist/html
```

This is the POSIX path to the file with the string `file://` added to the front of it.

Therefore, you could substitute the `open location` command in your program with the following command line to open the file in your default browser:

```
open location "file://" & POSIX path of HTMLFile
```

Try it to see how it works!

Obviously, if this were a true backup program, you would not be displaying your files for backup on a web page. Rather, you would take each file from the list and write it to a backup device, such as a removable Firewire drive.

Ignoring Application Responses

Normally, when you send a command to an application, AppleScript waits for a response. However, sometimes you don't need a response or you don't want to wait. For example, when you tell your e-mail application to send a message you've composed, or you ask your browser to open a window, you may not want to wait for the application to complete its task before continuing execution of your program.

You can tell AppleScript that you don't want it to wait for a reply or an error from a command sent to an application by enclosing such commands within an `ignoring application responses` block. The general format for such a block is as follows:

```
ignoring application responses
    statement
    statement
       ...
end ignoring
```

In the previous backup file list program, if you wrote this at the end of the program:

```
ignoring application responses
    tell application "Safari" to open HTMLFile
end ignoring
```

AppleScript would send the request to open the specified file to Safari, but it would not wait for a response. If additional statements followed in the program (none do here), they would be executed immediately.

In the following case, the dialog saying that you're done will probably appear before the HTML page gets displayed:

```
ignoring application responses
    tell application "Safari" to open HTMLFile
    display dialog "All done!"
end ignoring
```

This happens because AppleScript sends the command to Safari to open the file and then immediately proceeds to execute the display dialog command. Without the ignoring block, AppleScript waits for Safari to acknowledge completion of its `open` command.

You can resume the normal handling of application responses inside an `ignoring application responses` block by inserting an inner `consider application responses` block. This prove useful only if you are talking to different applications within the block and you want to temporarily resume normal handling of application responses.

Application Timeouts

As noted in the preceding section, AppleScript normally waits for a command sent to an application to complete before continuing execution. However, sometimes the application may hang, or it may end up waiting for access to a network or removable volume. Alternatively, you might ask it to perform a task that takes an inordinate amount of time, such as individually adding up the sizes of all files on your disk. You have at your disposal the capability to put a time limit on a command. AppleScript automatically sets the time limit for any individual command to one minute. If the command does not complete within that time, a timeout error occurs.

You can either decrease or increase this time limit. You want to set it to a very large value if you know that a command you are sending to an application may take a long time to execute.

The general format for the `with timeout` block statement is

```
with timeout of n seconds
    statement
    statement
    ...
end timeout
```

Each *statement* within this block that contains a command for another application is given up to *n* seconds to execute. If the command doesn't finish within that time, an error is generated. The error number is `-1712`, so you can catch it in your program if you want to handle it yourself.

It I noted for the backup program from an earlier section, the Finder may end up timing out if you ask it to search a folder containing many files. Here's how you can extend the Finder's search time so that it has five minutes to generate its list:

```
with timeout of 300 seconds
    tell application "Finder"
        set fileList to files of entire contents of folder backupFolder whose
            modification date is greater than ((current date) - modifiedDays)
    end tell
end timeout
```

Note that even if a command times out, the application that sent the command continues running. That is, AppleScript doesn't terminate the application that has timed out or in any way interrupts its processing of your request. However, AppleScript can timeout while waiting for the application to respond.

Applets and Droplets

You learned how to save an AppleScript program as an application in Chapter 3. Programs that are saved this way are called *applets* (although we use this term interchangeably with the term *application* here). They otherwise behave as normal applications: You can double-click them to launch them. You can also make them *Run Only* to prevent them from being opened and their code examined. If you save an application with the Run Only box checked, even *you* can no longer open the file and edit it in Script Editor. Therefore, you want to be sure to make a copy of your program before you save it as a Run Only application.

Stay Open Applications

If you check Script Editor's Stay Open option when you save your program as an application, the program does not quit when it has finished executing. Instead, it stays active or open. That's like launching the Finder. Even after you close the last Finder window, the application stays open, as you can tell just by looking at the Finder's icon in your Dock. (The little black triangle underneath the application's icon in the Dock tells you the application is active.) Keeping an application active can save time the next time you want to use it because it doesn't have to be reinitialized.

A Stay Open application can have an `idle` handler (described shortly). This handler is called automatically at specified intervals. The `reopen` handler is also useful in combination with Stay Open handlers. That too, is described in an upcoming section.

You quit a Stay Open applet by quitting it from the Dock, which you do by Control-clicking or click-holding its icon in the Dock and then selecting Quit from its popup menu. You can also quit an active applet by typing Command-Q or choosing Quit from the applet's menu.

The following sections describe four different handlers you can add to your applets. None take parameters, and you don't specify open and closed parentheses after their names either, as you do with normal handlers.

The run Handler

The `run` handler gets called when the applet is run. This happens if its icon has been double-clicked in the Finder, has been opened in the Finder, or has been run by another application. Specifying the applet as the target of a `tell` statement also causes its run handler to be executed. If your program has a `run` handler, it should not have any other statements that appear outside of any handler or script object (so-called *top-level* statements). AppleScript wants either one or the other. If there's a `run` handler, it gets called when the program starts. If there's no `run` handler, the top-level statements in the applet are executed.

The quit Handler

The `quit` handler is called after the last statement in an application has been executed. For a Stay Open application, it is called when the applet is asked to quit (see the previous discussion on how that's done). For a Stay Open application to terminate, you have to insert the following statement at the end of your `quit` handler:

```
continue quit
```

The reopen Handler

The `reopen` handler is called when an application that is already running gets activated by clicking its icon in the Dock or by double-clicking its name in the Finder.

The idle Handler

The idle handler gets called after the run handler finishes execution. Or, if there's no run handler, the idle handler gets called after the top-level statements finish execution. The idle handler is expected to return a value in seconds as a real number that represent the next time the handler is to be called. The default value is 30, which will be used if the handler returns 0. If the number is very small, the handler may get called too often, which can bog down your system's performance.

Obviously, the idle handler is only meaningful for Stay Open applications. It's useful when you want to write a script to do things on a periodic basic. For example, you can write an idle handler that periodically checks for a file to be updated, to inform you when new mail arrives, or to track a stock on a regular basis.

The following Try It Out demonstrates a simple applet handler.

Try It Out — Simple Applet Handlers

In this program, you see how applet handlers get called.

1. Type the following program into Script Editor:

```
-- Demonstrate various applet handlers

on run
    display dialog "Starting"
end run

on reopen
    display dialog "I've been reopened!"
end reopen

on idle
    display dialog "Idling every 15 seconds"
    return 15
end idle

on quit
    display dialog "Quitting!"
    continue quit
end quit
```

2. Choose File ➪ Save As.

3. When the dialog appears, select Application as the File Format, and check the Stay Open box. Make sure the Startup Screen and Run Only boxes are not checked.

4. Type Applet Handlers for the Save As name and click Save. Make sure you note the folder to which your application was written.

5. Quit Script Editor.

6. Locate Applet Handlers in the Finder and double-click it to start its execution. You get the dialog displayed in Figure 10-10.

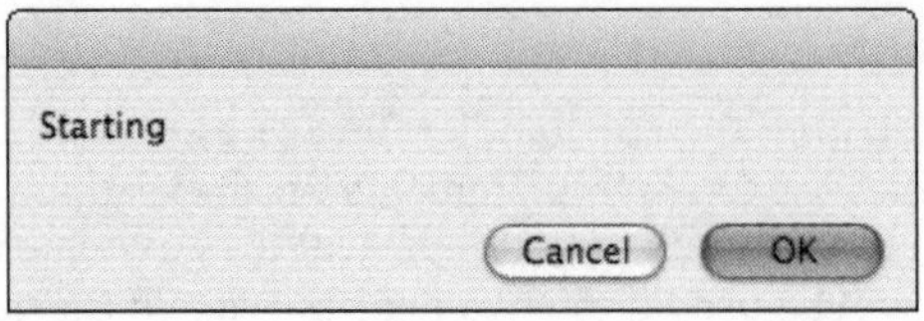

Starting

Cancel   OK

Figure 10-10

7. Click OK. You immediately get the dialog shown in Figure 10-11.

Idling every 15 seconds

Cancel   OK

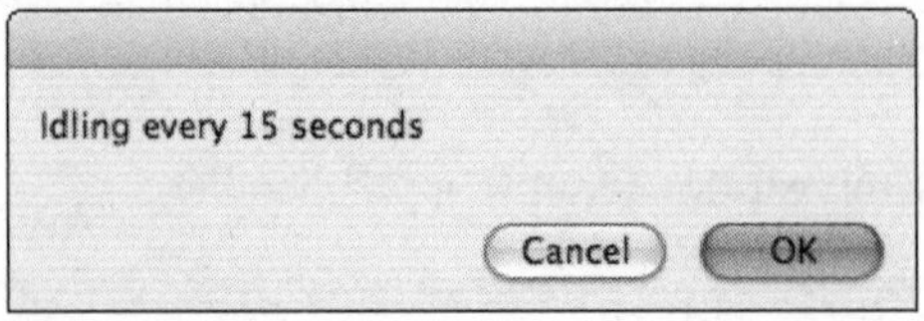

Figure 10-11

8. Click OK.

9. Wait about 15 seconds. After that time has elapsed, you again get the dialog shown in Figure 10-11.

10. Click OK in that dialog.

11. Locate the icon for the application in the Dock. Click the icon. You get the dialog shown in Figure 10-12.

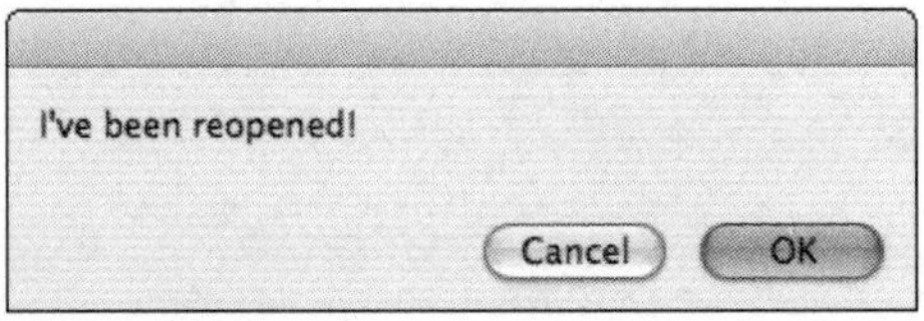

I've been reopened!

Cancel   OK

Figure 10-12

12. Click OK. You immediately get the dialog shown in Figure 10-11 again.

13. Click OK. On the menu bar, under Applet Handlers, select Applet Handlers Quit from the menu. You get the dialog shown in Figure 10-13.

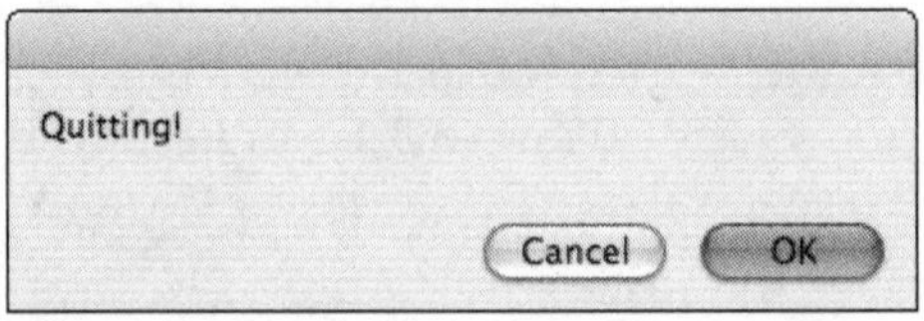

Quitting!

Cancel   OK

Figure 10-13

14. Click OK. Your applet quits and disappears from the Dock.

How It Works

The execution of this program is straightforward. Note once again that the `idle` handler gets called as soon as the `run` handler or the `reopen` handler finishes execution. Thereafter, it is called periodically based on the value it returns.

Droplets

A droplet is an AppleScript program that contains a special `open` handler. This handler gets called whenever you "drop" one or more files or folders onto the application's icon. The syntax of the `open` handler is as follows:

```
on open argName
    statement
    statement
    ...
end open
```

The files dropped on the applet get passed as the argument to the `open` handler as a list of file aliases. This list is stored in the variable *argName*. Even if a single folder is dropped, a list containing a single item is still passed to the `open` handler.

If you start an applet that contains an `open` handler by double-clicking its icon, the `open` handler doesn't get executed. Instead, the applet's `run` handler or top-level statements (whichever is present in the applet) is run. If you want, you can have the `run` handler prompt for files, for example, and then pass them along to the `open` handler. This is done by executing an `open` command, which calls your `open` handler. In this manner, you can write an applet that allows files to be dropped on it, or that starts in the normal way and then prompts for the files to be processed.

The next Try It Out provides a fitting way to end this chapter. It takes a folder of images (assume here that they're either GIF or JPEG files) dropped onto the applet's icon and makes a simple web page out of them. If the `run` handler is executed instead, the program prompts the user to select a folder containing the images and passes that along to the `open` handler.

Try It Out   Creating a Droplet

The following steps show you how to create a droplet.

1. Type the following program into Script Editor:

```
-- Droplet to make a web page from images in a folder

on open imageFolder
    -- make sure we have a single folder here

    set allIsWell to true

    if (count imageFolder)    1 then
        set allIsWell to false
    end if

    set imageFolder to item 1 of imageFolder
```

```
    set infoRec to get info for imageFolder
    if not folder of infoRec then
        set allIsWell to false
    end if

    if not allIsWell then
        display dialog "This droplet requires a  folder of images!" with icon stop ¬
                buttons {"OK"} default button 1
        return
    end if
     -- open the HTML file for writing

    set HTMLFile to (path to desktop folder as string) & "pics.html"
    set f to open for access HTMLFile with write permission
    set eof of f to 0

    -- write HTML header info to the file

    write "<HTML>
<HEAD>
<TITLE>Kids Pics</TITLE>
</HEAD>
<BODY>
<H1>Pictures of My Kids</H1>" to f

    -- process each image file in the folder

    repeat with imageFile in list folder imageFolder without invisibles
        set fullPath to (imageFolder as string) & imageFile
        set infoRec to get info for file fullPath

        if name extension of infoRec is not in {"JPG", "GIF"} then
            try
                display dialog "Can't process file " & (imageFile as string)
            on error -- if the user Cancels, clean up
                close access f
                tell application "Finder" to delete file HTMLFile
                return
            end try
        end if

        write "<img border=1 src=\"" & (POSIX path of fullPath) & "\"><p>" to f
    end repeat

    -- Close the HTML file

    write "</BODY>
</HTML>" to f

    close access f

    tell application "Safari" to open file HTMLFile
end open
```

```
-- Run handler if the applet is double-clicked

on run
    set theFolder to choose folder with prompt "Select a folder of images:"
    open {theFolder}
end run
```

2. Save the file as an application. Make sure Stay Open and Run Only are not checked.

3. Collect some image files and put them in a folder on your system. For this example, I created a folder that contained three JPEG images.

4. Drag the folder containing the images onto the icon for the applet you created. If all goes well, you get a web page in Safari that displays your images. On my system, I got a web page displayed, as shown in Figure 10-14.

Figure 10-14

5. Close the web page.

6. Double-click the application this time to run it. You get a dialog asking you to select a folder. Select the same folder you created in Step 3 and click Choose. You get the same web page displayed as you did in Step 4.

How It Works

When a folder of images is dropped onto the droplet, the on handler gets called. As noted, the handler gets passed a list that is stored in the variable imageFolder.

The program checks to make sure that just a single folder is dropped onto the droplet. If more than one item is dropped, or if that item is not a folder, the open handler displays a dialog and then returns. This causes the droplet to terminate.

Note that the code used to test for a folder by the program

```
set infoRec to get info for imageFolder
if not folder of infoRec then
    set allIsWell to false
end if
```

can be replaced by code that avoids the info for command and asks the Finder if the file is a folder. This is based on the fact that a kind property of a Finder's file reference is set to the string "Folder" if, in fact, the reference is to a folder. Here's the code to do that:

```
tell application "Finder"
    if kind of imageFolder is not "Folder" then
        set allIsWell to false
    end if
end tell
```

Getting back to the program, if a single folder is supplied, the program then opens a file to write HTML code into it. You saw this done with the backup program earlier in this chapter. The same approach is used here. After opening the file, some introductory HTML code is written to the file. Then the program proceeds to process each file in the folder. The program checks to make sure each file is a valid image type. This check is made by testing the extension of the file to see if it's either jpg or gif. Testing the file type property or the kind property are also options. However, in the former case, the property may not have a value. In the latter case, you can get JPEG image listed in some case and Adobe Photoshop JPEG image listed in others, for example.

If the file is not a JPEG or GIF file, a dialog is displayed. If the user cancels the dialog, an error is generated. If that happens, the HTML file is closed, the Finder is asked to delete the file, and the handler returns. This is a clean way to exit the program.

> *Sometimes JPEG files have the extension JPEG. You can add that extension to the program as an acceptable extension.*

As each image file is processed, a reference to the image is added to the HTML file with this statement:

```
write "<img border=1 src=\"" & (POSIX path of fullPath) & "\"><p>" to f
```

Recall that to include a double quote inside a string, you preface it with a backslash character. Also, the browser wants to see POSIX path names to files, not Mac paths. Here's what a line written to the HTML file might look like after this statement is executed:

```
<img border=1 src="/Users/steve/Desktop/images/kids1.jpg"><p>
```

After all the image files have been processed, the HTML file is closed and then opened in Safari. The program's execution is then complete.

When you run the application by double-clicking it, the droplet's `run` handler is called instead of the `open` handler. In the `run` handler, the user is prompted to choose a folder. The folder is then passed to the `open` handler as a list containing a single item as follows:

```
open {theFolder}
```

Processing continues from there in the manner just described.

Summary

In this chapter, you learned a lot about working with applications. You saw how to use the `tell` statement to target other objects. Most of the time, those objects are other applications. Often, one of those applications is the Finder.

In this chapter you also learned

- ❑ How to write a `tell` statement and understand targets
- ❑ How to work with Finder windows
- ❑ How to navigate the Finder's dictionary, and understand its classes and commands
- ❑ How to work with the Finder's containers
- ❑ How to interpret a Finder's file reference
- ❑ How to perform common operations on files and folders with the Finder
- ❑ How to distinguish Finder file objects from AppleScript file specifications
- ❑ How to write a filter
- ❑ How to ignore application responses and set timeouts on commands
- ❑ How to use the `run`, `reopen`, `idle`, and `quit` handlers when writing applets
- ❑ How to write a droplet

Chapter 11 continues this theme of working with applications. You learn how to use AppleScript to communicate with the programs that form part of the iLife package of applications: iPhoto, iTunes, iDVD, iMovie, and GarageBand. Before proceeding, however, try the exercises that follow to test your understanding of the material covered in this chapter. You can find the solutions to these exercises in Appendix A.

Exercises

1. Modify the program that slides the Finder window from the top-left corner down to the right so that it moves instead from the bottom-left corner up to the top right of the screen. Assume you're working with a screen size of 1280 × 854 pixels.

2. Type and run the following program, noting the output that appears in the Result pane:

```
tell application "Finder" to set fileRef to get home
fileRef
```

Based on the result, write the following AppleScript statements. Be sure to test them and verify that you get the correct result.

   a. Rewrite the file reference as nested `tell` blocks.

   b. Write an AppleScript statement to get the Mac path equivalent for `fileRef`.

   c. Write an AppleScript statement to get the POSIX path equivalent for `fileRef`.

   d. Write an AppleScript statement to coerce `fileRef` into an alias.

3. The following statement assigns the name of a text file in Linda's home folder to the variable `todoFile`.

```
set toDoFile to "Macintosh HD:Users:linda:ToDo.txt"
```

Given this assignment, write statements to do the following (as independent steps) in the Finder:

   a. Get the size of the file.

   b. Copy the file into your `Documents` folder.

   c. Rename the file to `ToDoOld.txt`.

   d. Delete the file.

   e. Create a new folder in your home directory called `ToDoFolder` and then move the file into the newly created folder.

   f. Count the number of files that start with `ToDo` in your home folder.

   g. Count the number of files that contain `ToDo` in their name in your home folder.

4. Write a program to use the Finder to create an Internet location file on your desktop with the URL set to `http://p2p.wrox.com`. Make sure your file works by double-clicking it in the Finder and ensuring that the specified page is opened in your browser. *Note:* This exercise requires some digging and experimentation because this wasn't covered in detail in this chapter. Good luck!

5. If you use the Address Book application, modify the example from this chapter to prompt for the person's first and last name. Then, if more than one match is found or more than one e-mail address exists, present the list of e-mails to the user and have him select a preferred e-mail address. *Note:* This is a difficult exercise. For each matching entry from the Address Book, you have to get every e-mail address and store it in a list.

6. Modify the backup program from this chapter to prompt for the number of days and allow the user to select the folder to be scanned for backup.

7. Turn the backup program developed in this chapter into a droplet so that it analyzes a single folder dropped onto its icon for files that are to be backed up. Make sure the program still runs correctly if it's launched from the Finder. That is, have it prompt for the folder as in the previous exercise. In either case, assume you are looking for files that have been modified within the last seven days.

8. Modify the droplet developed in this chapter so that the title of the web page (the text that appears between the HTML <TITLE> and </TITLE> codes) is the base name of the images folder. Use that name as the heading for the web page (the text that appears between the HTML <H1> and </H2> codes).

9. Modify the droplet developed in this chapter so that a list of folders and/or files can be dropped onto the droplet. Have the droplet create a web page from all the images in the folders (but not in any subfolders) and files.

10. Write a droplet called `File Me` that works as follows: The droplet maintains a list of records (in the example that follows, it's called `filingList`). Each record contains a file extension and a corresponding folder alias. Each file dropped on the droplet is filed (that is, moved) into its corresponding folder. The last record should have a file extension of `"*"` and a folder that indicates where any files not matching the previous extensions are to be filed.

Look over the following code:

```
set docs to (path to documents folder) as string

set filingList to { ¬
    {ext:"JPG", place:(docs  & "Images:") as alias}, ¬
    {ext:"GIF", place:(docs  & "Images:") as alias}, ¬
    {ext:"MP3", place:(docs  & "Music:") as alias}, ¬
    {ext:"MP4", place:(docs  & "Music:") as alias}, ¬
    {ext:"TXT", place:(docs  & "Text files:") as alias}, ¬
    {ext:"PDF", place:(docs  & "PDF:") as alias }, ¬
    {ext:"MOV", place:(docs  & "Movies:") as alias }, ¬
    {ext:"AVI", place:(docs  & "Movies:") as alias }, ¬
    {ext:"*",    place:(docs  & "Misc:") as alias } ¬
}
```

If a file called `ToDo.txt` is dropped on the droplet, it is filed in the folder `Text files` contained in your `Documents` folder. This is indicated by the `place` property for the matching `ext` property `"TXT"`. Similarly, if the file `Cover.jpg` is dragged onto the droplet, it is automatically be filed into the `Images` subfolder of your `Documents` folder. Any file whose extension does not match one in the list is filed in the place indicated by the last entry in the list or in the folder `Misc` in your `Documents` folder.

Your droplet should accept multiple files dropped on it. However, for this exercise, ignore any folders dropped on it.

11

Scripting iLife Applications

One of the key uses of AppleScript is to automate tasks. These may be simple tasks, like renaming the files in a folder, or more sophisticated tasks such as extracting images from the Internet and creating a slide show from them. In both cases, AppleScript can be used to automate the task for you. This is particularly valuable when you are required to type the same sequence of commands over and over again.

As of this writing, of the five applications that are part of iLife — iTunes, iPhoto, iMovie, iDVD, and GarageBand — only three of the five are scriptable. That is, only iTunes, iPhoto, and iDvd contain dictionaries that define classes and commands that you can use from an AppleScript program. All is not lost, however; through a process known as *GUI scripting* you can still get nonscriptable applications — such as iMovie and GarageBand — to do things for you from within an AppleScript program. GUI scripting is covered in Chapter 13.

In this Chapter, you learn how to start scripting iTunes, iPhoto, and iDVD. When you read through the sections in this chapter, notice the common approach that applies to scripting each of these applications. This will help you understand how to approach scripting new applications that you may encounter in the future.

If you don't have the iLife applications on your system, read through this chapter anyway. It will help reinforce the concepts taught in the previous chapters. Because iTunes is the most popular iLife application and is available separately for no charge, emphasis in this chapter is placed on scripting iTunes. iTunes is available from Apple's website at www.apple.com/itunes, so you may want to download and install it, and then add some songs to the library. Doing so enables you to try the program examples presented in the iTunes section of this chapter.

> *See the reference under Appendix C, "Resources," for Doug's AppleScripts for iTunes, which is a comprehensive website devoted to scripting iTunes.*

As noted, there's not enough space in this book to go into a detailed treatment of scripting each application. However, I have enough room to show you the basics and get you started.

Scripting iTunes

The first iLife application you learn is how to script is iTunes. You learn how to play a song, list the songs in a playlist, adjust the volume, and so on. The next couple of Try It Out examples help you become more familiar with iTunes. This section is based on version 4.6 of iTunes.

Try it Out | **Examining the iTunes Dictionary**

To begin scripting an application, look at the application's dictionary, if it has one. The iTunes application does have a dictionary, and you can look at it by following these steps:

1. Open the iTunes dictionary by dragging the iTunes icon onto Script Editor or by choosing File⇨Open Dictionary from Script Editor's menu bar and then choosing iTunes.

2. Under iTunes Suite, select Commands. Take a look at some of the iTunes-specific commands shown in Figure 11-1.

Figure 11-1

3. Under iTunes Suite, select Classes and look at the `application` class to see its elements and properties. How can you tell if iTunes is playing a song? How can you adjust the volume setting of iTunes, and what are the possible values?

4. Look at the other iTunes classes. See if you can determine the relationship among the classes. Make sure you examine the following classes: source, playlist, and track. How do you find the playing time of a track? How do you find the artist of a track? How do you find out how long it takes to play an entire playlist of tracks? Figure 11-2 shows information from the iTunes dictionary for the track class.

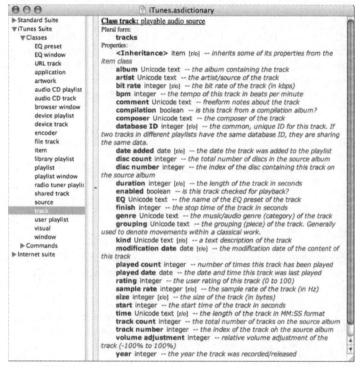

Figure 11-2

Figure 11-3 shows the information from the iTunes dictionary for the playlist class.

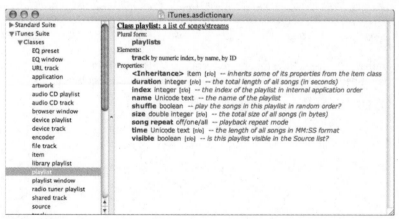

Figure 11-3

How It Works

By examining the iTunes dictionary, you learn about its classes and commands. As you gain more experience reading application dictionaries, you will find it easier to understand how the classes and commands work together. However, as noted earlier, these dictionaries are not always complete or accurate. So, although they provide a good starting point, the best way to learn about the application is by actually writing small scripts.

It's often a good idea to look at the `application` class entry in the dictionary first. This gives you global information that you can retrieve or set at the application level. For example, by examining iTunes' `application` class, you see that you can get access to the iTunes windows, the current state of iTunes with respect to playing a track, equalizer settings, the current selection, volume settings, and so on. Recall that any property listed as [r/o] in the dictionary is read-only, meaning you can retrieve its value, but not set it..

The iTunes hierarchy of classes consists of three basic levels:

❑   A `source` of music, such as a music library on your disk, an audio CD, a streaming radio, or an iPod

❑   A collection of music on that source in the form of `playlists`

❑   A collection of `tracks` in each playlist

If you have the Script Debugger application, you can get a graphic representation of the iTunes class hierarchy, which can give you a good understanding of the relationship between the classes. Such a representation is shown in Figure 11-4.

One recurring theme when you work with applications is the form of a *reference* to an object. For example, you saw in the previous chapter how the Finder makes a reference to a file. So, a full reference to the file `TextFile101.txt` in my Documents folder might look like this:

```
document file "TextFile101.txt" of folder "Documents" of folder "steve" of folder ¬
    "Users" of startup disk of application "Finder"
```

In iTunes (and in many other applications), references to objects are made in a similar way within the context of the application's classes. For example, here's a reference to a specific iTunes track:

```
file track id 3473 of user playlist id 3461 of source id 34 of application "iTunes"
```

Notice the similarity between the Finder's reference to a file and iTunes' reference to a track. In the case of iTunes, `id` numbers are used instead of names, but the similarity is obvious.

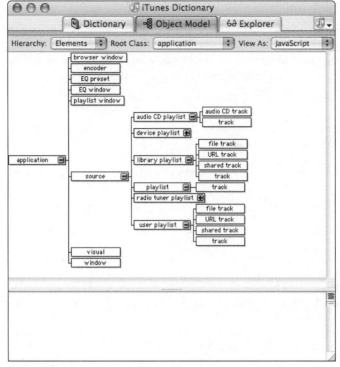

Figure 11-4

Working with Tracks and Playlists

The different types of tracks in the iTunes library (`device track`, `audio CD track`, `file track`, and `shared track`) all inherit from the `track` class. (In object-oriented programming terminology, they are all *subclasses* of the `track` class, which is their *superclass*.) Because of this inheritance chain, you can refer to an object from any of these track classes as simply a `track` in your AppleScript program. That's similar to the way a container can be used in the Finder to refer to a folder, a disk, or another container.

The `file track` class represents songs that are stored somewhere on your file system, so this class has an added property called `location`. The value of this property is an alias to the file containing the actual song (such as an MP3 or MP4 file).

Your tracks are stored inside playlists. If you're familiar with iTunes, this comes as no surprise. The identification of your library playlist, which contains all your tracks, is important. In the iTunes dictionary, this is an object of type `library playlist`. Although the iTunes model supports the idea of maintaining multiple libraries, no command in the current version of iTunes supports the creation of a new library. To identify your library playlist, you write the following:

```
first library playlist
```

Of course, you can also write `1st library playlist` or `library playlist 1`.

A specific playlist can be referenced by name. So if you have a playlist called Latin Jazz you can write

```
playlist "Latin Jazz"
```

Your library playlist is named `Library` *by default. You can change this name, so you shouldn't reference the playlist by this default name, as in* `playlist "Library"`.

When identifying tracks and playlists by name, case is not considered.

A playlist contains an ordered collection of tracks. You can identify the tracks by number, by name, or by Id. The latter method is used by iTunes.

To get a reference to the first track of your Latin Jazz playlist, you write the following:

```
first track of playlist "Latin Jazz"
```

To get a track named `"Here Comes the Sun"` from your library, you write a reference like this:

```
track "Here Comes the Sun" of first library playlist
```

There's generally no need to explicitly list a source when identifying a track or playlist. A source must be specified, however, if you're looking at playlists on your iPod, for example, or tracks on an audio CD.

To play the track called `"Caonao"` in your Latin Jazz playlist, you use iTunes' `play` command and follow it by an appropriate track reference, like so:

```
play track "Caonao" of playlist "Latin Jazz"
```

To get a list of references to all the tracks in a playlist, you can write the following:

```
tracks of playlist "Latin Jazz"
```

As you recall, you can also write the statement this way:

```
every track of playlist "Latin Jazz"
```

You can do a lot more with tracks, such as search for all tracks containing a specified string, get the name of a track, get all the tracks in a particular album, and so on. The following table shows the commands that accomplish these sorts of things, along with some examples.

Description	Code	Example
Get all the tracks in the library	`get tracks of first library playlist`	`get tracks of first library playlist`
Get a track by name from the library	`get track` *name* `of first library playlist`	`get track "This is Halloween" of first library playlist`
Get the name of all tracks in the library	`get name of tracks of first library playlist`	`get name of tracks of first library playlist`

Description	Code	Example
Get *all* tracks of a particular name from the library	`get tracks of first library playlist whose name is name`	`get tracks of first library playlist whose name is "This is Halloween"`

Get *all* tracks from the library whose name contains the specified characters	`get tracks of first library playlist whose name contains name`
	 -or-
	 `search first library playlist for name only songs`
		`get tracks of first library playlist whose name contains "winter"`
		 -or-
		 `search first library playlist for "winter" only songs`

Get all the tracks in a specific playlist	`get tracks of playlist name`	`get tracks of playlist "Dance Music"`
Get the names of all tracks in a specific playlist	`get name of tracks of playlist name`	`get name of tracks of playlist "Dance Music"`
Get a track by name and artist from a playlist	`get tracks of playlist whose name is name and artist is artist`	`tell application "iTunes" to get tracks of first library playlist whose name is "Light My Fire" and artist is "The Doors"`

Get all tracks in an album	`get tracks of first library playlist whose album is album`
	
	 -or-
	 `search first library playlist for album only albums`
		`get tracks of first library playlist whose album is "The Best of Sade"`
		
		 -or-
		 `search first library playlist for "The Best of Sade" only albums`

Change the name of a track	`set name of trackRef to name`	`set name of track "How Come" of first library playlist to "How Come?"`
Get the track(s) currently selected in iTunes	`get selection`	`set trackList to get selection`
Get all the tracks on your connected iPod	`get tracks of first library playlist of iPodSource`	`get tracks of first library playlist of (item 1 of (sources whose kind is iPod))`
Play a specific track	`play trackRef`	`play track "Lose Yourself" of playlist "Eminem"`
Play a random track from your library	`play some track of first library playlist`	`play some track of first library playlist`

Table continued on following page

Description	Code	Example
Pause currently playing track	`pause`	`pause`
Resume play of current track	`play`	`play`
Toggle play/pause of current track	`playpause`	`playpause`
Stop play of current track	`stop`	`stop`

Other commands not listed in the table enable you to do other things with tracks, such as rewind, fast forward, skip backward, and so on. These commands are listed in the iTunes dictionary, and you should discover and try them on your own.

In general, commands that specify a playlist can be `first library playlist` for the master library or `playlist name` for a specific library. Also, the filters in the examples use the properties `name`, `artist`, and `album`. You can use any `track` properties for your search, such as `genre`, `played date`, `rating`, `played count`, or `date added`. For example, to locate all tracks in your library playlist that were added in the last 30 days, you can write the following:

```
get tracks of first library playlist whose date added is greater than ¬
    (current date - 30 * days)
```

You can also get the names of those tracks in one line like this:

```
get name of tracks of first library playlist whose date added is greater than ¬
    (current date - 30 * days)
```

Remember that with all these constructs, you can substitute `in` for `of`, and liberally insert the word `the`. So you can also write the previous statement like so:

```
get the name of the tracks in the first library playlist whose date added is ¬
    greater than (current date - 30 * days)
```

The following table shows you how to perform operations with playlists, such as enumerating them, renaming them, adding tracks to them, creating new ones, and so on.

Description	Code	Example
Get a list of sources (`library`, `audio CD`, `MP3 CD`, `device`, `radio tuner`, `shared library`, `iPod`, or `unknown`)	`get sources`	`get sources`
Get all playlists	`get playlists`	`get playlists`

Description	Code	Example
Get playlists from all sources	`get playlists of sources`	`get playlists of sources`
Get playlists from a particular source	`get playlists of (sources whose kind is` *sourceType*`)`	`get playlists of (sources whose kind is audio CD)`
Get playlists of your connected iPod	`get playlists of` *iPodSource*	`get playlists of (sources whose kind is iPod)`
Get a reference to the playlist selected in the front iTunes window	`get view of front window`	`get view of front window`
Play the songs in a playlist	`play` *playlistRef*	`play playlist "Party Music"`
Make a new playlist	`make new playlist with properties` *propRec*	`make new playlist with properties {name: "Hip-Hop Plus"}`
Add a track to a playlist	`duplicate track` *trackRef* `to` *playlist*	`duplicate "Without You" of first library playlist to playlist "Cardio Mix"`
Add tracks from one playlist to another	`duplicate tracks of` *playlistRef* `to` *playlistRef*	`duplicate tracks of playlist "Dance" to playlist "Party Mix"`
Change the name of a playlist	`set name of` *playlistRef* `to` *name*	`set name of playlist "Dance Music" to "Club Dance Music"`
Delete a track from a playlist	`delete` *trackRef*	`delete track "Men in Black" of playlist "Cardio Mix"`
Delete a playlist	`delete` *playlistRef*	`delete playlist "On-the-Go 4"`

An iTunes Player Applet

In the following Try It Out, you write an applet that allows you to play a song by name.

Try it Out   An iTunes Song Player

In this program, you enter characters from a song's name, ask iTunes to find all songs containing those characters, and then play one of the matches.

1. Type the following program into Script Editor:

```
set trackName to text returned of (display dialog "Type in some characters from the
    song name" default answer "")
```

```
tell application "iTunes"
    set trackList to search first library playlist for trackName only songs

    if (count trackList) is 1 then
        set trackToPlay to item 1 of trackList
    else if (count trackList) > 1 then
            -- make a list of track names for the user to choose from

            set trackNameList to {}
            repeat with aTrack in trackList
                set end of trackNameList to name of aTrack
            end repeat

            choose from list trackNameList with prompt "Pick one:"
            set resultList to result

                if resultList is false then   -- User canceled?
                    return
                else
                    set trackSelected to item 1 of resultList
                end if

                -- now find the selected track in the list

                repeat with aTrack in trackList
                    if (name of aTrack) = trackSelected then
                        set trackToPlay to aTrack
                            exit repeat
                    end if
                end repeat
        else -- no matching tracks
            display dialog "I couldn't find any tracks containing " & trackName & ¬
                " in their titles" with icon note buttons {"OK"} default button 1
            return
    end if

    -- finally, play the track

    play trackToPlay -- AppleScript doesn't wait for the song to finish!
    display dialog "Playing " & name of trackToPlay buttons {"OK"} with icon note ¬
        default button 1 giving up after 3
end tell
```

2. Save the program as an application with the name Play Song. Your desktop is a good place for this applet. Keeping it accessible from the Dock is another good idea.

3. Run your Play Song applet. A dialog displays asking you to type in some characters from the song's name. Figure 11-5 shows an example of this dialog with the characters light entered.

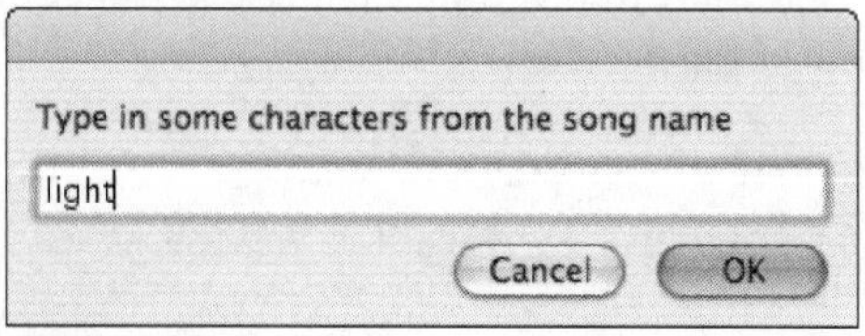

Type in some characters from the song name

light

Cancel   OK

Figure 11-5

4. Type some characters from one or more of the songs in your library and click OK.

5. If the characters you typed match one or more songs in your library, you get a dialog asking you to select one of the matching songs. Figure 11-6 shows the songs from my library whose name contains the characters *light*. Note that case is not considered for purposes of the match. If you get a dialog asking you to pick a song, select one of the songs and click OK.

Pick one:

Gimme the Light
Light My Fire
Northern Lights
Ray Of Light
The Light That Has Lighted The World
The Night That the Lights Went Out in NYC
When the Lovelight Starts Shining Through His Eyes (Single) [Mono]

Cancel   OK

Figure 11-6

6. The song you selected will begin playing in iTunes, and a dialog tells you the song it asked iTunes to play. If only one match was found, you do not get the dialog shown in Figure 11-6, but you still see a dialog like the one shown in Figure 11-7.

Playing The Night That the Lights Went Out in NYC

OK

Figure 11-7

How It Works

The program begins by prompting the user to enter some characters from the song's title. The result returned from `display dialog` is then stored in the variable `trackList`.

The first command sent to iTunes is a `search` command:

```
set trackList to search first library playlist for trackName only songs
```

The `search` command takes a playlist to search as its direct object. The `for` parameter specifies the text that can be located anywhere in the field being searched. The `only` parameter specifies the type of property to be searched. In this case, only song titles are searched. Other options are `albums`, `all`, `artists`, `composers`, and `displayed`.

You may have noticed from the preceding table that you can also do your search using a filter, like this:

```
set trackList to tracks of first library playlist whose name contains trackName
```

This type of search is more flexible because you can specify compound search criteria this way. You can also filter properties other than those searched by the search command. For example, you can get all tracks by a particular artist that were added in the last 30 days.

> *The iTunes* search *command does behave differently from the search done with a filter. If you use the* search *command on the string* "come in"*, it looks for the strings* "come" *and* "in" *in the specified property. However, these two strings do not have to appear consecutively within the strings.*

The search command returns a list of matching tracks, even if just one track matches. The program checks the number of items in the list. If there's only one item, meaning just one track matches, the rest is relatively easy: You have the track to be played.

If more than one matching track is returned, the program builds a list of track names from the list of matching tracks. This list is then presented to the user so that she can make a selection. After a track is picked, the program locates it in trackList to obtain the proper track reference to give to iTunes.

In the case of either a single matching track or a track being selected from a list of matches, trackToPlay is set to a reference to the track to be played. You can easily play the selection by executing the following command:

```
play trackToPlay
```

Note that when iTunes has finished playing a track you requested, it goes on to play the next song in your playlist. There's no simple way around this. For example, no command plays just a single track and stops. You can create a new playlist, add the song to the new playlist, and then play the song from that playlist. Or you can maintain a playlist with a special name that always has just one song in it. Each time a new song is selected, you remove whatever song is in the playlist, add the new song, and then play it. This is left as an exercise for you at the end of this chapter (Exercise #4).

An exercise at the end of this chapter (Exercise #1) enables you to resolve yet another flaw in this program. If you have more that one track in your library with the same name (they could be by different artists or on different albums, for example), you have no way to distinguish these songs from the list of choices presented by the program. That's because only each track's name, and no other information about the track, is added to the list.

This concludes your introduction to scripting with iTunes. Obviously, you can do a lot more with iTunes. I encourage you to try writing some of your own iTunes scripts.

Scripting iPhoto

The iPhoto application provides a convenient way for you to organize the images on your computer. Typically, these images are photographs; most often, these photographs have been imported from a digital camera that you connect to your Mac. The application can be set up to automatically import new photos into iPhoto whenever you connect a camera to your system. In iPhoto, you can easily set up slide shows with background music, create QuickTime movies, publish web pages, order prints, and do minor retouching of your photos.

iPhoto stores all your photos in a master library. From that library you can create albums of photos. If you spotted the analogy here to the iTunes library⇨playlist⇨track structure, you're one step ahead of the game. The next couple of Try It Out examples take a closer look at iPhoto. This section is based on version 4.0.3 of iPhoto. Please make sure you are using a current version of iPhoto. One command (import) did not exist in earlier versions of the application.

Try it Out   **Examining iPhoto's Dictionary**

Once again, examining an application's dictionary is a good place to start when you want to write scripts to work with the application. In the following steps, you look at the iPhoto dictionary:

1. Open the iPhoto dictionary by dragging the iPhoto icon onto Script Editor or by choosing File⇨Open Dictionary from Script Editor's menu bar and then choosing iPhoto.

2. Under iPhoto Suite, select Commands. Take a look at some of the iPhoto-specific commands shown in Figure 11-8. Notice the import command, which enables you to import an image file into iPhoto.

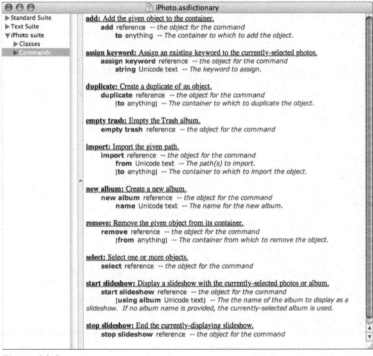

Figure 11-8

3. Look at the application class. Notice the different ways you can select an element such as a photo.

4. Look at the album and photo classes. The photo class is shown in Figure 11-9. As you can see, this class inherits from the item class. Can you get a list of all the properties of a photo by accessing its properties property? How you can find out where a photo is stored on your computer? What property gives you the size of a photo in pixels and how is that value expressed?

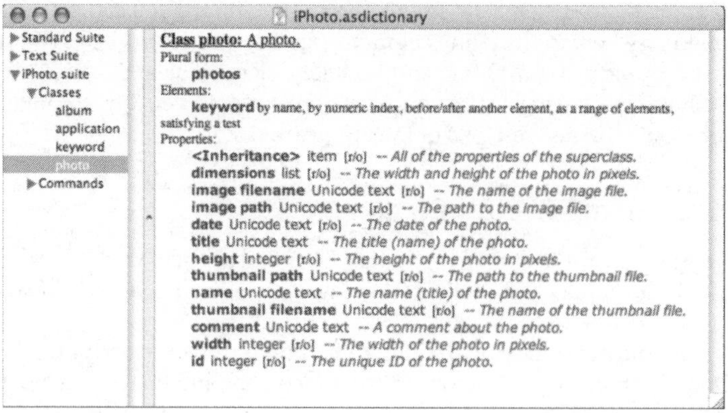

Figure 11-9

How It Works

There's a striking similarity between writing scripts for iTunes, which works with a library, playlists, and tracks, and writing scripts for iPhoto, which works with a library, albums, and photos.

Try it Out   **Making an Album from a Folder of Images**

The following program takes a folder of images and creates a new album in iPhoto from those images. The name used for the album is that of the folder.

1. Type the following program into Script Editor:

```
-- Make a new album from a folder of images

set imageFolder to choose folder with prompt "Select of a folder of images:"

set infoRec to info for imageFolder
set albumName to name of infoRec

tell application "iPhoto"
  activate

  -- make sure the album doesn't already exist

  if exists album albumName then
      display dialog "The album " & albumName & " already exists!  Change the
          folder name and try again!" with icon stop buttons {"OK"} default button 1
      return
  end if


  -- create the new album

  try
      new album name albumName
  on error
      display dialog "The album " & albumName & " could not be created!" with ¬
```

```
                  icon stop buttons {"OK"} default button 1
        return
    end try

    display dialog "Adding files to iPhoto album " & albumName buttons {"OK"} ¬
        default button 1 giving up after 3

    set fileList to list folder imageFolder without invisibles

    repeat with anImageFile in fileList
        set fullPath to (imageFolder as string) & anImageFile
        set infoRec to info for file fullPath

        -- import image files to the newly created album

        if name extension of infoRec is in {"JPG", "JPEG", "TIF", "TIFF", "GIF"} then
            try -- we ignore errors here
                import from (POSIX path of fullPath) to album albumName
            end try
        end if
    end repeat

    display dialog "Your album has been created!" buttons {"OK"}
            default button 1 giving up after 3

    -- display the album in iPhoto

    set current album to album albumName
end tell
```

2. Create a folder with some images in it. The images can be JPEG, GIF, or TIFF files. Give a name to the folder that will become the album name in iPhoto.

3. Run the program.

4. When prompted to select a folder, pick the folder you created in Step 2 and click Choose. You should get a dialog similar to that shown in Figure 11-10. This figure shows the dialog obtained from running the program and selecting a folder called My Kids. If an album already exists in iPhoto under the same name as the folder you selected, the program displays an error dialog and exits from the program. (The solution in Appendix A for Exercise 7 at the end of this chapter offers a more elegant approach.)

Figure 11-10

5. The program imports your image files into iPhoto. The amount of time it takes depends on the number of images in the selected folder. When processing is done, you get a dialog like the one shown in Figure 11-11.

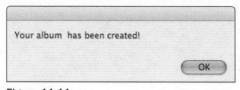

Figure 11-11

6. You should see your new album and its contents displayed in the iPhoto application. Figure 11-12 shows the window displayed in my iPhoto application after the program creates an album called My Kids containing 21 photos.

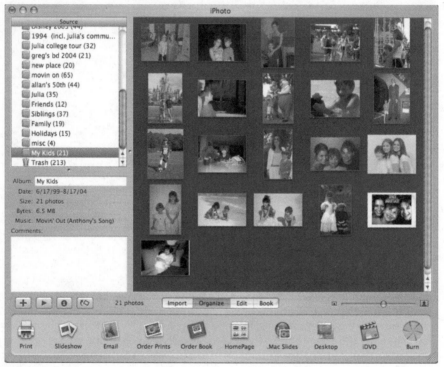

Figure 11-12

How It Works

The program prompts for a folder of images. The resulting alias that is returned is stored in the variable imageFolder. The name of the album that the program creates is the base file name from the folder. This is stored in the variable albumName.

The program then enters a tell block, and starts by sending the activate command to iPhoto to bring the application to the front.

The program uses the Standard Suite's `exist` command to test if an album named `albumName` already exists:

```
if exists album albumName then
    display dialog "The album " & albumName & " already exists!  Change folder name
        and try again!" with icon stop buttons {"OK"} default button 1
    return
end if
```

If the album already exists, the program puts up a dialog and exits.

Next, it's time to create the new album. Creation of new objects is often handled by the Standard Suite's `make` command. In this case, iPhoto has its own `new album` command, so the program uses that to create the new album with this code:

```
new album name albumName
```

Creation of a new album is executed inside a `try` block so that you can catch any error that might occur.

Now, you add the images from the selected folder to the new album. This is done with a `repeat` loop that cycles through each file in the folder. For each such file, you first get the full path to the file and store it in the variable `fullPath`. Then, you test the extension on the file to determine if it's a JPEG, TIFF, or GIF file. Any other files are just ignored. You could display a dialog to tell the user about the file not being added to the album, or you could build a list of all such files to display at the end of the program. There's no good reason why those strategies were not adopted in this program.

If the file type is okay, the program asks iPhoto to import the file into the new album, like so:

```
import from (POSIX path of fullPath) to album albumName
```

Notice that the `from` parameter takes a POSIX path to the file. But how did you know that? It's not specified in the dictionary under the description of the `import` command. You figure it out by trial and error. First, you specify a Mac-style path and get a not-too-specific error from iPhoto. So you try some other approaches, and this is the one that works. Unfortunately, this is a paradigm when working with applications, and I have pointed it out before. Dictionaries are sometimes imprecise and inaccurate, so you have to be creative and resourceful!

The `import` command is executed in a `try` block and, once again, any error that gets generated is simply ignored by the program. This allows the next image to be processed without interrupting the program's execution.

Note that the imported photos are added to your photo library as well as to the new album. So, if you delete the album or any individual photos in the album, they remain in your library unless you delete them from there as well.

When all images have been added to the album, the program executes the following statement:

```
set current album to album albumName
```

This causes the album you just created to be shown in iPhoto's viewer window, as depicted in Figure 11-12.

It's interesting to note that you could play the album of images as a slide show in iPhoto simply by adding the following command to the end of the program:

```
start slideshow
```

Try it and see!

Scripting iDVD

The last iLife application I cover in this chapter is iDVD. This application lets you create your own DVDs from images and movie clips. You can create slide shows with background music and select different types of effects for the transition from one slide to the next. iDVD comes with an assortment of built-in themes, which provide a good starting point for developing a new DVD. These themes allow you to easily add menus containing titles, buttons, movies, and slides and to provide a consistent overall look for your DVD. The following Try It Out examples help you become familiar with iDVD. This section is based on version 4.0.1 of iDVD.

Try it Out · · · Examining iDVD's Dictionary

As with the previous two iLife applications, you start to learn how to script iDVD by looking at its dictionary.

1. Open the iDVD dictionary by dragging the iDVD icon onto Script Editor or by choosing File⇨Open Dictionary from Script Editor's menu bar and then choosing iDVD.

2. Under iDVD, select Commands. Take a look at some of the iDVD-specific commands, as shown in Figure 11-13. Notice the `new project` command, which allows you to create a new iDVD project.

3. Examine the `application` class listed under iDVD. Notice that it inherits from the `application` class listed under the Standard Suite. Take note of the fact that the `current menu` property refers to the active menu of the current project (you'll be using it soon!) Notice some of the flags that you can query and/or set. How can you tell if iDVD is currently burning a disk? How can you get a list of all slide shows?

4. Examine other iDVD classes. In particular, look at the `menu` and `slideshow` classes. Can a menu contain a slide show? Can a menu contain a movie? Notice all the properties for a `menu`. For a slide show, how do you specify the background song to play? What are the different types of transitions that you can specify for a `slideshow`? Figure 11-14 shows the `slideshow` entry from the iDVD dictionary.

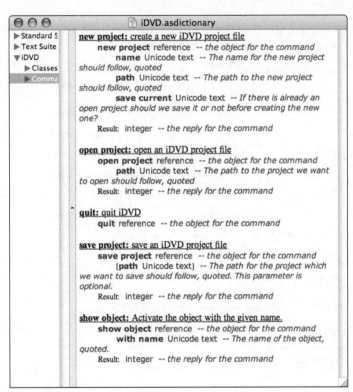

Figure 11-13

How It Works

You can ask the Script Debugger application to give you an object-model view of the iDVD dictionary. This helps you understand the relationships between the various classes. Figure 11-15 shows a screen shot from Script Debugger. You can see that a menu can contain text objects, buttons, slide shows, and movies. A slide show contains images.

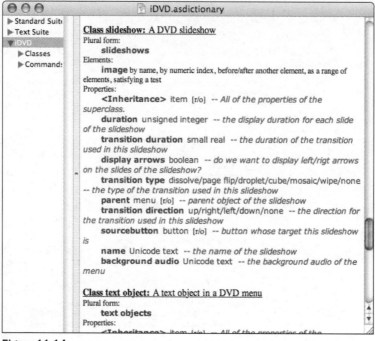

Figure 11-14

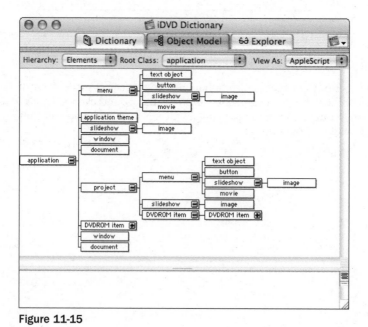

Figure 11-15

Try it Out   Making a DVD Slide Show from a Folder of Images

Similar to the way in which the iPhoto applet creates a new iPhoto album from a folder of images, the next program creates a DVD from a folder of images. The program sets up a slide show for the images, including background music.

1.   Type the following program into Script Editor:

```
-- Make a new DVD from a folder of images

on iTunesPick() -- get a track from iTunes
    tell application "iTunes" to get location of some file track of first ¬
        library playlist
end iTunesPick

set imageFolder to choose folder with prompt "Select of a folder of images:"
set projectLoc to choose file name with prompt "Select a name for your DVD
project:"

set infoRec to info for imageFolder
set folderName to name of infoRec
set fileList to list folder imageFolder without invisibles

display dialog "Creating DVD from images..." buttons {"OK"} default button 1 ¬
        giving up after 2

tell application "iDVD"
    activate

    -- start a new project and select a theme and background pic

    try
        new project name folderName path (projectLoc as string) save current "no"
    on error
        display dialog "I couldn't create a new iDVD project!" with icon stop ¬
                buttons {"OK"} default button 1
        return
    end try

    set motion mode to false
    set assigned theme of current menu to "Transparent Blue"

    -- set properties of the menu

    set menuName to "Menu1"
    set name of current menu to menuName
    set title of current menu to folderName

    -- create a new slide show

    make new slideshow at end of slideshows of current menu
    set the label of first button of current menu to "Slides!"
    set name of first slideshow of current menu to "Slides!"
    set transition type of first slideshow to cube

    set backgroundSet to false
```

```
    -- now add each image to the slide show

    repeat with anImageFile in fileList
        set fullPath to (imageFolder as string) & anImageFile
        set infoRec to info for file fullPath
        set pPath to POSIX path of fullPath

        -- import image files

        if name extension of infoRec is in {"JPG", "JPEG", "TIF", "TIFF"} then
            if not backgroundSet then
                set background asset of current menu to pPath
                set backgroundSet to true
            end if

            try -- we ignore errors here
                make new image at end of images of first slideshow with properties ¬
                    {name:anImageFile, path:pPath}
            end try
        end if
    end repeat

    set transition type of current menu to page flip

    -- select background music for the slide show and main menu

    set background audio of current menu to my iTunesPick()

    set motion mode to true
    set duration of current menu to 30 -- can't go any higher?

    set background audio of first slideshow to my iTunesPick()


    display dialog "Your DVD project has been created!" buttons {"OK"} default ¬
        button 1 giving up after 3
end tell
```

2. Create a folder containing some images. You can use the same folder of images you used in the iPhoto example. In this case, the name of the folder is used as the title on the DVD's menu screen.

3. Run the program.

4. When prompted to select a folder, select the one you created in Step 2. Click Choose.

5. Another dialog is displayed and asks you to select a name for your DVD project. Locate the folder in which you want to store your project, type a meaningful file name in the Save As box, and click Save. You should see a dialog like the one shown in Figure 11-16.

6. The iDVD application window comes to the front, and you can watch changes made to your project as your script runs. When the program has finished creating your project, you should hear some music start to play. The program then displays the dialog shown in Figure 11-17.

Creating DVD from images...

OK

Figure 11-16

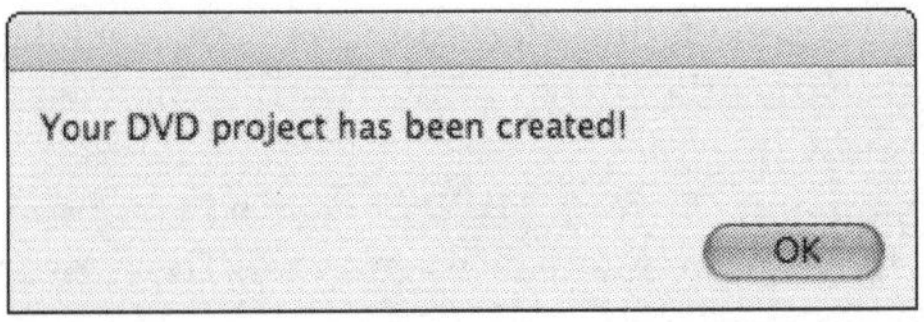

Your DVD project has been created!

OK

Figure 11-17

7. Click the iDVD application window. You should see a screen displaying the first image from your folder as its background. The title on the screen is the name of the folder you selected. Figure 11-18 shows the result of running the program on a folder of images called Kids Photos.

Figure 11-18

8. Click the Preview button. Then click the Slides! button inside the window. A slide show with background music begins playing, and you see the images from the folder you selected.

How It Works

When you create a new project in iDVD, you start with one of its installed themes. The program arbitrarily chooses the theme called Transparent Blue, but it's easy to modify the program to work with a different theme. A menu is the basic element that you work with when creating a DVD. Don't confuse the term *menu* as used by iDVD with the pull-down menus that appear at the top of your Mac's screen. A menu in your iDVD project is the entire window, as depicted in Figure 11-18. On that window you can place buttons that initiate slide shows, play movies, or enter another menu screen (a submenu).

iDVD shows your first menu based on the selected theme. You see text placed on the menu that serves as a placeholder. You're free to change the text or move it somewhere else in the window.

You can have many different menus in your iDVD project, so you need a way to identify them. In AppleScript, they can be referenced by name or by number. The menu you are currently working on can be referenced simply as `current menu`.

Various properties can be set for a menu. For example, you can set its `title` (including its font, size, and color), which normally appears somewhere on the screen (and there's normally a placeholder for the title in the theme template). You can also specify a background image or movie for the menu (known as its `background asset`), as well as a song to play (its `background audio` property) while the menu is on the screen. The `duration` property specifies how much of the song to play before it starts over again. You can set a menu's `transition type` to dictate how you want the menu to transition into the next menu/slide show/movie. Possible values for the transition, gleaned from the iDVD dictionary, are `dissolve`, `page flip`, `droplet`, `cube`, `mosaic`, `wipe`, and `none`.

You can add new objects to the menu. These objects can include other slide shows, movies, text, and buttons that take you to submenus. To add a new item to your menu in AppleScript, you make a new object of the specified type (using the `make` command), and set its properties. When you make an object like a `slideshow`, a button is also created for you. You can reference it from the `slideshow`'s `sourcebutton` property, or directly from the menu by number or name. You set the title on a button by setting its `label` property.

After you create a new slide show, you can add images to it. To do this, you again use the `make` command and specify where the image is located on the disk. You can set other properties of the image (such as its name) when you execute the `make` command or, subsequently, by using the `set` or `copy` command.

The `slideshow` properties include a `transition` property, which enables you to select a transition type between slides (like the `transition type` property of a menu); a `background audio` property, which allows you to specify a song to play during the slide show; and a `duration` property, which allows you to specify how long a slide is displayed before transitioning to the next slide. If you specify a background song, this value is automatically set to 0, meaning that the iDVD application sets the duration of each slide so that the last slide finishes at the same time the song ends (that's a nice feature!)

Now take a closer look at the program. The program starts by defining a handler called `iTunesPick` that selects a track from iTunes:

```
on iTunesPick() -- get a track from iTunes
    tell application "iTunes" to get location of some file track of first ¬
        library playlist
end iTunesPick
```

For the sake of simplicity, a random track is selected by the handler (recall the use of the some property from Chapters 5 and 6), which produces a random item from a list). A more practical approach might be to allow the user to select the track. You know how to do this from the program you wrote in the iTunes section of this chapter.

The location property of a file track is an alias to the location of the file containing the track. The iDVD must have this to specify background audio.

After the handler definition, the program prompts for a folder of images, as you've seen many times before. The program then enters a tell block to start its communication with iDVD.

After activating the iDVD application to bring it to the front, you make a request to create a new project, like so:

```
new project name folderName path (projectLoc as string) save current "no"
```

The arbitrary name you assign to the project is the same as the folder name, which is stored in the variable folderName. The path parameter specifies where you want to store the new project. The path projectLoc is returned by the choose file name command. The save current parameter takes a *string* (yes, that's correct), that is either "yes" if you want the iDVD application to save whatever project you may be currently working on, or "no" if you do not.

The iDVD application has a Motion button. When it's active, background movies (swaying curtains in one of the themes) and audio will play while you are working on the project. This can be a nuisance and, in some cases, can impact performance. You can turn off this mode while the program is running with the following statement:

```
set motion mode to false
```

The next command in the program sets the theme of the current menu to Transparent Blue by setting its assigned theme property:

```
set assigned theme of current menu to "Transparent Blue"
```

Other themes include Theater, Book, Projector, Blue, Orange, Lightbox, Montage, Blocks, Marquee, Transparent Green, and so on. You can get a list from the iDVD application by clicking its Customize button and selecting Themes.

The program sets some properties for the current menu, including its name and title, as follows:

```
set menuName to "Menu1"
set name of current menu to menuName
set title of current menu to folderName
```

The menu is named "Menu1". You can subsequently reference your first menu as current menu (it's the only menu you have in this project), first menu, or menu menuName. Setting the title property of the menu has the effect of replacing the text "Transparent Blue" with the specified name. You can see this happen as the script is running.

Now it's time to make your slide show. You start this process in the program with the following command:

```
make new slideshow at end of slideshows of current menu
```

The `make new` command is used to make a new slide show. You need the `at` parameter to tell the command where the `slideshow` is to go. It's a frequent paradigm to create new objects at the end of a list of objects. Even though you have no other `slideshows`, you can still specify `end of slideshows of current menu` as the location to place the new `slideshow`.

When a new `slideshow` is created, a new button that is associated with that `slideshow` also appears. You set the `label` property of that button (and not its `name` property) to determine the name that you see on the screen. In the program, you simply label the button `"Slides!"` as follows:

```
set the label of first button of current menu to "Slides!"
```

You don't need to name the slide show, just as you didn't need to name the menu. However, the program sets its name to `"Slides!"` anyway:

```
set name of first slideshow of current menu to "Slides!"
```

You can refer to a `slideshow` by its name, as in `slideshow "Slides!"` or by its number, as in `first slideshow`. The program uses the latter method to set the transition between slides to a revolving cube effect like so:

```
set transition type of first slideshow to cube
```

Now it's time to add each image from the folder to the slide show. A `repeat` loop is set up to do this. The POSIX path of the image file is obtained and stored in the variable `pPath`:

```
set pPath to POSIX path of fullPath
```

You use a POSIX path to set the background image of the menu, as well as for specifying the file path for each image to be added to the slide show. Unfortunately, you can't determine that you need POSIX paths from reading the iDVD dictionary.

You can set the background of your menu to any image or movie you want. The program arbitrarily uses the first image from the folder for the menu's background. If the background image for the menu hasn't been set, the first image file is used. You then set a flag so subsequent iterations through the loop recognize that the background has been set. You do this with the following code:

```
if not backgroundSet then
    set background asset of current menu to pPath
    set backgroundSet to true
end if
```

The flag `backgroundSet` was initially set `false` before the `repeat` loop was entered. It's set `true` only after the `background asset` property of the current menu has been set.

To add a new image to your `slideshow`, you use the `make` command. This command is executed in a `try` block to prevent the program from abruptly aborting if something goes wrong (that might happen if, for some reason, the image file can't be added to the slide show):

```
try -- we ignore errors here
    make new image at end of images of first slideshow with properties
        {name:anImageFile, path:pPath}
end try
```

The path property of the image is set to the POSIX path that identifies where the image file is located.

The program next sets the transition on the current menu to the flip page effect:

```
set transition type of current menu to page flip
```

This is the effect that occurs if you click the button to start the slide show when the DVD is running (or in Preview mode in iDVD). Note that the transition type of the menu must be set *after* you set the background asset. It does not work if you do it in the opposite order. This is determined by trial and error.

The background music for the menu is set with the menu's background audio property:

```
set background audio of current menu to my iTunesPick()
```

The file reference returned by the iTunePick handler is the value assigned to this property. You use the keyword my in front of your handler call. That's because the call occurs inside a tell block. I discussed this in Chapter 10.

In order to set the length of time the background audio plays (before it loops back to the beginning), you set the menu's duration property to the number of seconds. Here, this property is set to 30 seconds:

```
set motion mode to true
set duration of current menu to 30 -- can't go any higher?
```

You have to set motion mode true before setting the duration property. Otherwise, setting the property has no effect (once again, this is determined by trial and error and may be a bug). Furthermore, for some reason, iDVD does not allow you to set a value for the duration that is greater than 30 seconds. This is surely a bug; you can manually set the duration for the length of the song from within the application itself.

Because you turned motion mode on and set the duration to some nonzero value, the background audio for your iDVD slide show actually starts playing at this point. Program execution continues with a statement to set the background audio for your slide show to a track returned by your iTunesPick handler:

```
set background audio of first slideshow to my iTunesPick()
```

The program displays a dialog to announce it's finished, and execution is complete. Note that the program doesn't save the current project. You can insert the following statement at the end if you like:

```
save project
```

Alternatively, you can save the project yourself from iDVD.

You can do many more things with iDVD that I don't have space to cover here. As I noted, you can add more slide shows, movies, and submenus. You can also control the placement of your objects on the screen from within AppleScript. I hope that this provides a good start, however, and that it piques your interest to explore some of these features on your own.

Summary

In this chapter, you learned how to write scripts for three of the iLife applications: iTunes, iPhoto, and iDVD. You learned

- ❏ How to read the iTunes dictionary and how to work with sources, playlists, and tracks
- ❏ How to select and play tracks from the iTunes library
- ❏ How to read the iPhoto dictionary and how to work with albums and photos
- ❏ How to create a new iPhoto album and add images to it
- ❏ How to read the iDVD dictionary and how to work with projects, menus, and slide shows
- ❏ How to make a slide show in iDVD from a folder of images

In the next chapter, you learn about script objects and how to define them to group related variables, properties, handlers, and other script objects. Before proceeding, however, try the exercises that follow to test your understanding of the material covered in this chapter. You can find the solutions to these exercises in Appendix A.

Exercises

1. The iTunes applet you developed in this chapter does not distinguish among multiple matching tracks with the same name. For example, you may have two tracks with the same name that were recorded by a different artist or on a different album. The user won't know that when presented with the list of choices. Modify the program so that each track provides the artist and album in the list of choices presented to the user (you can use the format *name – artist – album*) in the list.

2. Modify the iTunes applet so that if an asterisk is entered for the song name a randomly selected track is played.

3. Modify the iTunes applet so the three buttons labeled Title, Artist, and Album are offered to the user instead of OK, and Cancel. (Because `display dialog` only supports three buttons, you can't offer a Cancel button here.) The track should be selected from iTunes based on the button that is clicked. So, for example, if the user enters `Springsteen` and then clicks Artist, you display all tracks in the library playlist whose artist is Springsteen.

4. As noted in the chapter, after you select a song, the next songs in your library continue to play. Implement the following strategy: Keep a playlist called `Play Just One` in your library. If the playlist doesn't exist, create it. Remove any previous track from the playlist, add the selected track, and then play it. After playing the single track, iTunes should stop playing. *Note:* You need to change the `playlist` property of the track reference to refer to the track from the `Play Just One` playlist in order for this to work. (Why?)

5. Based on your solution to Exercise 4, modify the iTunes applet so that more than one song can be queued for playing. After the track has been selected, check the player's state. If the state of the player is not `stopped`, and it's playing a track from your Play Just One playlist, simply add the song to that playlist. However, if the player's state is `stopped`, remove any tracks from the Play Just One playlist and add the selected track.

6. Turn the iPhoto applet into a droplet so that, if a folder of images is dropped on it, the applet creates a new album from the images in the folder. If the applet is started in the normal way, which is by opening it from the Finder or double-clicking its icon, the applet should prompt for the name of the folder as before.

7. The iPhoto applet generates an error if an album already exists with the same name as the selected folder. Modify the program so that when this happens, the user is prompted to key in a different name for the album.

8. Count the number of images added to the new album by the iPhoto applet. If none are added, display a dialog and delete the empty album. Use the iPhoto command

```
remove album name
```

to delete the album called *name*.

9. Based on the results of Exercise 8, display a dialog at the end of the program's execution that informs the user of the number of files that were added to the album. Also, have it list (using `choose from list`) the names of the files that were not added to the album.

10. Convert the iDVD applet into a droplet so that it creates a DVD from a folder of images dropped onto it.

11. Modify the IDVD applet to convert an iPhoto album to a DVD, instead of a folder of images. Base your changes on the following handler called `getAlbum`, which prompts the user to select an album in iPhoto and returns the selected album. Use the `image path` property of each photo in the album to get its path name:

```
on getAlbum()
    display dialog "Select an album in iPhoto and click Continue" buttons ¬
        {"Continue", "Cancel"} default button 1

    tell application "iPhoto"
        activate

        repeat
            try
                set sel to selection
                set theAlbum to first item of sel

                if (class of theAlbum) is not album or (count selection) is greater ¬
                    than 1 then
                    display dialog "Please pick one album"
                else
                    return theAlbum
                end if
            on error
                display dialog "Please select a photo album in iPhoto"
            end try
        end repeat
    end tell
end getAlbum
```

Script Objects

You've seen the word *scrip* used throughout this book. I have used it interchangeably with the word *program*. You used *Script* Editor to edit and run your programs, and you saved your files as *script* files with extensions of .scpt. But what exactly is a script? Technically, all the programs you have written in this book are scripts, or *script objects*. As you learn in this chapter, you can define other script objects to group related variables (or properties), handlers, and other script objects. If you're familiar with other object-oriented programming (OOP) languages like Objective-C or C++, you see in this chapter that script objects also share some OOP features. These features include inheritance, instantiation, data encapsulation, and polymorphism.

Defining a Script Object

In this section, you learn how to define a script object in AppleScript. This is done with a compound statement that begins with the keyword script.

In the following Try It Out, you define a simple script object called sayHi.

Try It Out   Defining a Script Object

The purpose of this script is to put up a dialog containing the message Hi!

1. Type the following program into Script Editor:

```
-- Define a simple script

script sayHi
    display dialog "Hi!" buttons {"OK"} default button 1
end script

run sayHi
```

2. Run the program. You should see the dialog shown in Figure 12-1.

Figure 12-1

How It Works

You define a script object in your program according to the following format:

```
script name
    statement
    statement
        ...
end script
```

This defines a script object called *name*. The script object consists of any statements that follow, ending in the `end script` statement. These statements can include other script definitions and handler definitions as well.

> *For all intents and purposes,* name *is treated like an ordinary variable; in this case, it stores a script object.*

Defining a script object does not cause any of the statements that comprise the script to be executed. To execute the script, you use the `run` command, followed by the script's name:

```
    run name
```

This causes all the statements in the compound `script` statement to be executed.

> *You can physically place the* run *command in your program before the script's definition; like handlers, however, script definitions are often defined first.*

Script Properties

As previously noted, you can use script objects for various purposes. Many times, you use them to take advantage of the persistent nature of their *properties*. A property is very similar to a variable. In fact, use of the term *property variable* is not inaccurate. Like ordinary variables, you can assign values to properties, use them in expressions, pass them as arguments to handlers, and so on.

To define a property, you write the keyword `property` followed by the name you choose, followed by a colon, followed by the initial value to assign to that property. This is the general format:

```
property  name : value
```

This defines a property called *name* with an initial value specified by *value*. You must specify an initial value for a property when you define it, whether it's 0, missing value, or the result of an expression.

The following Try It Out illustrates how script properties are initialized once and retain their values through repeated executions of a script.

Try It Out   Working with Script Properties

Follow these steps to work with script properties.

1.   Type the following program into Script Editor:

```
-- Script properties

script showXY
    property X : 100

    set Y to 100

    set X to X + 1
    set Y to Y + 1

    log "X = " & (X as string) & ", Y = " & Y as string
end script

run showXY
run showXY
run showXY
```

2.   Click the Event Log tab and run the program. You should see the following output recorded in the Event Log:

```
(*X = 101, Y = 101*)
(*X = 102, Y = 101*)
(*X = 103, Y = 101*)
```

How It Works

The script showXY defines a property called X with a value of 100. It also sets a variable Y to 100. The property is subsequently used in the script like a normal variable. The main difference between the two is that the property X is set to 100 only once, whereas the variable Y is set to 100 each time the script is run. This behavior is verified by the program's output, which shows the effect of running the script showXY three times. As you can see, the value of the property X is incremented by 1 each time, verifying that it retains its value through successive runs of the script.

As you'll see shortly, the property X can be accessed from outside the script showXY, whereas the variable Y cannot.

Initializing Script Properties

Note that properties in scripts get initialized when a script is *defined*, and not when the script is run. The following Try It Out shows how a script's properties are initialized without the script even being run.

Try It Out   Initializing Script Properties

In the following steps, you see how a script's properties are initialized.

1. Type the following program into Script Editor:

```
-- Initializing script properties

script foo
    property X : 100
    property Y : current date

    display dialog "Hello!"
end script

log X of foo
log foo's Y
```

2. Click the Event Log and run the program. You should see output similar to the following (your output will reflect the date and time that you ran the program):

```
(*100*)
(*Friday, July 30, 2004 12:31:48 PM*)
```

How It Works

You defined a script called `foo` that contains two properties and executes a `display dialog` command. The important thing to realize is that the two properties inside that script are initialized *even though the script itself is never run!* AppleScript initializes script properties when a script is defined and not when it is run. So, when you run this program, AppleScript encounters the script definition, sees the two properties X and Y, and initializes them. The program then proceeds to log the values of the properties X and Y. Note how that's done:

```
log X of foo
log foo's Y
```

You have to identify the script object to which these two properties belong; They're not directly accessible from outside the script as simply X and Y. The first method uses the familiar `of` notation, whereas the second method uses the apostrophe-s notation presented in an earlier chapter. Either notation is suitable and is simply a matter of personal preference.

You may have noticed that although the property X is initialized to a literal value of `100`, the property Y is initialized to the current date by executing the command of the same name. It's okay to use expressions involving other previously defined properties, handler calls, and so on for specifying the initialization value. However, you're not allowed to use variables here.

The `display dialog` command in the script *never gets executed*. That's because the script is never run. The command is inserted there to bring that point home; be sure you understand it.

Copying Script Objects

Script objects behave like lists and records when you pass them as arguments to handlers or assign them to other variables.

The following Try It Out shows the difference between using the set and copy commands when dealing with script objects.

The following steps illustrate how to copy a script object.

1. Type the following program into Script Editor:

```
-- Copying script objects

script scr
    property X : 100
end script

set scr2 to scr
copy scr to scr3

set X of scr to 200
copy scr to scr4

log X of scr
log X of scr2
log X of scr3
log X of scr4
```

2. Click the Event Log tab and run the program. This is what you get:

```
(*200*)
(*200*)
(*100*)
(*200*)
```

How It Works

The script scr is defined to contain just a single property called X with an initial value of 100.

The script scr contains no executable statements. If you try to run such a script, you get a stack overflow error from AppleScript, or Script Editor may just freeze on you!

The program sets the variable scr2 to scr with the following statement:

```
set scr2 to scr
```

This behaves just like a normal variable assignment. Like lists and records, scr2, after this assignment, references the same script object in memory as scr does. That is, a new copy of the script object is not made with the set command. This matters with respect to properties, which are part of the script object.

Because `scr` and `scr2` reference the same script object, they also reference the same property named `x` that is defined therein.

The program next uses the `copy` command to copy the script object from `scr` to `scr3`. This makes a fresh copy of the script object in much the same way as `copy` makes a fresh copy of a list or record.

After executing the `copy` command, `scr` and `scr2` reference the same script objects, whereas `scr3` references a copy of the script object. So, when the value of the property `x` from `scr` is changed from `100` to `200` with this statement:

```
set X of scr to 200
```

this affects the *same* property `x` contained in the *same* screen object referenced by both `scr` and `scr2`. However, it has no effect on the property `x` that is in `scr3`'s screen object. The first three lines of the log's output verify these conclusions.

When a script object is copied, the *current* values of its properties get copied as well. So, in the program, when you execute the statement

```
copy scr to scr4
```

the value of the property `x` that gets copied is its current value, which is `200`. Once again, this fact is reflected in the log's output.

Your Program Is a Script Object

You may not realize it, but all the programs you have worked with in this book have been script objects (which is why I've been referring to them as *scripts*). Think of your entire program as one big script object. You don't have to encapsulate it within `script.....end script` statements, but those statements are implicitly there.

Because the program itself is a script object, you can define properties at this top-most level. These properties persist through repeated executions of your program and even through repeated executions of your application! The property only gets reinitialized when the script is modified and recompiled.

Try It Out	Defining Properties at the Top Level

In the following steps, you define properties at the top level.

1. Type the following program into Script Editor:

```
property X : 100

set X to X + 1
```

2. Click the Result tab and run the program. You get the following output in the Result pane:

```
101
```

3. Run the program again. You get the following output in the Result pane:

```
102
```

4. Run the program again. You get the following output in the Result pane:

```
103
```

5. Add a comment to the beginning of the program so that your program now looks like this:

```
-- Initializing properties

property X : 100

set X to X + 1
```

6. Run the program. You get the following output in the Result pane:

```
101
```

7. Run the program again. You get the following output in the Result pane:

```
102
```

How It Works

The property X is initialized only once when the program is run and retains its value through repeated runs of the program. When a change is made to the program and it is subsequently recompiled (which happens when you go to run it again after making a change), the property gets reinitialized.

Just clicking the Run or Compile button does not guarantee that the properties are reinitialized. You have to actually make a change to the program (even if it's as simple as adding a comment) and then Run or Compile it in order for the properties to be reinitialized.

The following Try It Out illustrates that property values are recorded within an application.

Try It Out   **Properties in Applications**

As you see in the following steps, the values are retained unless the application gets rebuilt, at which point the properties are reinitialized.

1. Type the following program into Script Editor:

```
-- Illustrate script properties

property X : 100

set Y to 100

set X to X + 1
set Y to Y + 1

display dialog "X = " & (X as string) & ", Y = " & (Y as string) buttons {"OK"}
        default button 1
```

2. Save the program as an application.

3. Quit Script Editor.

4. Run the application you just created by locating it in the Finder and double-clicking. You should get the dialog shown in Figure 12-2.

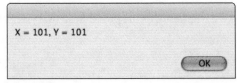

X = 101, Y = 101

OK

Figure 12-2

5. Rerun the application. You should get the dialog shown in Figure 12-3.

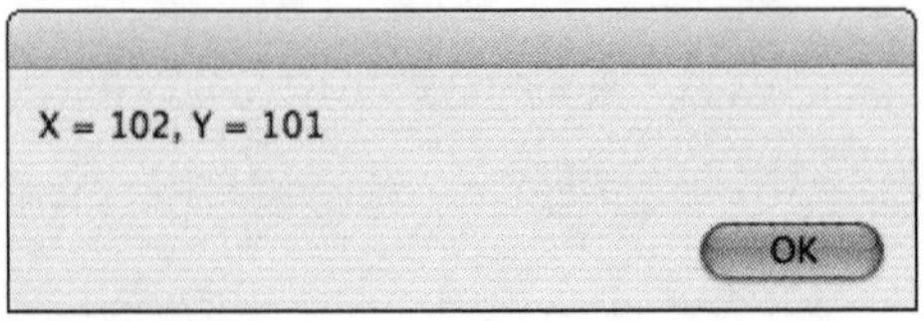

X = 102, Y = 101

OK

Figure 12-3

6. Run the application for a third time. You should get the dialog shown in Figure 12-4.

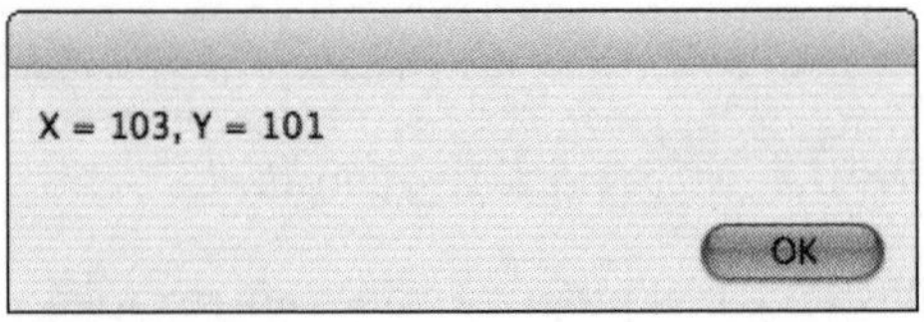

X = 103, Y = 101

OK

Figure 12-4

How It Works

If a program changes the value of a property, that modified value gets recorded with the application. This change persists until you modify and recompile the program, at which point the property is reinitialized.

The fact that the value of a property is saved with an application can be very useful because it allows you to save a user's preferences, for example, with the application. The next Try It Out is a good illustration of this idea.

<p>**Try It Out**   **Recording Values in Applications**</p>

In the following steps, you record values in applications.

1. Key the following program into Script Editor:

```
-- Storing script properties

property docFolder : path to documents folder

set docFolder to choose folder with prompt "Select a folder to store your work:"
default location docFolder

-- Following would be code that works with file in docFolder
```

2. Save the program as an application and quit Script Editor.

3. Locate the application you created and run it. A dialog asking you to select a folder should appear, and the window shows your Documents folder.

4. Select a different folder anywhere on your system and click Choose.

5. Rerun the application. Notice which folder is shown in the window this time. It is the folder you selected the last time you ran the application.

How It Works

The program defines a property called docFolder that is assigned as its initial value the path to your Documents folder. The choose folder command is executed by the program with the default location specified by this property. So the first time you run this application, the choose folder command is set to your Documents folder as its default location.

You store the folder location selected by the user in docFolder using the set command. Because docFolder is a property, its value is retained for the subsequent executions of the application. So the default location specified to the choose folder command the next time you run the program is the folder you selected the last time the program was run.

Scope of Properties

Like variables that you learned about in Chapter 8, script properties have scope associated with them.

Try It Out   **Scope of Script Properties**

The following program shows how properties defined at the top level can be accessed from within other script objects or handlers.

1. Type the following program into Script Editor:

```
-- Scope of properties

property X : 100

script fooS
    property Y : 200

    set X to X + 1
    log "X from fooS = " & X
end script

on fooH()
```

```
        set X to X + 1
        log "X from fooH = " & X
        log "Y from fooS = " & Y of fooS
    end fooH

    run fooS
    fooH()
    log "X at top level = " & X
    log "Y at top level = " & Y of fooS
```

2. Click the Event Log tab and run the program. You see this output in the log:

```
(*X from fooS = 101*)
(*X from fooH = 102*)
(*Y for fooS = 200*)
(*X at top level = 102*)
(*Y at top level = 200*)
```

How It Works

The property X is initialized to 100 when the program is compiled. This property is accessible directly by name from other script objects and handlers defined in the program. The script fooS defines its own property Y with an initial value of 200. This property is local to the fooS, but it can be accessed by other scripts and handlers as long as a reference to the script fooS is made. That is, it can be accessed as Y of fooS or as fooS's Y.

The fooS script increments the X property to verify that it can access and change a property defined at a higher level. Likewise, the fooH handler does the same thing with the X property. It also shows that it can access the Y property that is defined in the fooS script using the proper notation.

pi Is a Property

You may remember that you used pi in earlier examples in this book and that I referred to pi as a property. This property exists at the topmost level of your program. It is predefined, but it is nevertheless a normal property. You can even change its value if you like, and it persists until you make a change and recompile your program. However, I don't recommend that you do that!

Other predefined properties in your script include the following: minutes, hours, seconds, return, and text item delimiters.

Script Objects Containing Handlers

Your script objects can contain their own handler definitions. Like properties, those handlers are defined *at the time you define the script*. You can call the handlers directly from within the script object or from outside the script by using the notation *handler of script* (or the equivalent *script's handler*). In fact, that's what you did in Chapter 8 when you used the load script command to load your list handlers.

When you think of your program at the topmost level as a script object, you understand the idea of defining a handler inside a script. But in the next Try It Out, you explicitly create a script object and define three handlers inside that script object.

Try it Out   **Defining Handlers inside Scripts**

In this program, you define three handlers inside a script.

1. Type the following program into Script Editor:

```
-- Handlers inside script objects

script circle
    on area given radius:r
        return pi * r * r
    end area

    on circumference given radius:r
        return 2 * pi * r
    end circumference

    on volume given radius:r    -- okay, so it's a sphere
        return 4 * pi * (r ^ 3) / 3
    end volume
end script

-- now calculate and log various values

log (area of circle given radius:5)
log (circle's circumference given radius:10)   -- gets changed when compiled

tell circle
    log (volume given radius:2)
end tell
```

2. Click the Event Log tab and run the program. You should see this output:

```
(*78.539816339745*)
(*62.831853071796*)
(*33.510321638291*)
```

How It Works

The script called `circle` contains the definition for three handlers: `area`, `circumference`, and `volume`, whose purpose is to calculate the area and circumference of a circle and the volume of a sphere, respectively. (Okay, so technically, the volume of a sphere shouldn't be a handler categorized under *circles*, but I wanted a third example of a handler that takes a radius as its argument and performs a simple calculation!)

When the `circle` script is defined, so are its handlers. That means you don't have to run the script in order to use the handlers.

The handlers are defined inside the script called `circle`, so you need to inform AppleScript of that fact whenever you want to use one of the handlers. You do this in one of three ways: using the `of` notation, using the apostrophe-s notation, or using a `tell` statement. The program illustrates all three methods:

```
log (area of circle given radius:5)
log (circle's circumference given radius:10)
```

```
tell circle
    log (volume given radius:2)
end tell
```

In the first case, the area of a circle with a radius of 5 is calculated, and the result of 78.54 is logged. Notice how nicely that statement reads! That's because the script's name (circle), the handler's name (area), and the labeled parameter's name (radius) were each carefully chosen.

In the second case, the circumference of a circle with a radius of 10 is calculated. Notice, however, that after compilation, the statement

```
log (circle's circumference given radius:10)
```

gets automatically changed to the following:

```
log (circumference of circle given radius:10)
```

In the third and final case, the volume of a sphere with a radius of 2 is calculated and logged. Because the volume handler is invoked within the context of a tell circle command, AppleScript looks inside the circle script, finds a volume handler there, and executes it.

When you use the tell statement, understand that, although you can reference handlers directly by name, you can't reference properties that way. For example, if the circle script contains a property called twoPi, defined like this:

```
script circle
    property twoPi : 2 * pi
    ...
end script
```

you cannot access this property directly as twoPi from inside the tell statement:

```
tell circle
    log twoPi     -- this won't work!
end tell
```

You can access twoPi from inside the tell statement in the usual way (using twoPi of circle), or you can access it by placing the keyword its in front of it, like this:

```
tell circle
    log its twoPi     -- this works okay!
end tell
```

Here, the word its tells AppleScript to resolve the name twoPi within circle's context.

The Run Handler

You were first introduced to the run handler in Chapter 10. There I talked about defining a run handler at the top level of your program. Your own scripts can also have run handlers. Whenever you run a script using the run command, AppleScript examines the script to see if it contains a run handler. If it does, AppleScript executes it. As you've seen in prior examples, if there is no `run` handler, AppleScript executes any statements within the script that are outside any handlers. If you have such statements, you cannot also have a `run` handler. AppleScript complains if you do.

Recall the first program you wrote in this chapter:

```
-- Define a simple script

script sayHi
    display dialog "Hi!" buttons {"OK"} default button 1
end script

run sayHi
```

The `display dialog` command appears inside the `sayHi` script but outside any handler. So it is executed when you run the script with the `run` command.

You could have defined your `sayHi` script like this, and it would have functioned the same way:

```
script sayHi
    on run
        display dialog "Hi!" buttons {"OK"} default button 1
    end run
end script

run sayHi
```

Once again, when this script gets run, AppleScript finds the `run` handler and executes it. This has the effect of executing the `display dialog` command. Recall that you don't put parentheses after the `on run` when defining a `run` handler. That's because it's a special handler. A `run` handler can take arguments, but they must be passed to the handler as a single argument in the form of a list.

Handlers Containing Script Objects

You've seen how you can define handlers inside script objects. In the following Try It Out, you learn the opposite.

Try It Out   Defining Script Objects inside Handlers

In the following program, you practice defining a script object inside a handler.

1. Type the following program into Script Editor:

```
-- Script objects defined inside handlers

on callXY()
    script showXY
        property X : 100

        set Y to 100
```

```
            set X to X + 1
            set Y to Y + 1

            log "X = " & (X as string) & ", Y = " & (Y as string)
        end script

        run showXY
        run showXY
    end callX

callXY()
callXY()
```

2. Click the Event Log tab and run the program. You get the following four lines of output in the log:

```
(*X = 101, Y = 101*)
(*X = 102, Y = 101*)
(*X = 101, Y = 101*)
(*X = 102, Y = 101*)
```

How It Works

The callXY handler is defined to take no arguments. Inside the handler, a script is defined. The showXY script is analogous in function to the script object you defined earlier in this chapter. It defines a property called X with an initial value of 100 and sets and increments a variable called Y.

Because the showXY script is defined *inside* callXY, the script gets redefined each time the handler is called. That means that the property X is reinitialized each time the handler is called. But when the script is run from inside the handler, it does not get reinitialized each time the script is run, as the program illustrates.

The two statements that run the script follow the definition of the showXY script in the handler:

```
run showXY
run showXY
```

The idea is to see what happens to the property X and the variable Y.

When the callXY handler is called in the program, the following occurs:

1. The handler defines a script showXY that exists for the duration of the callXY handler's execution.

2. When the script is defined, the property variable X is initialized to 100.

3. After the script is defined, the script is run two times in succession from inside the handler.

The first time callXY is called, the script is defined and its property variable X is initialized to 100. The script showXY is then run twice from inside the handler. You can see from the log that both the property X and the variable Y are incremented by 1 in the script.

When you run the script for the second time you see that the property X retains its value from its previous execution and is incremented from 101 to 102. The variable Y, on the other hand, is reset to 100 when the script is rerun. This behavior is explained by the fact that the script is defined only once when the handler is called and not each time it is run. After the callXY handler call has completed and returned, it is called again. This has the effect of redefining the script showXY, which means that its property X gets reinitialized to 100. So the bottom line is that each time callXY is called, the script is redefined and its property value X is reinitialized. Make sure you follow this logic. If it isn't clear, go back over this section.

Storing, Loading, and Running Scripts from Files

You saw how the load script command was used in Chapter 8 to load a set of handlers from a file. In the following Try It Out, you see commands for storing a script in a file and running a script stored in a file.

Try It Out   Illustrating the store script and run script Commands

In the following program, you define a simple script, store it in a file, and then run the script you stored in that file.

1. Type the following program into Script Editor:

```
-- Illustrate the store script and run script commands

set scriptFileName to ((path to scripts folder as string) & "test.scpt")

script testScript
    display dialog "Hello" buttons {"OK"} default button 1
end script

-- write the script to a file

store script testScript in file scriptFileName replacing yes

-- run the script stored in the file

run script file scriptFileName
```

2. Run the program. You get the dialog shown in Figure 12-5.

Hello

OK

Figure 12-5

How It Works

You store a script object in a file using the `store script` command. The optional `replacing` parameter specifies whether to overwrite a preexisting file. If the file exists and you specify `replacing no`, the program terminates with an error (unless you catch it within a `try` statement). If you omit the `replacing` parameter completely, the program asks you if you want to overwrite a preexisting file.

After the script has been stored in a file, you can run it directly using the `run script` command. If the script contains a run handler, that's what is executed. If no run handler is present, any top-level statements in the file are executed (remember, you can't have both).

> *The script file you execute with the `run script` command doesn't have to be a file previously saved with the `store script` command. Indeed, any of the script files you have created in this book can be run using this command.*

The program stores the script `testScript` in the file `test.scpt` in the `scripts` folder. If a file of that name already exists there, it is replaced based on the use of the `replacing` parameter.

> *As you see in Chapter 13, when you store scripts in your scripts folder (~/Library/Scripts), you can easily access them later from the Script Menu.*

> *Only the statements that comprise the script are written to the file. This does not include the script's wrapper; that is, the `script testScript` and `end script` statements are not written to the file.*

After you store the script in the file, it is run using the `run script` command. This has the effect of executing the `display dialog` command contained within the script, which displays the message `Hello`.

If you have a run handler in your script and it takes parameters, they can be listed with the `run script` command. You do this by using the `with parameters` parameter, followed by a list of the parameters. A more detailed discussion of this concept is beyond the scope of this book.

In the next Try It Out, you see the difference between running a script with the `run script` command and first loading it with the `load script` command and then running it.

Try It Out   **Running and Loading a Script**

The following program shows you a couple of ways to run and load a script.

1.   Type the following program into Script Editor:

```
-- The run script and load script commands

set scriptFileName to ((path to scripts folder as string) & "test.scpt")

script testScript
    property X : 100

    display dialog "X = " & X
    set X to X + 1
end script

-- save the script to a file
```

```
store script testScript in file scriptFileName replacing yes

-- run the script stored in the file

run script file scriptFileName
run script file scriptFileName

-- load the script into memory and run it

set loadedScript to load script file scriptFileName
run loadedScript
run loadedScript
```

2. Run the program. You should see four successive dialogs containing the numbers 100, 100, 100, and 101, respectively.

How It Works

Each time the run script command is executed, the script contained in the file is defined. So the property X is initialized to 100 each time run script is executed on the file test.scpt. That explains the first two values of 100 that are shown in the dialog.

If you load a script using the load script command, it reads the script into memory but doesn't execute it. You need to run it. The program loads the script and stores it in the variable loadedScript. Loading a script file *does* have the effect of reinitializing the script file's properties.

The second time the script is run, the display dialog command shows you that the property X has the value 101, verifying that its value does persist and is not reinitialized each time the run command is executed.

Script Objects and Object-Oriented Programming

I mentioned at the start of this chapter that AppleScript supports many of the notions of object-oriented programming. You already know that it has the concepts of classes and objects. But it's not as obvious that AppleScript also supports some fundamental OOP features such as inheritance, instantiation, data encapsulation, and polymorphism.

There's not enough space in this book to teach OOP concepts. As a result, this section is geared for programmers with some OOP background. If you don't have such a background, you should read through this section anyway. Perhaps you'll learn something new!

Script objects provide the foundation for OOP programming in AppleScript because they provide the means for you to create an object that contains its own hidden variables (in OOP parlance *instance variables*), and to associate a set of handlers (*methods*) with that object. The script object also encapsulates those handlers, meaning that you can have handlers with the same name inside different script objects. This provides the mechanism for supporting OOP's concept of *polymorphism*, which I discuss in more detail in the next section.

Before I show you a program that uses OOP concepts, you need to know how to return script objects from handlers and why you might want to do that. The next Try It Out illustrates this concept.

Try It Out   Returning a Script Object from a Handler

The following program shows you how to return a script object from a handler.

1. Type the following program into Script Editor:

```
-- Returning a script object from a handler

on testHandler()
    script
        property X : 100

        log "This is from the script!"
    end script
end testHandler

set myScript to testHandler()
log class of myScript
log X of myScript

run myScript
```

2. Click the Event Log tab and run the program. You get the following results logged:

```
(*script*)
(*100*)
(*This is from the script!*)
```

How It Works

The program defines a handler called `testHandler` that takes no arguments. The only thing the handler does is define a script. Notice that there's no name on the script either! That's okay, because the script itself never needs to be referenced by its name.

As you know, the value returned from a handler is that of the last statement executed in the handler. When `testHandler` is called, the script inside the handler gets defined using the `end script` to close off the definition. The *value* of defining this script is a script object, which represents the script itself. That is the value the handler returns.

It may be a little clearer if you realize that you can define `testHandler` this way and achieve the same result:

```
on testHandler()
    script testScript
        property X : 100

        log "This is from the script!"
    end script

    return testScript
end testHandler
```

In this case, you name the script object `testScript` and then explicitly return the script object at the end of the handler's execution. Realize that this definition of `testHandler` and the previous definition are functionally equivalent. They both return a script object that defines a property called `X` and logs a message.

In your program, the handler is called with the following statement:

```
set myScript to testHandler()
```

The script object returned by `testHandler` gets stored inside the variable `myScript`. This may seem like a roundabout way of getting a script object stored inside a variable, but it works! And as you'll see, you gain the added capability to customize the script when you encapsulate it inside a handler.

The next statement in the program tests the class of `myScript`. As you can see from the log's output, the class is `script`.

The statement

```
log X of myScript
```

shows how you access the value of a property stored in the script variable `myScript`.

Finally, the statement

```
run myScript
```

runs the script stored inside `myScript`, which causes the string `"This is from the script!"` to be logged.

The next Try It Out program shows how a script can be customized so that you can create and store different versions of a script.

Try It Out   More on Returning Script Objects

These steps give you more practice in returning script objects. After working through this example, you'll be ready to learn about OOP techniques in AppleScript.

1.   Type the following program into Script Editor:

```
-- Returning a script object from a handler -- Part 2

on testHandler(n)
    script
        property X : n * n
    end script
end testHandler

-- create 2 script objects

set s1 to testHandler(10)
set s2 to testHandler(20)

-- get the properties of each script object
```

```
log X of s1
log X of s2

-- change the property in one script object

set (X of s1) to (X of s1) + 100

log X of s1
log X of s2
```

2. Click the Event Log tab and run the program. You get the following output in the log:

```
(*100*)
(*400*)
(*200*)
(*400*)
```

How It Works

The handler testHandler takes a single argument called n. The script defined inside the handler sets the property X to the square of this argument:

```
on testHandler(n)
    script
        property X : n * n
    end script
end testHandler
```

The script object, which contains a single property called X, with its initial value of n * n, is the value returned by testHandler whenever it gets called.

The program makes two calls to the handler. The first call has an argument of 10, and the second call has an argument of 20:

```
set s1 to testHandler(10)
set s2 to testHandler(20)
```

Let's follow the execution of the first call, in which testHandler gets called with an argument of 10. Inside the handler, this value of 10 is stored inside the variable n. The handler then defines a script object. In that script object, a property called X is defined and initialized to the value of n squared. Because the value of n is 10 in this example, the property X is initialized to the value 100. The handler testHandler then returns this script object to the caller, where it gets stored in the variable s1. So at the end of this first call to testHandler, s1 contains a script object. That script object has a property called X with a value of 100. The fact that you dynamically create a script object that contains a property initialized to a specific value is a key concept here. Reread this paragraph again if the sequence of events is still a little unclear.

After the second call to testHandler, s2 contains a script object having a property called X with a value of 400 (which represents the value of 20^2).

The remaining statements in the program show how the property X can be accessed from the two script objects stored in s1 and s2, respectively:

```
set (X of s1) to (X of s1) + 100

log X of s1
log X of s2
```

The logged values of 200 and 400, respectively, prove that the two properties stored in the two script variables are distinct, even though they share the same name. In fact, these properties are contained within their s1 and s2 objects, a principle in OOP terminology known as *data encapsulation*.

The next Try It Out shows how you use a script object to define a rectangle object.

Try It Out   Defining a Rectangle Object

In the following program, the script object stores the rectangle's width and height as instance variables (properties) and contains methods (handlers) to calculate a rectangle's area and perimeter.

1.   Type the following program into Script Editor:

```
-- Working with rectangles

on rectangle given width:w, height:h
    script
        property width : w
        property height : h

        on area()
            return width * height
        end area

        on perimeter()
            return (width + height) * 2
        end perimeter
    end script
end rectangle

-- instantiate two rectangles

set obj1 to rectangle given width:10, height:20
set obj2 to rectangle given width:5, height:10

-- calculate areas and perimeters of obj1 and obj2

log "Area of obj1 = " & area() of obj1
log "Perimeter of obj1 = " & perimeter() of obj1

log "Area of obj2 = " & area() of obj2
log "Perimeter of obj2 = " & perimeter() of obj2

-- set height of obj2; access values

set height of obj2 to 12
log "Width of obj2 = " & width of obj2
log "Height of obj2 = " & height of obj2
```

2. Click the Event Log tab and run the program. You get this output:

```
(*Area of obj1 = 200*)
(*Perimeter of obj1 = 60*)
(*Area of obj2 = 50*)
(*Perimeter of obj2 = 30*)
(*Width of obj2 = 5*)
(*Height of obj2 = 12*)
```

How It Works

Embedding a script object inside a handler is your way to implement a class in AppleScript. Each time the handler is called, it creates a new script object, which is, effectively, a new instance from the class (in OOP parlance, the handler works as a *constructor*). The script object contains properties that are unique to that object. These properties are analogous to an object's instance variables.

The `rectangle` handler takes two arguments that specify the width and the height of the rectangle. Each time the handler is called, it creates a new script object. That object defines two properties that are used to store the width and the height of the rectangle inside the script.

The script also defines two handlers that have direct access to the script's properties. The `area` and `perimeter` handlers calculate the area and perimeter, respectively, of a rectangle. These handlers are analogous to methods using OOP terminology.

In the program, two different `rectangle` objects are created (that is, *instantiated*) with these two statements:

```
set obj1 to rectangle given width:10, height:20
set obj2 to rectangle given width:5, height:10
```

The first rectangle stored in `obj1` has its width and height set to 10 and 20, respectively. The second rectangle stored in `obj2` has its width and height set to 5 and 10, respectively.

The last three statements in the program show how to set and get the values of instance variables:

```
set height of obj2 to 12
log "Width of obj2 = " & width of obj2
log "Height of obj2 = " & height of obj2
```

True OOP purists may not be happy with directly setting and getting the values of instance variables this way because this violates the OOP methodology of data encapsulation. Purists can write setters and getters in the `rectangle` handler to directly access the instance variables like this:

```
on setHeight to h
    set height to h
end setHeight

on setWidth to w
    set width to w
end setWidth

on getHeight()
    height
```

```
    end

    on getWidth()
        width
    end
```

You can also define a setter to set both the height and width at once, like this:

```
on setRect given width:w, height: h
    setWidth to w
    setHeight to h
end setRect
```

You might also want to define a constructor that just creates a new rectangle without setting the width and height (that is, without taking any arguments). If you did that, a new rectangle could be created and set to a width of 10 and a height of 20 like this:

```
set rect1 to rectangle()
setRect of rect1 given width:10, height:20
```

No matter which approach you use, realize that each time you instantiate a new rectangle object you create a new script object that contains the properties and the handler code. In these examples, the handlers are small in size. However, if you are creating a number of objects that contain a lot of handler code, you might need to separate the handlers from the constructors. Then you could have boilerplate handlers that pass along any necessary properties (that is, instance variables) to the actual handlers that are defined outside the script.

Polymorphism

One of the key features of OOP is the concept of *polymorphism*. It's a big word that can be confusing to novices. The following Try It Out clarifies the use of this terminology.

Try It Out   Polymorphism in AppleScript

In the following program, you see how a rectangle and a square object can be defined and how each object can have handlers with the same names.

1. Type the following program into Script Editor:

```
-- Working with rectangles and squares

on rectangle given width:w, height:h
    script
        property width : w
        property height : h

        on area()
            return width * height
        end area

        on perimeter()
```

```
            return (width + height) * 2
        end perimeter
    end script
end rectangle

on square given side:s
    script
        property side : s

        on area()
            return side * side
        end area

        on perimeter()
            return side * 4
        end perimeter
    end script
end square

-- instantiate a rectangle and a square

set obj1 to rectangle given width:10, height:20
set obj2 to square given side:9

-- calculate areas and perimeters of obj1 and obj2

log "Area of obj1 = " & area() of obj1
log "Perimeter of obj1 = " & perimeter() of obj1

log "Area of obj2 = " & area() of obj2
log "Perimeter of obj2 = " & perimeter() of obj2
```

2. Click the Event Log tab and run the program. You get the following output:

```
(*Area of obj1 = 200*)
(*Perimeter of obj1 = 60*)
(*Area of obj2 = 81*)
(*Perimeter of obj2 = 36*)
```

How It Works

The program defines a `rectangle` and a `square` object using the techniques previously described. Notice that both object constructors define script objects that themselves contains handlers called `area` and `perimeter`. There's no conflict here; the handlers are defined within the scope of their respective script objects.

The program creates a `rectangle` with a `width` of 10 and `height` of 20. It then creates a `square` with a side of 9:

```
set obj1 to rectangle given width:10, height:20
set obj2 to square given side:9
```

The program proceeds to calculate the area and perimeter of the rectangle with these two statements:

```
log "Area of obj1 = " & area() of obj1
log "Perimeter of obj1 = " & perimeter() of obj1
```

When you write `area() of obj1`, the handler that calculates the area of a rectangle gets called. That happens because the script object stored inside `obj1` is returned from the `rectangle` handler. In OOP parlance, the method belonging to the `rectangle` class, which is the class of the object stored inside `obj1`, gets called.

The correct handler to calculate the rectangle's perimeter is called in a similar manner and the result is logged.

The program then uses the `area` and `perimeter` handlers from `obj2` to calculate the area and perimeter, respectively, of the object stored in that variable. Because `obj2` stores a script returned by the `square` handler, the correct handlers for working with squares are called.

Given that the variable `myShape` contains either a `square` or `rectangle` object, the fact that the expression

```
area() of myShape
```

calculates the area of that object, and the expression

```
perimeter() of myShape
```

calculates its perimeter is known as *polymorphism*. Polymorphism gives you the capability to write the same method name for different objects. Or, more in line with OOP parlance, polymorphism gives you the capability to send the same message to objects from different classes.

Inheritance

In line with the basic principles of OOP, AppleScript supports the notion of *inheritance*. Inheritance implies a notion of a *parent* and a *child*, and that the child *inherits* some or all the characteristics of the parent.

You specify that a child script is to inherit the properties and handlers of a parent script called *parentScript* by using this line in your script:

```
property parent : parentScript
```

The child script can define its own properties, and override properties and handlers that it inherits from its parent. If you need to execute a handler in the parent that has been overridden by the child, you can use the `continue` command (which is described later in this section), or explicitly refer to the parent script by the name `parent`.

Work through the following Try It Out to learn more about inheritance.

Try It Out   Illustrating Inheritance

The following program may help you gain a better understanding of the concept of inheritance.

1. Type the following program into Script Editor:

```
-- Show inheritance

script theParent
    property X : 100

    on logX()
        log X
    end logX
end script

script theChild
    property parent : theParent

    set my X to (my X) + 1
    logX()
end script

logX() of theParent
run theChild

logX() of theParent
logX() of theChild

log X of theChild
```

2. Click the Event Log tab and run the program. You get the following results:

```
(*100*)
(*101*)
(*101*)
(*101*)
(*101*)
```

How It Works

The program defines two scripts called `theParent` and `theChild`. The first script defines a property called `X` with an initial value of `100` and a handler called `logX` that logs the value of this property.

The script called `theChild` is defined like this:

```
script theChild
    property parent : theParent

    set my X to (my X) + 1
    logX()
end script
```

The first line of this script is as follows:

```
property parent : theParent
```

If you write `property parent`, followed by a colon and then write the name of a previously defined script object, you inherit the properties and handlers from the specified script. In this case, the script `theChild` inherits the property X and the handler `logX` from `theParent`.

When a property is inherited from a parent, that same property exists in both the parent and the child. That means that you can change its value in either the parent or the child. To reference a property defined in a parent and inherited by the child, you include the keyword `my` in front of the name of the property.

The statement

```
set my X to (my X) + 1
```

says to increment by 1 the property X that is inherited from the parent. If you omit the keyword `my` and write the statement like this:

```
set X to X + 1
```

AppleScript assumes that you are referencing a local variable called X. Because no such variable exists, when you run the program, this statement ends up generating the error `The variable X is undefined`.

Note that you can also reference the property X defined in the parent this way:

```
set X of parent to (X of parent) + 1
```

A child script can call a handler defined in a parent directly by name. This is demonstrated in `theChild` script by the line that reads

```
logX()
```

After defining the two scripts, the program executes the `logX` handler defined in `theParent`:

```
logX() of theParent
```

This has the effect of logging the value of `theParent`'s X property, which is 100.

The program next runs `theChild` script. This has the effect of incrementing the property X, thereby setting its value to 101. The `logX` handler that is inherited from the parent is then called directly to log the value of this property.

The next two statements in the program illustrate that the handler defined in a parent script can be accessed through either the parent or the child:

```
logX() of theParent
logX() of theChild
```

These two statements call the same handler, with the obvious effect.

The last program statement shows that an inherited property can be accessed from outside a script in the normal fashion:

```
log X of theChild
```

Of course, writing this statement instead:

```
log X of theParent
```

retrieves the same value.

In the following Try It Out, you practice using inheritance by defining a square in terms of a rectangle.

Try It Out   Defining a Square Using Inheritance

In the following program, you use inheritance to define a square as a rectangle whose width and height are identical.

1. Replace with the following the definition of the `square` handler from the earlier Try It Out "Polymorphism in AppleScript":

```
on square given side:s
    script
        property parent : rectangle given width:s, height:s
        property side : s
    end script
end square
```

2. Click the Event Log tab and run the program. You get the following output, which is identical to the output from the previous version of the program:

```
(*Area of obj1 = 200*)
(*Perimeter of obj1 = 60*)
(*Area of obj2 = 81*)
(*Perimeter of obj2 = 36*)
```

How It Works

The `square` handler takes a single argument that represents the side of a square. The handler then defines a script that contains this as its first property statement:

```
property parent : rectangle given width:s, height:s
```

Here, the `parent` property is set to the script returned from the `rectangle` handler. This handler is called with the width and height set to the side of the square.

The square inherits the rectangle's `area` and `perimeter` handlers, allowing them to be called directly by any square object. The `side` property stores the square's side, allowing you to get or set the side of the square directly by accessing this property.

Using its in Inherited Handlers

If you want an inherited handler access a property defined within the context of your current script, you use the keyword my in front of the property.

Using my in Handlers

In the following program you see why you need my to access a property inside a handler.

1. Type the following program into Script Editor:

```
-- Illustrate inherited handlers

script theParent
    property X : 100

    on logX()
        log X
        log my X
    end logX
end script

script theChild
    property parent : theParent
    property X : 200
end script


logX() of theParent
logX() of theChild
```

2. Click the Event Log tab and run the program. You get the following results in the log:

```
(*100*)
(*100*)
(*100*)
(*200*)
```

How it Works

The statement

```
logX() of theParent
```

calls the logX() handler defined in theParent. The two statements

```
log X
log my X
```

both have the same effect of logging the value of the property X, which is defined as 100 in the script theParent[S&IS1].

Next, the program executes the inherited logX() handler in theChild script like so:

```
logX() of theChild
```

This time, the two statements in the `logX` handler produce different results. The first logs the value `100`, and the second logs the value `200`. When you use the keyword `my`, AppleScript looks for the property defined within its current context. When you run the `logX` handler of `theChild`, the context is `theChild`, so its `X` property is referenced when the keyword `my` is used.

The continue Command

If a child script defines its own properties or handlers, it overrides any inherited properties or handlers that have the same name. Sometimes, you may want to access the parent's handler. You do this by using the `continue` command, followed by the handler call.

In the next Try It Out, you practice calling a parent's handler.

Try It Out   **Calling a Parent's Handler Using the continue Command**

In the following program, when the child's handler is called, it logs a message and then uses the `continue` command to call the handler defined in the parent script under the same name.

1. Type the following program into Script Editor:

```
-- Illustrate the continue command

script theParent
    property X : 100

    on logX()
        log my X
    end logX
end script

script theChild
    property parent : theParent
    property X: 200

    on logX()
        log "The value of X is on the next line"
        continue logX()
        logX() of parent
    end logX
end script

logX() of theChild
```

2. Click the Event Log tab and run the program. You get the following three lines in the log:

```
(*The value of X is on the next line*)
(*200*)
(*100*)
```

How It Works

The program defines a script called `theParent` that contains a property called `X` and a handler called `logX`. The `logX` handler logs the value of the property `X`, using the keyword `my` in front of the variable.

The script theChild specifies theParent script as its parent. That means it inherits its X property and the logX handler from theParent. The theChild script defines its own property called X with an initial value of 200, and its own handler called logX like this:

```
on logX()
    log "The value of X is on the next line"
    continue logX()
    logX() of parent
end logX
```

Because a handler by this name also exists in the parent script, this handler overrides the inherited one. This version of the handler first adds a message to the log and then calls the similarly-named handler defined in the parent two times. The first time the handler is called by executing a continue command like this:

```
continue logX()
```

When you call a handler this way, you are calling the handler within your current context (almost as if you had typed it in right there). For that reason, the value of X that is logged is its value as defined in theChild script. However, the keyword my must still appear in theParent script for this to work correctly.

The program shows another way to call a parent's handler:

```
logX() of parent
```

This causes the logX handler to be executed within the context of theParent script, causing the property X defined inside that handler to be logged.

You can also use the continue command to force AppleScript to look outside its current context to execute a command. This technique is described in Chapter 13.

Summary

In this chapter, you learned how to work with script objects. In particular, the following key points were covered:

❑ A script object is defined by encapsulating one or more statements within a compound script statement.

❑ When the script object is defined, any properties defined within the script object are initialized.

❑ A script's properties are only initialized once when the script is defined and not when it is run.

❑ Your entire program is a script object, and thus it can define its own properties at the topmost level. Those properties are initialized once and are only reinitialized if the program is modified and recompiled.

❑ A script that has been saved as an application stores it properties within the application. Those property values persist through repeated executions of the program.

❑ Scripts behave like lists and records when they are assigned or passed as arguments to handlers. The `set` command just makes a new reference to a scrip object; the `copy` command makes a new copy of the current script object.

❑ A handler can define and return a script object.

❑ A `script` object can contain handler definitions.

❑ A script can inherit properties and handlers from its parent; it can also override properties and handlers inherited from the parent script.

❑ A script can be stored in a file using the `store script` command. A script stored in a file can be run using the `run script` command and loaded into your program using the `load script` command.

❑ A handler or property defined in a parent can be explicitly referenced through its `parent` property.

❑ A handler in a parent can be run within the context of the child by using the `continue` command.

❑ Scripts can be used to implement many of the OOP paradigms, such as instantiation, methods, instance variables, data encapsulation, and polymorphism.

In the next chapter, I take a look at some miscellaneous material that was either a little advanced or just didn't quite fit in any other chapter of the book. Before proceeding, however, try the exercises that follow to test your understanding of the material covered in this chapter. You can find the solutions to these exercises in Appendix A.

Exercises

1. Write a script called `countMe` that logs the number of times it's been called. Then run the script 10 times in a `repeat` loop to test it out.

2. The surface area of a sphere with radius *r* is given by the following formula:

   $$Surface\ area = 4\ \pi\ r^2$$

   Add a handler called `surfaceArea` to the `circle` script object developed in this chapter and test it out.

3. AppleScript has a built-in class called `point` that is simply a two-item list of numbers that you can use to conveniently represent a coordinate point. For example, the following creates a point with coordinates (100, 200) and assigns it to the variable P1:

```
set P1 to {100, 200} as point
```

   Extend the `rectangle` and `square` classes to contain a `point` property called `origin` that stores the object's origin, with a default value of (0, 0). Add methods called `setOrigin` and `getOrigin` to set and get the values of this origin.

4. In Script Editor, save your definitions of the `rectangle` and `square` handlers in a file called `rects.scpt` in your folder. (Why can't you use the `store script` command to do this?) Then, use the `load script` command to load the script file you created in Exercise 3. Create a rectangle with a width of 15 and a height of 20 and a square with sides of 12. Calculate and log the area of the rectangle and the perimeter of the square.

5. A dictionary is a data structure used in many programming applications (not to be confused with the application dictionaries that you deal with in AppleScript). For example, on the Mac, the Cocoa programming environment supports dictionaries. A dictionary is defined as an unordered list of entries, where each entry consists of a key and a corresponding value. Each key in a dictionary must be unique.

You don't necessarily use a dictionary to store words and their definitions, although that's certainly one application. Here's an example of how you might store a concise dictionary of some OOP terms in AppleScript:

```
set OOPDict to { ¬
    {"instance", "A concrete representation of  a class"}, ¬
    {"OOP", "Abbreviation for Object-Oriented Programming"}, ¬
    {"message", "The method and its associated arguments sent to an object"}, ¬
    {"method", "A procedure belonging to a class"}, ¬
    {"instance variable", "A variable that belongs to an instance of an object"}, ¬
    {"class", "A set of instance variables and associated methods"} ¬
    }
```

For this exercise, define a new constructor handler called `makeDict`. The constructor creates a script object that contains a dictionary and associated methods. The dictionary should simply start out as a null list. Define the following methods for your dictionary object:

```
on setEntry given key:theKey, value:theValue -- replace value if key already exists
on getValue given key:theKey  --  return value for given key
on delEntry given key:theKey  -- remove entry for given key
on listKeys ()  -- returns a list of keys
```

Given these methods, here's how you create the previously listed `OOPdict` dictionary and add two entries to it:

```
set OOPDict to makeDict ()
setEntry of OOPDict given key: "instance", value:"A concrete representation of a
    class"
setEntry of OOPDict given key:"OOP", value:"Abbreviation for Object-Oriented
    Programming"
```

Here's how you look up class in the dictionary:

```
getValue of OOPDict given key: "class"
```

Hint: It will help to write a handler that searches your dictionary for a specific key and returns an index number in the list if the key is present.

Loose Ends

This chapter contains material that didn't make it into any of the previous chapters. Subjects like transactions, AppleEvents, and the `do shell script` command are more advanced topics that I chose not to cover earlier. Subjects like using the clipboard, using Script Editor's record mode, and Folder Actions fall into the miscellaneous category and don't quite fit in anywhere else.

The topics discussed here are not presented in any particular order, so feel free to skip around and read the sections that pique your interest. Because of the nature of the subject matter, as well as the scope and size of this book, I provide just an introduction to each topic.

Command Handlers

You've already seen how to write special handlers that do not conform to the normal syntax of the handlers you learned about in Chapter 8. These special handlers can take direct objects that you specify immediately after their name. In Chapter 10 you saw this used for the special `run`, `open`, `quit`, and `idle` handlers. In addition to these special handlers, as you see in Chapter 14, AppleScript Studio sends special commands to respond to events that occur with objects in your application. You provide the handlers to process these events by attaching the handler to the object.

These special handlers, called *command* handlers, respond to a command sent to an application. In some situations, you can also write a command handler that redefines an application's command. You can do this with commands built into AppleScript, including any of the Standard Addition commands.

The easiest command I can use to illustrate this technique is the `beep` command. Recall that you can use it without an argument to generate a single beep, as in

```
beep
```

You can also specify an integer number to generate more than one beep, as in

```
beep 5
```

In the next Try It Out you see how to write a command handler for the beep command.

Try It Out   Writing a Command Handler

The following program uses the continue command to execute the built-in beep command after the handler finishes.

1.   Type the following program into Script Editor:

```
-- Command handlers

on beep n
    activate
    display dialog "BEEP!" with icon caution buttons {"OK"} giving up after 2
    continue beep n
end beep

beep 5   -- try it out
```

2.   Run the program. You get a dialog containing the message BEEP! that goes away after a couple of seconds. This is followed by five audible beeps.

How It Works

The program defines a command handler for the beep command. The optional argument, which is the number of beeps, is called n. The handler issues the activate command to bring the current application to the front. This ensures that the dialog that follows is frontmost. If you execute the display dialog command when your application is not frontmost, your application bounces in the Dock, indicating it requires attention.

After the program puts up a dialog to display the message "BEEP!" it executes the following command:

```
continue beep n
```

You may recall that I used the continue command in Chapter 12 to call a handler defined in a parent script object. This example illustrates a different use for the command.

Perhaps this wasn't the most practical example, but you get the point. Besides, this could be used to give you a visual beep, which might be useful, for example, if your volume setting is turned all the way down or is muted.

Using terms from

You know about references to objects. In Chapters 10 and 11, I discussed references to Finder and iTunes objects in detail. For example, the following tell statement asks iTunes to give you a reference to the first track of your library:

```
tell application "iTunes" to set track1 to first track of first library playlist
```

This stores the following reference in the variable `track1` (your id numbers will be different):

```
file track id 1138 of library playlist id 1103 of source id 34 of application
"iTunes"
```

This is a complete reference to the specified track. With this reference stored in your variable, you can subsequently look for some information about that track. For example, if you want the artist's name you could write the following:

```
get artist of track1
```

If you execute this statement outside of a `tell` block, you get an error. Why? Because AppleScript doesn't know what an `artist` is. An `artist` is a property of a `track`, and it's defined in the iTunes dictionary. Because you're not executing the previous statement inside a `tell` block, that dictionary is not consulted when Script Editor compiles your program. Because the reference includes a reference to iTunes, iTunes will be given this statement to execute. The fact that iTunes wasn't consulted at compile time to resolve the term `artist` results in an error when you execute the statement.

> *You can tell something's amiss from the color that Script Editor gives to the word `artist` after compilation: it's green, meaning that Script Editor thinks it's just one of your variables.*

To tell Script Editor to reference terms from an application's dictionary, you can enclose statements inside a `using terms from` compound statement. This can fix the previous problem, like so:

```
using terms from application "iTunes"
    get artist of track1
end using terms from
```

Note that the word `artist` is blue after compilation. That means that Script Editor has resolved this word against a dictionary (in this case, the iTunes dictionary). Unlike a `tell` statement, the application object specified with the `using terms from` statement does not become a target. It's merely consulted to resolve terminology. A `using terms from` statement is often a handy way to get terms from an application inside a `tell` statement that talks to a different application. You can use this method to avoid conflicts that can occur with nested `tell` blocks.

> *You can still use a `tell` block in the previous example if you like. In this example it makes no difference. However, as mentioned, this technique is useful for resolving terms from a dictionary when you don't want to target commands to the application.*

Using the clipboard

You can use the `clipboard` to transfer data between your programs by using some Standard Additions commands that work with the `clipboard`. To access the contents of the `clipboard` in your program, write the following:

```
the clipboard
```

Here's what the clipboard contains after I copy this section's title from my Word file to the clipboard:

```
"Using the Clipboard"
```

Here's what the clipboard contains if I copy an image from Safari to the clipboard:

```
«data
PICT00000000000000950073001102FF0C00FFFE00000048000000480000000000000095007300000000
0001E
   ...
»
```

You can also copy something from your AppleScript program to the clipboard by using the set the clipboard to command, like so:

```
set the clipboard to "This is going onto the clipboard."
```

You can even tell some applications to paste whatever's on the clipboard at the current selection point in the active document, like so:

```
tell application "Microsoft Word"
    activate
    paste
end tell
```

This works because Word has a paste command. It's an easy way for you to get some data from AppleScript into your document. You can also do it like this:

```
tell application "Microsoft Word"
    activate
    set selection to the clipboard
end tell
```

You can have Word copy the current selection as a string onto the clipboard like so:

```
tell application "Microsoft Word"
    set the clipboard to the selection as string
end tell
```

If you don't specify the as string part, you get a reference to an object in Word instead. Also, in general, many applications put styled text onto the clipboard. That is, text that includes font, size, and style information. You have to be aware of that if you just want to work with a string.

The following example tells Safari to put the text of the first document window (your frontmost browser window) onto the clipboard as a string

```
tell application "Safari"
    activate
    set the clipboard to text of first document as string
end tell
```

The Script Menu

Apple provides a utility known as Install Script Menu that enables you to easily access and run scripts from your menu bar. When you run this utility, which is located in your `/Applications/AppleScript` folder, it silently runs and installs an icon in your menu bar. In Figure 13-1, the Script Menu icon is the leftmost icon.

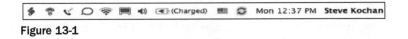

Figure 13-1

If you click the Script Menu icon, you get a drop-down menu showing all the scripts installed in the system's script folder, `/Library/Scripts`, followed by a list of scripts (or folders containing scripts) that you have installed in your own `Scripts` folder, `~/Library/Scripts` (see Figure 13-2).

There is also a way to display scripts associated with the frontmost application in the lower pane of this menu, but that's not shown here.

```
Open Scripts Folder
Hide Library Scripts

   Address Book Scripts      ▶
   Basics                    ▶
   ColorSync                 ▶
   Finder Scripts            ▶
   Folder Actions            ▶
   FontSync Scripts          ▶
   Info Scripts              ▶
   Internet Services         ▶
   Mail Scripts              ▶
   Navigation Scripts        ▶
   Printing Scripts          ▶
   Safari Scripts            ▶
   Script Editor 1.9 Scripts ▶
   Script Editor Scripts     ▶
   Sherlock Scripts          ▶
   UI Element Scripts        ▶
   URLs                      ▶

   AIM® Handler Scripts      ▶
   ASLibraries               ▶
   iPhoto Librarian
   iPod                      ▶
   iTunes                    ▶
   List Handlers
   QuickTime Player Scripts  ▶
   rects
   Safari Scripts            ▶
```

Figure 13-2

You can choose to hide the system library of scripts by selecting Hide Library Scripts from the pull-down menu. You can also open your own `Scripts` folder by selecting Open Scripts Folder. You can execute a script simply by selecting it from the Script Menu.

Folder Actions

The Mac allows you to attach a script to a folder. If you have attached a script to a folder, that script is automatically executed whenever one of five specific folder actions occurs. This action causes a specific handler in your script to be called. The following table summarizes the folder action and the corresponding handler that gets called.

Folder Action	Handler that Gets Called
opening a folder	`opening folder folder`
closing a folder window	`closing folder window for folder`
adding items to a folder	`adding folder items to folder after receiving fileList`
removing items from a folder	`removing folder items from folder after losing fileList`
moving or resizing a folder window	`moving folder window for folder from boundingRectangle`

These handlers get called when one of the listed actions occurs on a folder that is open in the Finder. These handlers each get passed an alias to the folder attached to the script. The alias is passed because you can attach the same script to as many folders as you like. You can test the argument to see which folder caused the handler to be called.

You don't have to handle all five of these folder actions. Instead, you just write the handlers for the actions you want to handle.

A list of files is also passed to the `adding items to` and `removing folder items from` handlers. In all cases, these actions only work for folders that are open in the Finder.

Make sure you distinguish a folder action from a droplet, which was covered in Chapter 10. A folder action allows you to attach a script to a folder in order to execute the script whenever an action occurs on the folder. A droplet is an application that gets launched whenever one or more files or folders are dropped onto its icon.

The next Try It Out shows how to work with Folder Actions.

Try It Out   Working with Folder Actions

This Try It Out shows how to attach a script to a folder. Assume that the folder is used to store image files that you want to rotate. Whenever you add one or more files to the folder, your attached script is automatically executed. Your script uses the Image Events application to rotate JPEG and TIFF images by 90 degrees.

1. Type the following program into Script Editor:

```
-- Rotates JPEG and TIFF images that are placed in the folder

on adding folder items to theFolder after receiving fileList
    display dialog "Rotating Files..." buttons {"OK"} default button 1 giving up
after 2

    repeat with theFile in fileList
        set infoRec to info for theFile

        if (name extension of infoRec) is in {"JPG", "JPEG", "TIF", "TIFF"} then
            tell application "Image Events"
                launch
                set thePic to open file (POSIX path of theFile)
                rotate thePic to angle 90
                close thePic saving yes
            end tell
        else
            display dialog "false"
        end if
    end repeat
end adding folder items to
```

2. Save the file under the name `Rotate90` in the following folder: `~/Library/Scripts/Folder Action Scripts`. If the folder does not exist, create it.

3. Create a folder on your desktop called `Rotated Images`.

4. Ctrl-click (or right-click if you have a two-button mouse) on your `Rotated Images` folder. You should get a menu like the one shown in Figure 13-3. If your menu does not show Enable Folder Actions, Folder Actions are already enabled on your system. In that case, your window should look like Figure 13-4, and you can skip to Step 6.

5. Click Enable Folder Actions.

6. Ctrl-click (or right-click if you have a two-button mouse) your `Rotated Images` folder. You will get the menu shown in Figure 13-4. Select Attach a Folder Action.

7. You should get a window asking you to Choose a File. Locate the script file `Rotate90` that you stored in `~/Library/Scripts/Folder Action Scripts` and click Choose.

8. Locate some JPEG or TIFF images on your system and drag them into the `Rotated Images` folder. When you drag an image file into the folder, you get the dialog shown in Figure 13-5.

9. Examine the images in your folder. Notice that they have all rotated 90 degrees.

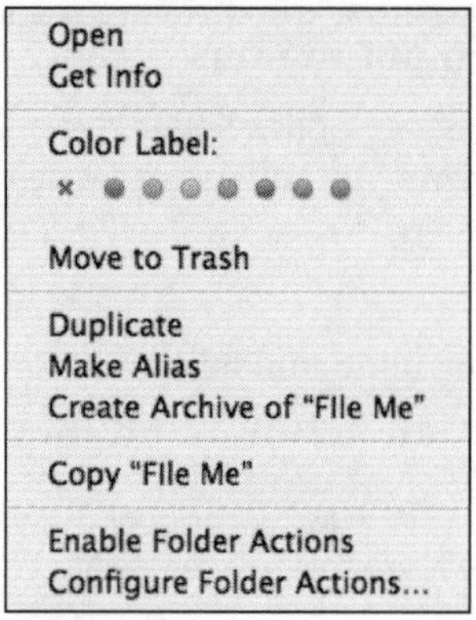

Open
Get Info

Color Label:
× ● ● ● ● ● ● ●

Move to Trash

Duplicate
Make Alias
Create Archive of "FIle Me"

Copy "FIle Me"

Enable Folder Actions
Configure Folder Actions...

Figure 13-3

Open
Get Info

Color Label:
× ● ● ● ● ● ● ●

Move to Trash

Duplicate
Make Alias
Create Archive of "FIle Me"

Copy "FIle Me"

Disable Folder Actions
Configure Folder Actions...
Attach a Folder Action...

Figure 13-4

Rotating Files...

OK

Figure 13-5

How It Works

You have to select Enable Folder Actions in order to attach scripts to a folder. The scripts have to be stored in a folder called `Folder Actions`. You can have a system-wide Folder Action script, which you store in `/Library/Scripts/Folder Actions`, that allows all users to use the script. Alternatively, you can store your script for your own use in `~/Library/Scripts/Folder Action Scripts`.

Your program to rotate an image 90 degrees is saved under the name `Rotate90` in your `Folder Actions` folder. When you Ctrl-click that folder in the Finder, you bring up its Contextual menu, which allows you to attach a script to that folder. After you've attached a script, when one of the five actions listed in the previous table occur on that open folder, your script is executed. Depending on the action, the appropriate handler that matches that action inside your script (if present) is executed.

Your program defines an `on adding folder items to` handler. Whenever one or more files get added to any folder you attach to this script, this handler is executed. The handler gets passed an alias to the folder that initiated the execution of the handler and a list of files.

The handler checks to see if the file is either a JPEG or TIFF. If it is one of those two formats, the Image Events application rotates the image. This is done in the following `tell` block:

```
tell application "Image Events"
    launch
    set thePic to open file (POSIX path of theFile)
    rotate thePic to angle 90
    close thePic saving yes
end tell
```

The Image Events application is a background process that does not have a user interface; therefore, no windows are open while it's running, and it doesn't appear in the Dock. You don't activate Image Events. Instead, you start it by issuing a `launch` command. Image Events provides commands to perform all sorts of useful image manipulations. For example, certain commands allow you to flip, scale, crop, resize, and rotate images. You can also open an image file and save it under a different format, giving you the ability to convert images from one type to another. Image Events supports many different image types in addition to JPEG and TIFF formats: JPEG2, PICT, BMP, PSD, PNG, and QuickTime Image. You can easily extend the example program to handle these other image types.

The program opens the image file and stores a reference to the image in the variable `thePic`. Note that POSIX paths are required. The `rotate` command is used to rotate the image by 90 degrees, but any positive angle can be specified. After the rotation is done, the image is saved by closing it with the `saving` parameter specified as `yes`. You can also save an image to another file by using Image Event's `close` command.

Open Scripting Architecture

The Open Scripting Architecture (OSA) is an Apple concept that allows applications, such as Script Editor and others, to support multiple scripting languages in a way that is independent of the actual scripting language. Under this design, a scripting language can be dynamically installed as a component on your system. As of this writing, AppleScript is the only OSA language that Apple releases with OS X.

The Script Editor application is designed to work under this OSA architecture. It really doesn't know any AppleScript at all; it just knows that AppleScript is an installed OSA component. If you look under the toolbar in your Script Editor window, you see a pop-up menu in the Navigation Bar that enables you to select any OSA component. (If you don't see your Navigation Bar, choose View➪Show Navigation

Bar.) You probably see only AppleScript here. On my system, I have two additional OSA components that I can choose from: JavaScript and AppleScript Debugger, both of which are available from Late Night Software (refer to Appendix C for more information).

Scripting Additions

When you learned how to examine the Standard Additions dictionary in Chapter 4, I briefly mentioned the term *osax*, which stands for Open Scripting Architecture extension. The Standard Additions osax is stored on your system in the folder `/System/Library/ScriptingAdditions` under the file name `StandardAdditions.osax`. Because the Standard Additions is available on all Mac OS X systems, the commands in this text have been treated as an integral part of the AppleScript language. A scripting addition can be written by anyone. After an addition is installed in your `ScriptingAdditions` folder, the addition's commands and terms become immediately available for use in your AppleScript programs, as if they were built into the language.

Satimage is a company that offers several scripting additions. These include a math addition that provides arithmetic and transcendental functions; a text addition for performing search and replace operations and formatting numbers; a files addition that enhances some of the Standard Additions commands; and a regular expressions addition for working with regular expressions.

As an example, the Satimage osax contains a command called `change` that performs a search and replace on a character string. By placing that osax file into the ScriptingAdditions folder, I can write a command like this directly in my program:

```
change " " into "X" in "This is a test of the Emergency Broadcast System"
```

This changes all occurrences of a space character to the letter X, producing the following result:

```
"ThisXisXaXtestXofXtheXEmergencyXBroadcastXSystem"
```

If you start using osax commands in your programs, make sure that the osax is installed on any system on which you want to run your program. As previously noted, this is not an issue with the Standard Additions osax because it's available on all Mac OS X systems.

AppleEvents

Applications talk to each other through packets of information known as *AppleEvents*. When you send a command to an application, AppleScript composes an AppleEvent that consists of the command and its parameters. It then sends the event to the application and waits for a response. The application responds to AppleScript through another AppleEvent. The event may specify that it doesn't understand the command; or if it can handle the command, it will reply with the result (which may be an error), if any, after executing the command.

Here's an example: Suppose you ask the Finder to delete a file. AppleScript composes an event consisting of the command, which is `delete`, and its direct object, which is a file reference. Then it sends the event to the Finder and waits for a reply. The Finder gets the event and looks at what it's been asked to do. Because Finder understands the `delete` command, it handles the command itself. The file reference that is part of the event specifies the file to delete. If the file is successfully deleted, the Finder sends back an event to AppleScript containing the reference to the deleted file.

As you see in the next Try It Out, communication with scripting addition commands are also managed through AppleEvents. That includes the Standard Additions commands.

Try It Out   **AppleEvents in the Event Log History**

To examine AppleEvents with Script Editor, follow these steps:

1.   Choose Script Editor⇨Preferences.

2.   Select History from the toolbar.

3.   Check Enable Event Log History and then close the window.

4.   Choose Window⇨Event Log History. A window titled Event Log History opens.

5.   Select Log Events and Results from the pop-up menu located at the top of the window.

6.   Type the following program into Script Editor:

```
tell application "Finder" to count files in home
display dialog current date
```

7.   Run the program. You get the following AppleScript error: `Can't make date "Thursday, August 26, 2004 10:24:14 AM" into a string`. The date shown on your system is the current date when you run the program. Click OK to dismiss this sheet.

8.   Figure 13-6 shows the Event Log History window after running your program. In that figure, all entries have been *unfolded* by clicking the ▶ character (the disclosure button) that appears in front of each line in the window. You can unfold all the disclosure buttons at once by Option-clicking the top one.

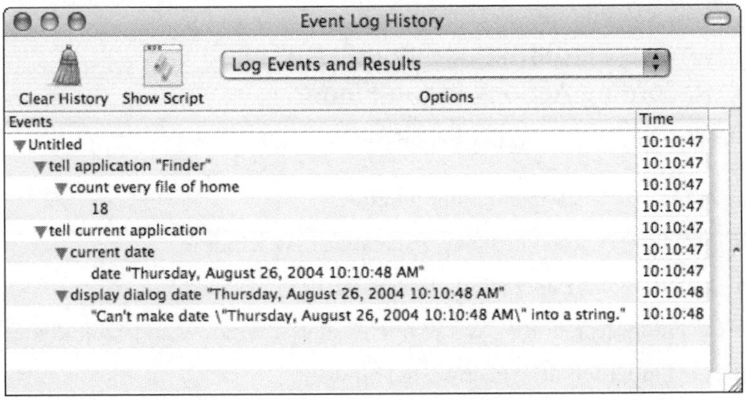

Figure 13-6

How It Works

Script Editor's Event Log records AppleEvents and not just the output from your `log` commands. In the Event Log History window, you see a record of the event: the command sent to the application or osax, its parameters, and the result that is returned.

When you run these two statements, you get an error. Looking in the Event Log pane or in the Event Log History window can prove enlightening. The Event Log History window displayed in Figure 13-6 shows that one event is sent to the Finder to count every file of home. The event returns the value 18. Because the `current date` and the `display dialog` commands are Standard Addition commands, AppleScript sends events to the current application to be handled. In the case of the `current date` command, you can see the resulting date in August that is returned. Notice that the date returned by the `current date` command is passed to the `display dialog` command. The command returns an error because it cannot coerce the date into a string.

You can also look at Apple Events at a much lower level, where you can see the actual bytes of information that are sent in each AppleEvent. I won't go into that here.

Recording Scripts

Mac OS X provides a couple of solutions to help you in the situations where an application has limited or no scriptability. One of these is the capability to record events inside Script Editor while you do work in the application that you want to script. In many ways, it's analogous to a macro record mode in a word processor like Microsoft Word. The actions you want to later repeat are recorded as you press keys, select menu items, and click buttons.

When you tell Script Editor to stop recording, you have a program you can run to duplicate the actions that you performed in the application. Well, that's the theory anyway. In practice, applications have to support recordability, and most offer very limited support, if any, for this feature. BBEdit, a text and HTML editing application, is one of the few applications that is fully recordable.

The Finder is also recordable, as you see in the next Try It Out.

Try It Out	Recording Actions in the Finder

Follow these steps to practice recording actions in the Finder:

1. In the Finder, close all open Finder windows.
2. In Script Editor, choose File⇨New to create a new window.
3. In the toolbar of your new window, click Record.
4. Click the Finder icon in the Dock to open a Finder window and carefully follow the next steps.
5. Resize the Finder window to any size you want.
6. Move the Finder window to some other place on the screen.

7. In the Finder window, locate your Documents folder and select the file TextFile101.txt that you created in Chapter 7. If the file is no longer there, select any file.

8. Click the file's name (but don't double-click) so that you can change it. Rename the file TextFile102.txt. If you selected a different file in the previous step, change its name to anything you like.

9. Switch back to your Script Editor window and click Stop in the toolbar of the window.

10. A program is created in your Editor window like that shown in Figure 13-7. Your window's contents can differ substantially from what is shown, especially if you didn't follow Steps 2 through 7 precisely.

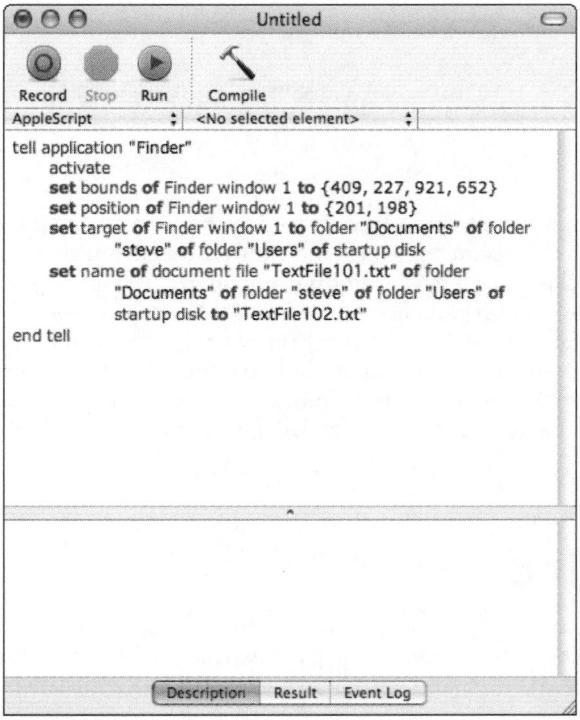

Figure 13-7

How It Works

When you click Record in Script Editor's toolbar, Script Editor starts recording commands from the applications you use. If the application is not recordable, Script Editor cannot record any commands. In the case of the Finder, which is recordable, Script Editor recorded the following operations:

❑ The resizing of the Finder window, which is done in AppleScript by setting the window's bounds property

❑ The relocation of the Finder window, which is done in AppleScript by setting the window's position property

❑ The selection of a folder in the window, which is done in AppleScript by setting the window's `target` property

❑ The renaming of a file, which is done in AppleScript by setting the file's `name` property

As you can see, this is a valuable tool when supported by the application. It's a good starting point for developing a script to work with an application.

QuickTime is another application that is recordable. To test it out, I turned on record mode in Script Editor, switched to QuickTime, and then chose File⇨Open Movie in New Player to select a movie to play. I adjusted the volume slider on the movie as well. After the movie finished playing, I closed the QuickTime window and told Script Editor to stop recording. Here's what I got:

```
tell application "QuickTime Player"
    activate
    open file "Macintosh HD:Users:steve:Movies:kids.mov"
    set sound volume of movie "kids.mov" to 170
    close movie "kids.mov" saving no
end tell
```

When I ran this recorded script, QuickTime opened my movie and then immediately closed it. What happened? Well, the movie started playing when it was opened, but after the action of setting the sound volume, QuickTime closed the movie! Unfortunately, no AppleScript code was generated while I was waiting for the movie to finish playing in Record mode. The good news is that this approach easily taught the AppleScript commands to get QuickTime to play a movie file for me. The bad news is that even recordable applications can have quirks and need fine-tuning. You won't get a polished, ready-to-go script in most cases. For this example, I removed the `close` command and the movie played just fine. However, I didn't bother to figure out how to wait for the movie to finish playing so I could close the QuickTime window.

GUI Scripting

GUI Scripting gives you the ability to script almost any application on the Mac. It does this by mimicking the actions of clicking the mouse, selecting menu items, and typing keystrokes. The next Try It Out gives you a quick look at how to use this technique for scripting applications.

Try It Out   Introduction to GUI Scripting

This program shows how you can copy the text inside your TextEdit window to your application without knowing the specific AppleScript command to do this. You saw how to use the clipboard commands earlier in this chapter to accomplish this; these steps provide another approach.

1. Select System Preferences from the Apple Menu.

2. In the System Preferences window, click the icon labeled Universal Access.

3. Check Enable Access for Assistive Devices. Enter your administrative password when prompted.

4. Close the System Preferences window.

5. Launch the TextEdit application.

6. Type some lines of text into the TextEdit Window.

7. Type the following program into Script Editor:

```
-- Copy the text from TextEdit's window to the clipboard

tell application "System Events"
    tell application process "TextEdit"
        set frontmost to true
        click menu item "Select All" of menu "Edit" of menu bar item "Edit" ¬
                of menu bar 1
        click menu item "Copy" of menu "Edit" of menu bar item "Edit" of menu bar 1
    end tell
end tell

delay 1
the clipboard
```

8. Click the Result tab and run the program. The text from the web page you loaded should be displayed in the Result pane.

How It Works

By enabling access for assistive devices you turn on an option in Mac OS X that allows software commands to simulate physical actions like clicking a button or selecting a menu item. This feature (or *interface*) enables people who may have physical limitations to use applications that they otherwise might not be able to work with. As an additional benefit, you can access this interface to write AppleScript programs that also simulate these physical actions.

GUI Scripting is handled by the System Events application. Inside a `tell` block to that application, you select an application process to talk to. Application processes are managed by System Events. To make the application process the frontmost process (and thus the target of your GUI requests), you set its `frontmost` property to `true`. This program assumes that Safari is already launched. If it's not, you get an error.

> *You don't activate the process; you activate an application, not an application process.*

The `click` command is a System Events command and is followed by a UI element that you want to "click" in software. UI elements can be menu buttons, progress indicators, sheets, menus, tool bars, radio buttons, scroll bars, text fields, and so on. These are all classes defined in Systems Events.

In the program, you simulate the action of clicking a `menu item` in the toolbar. You see from the program how to specify a complete reference to such a menu item. The first `click` command simulates choosing Select All from the Edit menu, as if you typed it directly in TextEdit. This has the effect of selecting the entire contents of the frontmost document's window. The second `click` command simulates selecting Copy from the Edit menu. This has the effect of copying everything to the clipboard. The program uses the `delay 1` command to enable data transfer between the application and your program. Without it, the program sporadically gives an error when it's run (when I used Safari instead of TextEdit for this test, I got an error every other time I ran the program without the `delay` command).

Because many applications have an edit menu that allows you to copy things to the clipboard, this program can be used to get data from these applications into your program via the clipboard.

With an interactive application like Smile or Script Debugger, you can look at the UI elements in a particular application process and try to deduce how to make the application do what you want. You can also use a tool such as UI Element Inspector (available free from Apple) or PreFab UI Browser (a more sophisticated utility) to more easily examine an application's UI Elements.

Before and After

Some applications let you specify an item relative to another one by using the keywords `before` and `after`, or their corresponding synonyms `in front of`, `behind`, and `in back of`.

For example, you can ask the Finder to give you the file after the first file on your desktop by sending it a command like this:

```
file after first file on desktop
```

This approach is more practical when you are talking to text editors from your program. You can give this command to TextEdit to give you the paragraph after the first one in your front document window:

```
paragraph after first paragraph of front document
```

Of course, this is equivalent to writing the following:

```
second paragraph of front document
```

You should note that you can't use `before` and `after` to refer to items or properties in a list or record. That means the following will not work:

```
item after first item of myList  -- Sorry, doesn't work!
```

The `before` and `after` keywords are used primarily when working with word processing applications like TextEdit. They allow you to insert text before and after other text in a document, typically at an insertion point.

Creating a Reference to an Object

AppleScript has an operator called `reference to` that allows you to explicitly create a reference to another object. Here's a small example:

```
set x to 100
set y to a reference to x
y
```

When you run this program, you get the following in the Result pane:

```
x of «script»
```

The variable y doesn't contain x, but rather a reference to it. In some situations, AppleScript automatically dereferences the value for you (for example, in arithmetic expressions). So this works

```
y + 1
```

and results in the value 101.

However, in inequality and equality tests, AppleScript does not do the dereferencing for you, so this expression

```
y = 100
```

is false. You can dereference the value yourself by asking for the contents of the reference. The following comparison produces a true result:

```
contents of y = 100
```

For the most part, you don't need to worry about making references like this (particularly as a beginning AppleScript programmer). However, you may see programs that use this operator. In particular, creating a reference to a list is a paradigm for working efficiently with large lists. So you may see code that looks like this:

```
set listRef to a reference to bigList
set sum to 0
set  numItems to count bigList

repeat with i from 1 to numItems
    set sum to sum + item i of listRef
end repeat
```

Here, you want to sum all the numbers in bigList, which is presumably a large list of numbers. By working with a reference to the list, you dramatically improve the speed of processing the elements in the list. This speed improvement doesn't apply if you insert elements at the beginning of the list or add elements to the end of the list. That's already efficient; therefore, you don't use a list reference in such cases.

In Chapter 6, a method that used my showed how to work efficiently with large lists. So, for the most part, you can bypass using the reference to operator altogether.

Web Services: XML-RPC and SOAP

XML-RPC and *SOAP* are services that work over the Internet. They let you access software over the web, so they are referred to as *web services*. Just in case you're curious, XML stands for Extensible Markup Language, RPC is an abbreviation for Remote Procedure Call, and SOAP stands for Simple Object Access Protocol. XML-RPC was developed in the late 1990s. SOAP, which came after XML-RPC, is more complex than XML-RPC and is still an evolving standard.

You can use web services to execute the software that they store by targeting an HTTP address to the application in a `tell` block. Inside the `tell` block, you make the call to the service, passing along any required parameters. This request is translated into XML and then sent to the specified location. The result is returned (also as XML) to your program, where it can be assigned to a variable, copied to the clipboard, and so on. This translation to and from XML is automatically handled for you, so you don't need to learn XML to use these services.

AppleScript supports interaction with SOAP and XML-RPC through two commands: `call soap` and `call xmlrpc`.

You can explore various websites to find SOAP and XML-RPC services. Some are free of charge; other services may require you to subscribe. The website `http://xmethods.net` is a good place to look. Consult Appendix C for some more resources.

The general format for making an XML-RPC request from AppleScript is as follows:

```
tell application XML-RPC-URL
    set resultVar to call xmlrpc {method name: method, parameters:  paramList}
    ...
end tell
```

Here `XML-RPC-URL` is an http address for the XML-RPC service. For the `call xmlrpc` command, a record with two properties is supplied. The property called `method name` has as its value a string specifying the action you're requesting. The property called `parameters` has as its value a list of parameters to be passed to the action. The result of the action, if any, is returned to your program. In the general format shown previously, this value is assigned to a variable.

Here's the general format for a `call soap` command:

```
tell application SOAP-URL
    set resultVar to call soap {method name: method, parameters:  paramList, ¬
        method namespace uri: namespace, SOAPAction: action}
    ...
end tell
```

This command takes five parameters, some of which are optional. You know what values to supply for the properties of the record by looking at the documentation for a particular XML-RPC or SOAP service. Admittedly, it is often not easy to decipher the documentation and determine how to translate it into an appropriate AppleScript call. I recommend you experiment and look at other examples.

Here's how to use a SOAP service to get a temperature for a given zip code in the United States. It uses a method named `getTemp` at the following URL: `http://services.xmethods.net:80/soap/servlet/rpcrouter`. The zip code used in the example is mine, `07405`. Note that it has to be passed as a string:

```
tell application "http://services.xmethods.net:80/soap/servlet/rpcrouter"
    set theTemp to ¬
        call soap { ¬
                method name:"getTemp", ¬
            method namespace uri:"urn:xmethods-Temperature", ¬
```

```
                                    parameters:{zipcode:"07405"}, ¬
                                    SOAPAction:"/TemperatureService" ¬
                            }
    end tell
```

The record for the `call soap` command is formatted just to aid readability.

Unfortunately, the documentation for this service on the `xmethods.net` website describes the call in XML. This is typical for most SOAP calls:

```
Sample Request envelope:

<SOAP-ENV:Envelope xmlns:SOAP-ENV="http://schemas.xmlsoap.org/soap/envelope/"
xmlns:xsi="http://www.w3.org/1999/XMLSchema-instance"
xmlns:xsd="http://www.w3.org/1999/XMLSchema">
<SOAP-ENV:Body>
<ns1:getTemp xmlns:ns1="urn:xmethods-Temperature" SOAP-
ENV:encodingStyle="http://schemas.xmlsoap.org/soap/encoding/">
<zipcode xsi:type="xsd:string">94041</zipcode>
</ns1:getTemp>
</SOAP-ENV:Body>
</SOAP-ENV:Envelope>
```

From this documentation, you deduce the `method name` (from the `ns1` field), the `method namespace uri` (from the `xmlns` field), and the `parameters` (see the `<zipcode. . . >` line in the listing).

In the next Try It Out, you use SOAP services to get a delayed stock quote for a stock symbol entered by the user.

Try It Out   Using SOAP Services

In the following program example, the method named `getQuote` takes a stock symbol as a string and returns a real number representing a quote for the stock. An error is returned as the number `-1.0`, which can happen if you type an invalid stock symbol.

1. Type the following program into Script Editor:

```
-- Use SOAP to get a stock quote

display dialog "Enter your stock symbol: " default answer ""
set theSymbol to text returned of result

set theQuote to missing value

try
  tell application "http://services.xmethods.net:9090/soap"
      set theQuote to call soap { ¬
                  method name:"getQuote", ¬
          method namespace uri:"urn:xmethods-delayed-quotes", ¬
                  parameters:{symbol:theSymbol}, ¬
                  SOAPAction:"urn:xmethods-delayed-quotes#getQuote" ¬
                  }
```

```
    end tell
  on error
    return
  end try

  if theQuote = -1.0 or theQuote = missing value then
    display dialog "Can't get quote for " & theSymbol with icon note buttons {"OK"} ¬
            default button 1
  else
    display dialog "The price for " & theSymbol & " is " & theQuote as string
  end if
```

2. Run the program. When prompted by the dialog, type in a stock symbol (like AAPL) and click OK.

3. You should get a dialog that gives the price of the requested stock. If a price can't be obtained or an error occurs, a dialog alerting you to this fact is displayed.

How It Works

The program prompts the user to key in a stock symbol. The call soap command takes the resulting quote that is returned and stores it in the variable theQuote. The call is made inside a try block in case something goes wrong, for instance if you can't connect to the website for some reason. The resulting quotation is then displayed by the program.

> I can't guarantee that the SOAP methods used in this section will be available. If for some reason the request fails, look at the website and try using a different method. Also check this book's pages on www.wrox.com. They give you another method to use.

Running Scripts from Terminal

Mac OS X contains a command called osascript that allows you to execute AppleScript commands and files from the command line. If you're used to using the Terminal application to enter UNIX commands, you may find the osascript command to be a nifty little program.

The general format of the osascript command is as follows:

```
osascript scriptFile
```

Here scriptFile is a POSIX path to a script file, perhaps one that you previously created in Script Editor. To execute a single AppleScript statement, you use this form of the osascript command:

```
osascript -e commands
```

Here's a command you can type to the shell to have iTunes play the song called "The Reason":

```
osascript -e 'tell app "iTunes" to play track "The Reason" of first library
playlist'
```

If you know how to write shell scripts, you can create a small shell script called play, *for example, that takes the name of the song as its argument and executes an* osascript *command like that shown previously to play the specified song.*

Here, the entire AppleScript statement is enclosed in a pair of single quotes, but they're removed before the statement gets executed. Using single quotes is generally recommended because they hide any double quotes inside the AppleScript statement from the command line shell.

You can use osascript to execute more than a single line. Simply type your open single quote, write as many lines as you need, and then type another single quote to close everything off. The entire set of lines is then be given to the osascript command to execute.

The following example asks the Finder to count the files in your home directory. (Here your command prompt is shown as a $ and the text you type is shown in bold. The > character is also displayed by the shell when you continue a command line. Your command prompts may differ.)

```
$ osascript -e '
> tell app "Finder"
>     count files in home
> end tell
```

...g these lines, I got the following output, indicating I have 18 files in my home folder:

...advice: You can't execute an interactive command like display dialog with osascript ...ectly from the command line or from inside a script that you run). That means that this won't

```
osascript -e 'display dialog "Hello"'
```

Interactive commands have to be executed indirectly, that is through another application. To put up a dialog, for example, you can go through the Finder, like this:

```
$ osascript -e '
> tell app "Finder"
>     display dialog "Hello"
> end tell
'
```

The do shell script Command

Sometimes, you just can't do everything you need to do in AppleScript. The do shell script command lets you execute any other command on the system and capture its output. If you're an experienced UNIX user, you understand that this command passes a command line to the UNIX shell for execution and captures its output (written to standard output).

The `ls` command without any additional arguments lists the files in your current directory. Here's how to execute the command from AppleScript and capture its output in your program:

```
set files to do shell script "ls"
```

This is a less efficient approach than using AppleScript's `list files` command, which is handled directly by AppleScript. The `do shell script` command must start up another process (the shell) and ask it to execute the specified command line.

To get a list of the files in your `Documents` folder, you could give `ls` the name of the folder to list as an argument:

```
do shell script "ls " & POSIX path of (path to documents folder as string)
```

All UNIX commands use POSIX paths, so you convert any Mac-style paths as necessary. In the next example, the shell's `printf` command is used to format the value of `pi` to two decimal places:

```
set x to pi
set cmdLine to "printf " & "%.2f" & " " & pi
do shell script cmdLine
```

Here's the result that is returned from the `do shell script` command:

```
"3.14"
```

This is useful for formatting numbers, which is not easy to do in AppleScript (you can write a special handler to do it).

Because the shell processes your command line, you have to be careful about any quotation marks or special character that may be in your command line. That's because quotes (single, double, and back quotes!) and other special characters (including a space!) have a special meaning to the shell. A safe way to protect your command line for the shell is by supplying the `quoted form` property of your command line string as the argument to the `do shell script` command, like so:

```
do shell script quoted form of myCommand
```

When you use the `quoted form` property of a string, the entire string is enclosed in a pair of single quotes (which provides maximum protection from the shell), and any embedded double quotes are escaped to the shell (that is, are preceded by a backslash character).

Don't use `quoted form` on the entire command line if it contains a command with one or more arguments because the shell sees the entire command line as the name of the command. This causes an error. You can use the `quoted form` on individual arguments. For example, consider the following statement:

```
set bookDirectory to POSIX path of ((path to documents folder as string) & ¬
        "Beginning AppleScript")
```

On my system, this sets the variable `bookDirectory` to the following POSIX path:

```
/Users/steve/Documents/Beginning AppleScript
```

The wc command counts characters, words, and lines in a file. The –1 option to this command counts the number of lines. If I wanted to ask the shell to count the number of files in my book directory (and you know how to use the Finder in AppleScript to do that), you might be tempted to write the following:

```
set fileCount to (do shell script "ls " & bookDirectory & " | wc -l ") as number
```

The | character is the UNIX pipe symbol that allows the output from the command to its left to be connected to the input of the command to its right.

If you try this it won't work because of the embedded space in the directory name Beginning AppleScript; the shell sees this as an argument delimiter. In order to keep these two words together, you can write your command line like this:

```
set fileCount to (do shell script "ls " & quoted form of bookDirectory & ¬
        " | wc -l ")  as number
```

Seasoned AppleScript users take maximum advantage of the do shell script command to do all sorts of things: run Python, Ruby, and Perl scripts, grab web pages (using the curl command), and so on.

The with transaction Statement

The with transaction statement is a compound statement that enables you to lock communication with an application so that no one else can send commands to the application and potentially foul up the works. This is useful when you are issuing a series of commands to an application to accomplish a certain task. By enclosing those commands inside a with transaction block (which is terminated by an end transaction), you effectively gain exclusive rights to talk to that application. The only *caveat* is that the application must support this mechanism; how it's implemented is up to the application. The application can implement transactions in a non-exclusive way, as long as it guarantees that no one else can interfere with your transactions. An application may also choose not to support transaction processing at all.

Normally, you would place the with transaction block inside the tell block that talks to the application.

Delayed Evaluation with the run script Command

AppleScript's run script command lets you execute a string as if it were a statement in your program. For example, suppose you have a command that's stored inside a string, like so:

```
set myCommand to "display dialog \"Hello!\""
```

You can't execute the command in the string just by writing

```
myCommand
```

because that just gives you the string. However, you can give the string to the `run script` command to execute, like so:

```
run script myCommand
```

The string specified as the argument to `run string` is compiled and executed, resulting in a dialog with the message "Hello!"

Perhaps you have handler calls stored as a table of strings in a list. Suppose you want to call one of those handlers based on some criteria, such as a choice selected by the user. This type of structure is often referred to as a *dispatch table*. You can pull the appropriate command string from the list based on the criteria and then give it to `run script` to execute.

With the `run script` command you can dynamically build a command based on parameters and then have it evaluated. This can be a powerful technique. You should note that, inside your command string, you use `my` to preface variables and properties that you want to access or modify (if they are defined outside the command string). You can do the same thing by following the variables or properties with `of me`.

The following shows how you can get a value from a variable whose name is stored in a string:

```
set x to 100
set varName to "x"
set y to run script "my " & varName
```

This results in the value of the variable `x`, which is `100`, being assigned to `y`. Note that the variable must be previously assigned a value before you execute the `run script` command.

Scheduling Scripts to Run with the cron

In Chapter 3, I showed you how to schedule your salutation application to run every time you log in to the system. You can also schedule programs to run at particular times, such as on the first of every month, every morning at 6 AM, or every 10 minutes. You do this with a feature of OS X known as *cron*.

The cron process is always running in the background on your computer. The process checks for scheduled events and, when necessary, initiates their execution. An event is scheduled for execution through a text file known as the *crontab*. There is a system crontab (stored in `/etc/crontab`), where the administrator can specify system programs to run on a periodic basis. A program scheduled this way might clean up temporary files or backup files, for example.

You can also have your own crontab and store it where you like. The next Try It Out shows you how to schedule a program to run once an hour and to sound a chime like a big clock. It's called Big Ben!

Try It Out   **Chime the Hour!**

In this program, you make your program chime every hour.

1.   Type the following program into Script Editor:

```
-- Big Ben!

-- Get the hour

set theTime to time string of (current date)
set theHour to first word of theTime as integer

-- adjust for a 24-hour clock

if theHour is 0 then
    set theHour to 12
else if theHour is greater than 12 then
    set theHour to theHour - 12
end if

-- Ring the hour

repeat theHour times
    say "ding" using "Bells"
end repeat
```

2. Save the program as an application in your home directory under the name `Big Ben`.

3. Start up a text editor like TextEdit to create a file called `myCrontab` in your home directory and type the following lines, replacing the path in the last line with a full path to your Big Ben application. Be sure to separate each of the six fields on the last line with a single tab character. This is critical; you can't use spaces or multiple tabs. The cron program uses tabs to delimit fields in your `crontab` file.

```
SHELL=/bin/sh
PATH=/etc:/bin:/sbin:/usr/bin:/usr/sbin
HOME=/var/log
#
#minute hour    mday    month   wday    command
#
0       *       *       *       *       "/Users/steve/Big Ben.app"
```

4. Save your file and exit the text editor. Now, locate the application Terminal, which is in your `/Applications/Utilities` folder. Launch this application. A window opens with some lines that look similar to this:

```
Last login: Wed Aug 25 09:09:52 on ttyp2
Welcome to Darwin!
$
```

The Terminal application enables you to type commands to the UNIX shell. These are typed on the line after your *prompt*, which is $ in the previous listing.

Your prompt may be set to something else, like the name of your current directory.

Commands are sent to the shell for processing by pressing the Return key.

5. When the Terminal application starts, you should be in your home directory. You can verify this by typing the command `pwd` followed by Return. The name of your current working directory will be listed, which should be your home directory.

6. The application file, `Big Ben.app`, and the `crontab` file, `myCronTab`, you created in the previous steps should be located in this directory. This can be verified by typing the `ls` command and pressing Return. You should see these two files among the list of files in your current directory.

7. Type the following `crontab` command to schedule your Big Ben program to run once an hour:

```
$ crontab myCrontab
```

8. If you get just a prompt after typing the previous command, the `crontab` command was successful. You can also verify this by using the `-l` option to the `crontab` command, which lists the contents of the crontab it "has on file" for you:

```
$ crontab -l
```

9. Wait for the time to reach the next hour. When it does, your Big Ben program should run and chime the hour.

How It Works

Your program extracts the hour of the current date by getting the first word of the time string. This works because the colon that delimits the hours from the minutes is considered a word delimiter character by AppleScript. Therefore, the first word of the time string is whatever appears to the left of the first colon, or the hour.

If the hour is zero, which it may be if you're using a 24-hour clock, the variable `theHour` is set to 12. You must also make an adjustment for hours between 1 PM and midnight to handle those times when a 24-hour clock is being used.

The word "ding" is then spoken once for each hour using the Bells voice. This sounds like a bell (well, almost). The `using` parameter is followed by the name of a voice to use. You can use any voice that's listed under System Preferences⇨System⇨Speech. I chose Bells for obvious reasons.

The first three lines of your crontab file contain a header that you can just leave there. The remaining lines from the file are shown here:

```
#
#minute hour    mday    month   wday    command
#
0       *       *       *       *       "/Users/steve/Big Ben.app"
```

The cron treats lines in your `crontab` file that start with # character as comments. The first three lines serve to remind you of the format of the fields in the `crontab` file. The first field specifies a minute of the hour (as a number from 0 to 59), the second field the hour (as a number from 0 to 23), the third field the day of the month (as a number from 1 to 31), the fourth field the month (as a number from 1 to 12), the fifth field the day of the week (as a number from 0 to 6, with 0 representing Sunday), and the last field is a full path to the command to be executed at the scheduled time(s). An asterisk used for a field means "every."

Based on this, the last line of your `crontab` file says to run the program /Users/steve/scripts/ch13/ Big Ben.app (the quotes around the path name are needed because of the space between Big and Ben) every time the minutes are equal to zero — that is every hour on the hour.

Here are some more examples of crontab entries. The following entry would run a backup program at 5:30 AM on Saturdays:

```
30      5       *       *       6       "/Users/steve/MyApplications/Backup.app"
```

This entry specifies a program called `taxReminder` to be run at 9 AM on April 15th:

```
0       9       15      4       *       "/Users/steve/scripts/ch13/taxReminder.app"
```

The notation `*/n` can be used in a field to specify *n* as an interval. For example, the following says to run the Big Ben application every 15 minutes:

```
*/15    *       *       *       *       "/Users/steve/Big Ben.app"
```

If you had a version of Big Ben that sounded a chime every 15 minutes, that's how you would schedule it to run. (I created such an application, using actual recordings of Big Ben's chimes that I play from iTunes!)

Commas can be used to list multiple entries for a field, as in:

```
30      5       1,15    *       *       "/Users/steve/MyApplications/Backup.app"
```

This says to run the backup program at 5:30 AM on the 1st and 15th of every month.

Finally, a dash can be used to specify a range. The following says to run the `checkFiles` program every hour on the hour between 1 AM and 6 AM, inclusive:

```
0       1-6     *       *       *       "/Users/steve/MyApplications/checkFiles.app"
```

After you schedule a program to run with the cron, it remains scheduled through logoffs and system restarts. To cancel the scheduling, you remove the entry from your `crontab` *file (or just insert a # character at the beginning of the line) and rerun the* `crontab` *command with the modified* `crontab` *file.*

Summary

This chapter provided a tapestry of various techniques, features, and commands. In particular, you learned

❑ How to write a command handler

❑ When to use a `using terms from` block

❑ How to work with the clipboard

❑ How to activate the Script Menu and install and remove scripts

❑ How to attach a script to a folder using the Folder Actions feature

❑   The principle of the Open Scripting Architecture

❑   What a Scripting Addition is

❑   How to get scripts from recordable applications

❑   How to use the GUI Scripting feature to write scripts for unscriptable applications

❑   The use of the keywords `before` and `after`

❑   What an AppleEvent is

❑   How to use web services XML-RPC and SOAP

❑   How to use `osascript` to execute an AppleScript program or command from the Terminal application

❑   How to use the `do shell script` command to execute UNIX command lines

❑   How to use the `with transaction` statement

❑   How the `run script` command works

❑   How to schedule scripts to run with the cron

In the next chapter, you are introduced to AppleScript Studio, which is a powerful development environment that enables you to create sophisticated Graphical User Interfaces (GUIs) for your programs. Before proceeding, however, try the exercises that follow to test your understanding of the material covered in this chapter. You can find the solutions to these exercises in Appendix A.

Exercises

1.   Modify the program that chimes the hour to also chime the quarter-hour. Be creative in how you chime each quarter hour. You should be able to distinguish 15, 30, and 45 minutes after the hour. One possibility is to download some Westminster chime audio from the Internet, install it in iTunes, and then play the appropriate quarter-hour song from iTunes.

Install your program into the crontab so that it is executed every 15 minutes.

2.   Here's some documentation for a SOAP service at `http://www.xmethods.net:80/soap/servlet/rpcrouter` that provides a price quote for a book given its ISBN number:

```
Sample Request envelope:

<SOAP-ENV:Envelope xmlns:SOAP-ENV="http://schemas.xmlsoap.org/soap/envelope/"
xmlns:xsi="http://www.w3.org/1999/XMLSchema-instance"
xmlns:xsd="http://www.w3.org/1999/XMLSchema">
<SOAP-ENV:Body>
<ns1:getPrice xmlns:ns1="urn:xmethods-BNPriceCheck" SOAP-
ENV:encodingStyle="http://schemas.xmlsoap.org/soap/encoding/">
<isbn xsi:type="xsd:string">0439139597</isbn>
</ns1:getPrice>
</SOAP-ENV:Body>
</SOAP-ENV:Envelope>
```

Write an AppleScript program that enables a user to key in an ISBN number for a book and looks up its price. Find the current selling price for this book, whose ISBN number is 0764574000.

3. Examine the Image Events dictionary to see what capabilities it has for performing image manipulation. Then write a Folder Action script that will scale an image file added to a folder by 50%.

4. Recall the File Me droplet from Chapter 10. That droplet took a list of files and filed them into various folders based on their extensions. Rewrite that program so that it works as a Folder Action instead of a droplet. Attach it to a folder called `File Me` on your desktop.

5. Use the GUI Scripting example from this chapter to copy data from different applications into your program.

Introducing AppleScript Studio

So far throughout this book, you've developed programs that have a simple user interface. You relied on the trustworthy `display dialog` command to display a message or to get input from the user. As useful as this command is, however, it is very limited in its capabilities. For example, this command only allows one field for data input and cannot display multiple fields of output. In fact, I showed you how to build a list and use the `choose from list` command to display multiple lines of output in a not-so-straightforward manner.

Certainly, other programs you use on the Mac are friendlier than AppleScript. In fact, the Mac's reputation is based on its user-friendly dialogs and ease of use. It would be great if AppleScript could somehow tap into that paradigm and support interfaces that provide for multiple inputs and outputs and perhaps even show tabular data, images, and so on.

You are lucky; this is where AppleScript Studio comes to the rescue! Not only does AppleScript Studio provide the tools for developing sophisticated graphical user interfaces (GUIs), but it also provides a powerful environment for program development, consisting of editing and debugging tools and convenient access to online documentation.

To do it justice, a sophisticated tool like AppleScript Studio requires a book at least as long as this one. Therefore, this chapter can provide only an introduction. But I offer sufficient coverage here to give you a solid understanding of what AppleScript Studio is all about.

Installing AppleScript Studio

In order to work with AppleScript Studio, you have to install the developer tools. If you have a folder called `/Developer` on your system, the tools are probably already there. If not, you'll have to install the Xcode Tools from your OS X installation CDs in order to try the examples in this chapter.

If your Mac didn't ship with a separate Xcode CD, you may have a compressed disk image inside `/Applications/Installers` that you can use to install Xcode.

You can get the latest version of the tools for free from Apple's Developer Connection website. First, you have to register as a developer. Go to http://developer.apple.com, where you can register as an online developer for no charge. After you've registered, you can sign in and download the Xcode Tools.

The discussions in this chapter are based on Xcode 1.5 and Interface Builder 2.4.2.

Developing a Simple Application

In this chapter, you develop an application with a simple user interface. Recall the program from Chapter 13 that you used to fetch a stock quote. That program allowed you to enter a stock symbol with one dialog, and then it displayed the resulting stock price with another. Here, you use AppleScript Studio to develop a better user interface. Instead of asking for the stock and then separately displaying the result, you design an interface that enables you to enter the stock's ticker symbol and show the quote in the same window. This is a fairly simple example, but you can't do it in AppleScript using only the built-in commands.

Figure 14-1 shows the interface for the application you'll develop in AppleScript Studio.

Figure 14-1

Figure 14-2 shows the result of typing AAPL into the Enter Symbol field and clicking the Get Quote button (or pressing Return). As you can see, Apple Computer's stock was selling for 30.8 when this program was run.

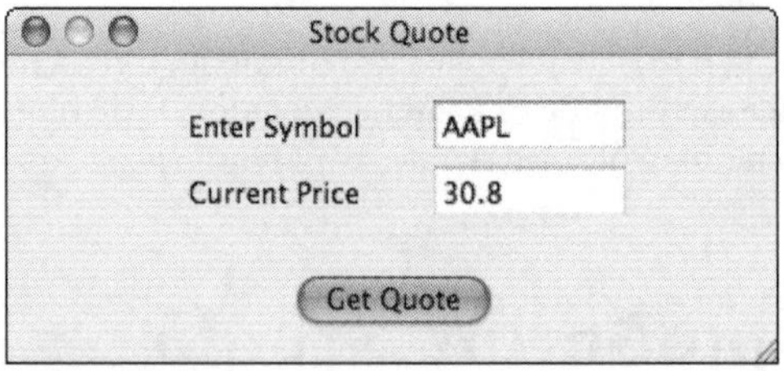

Figure 14-2

Now it's time to develop your Stock Quote application, which you do in the following Try It Out.

Try It Out   **Working with AppleScript Studio**

It's important that you follow all these steps in order. It's easy to get lost using AppleScript Studio at first. You need to gain the experience of working with two applications simultaneously.

1.   Locate the Xcode application. It's inside `/Developer/Applications`, with the icon shown in Figure 14-3.

Figure 14-3

2.   To start a new project in AppleScript Studio, launch the Xcode application. You get a window like that shown in Figure 14-4. If this window does not appear, choose File⇨New Project from the menu bar, which produces the Assistant window shown in the figure.

```
○ ○ ○                          Assistant

        ▮▮        New Project


        Empty Project
        ▼ Application
           AppleScript Application
           AppleScript Document-based Application
           AppleScript Droplet
           Carbon Application
           Cocoa Application
           Cocoa Document-based Application
           Cocoa-Java Application
           Cocoa-Java Document-based Application
        ▼ Bundle
           Carbon Bundle
        ▼ Command Line Utility

        This project builds a simple Cocoa application written in AppleScript.



        ( Cancel )                    ( Previous )   ( Next )
```

Figure 14-4

3.   Select AppleScript Application under the Application category and click Next. This results in a new Assistant window.

4.   Name your new project and tell Xcode where to store the files associated with that project. Here, I've typed stock quote in the Project Name field. Notice that the Project Directory field automatically changes, as depicted in Figure 14-5. Recall that ~ indicates your home directory. According to the figure, the files associated with your new project will be stored in a directory called stock quote in your home directory.

Figure 14-5

5.   Click Finish. The Assistant window closes and a new window opens, as shown in Figure 14-6.

Figure 14-6

The contents of your window may differ slightly, particularly if you've used Xcode before. If your right pane doesn't look like what's shown in Figure 14-6, click the Editor icon in the toolbar. This toggles the view of the right pane. (You can also split the view in the right pane by pulling on the dot just below the bar at the bottom of the pane.)

6. Notice the categories in the left pane of your window. The right pane shows the contents of the selected item in the left pane. If stock quote is not selected, select it now so that your window conforms to what is shown in Figure 14-6.

7. Navigate in the left pane to get familiar with its contents. The Scripts folder is used to store your AppleScript files associated with your project. Open this folder and reveal its contents by clicking the disclosure button (▶). You should see a file called stock quote.applescript listed here. This file is a template for your program. It was created by Xcode when you created your new project.

8. Select stock quote.applescript in the left pane. Next, click the Editor icon in the toolbar. Your window's content should resemble what's shown in Figure 14-7.

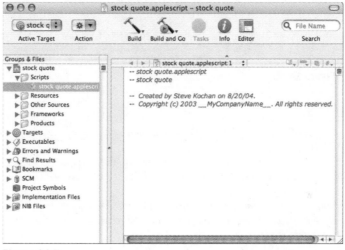

Figure 14-7

9. In the left pane, reveal the contents of the folder listed under Resources by clicking its disclosure button (▶). Select the file AppleScriptKit.asdictiontary. Your window should look like the one shown in Figure 14-8.

10. The right pane shows the contents of the dictionary. In addition to viewing and editing your program files, Xcode enables you to view dictionaries and other documentation. Here you are looking at the AppleScript Studio Kit dictionary. You will reference this key dictionary as you develop programs with AppleScript Studio. Spend some time navigating through this dictionary, as you have done with other dictionaries. Look at the various categories, and examine the classes and commands under each category. These classes represent various objects you can use with your interface.

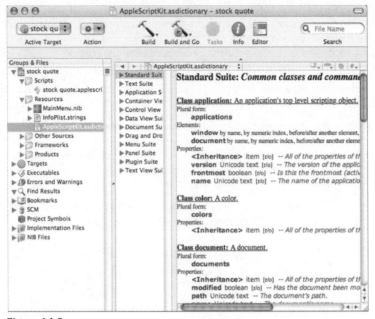

Figure 14-8

You can open any file in its own window by double-clicking the file in the left pane. When you first start using AppleScript Studio, it's a good idea to avoid confusion by having as few open windows as possible.

11. When you're finished examining the dictionary, open the `NIB Files` folder in the left pane. You see a file listed there called `MainMenu.nib`, as depicted in Figure 14-9.

A nib *file contains all the information about the user interface for your program, including information about its windows, buttons, menus, sliders, text fields, and so on. Of course you don't have a user interface yet! That's the next step.*

Figure 14-9

12. Double-click the `MainMenu.nib` file. This action causes another application, Interface Builder, to launch.

You can also access the NIB file from the `Resources` *folder of your project.*

When Interface Builder starts, you get a series of windows drawn on your screen, as depicted in Figure 14-10. The actual windows opened, as well as their position on your screen, may differ from what's shown in the figure.

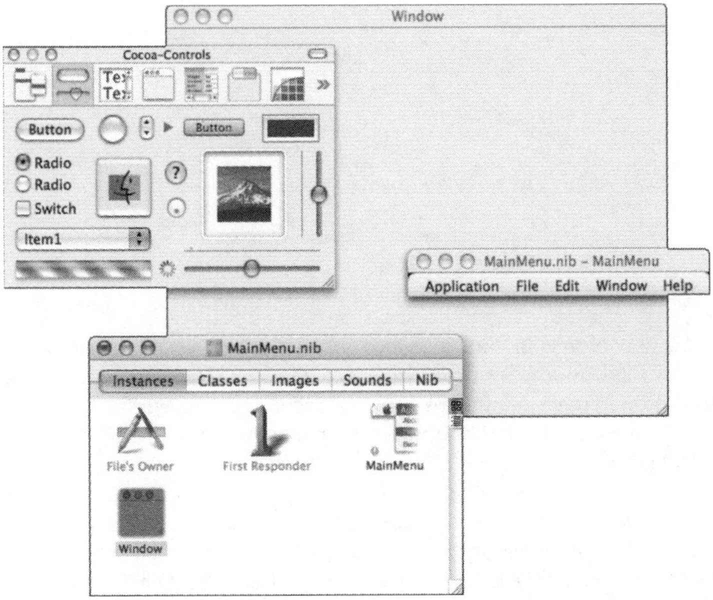

Figure 14-10

13. Before going any further, it's a good idea to clean up your screen. Otherwise, you'll have Xcode and Interface Builder windows open simultaneously. This may confuse you (and it can get a lot worse when you start debugging your program and switching back and forth between the two applications). From the menu bar, choose Interface Builder⇨Hide Others. This hides all other application windows.

14. Examine the various windows open on your screen. Notice their titles:

❑ **Window:** This is your *interface* window. It's a blank slate on which you will design your interface.

❑ **MainMenu.nib:** This window gives you control over all the components of your interface, including images, sounds, and menus.

❑ **MainMenu.nib – MainMenu:** This window is where you work on the menu for your application. In this window you can add to, rename, and remove items from the menu.

❑ **Cocoa-Controls:** This window is your palette for selecting user interface (UI) elements. The various icons in the toolbar represent different categories of elements you can use in your interface. When you select a category from the toolbar, the window changes to display the UI elements from that category. (The window's title also changes to reflect the selected category.) It's then simply a matter of selecting one of those elements and dragging it onto the Window window. Figure 14-10 shows the Cocoa-Controls window with the display of the various buttons and sliders that you can use in your interface design.

15. To begin designing your interface, click the window titled Window. Resize the window so that it is smaller and more rectangular, as shown in Figure 14-11. It doesn't have to precisely match the size of the window shown in the figure. You can always resize it again later if you need to.

Figure 14-11

16. You create new objects in your interface window by click-dragging one of the objects from the Cocoa-Controls window into your interface window. Click-drag an oblong button (the one labeled Button in the top-left corner of the Cocoa-controls window) into your interface window. Release the mouse when the button is near the center of the window, close to the bottom, as shown in Figure 14-12.

Blue guide lines appear in your window as you move the control around. Sometimes they appear to help you align objects with other objects previously placed in the window. At other times, they appear to make sure your objects are spaced far enough apart from other objects and from the edges of the window. This is consistent with Apple's interface guidelines, known as the Apple Human Interface Guidelines, which you can obtain using the following URL: `http://developer.apple.com/documentation/UserExperience/Conceptual/OSXHIGuidelines/OSXHIGuidelines.pdf[S&IS1].`

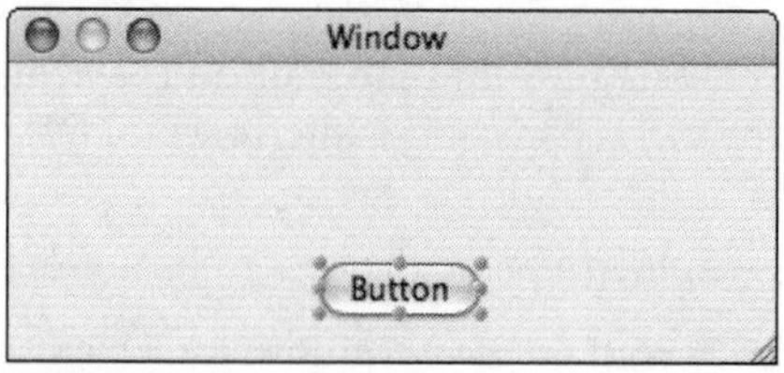

Figure 14-12

You can always reposition the button in the window by click-dragging it to another spot inside the window.

17. Double-click the button you just created. The text field of the button is selected, allowing you to change its title. Type Get Quote to change the button's title. Notice how the size of the button automatically expands to accommodate the width of the label. Your interface window now has a button called Get Quote, as depicted in Figure 14-13!

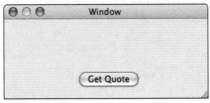

Figure 14-13

18. Now you're going to create two text fields: one for entering the stock symbol and the other for displaying the resulting price. Go to the Cocoa-Controls window and select the third icon from the left (the icon that contains two rows of characters starting with Tex) from the toolbar. This opens the text palette, as shown in Figure 14-14, and the window should be titled Cocoa-Text.

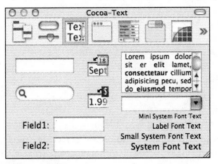

Figure 14-14

19. Click-drag the top leftmost text box from the Cocoa-Text window into your interface window. Repeat this process to create a second text box. Align the two text boxes as shown in Figure 14-15.

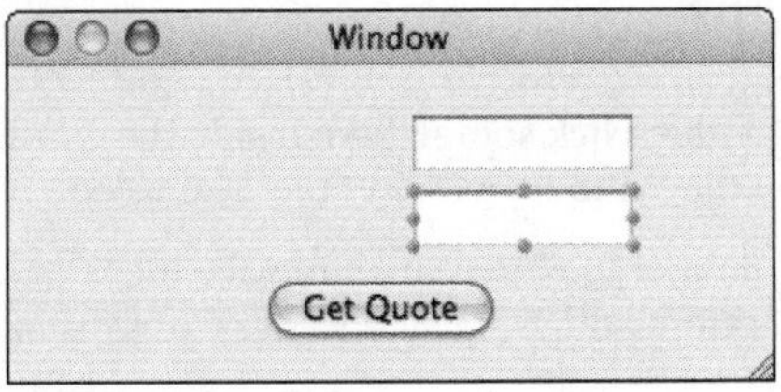

Figure 14-15

20. From the Cocoa-Text window, select the line labeled System Font Text. Click-drag this line (which represents an object) into your window and place it to the left of your topmost text box. Repeat this process, placing the second label to the left of your lower text box. Align your labels and boxes as shown in Figure 14-16. Use the blue guidelines to aid in your alignment.

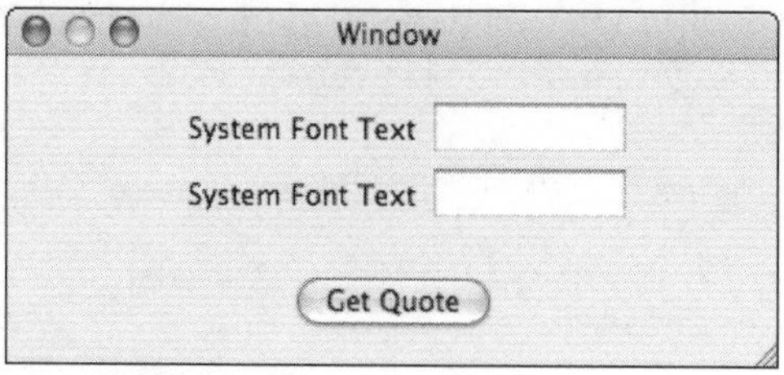

Figure 14-16

21.	Double-click the top label and change its title to `Enter symbol`. Next, double-click the lower label and change its title to `Current price`. Your interface window should now look like Figure 14-17.

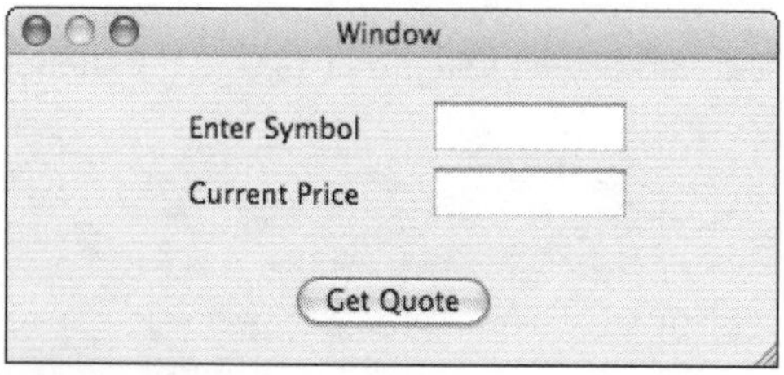

Figure 14-17

22.	Open the Info panel by choosing Tools⇨Show Info. This is a window that allows you to specify *events* and *attributes* for the objects you create for your interface. For example, you must define what happens when the Get Quote button is clicked. You do this by forming a connection between the event of clicking the button and the AppleScript code that handles the click. Also, you don't want the title of your application's window to remain simply *Window,* as it is currently. You change its name by changing one of the window's attributes, namely its title.

23.	In your interface window, click various objects and notice how the Info Panel window changes to display information about that object. The title of the Info Panel reflects the type of object you have currently selected.

24.	To get the Info panel displayed for your interface window (and not for any particular element within the window), either click somewhere inside the window (making sure you don't select an object), or click on the Window icon in your MainMenu.nib window.

25.	In the Window Title field of the Info panel, replace the text `Window` with `Stock Quote` and uncheck the Resize option, which is listed under Controls in that same panel (see Figure 14-18).

	You don't want to give your users the capability to resize your interface's window, which is why you want to uncheck the Resize option. Make sure your Info panel matches the one shown in this figure. Your interface window should now have a new title, as shown in Figure 14-19.

26.	In your Stock Quote window, click the top rightmost text field. That's the field where you want the user to enter his stock symbol. You should notice that the Info panel changes to what you see in Figure 14-20 as soon as you click this text field. In this Info panel, you can see that Editable is checked. You want that option checked because you want the user to enter information into this text field.

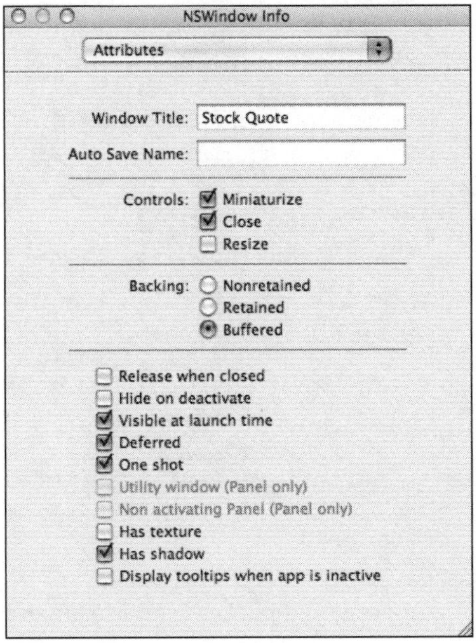

Figure 14-18

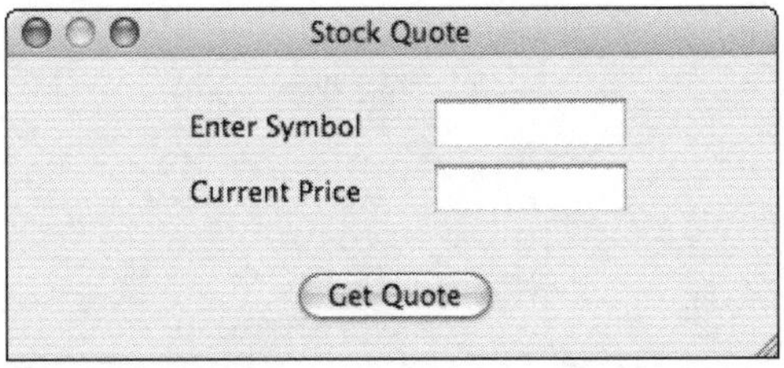

Figure 14-19

27. In the Stock Quote window, select the lower-right text field, which is the output field for Current Price. In the Info panel, deselect Editable. This is an output field where you will place the stock price, so you don't want to allow the user to edit this field. The contents of your Info panel should now match Figure 14-21.

When you change any field in the Info panel, make sure you're changing the field for the right object, that is, the one selected in your interface window. It's easy to get confused here, especially when you're switching back and forth between windows. You can inadvertently change the attributes for the wrong object because you accidentally selected it by clicking in your interface window.

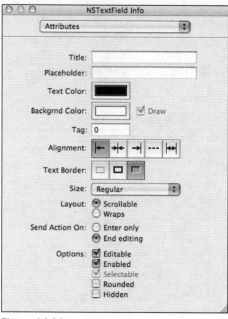

Figure 14-20

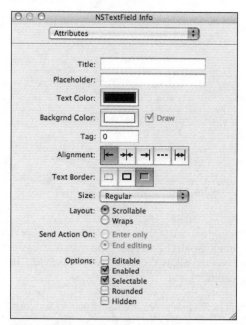

Figure 14-21

Now that you've set the attributes of your input and output text fields, it's time to turn your attention to the Get Quote button.

The two labels you placed in front of the fields in the Stock Quote box are also text field objects, even though they look like static text. Because they are text fields, they can be selected and their attributes can be changed in the Info panel.

28. In the Stock Quote window, select the Get Quote button. You want this button to be the default action if the Return key is pressed. So back in the Info panel, under the Key Equiv field, select Return from the list of choices in the pop-up menu. The Info panel for your button should now look like Figure 14-22.

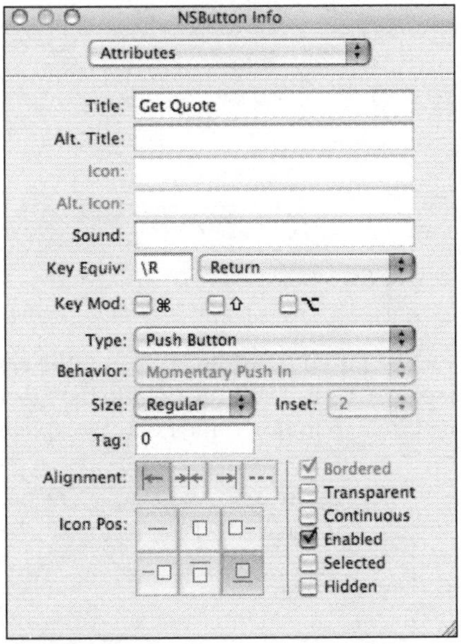

Figure 14-22

29. Now you've set all the attributes for your objects. You also want the capability to reference your input and output text fields from within your AppleScript application. To do that, you have to give names to these two fields. Let's start with the first field. In your Stock Quote window, select your input field (that's the top-right text box). From the top pop-up menu in your Info panel, select AppleScript (you can also get to the AppleScript window directly by pressing the keyboard shortcut Command-7). In the Name field, type stockSymbol. Your Info panel should now look like Figure 14-23.

Don't confuse the Name field under AppleScript with the Title field under Attributes. The former is the variable name used to reference the field from within your AppleScript code. The latter is the content initially assigned to the field.

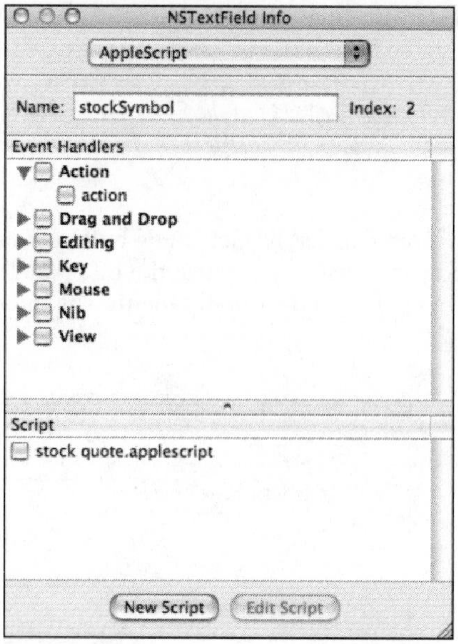

Figure 14-23

30. Follow the same procedure for your output text field (the bottom-right field where you're going to display the current price). First, select the field in the Stock Quote window, switch to the Info panel, and type `currentPrice` in the Name field, as depicted in Figure 14-24.

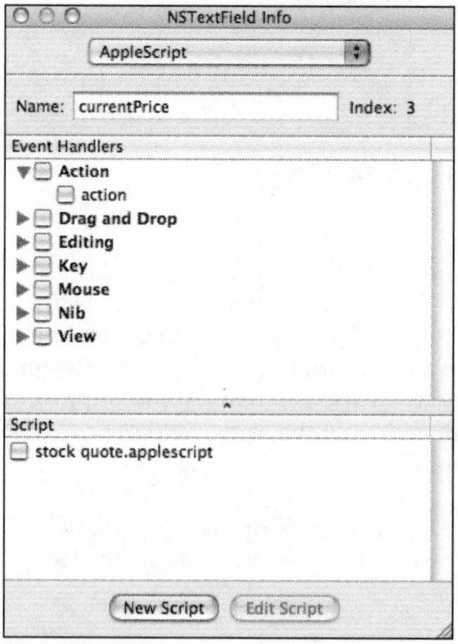

Figure 14-24

31. While you're naming things, give a name to your Stock Quote window so you can easily refer to it from within your application. Click somewhere to select the window (and not an object); then, in the Info panel, set the Name field to main.

32. Select the Quote button and give it a name in the Info panel. In the Name field, specify its name as quoteButton.

33. In your button's Info panel, check the Clicked box under Action. By checking this option, you're specifying that you want a handler called whenever the button is clicked. The file containing the handler is specified in the lower pane of your Info panel. Fortunately, when Xcode first launched Interface Builder for you, it automatically placed the file stock quote.applescript there for you. But that file won't be used unless you've completed the connection, which you do by checking the box next to the file name. After making the connection between the event and the script file, your Info panel looks like Figure 14-25.

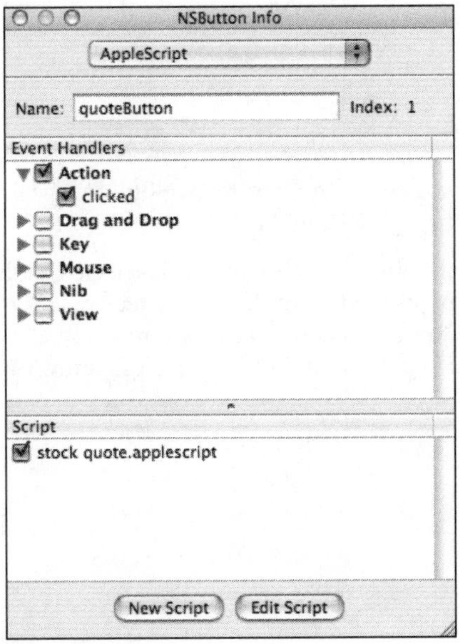

Figure 14-25

34. Switch to the window that contains your menu. It's titled MainMenu.nib – MainMenu. Double-click Application in the menu bar to select the text; then change the text to Stock Quote. This is now the name that appears in the menu bar when your program is running. Figure 14-26 shows how your menu window looks after you make this change.

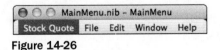

Figure 14-26

35. Click on Stock Quote in the menu bar to reveal the drop-down menu. In that menu, double-click the About Application entry and change the word *Application* to `Stock Quote`. Your window should look like Figure 14-27. While you're at it, you can also change the selection that reads Hide Application to read Hide Stock Quote; and you can also change Quit Application to Quit Stock Quote, although that selection is not shown in the figure.

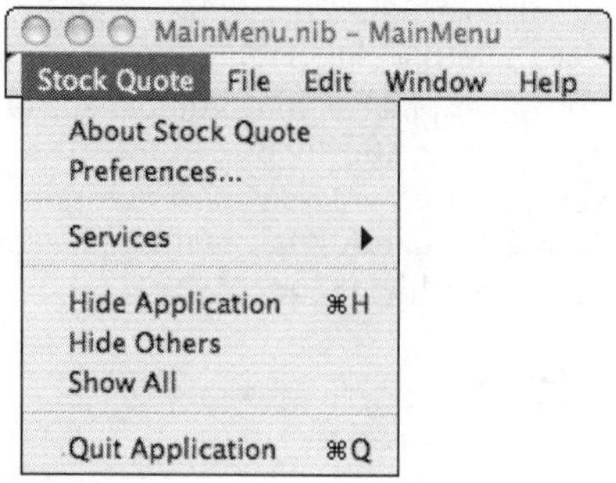

Figure 14-27

36. You have just two things left to do in Interface Builder (yeah!). First, go to the MainMenu.nib window and select the icon labeled File's Owner.

37. In the Info panel, make sure AppleScript is still selected in the pop-up menu at the top. Look in the Event Handlers pane. Under Application, check *should quit after last window closed*. Make the connection between this event and your program file by checking *stock quote.applescript* in the Script pane. Your Info panel should now look like Figure 14-28.

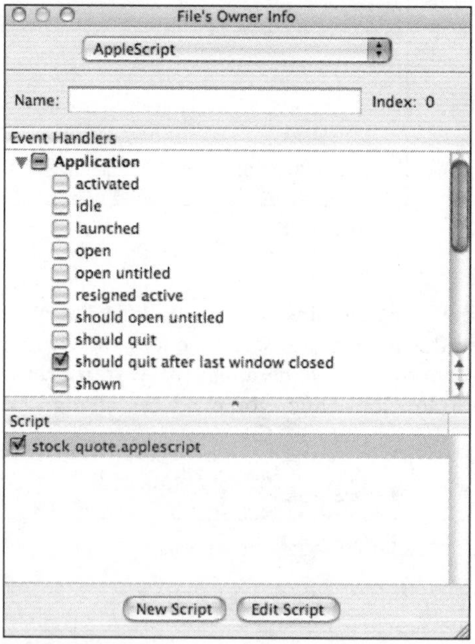

Figure 14-28

38. You're finished with Interface Builder. Save your interface by choosing File⇨Save.

39. Click the Xcode icon in your Dock to activate its windows (recall that you hid them earlier).

40. Hide the Interface Builder windows so they don't clutter up your screen by choosing Xcode⇨Hide Others.

41. Select the AppleScript file `stock quote.applescript` from the left pane of the Xcode project window. Notice that a template for two handlers has been automatically inserted into the file for you because of the work you did in Interface Builder. This is depicted in Figure 14-29.

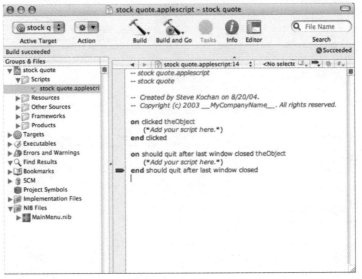

Figure 14-29

42. Before entering any code, set Interface Builder to wrap and indent your lines (you're used to that from Script Editor) by choosing Xcode⇨Preferences. Click Text Editing in the toolbar. In the lower pane that appears, check Wrap Lines and also Indent Wrapped Lines by: 4. Click OK.

43. Modify the two template handlers that were created for you by adding the code shown in Figure 14-30. Be sure to type long lines (such as the `call soap` line) as a single line; alternatively, you can manually break them by using Option-return at the end of each line.

44. Click the button labeled Build and Go in the toolbar. The dialog shown in Figure 14-31 asks whether you want to save your files before building. Click Save All.

45. If you have any AppleScript errors, correct them in your file and go back to the preceding step to attempt another build (your lines that have errors in them will be identified by red Xs down the left side of your Editor pane. If you click an X, you see a description of the error listed right below the toolbar). If you have no errors and you have diligently followed all the steps up to this point, you should get the dialog shown in Figure 14-1 at the start of this chapter.

46. Enter a stock symbol (AAPL is always a good choice!) and click Get Quote. You should get the latest stock quote for Apple Computer, as depicted in Figure 14-2. If you lose your Internet connection or some other problem occurs, you may get N/A displayed instead.

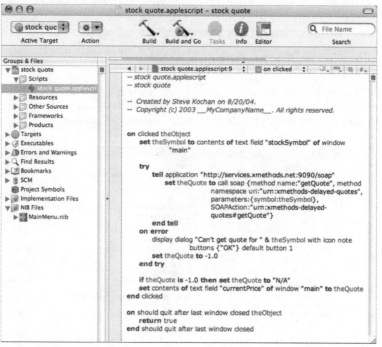

Figure 14-30

Figure 14-31

How It Works

The name *AppleScript Studio* collectively refers to two applications: Xcode and Interface Builder. These two applications are designed to support development and debugging of applications in many different programming languages, including C, C++, Objective-C, Java, and yes, AppleScript.

Writing a new application in AppleScript Studio involves the following steps:

1. Creating a new project in Xcode

2. Creating a user interface in Interface Builder and making connections betweens events in your interface and code that will be called by the system to handle those events

3. Writing the code in Xcode to implement the connections you made in the preceding step

4. Building and running your application

5. Reiterating Steps 3 through 5 as necessary to get your program to run and produce the desired results

After you design your user interface with Interface Builder and switch back to Xcode, you find that two handler templates have been created for you as shown:

```
on clicked theObject
    (*Add your script here.*)
end clicked

on should quit after last window closed theObject
    (*Add your script here.*)
end should quit after last window closed
```

When you make a connection in Interface Builder, a corresponding handler template is automatically added to the script file that you connect it to. The second handler, should quit after last window closed, gets called when the last window of your application is closed. The handler is expected to return a Boolean value: true if the application should quit, and false if it should not. Because you want your stock quote application to quit when its window is closed, you return true from this handler:

```
on should quit after last window closed theObject
    return true
end should quit after last window closed
```

If you were writing a Stay Open application, you might not want your application to quit. In that case, you would return false.

As you can see, an argument gets passed to your template handlers. The argument is called theObject, and its value is a reference to the object that caused the event to occur. In the case of the should quit after last window closed handler, theObject is the window that was closed. You only have one window called Stock Quote, so it's a reference to that window that is passed to the handler when it is closed.

You can have the same handler respond to the same event that can occur on different objects. In such cases, the argument that is passed to the handler can be used to discern the object that triggered the event. For example, if your application has several buttons, theObject can be tested by the clicked handler to see which button was clicked. You can do this by looking at the argument's `name` property, for example.

Speaking of the `clicked` handler, it is called when you click the Get Quote button (or press the Return key). Recall that you made that connection in Interface Builder; namely, you specified that when the button is clicked, a `clicked` handler from the file `stock quote.applescript` is to be called (refer to Figure 14-25).

You have only one button in your interface, so you know that your `clicked` handler is called only as the result of someone clicking your application's Get Quote button. Therefore, the handler doesn't need to discern the object that initiated the call. If you do want to determine the object that causes the handler to be called, you can look at the `name` property for `theObject`.

The `clicked` handler must retrieve the stock symbol from the appropriate text field and then use SOAP services to get a quote. The following line from your handler retrieves this value from the field you named `stockSymbol`:

```
set theSymbol to contents of text field "stockSymbol" of window "main"
```

Notice that even though you have a name for your text field, it's still not a complete reference. You have to identify which window the text field belongs to (even though you have only one window). Recall that you named the window `main`; also remember that the Name field, not the Title field, becomes the variable name.

When your handler needs to make many references to your window (this one obviously doesn't), a `tell` block is often used to reduce the typing required and make the program easier to read, like this:

```
tell window "main"
    set theSymbol to contents of text field "stockSymbol"
    ...
end tell
```

Text fields store data, as well as text! If you want the contents of the field to be interpreted as a number, you can coerce it in your program. Be sure to do that inside a `try` block in case a nonnumeric value is keyed by the user. When assigning a value back to a text field, it's okay to assign a number because it will be coerced into text.

With the symbol in hand, the program proceeds to look up the symbol and assign the result to the variable `theQuote`. If an error occurs in the `try` block, a dialog is displayed and the value of the `theQuote` is set to -1.0, which is the same value that the `soap` call returns if you try to look up a nonexistent stock.

> Consistent with what you learned about timeouts in Chapter 10, the `soap` call times out if there's no response after one minute. As you know, you can change this time by encapsulating the call in a `with timeout` statement block.

If the value of `theQuote` is -1.0, then its value is set to the text characters N/A for display in the output text field. This text value, which you named `curerntPrice` in Interface Builder, is set to the value of `theQuote` with the following statement:

```
set contents of text field "currentPrice" of window "main" to theQuote
```

After the `currentPrice` field has been set, you're done with this handler, so execution returns. Your program does not terminate, but remains active. You can quit the application from the menu bar, the dock, or by closing its window (recall the handler you wrote to take care of that event).

Congratulations on creating your first AppleScript Studio application! Although many steps are involved in this process, you can be sure that these steps will become second nature after you gain experience working with Xcode and Interface Builder.

An iTunes Remote

Before leaving this chapter, I want to give you a glimpse of a slightly more complex AppleScript Studio application called iTunes Remote. Just an overview is presented here. I hope to give you enough information to arouse your curiosity. The complete Xcode project is available for you to download from this book's companion website at `wrox.com`. You are encouraged to download the project, build it, and run it. Then try making some enhancements. If you do, you'll really get your feet wet and gain a better working knowledge of AppleScript Studio.

iTunes Remote offers the following features:

❑   Displays the title, artist, and album for the current track

❑   Displays artwork for the current track, if available

❑   Provides controls that allow you to play the previous track, pause/resume play, and skip to the next track

❑   Allows you to adjust the volume with a slider control

Figure 14-32 shows the iTunes Remote window. As you can see from the figure, a track from the Spider-Man 2 soundtrack was playing when this window was captured.

Figure 14-32

As you might expect, iTunes is intimately involved with this application. Three events are connected to the clicking of the three buttons. When the leftmost button is clicked, iTunes is asked to play the previous track, using its `previous track` command. When the middle button is clicked, the pause/play state of iTunes is toggled, and the button's title (not its name!) is changed from Pause to Play and vice versa. Clicking the rightmost button causes the `next track` command to be sent to iTunes. Because you have three buttons that can be clicked, the `clicked` handler for this application checks its argument to determine which button triggered the event.

Another event deals with the slider. In Interface Builder, you can specify a minimum and maximum value for a slider with 0 and 100, respectively, being the defaults. You can also specify that your handler be called while the slider is being moved instead of just when the movement ends. That's good for a volume control slider because it allows you to hear the volume getting louder or softer as you move the slider. Inside the `action` handler for this slider, you get the value of the slider control by accessing its `float value` property. Then you set the volume in iTunes to the corresponding value by setting the application's `sound volume` property.

iTunes allows you to set its volume to a value between 0 and 100 with a command like this:

```
tell application "iTunes" to set sound volume to 50
```

You want this application to do things while it's just "hanging around," so you check the `idle` attribute for the File's Owner in Interface Builder. This causes a template `idle` handler to be added to your script file. Having the application idle enables you to periodically update your iTunes Remote window if the song changes or the state of the player changes from somewhere else (like from directly within the iTunes application).

The artwork is displayed using an object known as an `image view`. Getting the artwork for the current track from iTunes is straightforward (iTunes allows for multiple images to be associated with a track):

```
tell application "iTunes" to get data of first artwork of current track
```

Setting the `image` property of the `image view` object in your interface window to the resulting artwork is a little tricky. You can't assign the pixel data that iTunes gives you directly to this `image` property. Instead, you have to first write the data to a file and then use the `load image` command (as documented in the AppleScript Studio Kit dictionary) to load the data into your application. You can then set the `image` property of the `image view` object in your window to the result.

The entire iTunes Remote application requires about 115 lines of AppleScript code. That's fairly impressive when you consider how much is going on in the application. You are leveraging the power of Interface Builder, AppleScript, and iTunes to accomplish all this work in a small amount of code.

Again, I encourage you to download the project and get it running on your system. One interesting extension would be to allow for a song title to be keyed in, as you did in the iTunes applet in Chapter 11.

Summary

This chapter introduced you to AppleScript Studio. You learned that

❑   AppleScript Studio really consists of two applications: Xcode and Interface Builder.

❑   Xcode provides a powerful environment for editing, building, running, and debugging applications. It also allows you to easily manage all the files associated with a project and to view online documentation.

❑   Interface Builder is a tool for developing graphical user interfaces. It allows you to drag UI elements into a window, set attributes for those elements, and make connections. A connection specifies the code that is to be executed whenever a specific event occurs, such as a button being clicked, a window being opened or closed, or a text field being edited.

Congratulations! You've persevered and made it through the final chapter of this book. I hope you feel that you can begin writing your own AppleScript programs with confidence. Before you move on to check out the additional information provided in the appendixes, try the exercises that follow to test your understanding of the material covered in this chapter. You can find the solutions to these exercises in Appendix A.

Exercises

1. Based on the AppleScript Studio application you developed in this chapter:

   a. Change the title of the first label from `Enter symbol` to `Symbol name:`.

   b. Change the name of the variable associated with the program's output from `currentPrice` to `quotedValue`. Make sure you make the change in all required places.

   c. Change the color of the text for both the stock symbol and the price from black to red.

2. Write an AppleScript Studio application that will allow a radius of a circle to be entered and then will display the circle's circumference and volume. Design your interface to match the one shown in Figure 14-33. The figure shows the result of entering 2 for the circle's radius.

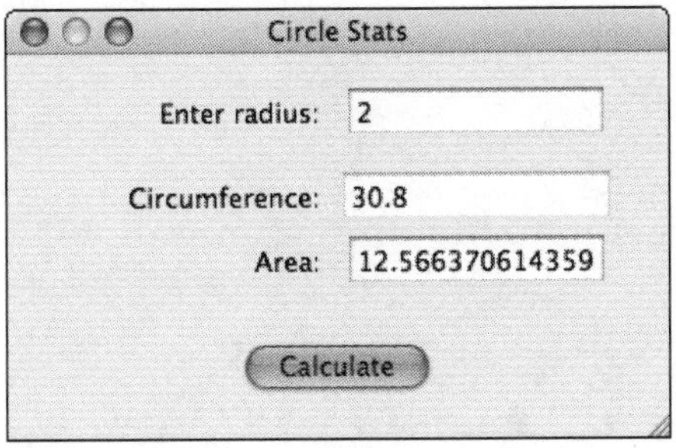

Figure 14-33

Exercise Answers

Chapter 1

Exercise 1 solution

```
2 * pi * 1.48
```

Exercise 2 solution

```
display dialog "Do you think this is a great book?" buttons { "Yes", "No" }
    default button {"Yes"}
```

Exercise 3 solution

```
-- This program will ask the user for her opinion

display dialog "Do you think this is a great book?" buttons { "Yes", "No" }
    default button {"Yes"}
```

Exercise 4 solution

Click on the Description tab in the Script Editor window and enter the text "A program to ask a profound question!"

Exercise 5 solution

```
display dialog "Pick a color" buttons {"Red", "Yellow", "Blue"} ¬
    default button "Red"
```

Exercise 6 solution

Yes, you can alter the order of the optional parameters. However, they must appear after the message that you want to display.

Exercise 7 solution

```
beep 3
display dialog "Couldn't find myFavorites" buttons { "OK" } default button "OK"
    with icon stop
```

Exercise 8 solution

```
say "Programming in AppleScript is fun."
```

Chapter 2

Exercise 1 solution

The following variable names are not valid for the listed reasons.

```
integer          -- can't use a reserved word
6_05             -- can't start with a digit
month            -- can't use a reserved word
a$               -- can't use a $
weekday          -- can't use reserved word
file extension   -- can't use embedded spaces
```

Exercise 2 solution

The following are invalid literal constants:

```
e-02            -- need a number before the exponent
2.44  e -03     -- no spaces allowed between the  number, the 'e', and the exponent
```

Exercise 3 solution

```
200 mod 7                                      -- 4
100 / 25 * 4                                   -- 16.0
((100.5 as integer) - (50.99 as integer) ) ^ 2  -- 2401.0
(1.234e+2 + 2.345e+3)                          -- 2468.4
2 ^ 0.5  -- this calculates the square root of 2 (1.414213562373)
(6 ^ 2 + 8 ^ 2) ^ 0.5                          -- 10.0
100.25 + 7.5 div 5 - 29 mod 8                  -- 96.25
```

Exercise 4 solution

```
log 5 * (100 - 32) / 9
log (100 as degrees Fahrenheit) as degrees Celsius

log 5 * (32 - 32) / 9
log (32 as degrees Fahrenheit) as degrees Celsius

log 5 * (0 - 32) / 9
log (0 as degrees Fahrenheit) as degrees Celsius

log 5 * (55 - 32) / 9
log (55 as degrees Fahrenheit) as degrees Celsius
```

Exercise 5 solution

```
(3.31E-8 + 2.01E-7) / (7.16E-6 + 2.01E-8)
```

Exercise 6 solution

```
log 365 + 7 - 365 mod 7
log 12258 + 23 - 12258 mod 23
log 996 + 4 - 996 mod 4
```

Exercise 7 solution

```
set D1 to date "Friday, July 22, 2005 8:34:35 PM"
set D2 to date "Sunday, August 14, 2005 8:44:50 PM"

set diff to D2 - D1

set numWeeks to diff div weeks
set diff to diff - numWeeks * weeks

set numDays to diff div days
set diff to diff - numDays * days

set numMinutes to diff div minutes
set numSeconds to diff - numMinutes * minutes

log numWeeks
log numDays
log numMinutes
log numSeconds
```

Chapter 3

Exercise 1 solution

```
-- Program to give a greeting

set today to current date
set weekdayToday to the weekday of today

if weekdayToday = Monday then
    set message to "Hope you had a great weekend!"
else if weekdayToday = Wednesday then
    set message to "Happy Hump Day!"
else if weekdayToday = Friday then
    set message to "TGIF!"
else if weekdayToday = Saturday or weekdayToday = Sunday then
    set message to "What are you doing here on the weekend?"
else
    set message to "Have a Great Day!"
end if

display dialog message with icon note buttons {"Thanks!"}
```

Exercise 2 solution

The steps to do this are outlined in the chapter.

Exercise 3 solution

```
true and true                    -- true
true and false                   -- false
true or false                    -- true
false or false                   -- false
not true and false               -- false
true and not false or true       -- true
true and not (false or true)     -- false
```

Exercise 4 solution

1986 – yes , 1989 – no , 2000 -- yes, 2010 -- no, 2100 – no

Exercise 5 solution

The null string becomes 0 when coerced into a number.

Exercise 6 solution

```
-- Speak salutation based on the time

set secsSinceMidnight to time of (current date)
set sixPM to time of date "6 PM"
set noon to time of date "12 PM"

if secsSinceMidnight < noon then
    say  "Good morning!"
else if secsSinceMidnight    noon and secsSinceMidnight < sixPM then
    say "Good afternoon!"
else
    say "Good evening!"
end if
```

Exercise 7 solution

```
-- Simple alarm clock program
-- sets an alarm a specified number of seconds in the future

display dialog "Enter sleep time in seconds" default answer "60"
set delayTime to text returned of result as number

display dialog "Enter Message to Display" default answer "Your time is up!"
set message to text returned of result

-- pause execution for the specified number of seconds

delay delayTime

-- time is up; display the message

display dialog message with icon note buttons {"Thanks!"} default button 1
```

Exercise 8 solution

```
-- Program to test for a leap year

set testYr to missing value
display dialog "Enter the year:" default answer ""

try
    set testYr to text returned of result as integer
end try

if testYr = missing value then
    display dialog "You didn't enter a valid year!" with icon stop buttons {"OK"}
else if testYr mod 4 = 0 and (testYr mod 100   0 or testYr mod 400 = 0) then
    display dialog "Remember that February has 29 days!"
else
    display dialog "Just another ordinary year!"
end if
```

Chapter 4

Exercise 1 solution

```
-- Calculate a triangular number specified by the user

set triangularNumber to missing value
set sum to 0 -- the sum so far

display dialog "Enter your integer" default answer ""

-- make sure an integer was entered
try
    set triangularNumber to text returned of result as integer
end try

if triangularNumber = missing value then
    display dialog "You didn't enter an integer" with icon stop ¬
            buttons {"OK"} default button 1
else
    -- now calculate the requested number

    set sum to (triangularNumber * (triangularNumber + 1) / 2) as integer

    display dialog (sum as string)
end if
```

Exercise 2 solution

```
-- Calculate a triangular number specified by the user

set triangularNumber to missing value
set sum to 0 -- the sum so far

display dialog "Enter your integer" default answer ""
```

```
-- make sure an integer was entered
try
    set triangularNumber to text returned of result as integer
end try

if triangularNumber = missing value then
    display dialog "You didn't enter an integer" with icon stop ¬
            buttons {"OK"} default button 1
else
    -- now calculate the requested number

    set n to 1

    repeat triangularNumber times
        set sum to sum + n
        set n to n + 1
    end repeat

    display dialog (sum as string)
end if
```

Exercise 3 solution

```
-- Calculate a triangular number specified by the user - Version 3

set sum to 0 -- the sum so far
set validNumber to false
set tries to 1

repeat while tries    3 and not validNumber
    display dialog "Enter your integer" default answer ""
    try
        set textEntered to text returned of result
        set triangularNumber to textEntered as integer

        -- if this statement is reached, an integer was entered
        set validNumber to true
    end try

    if not validNumber then
        display dialog textEntered & " is not a valid integer" with icon note
        set tries to tries + 1
    end if
end repeat

if not validNumber then
    display dialog "I give up!" with icon note buttons {"OK"} default button 1
else
    -- now calculate the requested triangular number

    repeat with n from 1 to triangularNumber
        set sum to sum + n
    end repeat
```

```
            -- display the result
            display dialog "The triangular number is " & (sum as string)
    end if
```

Exercise 4 solution

```
    -- Calculate the sum of the squares from 1 to n

    set sum to 0 -- the sum so far
    set validNumber to false
    set tries to 1

    repeat while tries   3 and not validNumber
        display dialog "Enter your integer" default answer ""
        try
            set textEntered to text returned of result
            set n to textEntered as integer

            -- if this statement is reached, an integer was entered
            set validNumber to true
        end try

        if not validNumber then
            display dialog textEntered & " is not a valid integer" with icon note
            set tries to tries + 1
        end if
    end repeat

    if not validNumber then
        display dialog "I give up!" with icon note buttons {"OK"} default button 1
    else
        -- now calculate the requested sum

        repeat with x from 1 to n
            set sum to sum + x * x
        end repeat

        -- display the result
        display dialog "The sum of the squares from 1 to " & (n as string) & ¬
            " is "  & (sum as string)
    end if
```

Exercise 5 solution

```
    -- Simple guessing game

    -- Pick a number

    set myNumber to random number from 1 to 10

    set tries to 0 -- Number of tries so far
    set guess to missing value -- Not a valid guess

    -- Introductory dialog
```

```
display dialog "I'm thinking of a number from 1 to 10"

repeat until guess = myNumber
    set guess to missing value

    display dialog "Enter your guess" default answer ""

    try
        set guess to text returned of result as integer
    end try

    -- Now see if a valid number was entered

    if guess = missing value or guess < 1 or guess > 10 then
        display dialog "I asked for a number from 1 to 10!" with icon note
    else
        set tries to tries + 1
    end if

    if guess > myNumber then
        display dialog "Your guess is too high!" with icon note
    else if guess < myNumber then
        display dialog "Your guess is too low!" with icon note
    end
end repeat

display dialog "Great!  You got it in " & (tries as string) & " guesses!" ¬
        with icon note buttons {"OK"}
```

Exercise 6 solution

```
-- Simple guessing game

-- Pick a number

set myNumber to random number from 1 to 10

set tries to 0 -- Number of tries so far
set guess to missing value -- Not a valid guess

-- Introductory dialog

display dialog "I'm thinking of a number from 1 to 10"

repeat until guess = myNumber
    set guess to missing value

    display dialog "Enter your guess" default answer ""

    try
        set guess to text returned of result as integer
    end try
```

```
        -- Now see if a valid number was entered

    if guess = missing value or guess < 1 or guess > 10 then
        display dialog "I asked for a number from 1 to 10!" with icon note
    else
        set tries to tries + 1
    end if
end repeat

if tries < 4 then
    display dialog "Wow!  You got it in only " & (tries as string) & " guesses!" ¬
        with icon note buttons {"OK"}
else if tries > 7 then
    display dialog "It took you " & (tries as string) & " guesses! Better luck next
            time!"
else
    display dialog "You got it in " & (tries as string) & " guesses!" ¬
        with icon note buttons {"OK"}
end
```

Exercise 7 solution

```
-- Simple guessing game

set totalTries to 0 -- total tries for all games


repeat with timesPlayed from 1 to 5
    -- Pick a number
    set myNumber to random number from 1 to 10

    set tries to 0 -- Number of tries so far
    set guess to missing value -- Not a valid guess

    display dialog "Game #" & (timesPlayed as string) & ¬
            ": I'm thinking of a number from 1 to 10"

    repeat until guess = myNumber
        set guess to missing value

        display dialog "Enter your guess" default answer ""

        try
            set guess to text returned of result as integer
        end try

        -- Now see if a valid number was entered

        if guess = missing value or guess < 1 or guess > 10 then
            display dialog "I asked for a number from 1 to 10!" with icon note
        else
            set tries to tries + 1
        end if
    end repeat
```

```
        display dialog "Great!  You got it in " & (tries as string) & " guesses!" ¬
            with icon note buttons {"OK"}

        set totalTries to totalTries + tries
    end repeat

-- calculate and display the average

set average to totalTries / 5
display dialog "You're average score was " & (average as string) & " guesses" ¬
        buttons {"Thanks"} default button 1
```

Exercise 8 solution

```
-- Simple guessing game

set totalTries to 0 -- total tries for all games
set timesToPlay to missing value

display dialog "How many times do you want to play?" default answer "1"
try
    set timesToPlay to text returned of result as integer
end try

if timesToPlay = missing value then
    display dialog "You didn't type a number!" with icon stop buttons {"OK"}
else

repeat with timesPlayed from 1 to timesToPlay
        -- Pick a number
        set myNumber to random number from 1 to 10

        set tries to 0 -- Number of tries so far
        set guess to missing value -- Not a valid guess

        display dialog "Game #" & (timesPlayed as string) & ¬
            ": I'm thinking of a number from 1 to 10"

        repeat until guess = myNumber
            set guess to missing value

            display dialog "Enter your guess" default answer ""

            try
                set guess to text returned of result as integer
            end try

            -- Now see if a valid number was entered

            if guess = missing value or guess < 1 or guess > 10 then
                display dialog "I asked for a number from 1 to 10!" with icon note
            else
                set tries to tries + 1
            end if
```

```
            if guess > myNumber then
                display dialog "Your guess is too high!" with icon note
            else if guess < myNumber then
                display dialog "Your guess is too low!" with icon note
            end if

        end repeat

        if tries < 4 then
            display dialog "Wow!  You got it in only " & (tries as string) & ¬
                " guesses!" with icon note buttons {"OK"}
        else if tries > 7 then
            display dialog "It took you " & (tries as string) & " guesses!
                Better luck next time!" with icon note buttons {"OK"}
        else
            display dialog "You got it in " & (tries as string) & " guesses!" ¬
                with icon note buttons {"OK"}
        end if

        set totalTries to totalTries + tries
    end repeat

-- calculate and display the average

    set average to totalTries / timesToPlay
    display dialog "You're average score was " & (average as string) & ¬
        " guesses" buttons {"Thanks"} default button 1
end if
```

Exercise 9 solution

The giving up after parameter specifies the number of seconds the dialog will be shown on the screen before it is closed. For example, the command

```
display dialog "You didn't enter a number!" with icon note giving up after 5
```

will display the given message for five seconds (or less than five seconds if the user clicks OK or Cancel before five seconds have elapsed).

Chapter 5

Exercise 1 solution

```
-- Counting special characters

set theText to "AppleScript is a flexible language that allows you to easily work
    with elements in strings and lists."

set wordChars to 0
-- sequence through each word in the string

repeat with theWord in (get every word in theText)
    set wordChars to wordChars + count theWord
end repeat
```

```
-- log the Answer

set specialChars to (count theText) - wordChars
log "There are " & specialChars & " special characters in the text."
```

Exercise 2 solution

No answer shown.

Exercise 3 solution

```
-- Get the last ocmponent in a path

set myPath to "Macintosh HD:Users:steve:mysrc:scripts:ch05:enum1.scpt"

-- save the old delimiters and change to a :

set saveTextItemDelimiters to text item delimiters
set text item delimiters to ":"

-- get the last text item; if it's null, get the one before it

set component to text item -1 of myPath
if component = "" then
    set component to text item -2 of myPath
end if

log component

-- restore the old delimiters

set textItemDelimiters to saveTextItemDelimiters
```

Exercise 4 solution

Here's the output from the Event Log:

```
(*Don't get*)
(*t get *)
(*thru!*)
tell current application
    offset of "from" in "Don't get from-to mixed up with thru!"
11
    (*Don't get *)
    (*D, o, n, ', t,  , g, e, t,  *)
end tell
```

Exercise 5 solution

```
-- count the number of occurrence of a word

set searchWord to "the"
set someText to "The word \"the\" is the most common word in the English language"
set wordCount to 0
```

```
repeat with theWord in (get every word in someText)
    if contents of theWord = searchWord then
        set wordCount to wordCount + 1
    end if
end repeat

display dialog "The word \"" & searchWord & "\" occurs " & (wordCount as string)
    & " times in the text."
```

Exercise 6 solution

Note: This is just the modified section of the alarm clock program related to testing for hours, minutes, or seconds.

```
-- see if a relative time was entered

if textEntered ends with "seconds" or textEntered ends with "secs" then
    set units to 1
else if textEntered ends with "minutes" or textEntered ends with "minute" or
    textEntered ends with "min" or textEntered ends with "mins" then
    set units to minutes
else if textEntered ends with "hours" or textEntered ends with "hour" or
    textEntered ends with "hr" or textEntered ends with "hrs" then
    set units to hours
end if
```

Exercise 7 solution

```
-- Remove a substring from a string

-- These are two test strings...experiment with others

set myText to "There's got to be some way out of here!"
set removeString to "got to be "

-- startOffset is the offset of the substring in the string

set startOffset to offset of removeString in myText
set firstPart to ""

if startOffset = 0 then
    display dialog removeString & " doesn't exist in " & myText with icon note
        buttons {"OK"} default button 1
else

    -- first get the characters from the start of the string up to the
    -- beginning of the substring; check for special case where substring is at
    -- the very beginning of the string

    if startOffset    1 then
        set firstPart to text from character 1 to character (startOffset - 1)
            in myText
    else
set firstPart to ""
    end if
```

```
    -- now get the characters starting after the substring to the end of the string

    set endOffset to startOffset + (count removeString)

    if endOffset    (count myText) then
        set secondPart to text from character endOffset to end in myText
    else
        set secondPart to ""
    end if

    -- now log the result

    log firstPart & secondPart
end if
```

Exercise 8 solution

```
(*false*)
(*true*)
(*true*)
(*false*)
```

Chapter 6

Exercise 1 solution

```
-- Calculate the first 20 Fibonacci numbers

-- Define F1 and F2

set fibList to {0, 1}

-- Now calculate the next 18 numbers

repeat 18 times
    set end of fibList to (item -1 of fibList) + (item -2 of fibList)
end repeat

-- log the result

log fibList
```

Exercise 2 solution

```
set USCities to {{"Boston", 574000}, {"Chicago", 2784000}, {"Dallas", 1007000}, ¬
    {"Houston", 1631000}, {"Los Angeles", 3485000}, {"Philadelphia", 1586000}, ¬
    {"San Diego", 1111000}, {"San Francisco", 724000}, {"New York", 7323000}}

-- set the mix and max to the population of the first city

set min to item 2 of item 1 of USCities
set max to min
```

```
-- keep track of the list item that contains the max and min populations

set minIndex to 1
set maxIndex to 1

repeat with i from 2 to count USCities
    set population to item 2 of (item i of USCities)
    if population > max then
        set maxIndex to i
        set max to population
    end if

    if population < min then
        set minIndex to i
        set min to population
    end if
end repeat

display dialog "The city with the smallest population is " & item 1 of (item ¬
    minIndex of USCities) & return & "The city with the largest population is " ¬
    & item 1 of (item maxIndex of USCities)
```

Exercise 3 solution

```
set USCities to {¬
    {name:"Boston", population:574000}, ¬
    {name:"Chicago", population:2784000}, ¬
    {name:"Dallas", population:1007000}, ¬
    {name:"Houston", population:1631000}, ¬
    {name:"Los Angeles", population:3485000}, ¬
    {name:"Philadelphia", population:1586000}, ¬
    {name:"San Diego", population:1111000}, ¬
    {name:"San Francisco", population:724000}, ¬
    {name:"New York", population:7323000}}

-- set the mix and max to the population of the first city

set min to population of item 1 of USCities
set max to min

-- keep track of the list item that contains the max and min populations

set minIndex to 1
set maxIndex to 1

repeat with i from 2 to count USCities
    set population to population of (item i of USCities)
    if population > max then
        set maxIndex to i
        set max to population
    end if

    if population < min then
```

```
            set minIndex to i
            set min to population
        end if
    end repeat

display dialog "The city with the smallest population is " & name of (item ¬
    minIndex of USCities) & return & "The city with the largest population is " ¬
    & name of (item maxIndex of USCities)
```

Exercise 4 solution

The following program can be used to test the general list item insertion and deletion code. The values of L and n can be changed in the program to verify that all cases are working correctly.

```
-- Arbitrary list item deletion and insertion

-- remove item n from list L

set L to {1, 2, 3, 4, 5}
set n to 3

if n > 0 and n   (count L) then -- make sure  n is valid
    if n = 1 then
        set L to rest of L -- remove first item
    else if n = (count L) then
        set L to items 1 thru -2 of L -- remove last item
    else
        set L to (items 1 thru (n - 1) of L) & (items (n + 1) thru -1) of L
    end if
end if

log L

-- add item insertItem in front of item n in list L
-- special case of n = -1 for insertion at end of list

set L to {1, 2, 3, 4, 5}
set n to 5
set insertItem to {100, 200}

if n = -1 or (n   1 and n   (count L)) then -- make sure n is valid
    if n = 1 then
        set beginning of L to insertItem -- insert at front of list
    else if n = -1 then
        set end of L to insertItem -- add to end of list
    else
        set L to (items 1 thru (n - 1) of L) & insertItem & (items n thru -1 of L)
    end if
end if

log L
```

Exercise 5 solution

Just change the USCities list accordingly. The rest of the program remains unchanged. Here's what the list would look like for the fourth version of the population program:

```
set USCities to {¬
  {name:"Boston", population:574000}, ¬
  {name:"Chicago", population:2784000}, ¬
  {name:"Dallas", population:1007000}, ¬
  {name:"Houston", population:1631000}, ¬
  {name:"Los Angeles", population:3485000}, ¬
  {name:"Philadelphia", population:1586000}, ¬
  {name:"San Diego", population:1111000}, ¬
  {name:"San Francisco", population:724000}, ¬
  {name:"New York", population:7323000}, ¬
  {name:"Baltimore", population:736000}, ¬
  {name:"Columbus", population:633000}, ¬
  {name:"Detroit", population:1028000}, ¬
  {name:"Memphis", population:610000}, ¬
  {name:"Phoenix", population:983000}}
```

Exercise 6 solution

```
-- Show the population of a given city

set USCities to {"Boston", 574000, "Chicago", 2784000, "Dallas", 1007000, ¬
        "Houston", 1631000, "Los Angeles", 3485000, "Philadelphia", 1586000, ¬
        "San Diego", 1111000, "San Francisco", 724000, "New York", 7323000}

display dialog "Enter your city: " default answer ""
set cityEntered to text returned of result

-- now look for the city in the list

set found to false

set n to 1

repeat while not found and n    (count USCities)
    if item n of USCities = cityEntered then
        set found to true
    else
        set n to n + 2  -- skip past population in list
    end if
end repeat

-- Either show the population or give a message that the city wasn't found

if not found then
    display dialog "Sorry, I don't know the population of " & cityEntered with ¬
    icon note buttons {"OK"} default button 1

else
```

```
        set cityPopulation to item (n + 1) of USCities
        display dialog "The population of " & cityEntered & " is " & (cityPopulation ¬
            as string)
    end if
```

Exercise 7 solution

```
-- Show the population of a given city
-- Version with Land Area Property added

set USCities to {¬
    {name:"Boston", population:574000, landArea:48}, ¬
    {name:"Chicago", population:2784000, landArea:227}, ¬
    {name:"Dallas", population:1007000, landArea:342}, ¬
    {name:"Houston", population:1631000, landArea:540}, ¬
    {name:"Los Angeles", population:3485000, landArea:469}, ¬
    {name:"Philadelphia", population:1586000, landArea:135}, ¬
    {name:"San Diego", population:1111000, landArea:324}, ¬
    {name:"San Francisco", population:724000, landArea:47}, ¬
    {name:"New York", population:7323000, landArea:309}}

-- Now build a list of city names to give to the
-- choose from list command

set USCityNames to {}

repeat with cityRecord in USCities
    set end of USCityNames to name of cityRecord
end repeat

choose from list USCityNames with prompt "Pick a city to find its population:"

set theSelection to result

-- see if Cancel was clicked
if theSelection = false then
    return -- stops the program's execution
end if

set cityEntered to item 1 of theSelection

-- now look for the city in the list of records

set found to false
set n to 1

repeat while not found and n    (count USCities)
    if name of (item n of USCities) = cityEntered then
        set found to true
    else
        set n to n + 1
    end if
end repeat
```

```
-- Show the population and area or give a message if the city wasn't found

if not found then
    display dialog "Sorry, I don't know the population of " & cityEntered ¬
        with icon note buttons {"OK"} default button 1
else
    set cityPopulation to population of (item n of USCities)
    set area to landArea of (item n of USCities)
    display dialog "The population of " & cityEntered & " is " & ¬
        (cityPopulation as string) & return & "The land area is " & ¬
        (area as string) & " square miles" buttons {"OK"} default button 1
end if
```

Exercise 8 solution

Here are the original four tracks with three additional tracks and the `playTime` property added:

```
set track1 to {name:"By Your Side", artist:"Sade", album:"Lovers Rock", ¬
    playTime:4 * minutes + 34}
set track2 to {name:"Lose Yourself", artist:"Eminem", album:"8 Mile", ¬
    playTime:5 * minutes + 27}
set track3 to {name:"Riders on the Storm", artist:"The Doors", album:"The Best ¬
    of the Doors", playTime:7 * minutes + 12}
set track4 to {name:"Someday", artist:"Sugar Ray", album:"14:59", ¬
    playTime:4 * minutes + 2}
set track5 to {name:"Old Friends", artist:"Simon & Garfunkel", album:"Bookends", ¬
    playTime:2 * minutes + 35}
set track6 to {name:"Who Can See It", artist:"George Harrison", album:"Living ¬
    in the Material World", playTime:3 * minutes + 53}
set track7 to {name:"Fields of Gold", artist:"Sting", playTime:3 * minutes + 39}

set playList to {track1, track2, track3, track4, track5, track6, track7}
```

Note here how you let AppleScript calculate the time in seconds for each song.

Exercise 9 solution

Just add the following code to the end of the code shown from the previous exercise:

```
set totalTime to 0

repeat with track in playList
    set totalTime to totalTime + (playTime of track)
end repeat
```

Exercise 10 solution

```
-- Get information about a song

set track1 to {name:"By Your Side", artist:"Sade", album:"Lovers Rock", ¬
    playTime:4 * minutes + 34}
set track2 to {name:"Lose Yourself", artist:"Eminem", album:"8 Mile", ¬
    playTime:5 * minutes + 27}
```

```
    set track3 to {name:"Riders on the Storm", artist:"The Doors", album:"The Best ¬
        of the Doors", playTime:7 * minutes + 12}
    set track4 to {name:"Someday", artist:"Sugar Ray", album:"14:59",
        playTime:4 * minutes + 2}
    set track5 to {name:"Old Friends", artist:"Simon & Garfunkel", album:"Bookends", ¬
        playTime:2 * minutes + 35}
    set track6 to {name:"Who Can See It", artist:"George Harrison", album:"Living ¬
        in the Material World", playTime:3 * minutes + 53}
    set track7 to {name:"Fields of Gold", artist:"Sting", playTime:3 * minutes + 39}

    set playList to {track1, track2, track3, track4, track5, track6, track7}

    -- Build a list of songs from the playList

    set songList to {}

    repeat with track in playList
        set end of songList to name of track
    end repeat

    -- Let the user choose from the playList

    choose from list songList with prompt "Pick a song for more information"

    set theSelection to result

    -- See if Cancel was clicked

    if theSelection = false then
        return
    end if

    set songPicked to item 1 of theSelection

    -- now find the song in the playList

    set found to false
    set n to 1

    repeat while not found and n    (count playList)
        if name of (item n of playList) = songPicked then
            set found to true
        else
            set n to n + 1
        end if
    end repeat

    -- Show info about the song

    if not found then
        display dialog "Sorry, Something is wrong...I don't know about song " & ¬
            songPicked with icon note buttons {"OK"} default button 1
    else
```

```
        set theTrack to item n of playList
        set artist to artist of theTrack
        set album to album of theTrack
        set playTime to playTime of theTrack

        display dialog songPicked & ":" & return & return & "Artist: " & artist & ¬
            return & "Album: " & album & return & "Play time: " & ((playTime div 60) ¬
            as string) & " mins. " & ((playTime mod 60) as string) & " secs." buttons ¬
            {"OK"} default button 1
    end if
```

Exercise 11 solution

```
-- Sort a List L in ascending order

set L to {20, 10, 5, -3, 100, 15, 6}

-- Simple exchange sort algorithm

set n to count L

repeat with i from 1 to n - 1
    repeat with j from i + 1 to n
        if item i of L > item j of L then
            set temp to item i of L
            set item i of L to item j of L
            set item j of L to temp
        end if
    end repeat
end repeat

log L
```

For a descending sort, just change the line from the program that reads

```
if item i of L > item j of L then
```

to the following:

```
if item i of L < item j of L then
```

Exercise 12 solution

Add the following code after the list songList is created but before it is presented to the user with the choose from list command:

```
set n to count songList

repeat with i from 1 to n - 1
    repeat with j from i + 1 to n
        if item i of songList > item j of songList then
            set temp to item i of songList
            set item i of songList to item j of songList
```

```
            set item j of songList to temp
        end if
    end repeat
end repeat
```

Chapter 7

Exercise 1 solution

```
info for (path to documents folder)
```

Exercise 2 solution

```
set infoApp to info for (path to application "Script Editor")
short version of infoApp
```

Exercise 3 solution

```
-- Implement a simplified "Get info" command

set theFile to choose file default location (path to home folder)

set infoRec to info for theFile

set theResult to "Info for " & (theFile as string) & return & return
set theResult to theResult & "Size (bytes):  " & (size of infoRec as integer) & ¬
        return
set theResult to theResult & "Created:  " & (creation date of infoRec as string) ¬
        & return
set theResult to theResult & "Last Modified: " & (modification date of infoRec ¬
        as string) & return
set theResult to theResult & "File Extension: " & (file extension of infoRec) & ¬
        return
set theResult to theResult & "Alias: "

if alias of infoRec is true then
    set theResult to theResult & " Yes"
else
    set theResult to theResult & " No"
end if


display dialog theResult buttons {"OK"} default button 1
```

Exercise 4 solution

```
-- Sum the size of the files in the Documents folder

set folderPath to (path to documents folder) as string
set fileList to list folder folderPath

set totalSize to 0
```

```
repeat with aFile in fileList
    set theFile to contents of aFile
    set infoRec to info for file (folderPath & theFile)
    set totalSize to totalSize + (size of infoRec)
end repeat

display dialog "Your files in " & folderPath & " take up " & (totalSize as ¬
    string) & " bytes"
```

Exercise 5 solution

```
-- Find the oldest file in the Applications folder

set folderPath to (path to applications folder) as string
set fileList to list folder folderPath

set oldestFile to missing value
set oldestDate to current date

repeat with aFile in fileList
    set theFile to contents of aFile
    set infoRec to info for file (folderPath & theFile)

    if folder of infoRec is false and creation date of infoRec < oldestDate then
        set oldestDate to (creation date of infoRec)
        set oldestFile to theFile
    end if
end repeat

display dialog "The oldest file in " & folderPath & "is " & theFile & ¬
    "; it was created on " & oldestDate as string buttons {"OK"} default button 1
```

Exercise 6 solution

```
-- Update the population list in a file

-- open the file, first to read, then to write back the new results

set fileName to (path to documents folder as string) & "ListFile101"
set citiesFile to open for access file fileName with write permission

-- now read in the existing list

set USCities to read citiesFile as list

-- prompt the user for a new city and population

set gotThrough to false

-- do the following in a try in case an error occurs...

try
    display dialog "Enter your new city: " default answer ""
```

```
      set newCity to text returned of result
      display dialog "Enter the population for " & newCity default answer ""
      set newPopulation to text returned of result as integer

      -- add the new record to the list
      set end of USCities to {name:newCity, population:newPopulation}

      -- write the update list out to the file
      write USCities to citiesFile starting at 0
      set gotThrough to true
   end try

   close access citiesFile

   -- See if any error occurred

   if gotThrough = true then
      display dialog "The file has been updated" buttons {"OK"} default button 1
   else
      display dialog "An error occurred during this operation, I couldn't update the
   file!"
             buttons "OK" default button 1
   end if
```

Exercise 7 solution

Assuming the population list is stored in the file ListFile101 in the user's Documents Folder (and be careful to note here that you're talking about the user running the program), you can simply replace the lines from the population program in Chapter 6 that read:

```
set USCities to {¬
   {name:"Boston", population:574000}, ¬
   {name:"Chicago", population:2784000}, ¬
   {name:"Dallas", population:1007000}, ¬
   {name:"Houston", population:1631000}, ¬
   {name:"Los Angeles", population:3485000}, ¬
   {name:"Philadelphia", population:1586000}, ¬
   {name:"San Diego", population:1111000}, ¬
   {name:"San Francisco", population:724000}, ¬
   {name:"New York", population:7323000}}
```

with the following lines:

```
set fileName to alias ((path to documents folder as string) & "ListFile101")
set citiesFile to open for access fileName with write permission
set USCities to read citiesFile as list
close access citiesFile
```

These lines read the list from the file instead of defining it in the program. The rest of the program remains unchanged.

Exercise 8 solution

```
-- A simple file copy program

-- get the file to be copied

set fromFile to choose file with prompt "Select the file to be copied:"

set fromFileID to open for access fromFile

-- now get the destination file name

set toFile to choose file name with prompt "Select the name of the file for the copy"

set toFileID to open for access toFile with write permission
set eof toFileID to 0      -- truncate if it exists

-- now copy the files

set theData to read fromFileID
write theData to toFileID

-- close the files

close access fromFileID
close access toFileID
```

Chapter 8

Exercise 1 solution

```
-- Add three numbers and return the result

on sum(x, y, z)
    if class of x is in {real, integer} and class of y is in {real, integer} and ¬
        class of z is in {real, integer} then
        return x + y + z
    else
        return 0
    end if
end sum
```

Exercise 2 solution

```
-- sum all the numbers in a list

on listSum(L)
    set theSum to 0

    if class of L is list then
        repeat with num in numbers in L
```

```
                set theSum to theSum + num
         end repeat
    end

    return theSum
end listSum
```

Exercise 3 solution

```
-- remove numItems items from L starting at n

on removeItems(L, n, numItems)
   if n > 0 and numItems > 0 and n + numItems - 1    (count L) then
      if n = 1 then                                  -- remove leading items
         if N + numItems - 1 = (count L) then
            set L to {}                              -- remove all items
         else
            set L to items (n + numItems) thru -1 of L
         end if
      else if n + numItems - 1 = (count L) then      -- remove ending items
         set L to items 1 thru (n - 1) of L
      else                                           -- remove in between items
         set L to (items 1 thru (n - 1) of L) & (items (n + numItems) thru -1) of L
      end if
   end if

   return L
end removeItems

-- test case
removeItems({1,2,3,4,5}, 2, 3)
```

Exercise 4 solution

The call

```
reverse of listSort(L)
```

would give you a list sorted in descending order.

Exercise 5 solution

```
on listSort of L given ascendingSort:ascendingFlag
    if ascendingFlag then
        return quickSort(L, 1, count L)
    else
        return reverse of quickSort(L, 1, count L)
    end if
end listSort
```

Bonus:

```
-- Recursive quick sort

on listSort of L given ascendingSort:ascendingFlag
    return quickSort(L, 1, count L, ascendingFlag)
end listSort

on quickSort(L, leftIndex, rightIndex, ascendingFlag)
    if L = {} then
        return L
    end if

    set lHold to leftIndex
    set rHold to rightIndex

    set pivot to item leftIndex of L

    repeat while leftIndex < rightIndex
    repeat while ((ascendingFlag and item rightIndex of L ≥ pivot) or (not ¬
            ascendingFlag and item rightIndex of L ≤ pivot)) and ¬
            leftIndex < rightIndex
        set rightIndex to rightIndex - 1
    end repeat
    if leftIndex ≠ rightIndex then
        set item leftIndex of L to item rightIndex of L
        set leftIndex to leftIndex + 1
    end if

    repeat while ((ascendingFlag and item leftIndex of L ≤ pivot) or (not ¬
            ascendingFlag and item leftIndex of L ≥ pivot)) and ¬
            leftIndex < rightIndex
        set leftIndex to leftIndex + 1
    end repeat
    if leftIndex ≠ rightIndex then
        set item rightIndex of L to item leftIndex of L
        set rightIndex to rightIndex - 1
    end if
    end repeat

    set item leftIndex of L to pivot
    set oldLeft to leftIndex
    set leftIndex to lHold
    set rightIndex to rHold

    if leftIndex < oldLeft then
        quickSort(L, leftIndex, oldLeft - 1, ascendingFlag)
    end if
    if rightIndex > oldLeft then
        quickSort(L, oldLeft + 1, rightIndex, ascendingFlag)
    end if

    return L
end quickSort
```

Appendix A

Exercise 6 solution

The program generates an error because x is declared to be a local variable. Therefore, its value cannot be accessed from inside any handler, even with the use of the my keyword.

Exercise 7 solution

```
-- Generate a sorted list of words in a file

set listHandlers to load script file ((path to scripts folder as string) &
    "List Handlers.scpt")

-- get the file

set textFile to choose file with prompt "Select a file with some words in it"

-- open the file and read its contents (up to 32KB)

set fileID to open for access textFile

-- limit read to 32KB characters
set fileSize to get eof fileID
if fileSize > 32767 then set fileSize to 32767

set textData to read fileID for fileSize
close access fileID

set wordList to words of textData

-- get a sorted list of words

set sortedWords to listSort(wordList) of listHandlers
log sortedWords
```

Exercise 8 solution

```
-- Remove duplicate items from a sorted list

on removeDuplicateItems from L
    set listSize to count L
    set uniqueItems to {}    -- the output list
    set i to 1

    repeat while i     listSize
        set curItem to item i of L
        set end of uniqueItems to curItem

        -- skip any repeats of curItem in the list

        set i to i + 1
        repeat while i < listSize and curItem = item i of L
            set i to i + 1
        end repeat
    end repeat
```

```
        return uniqueItems
end removeDuplicateItems

-- code that follows tests the handler

-- load the list handlers to use listSort

set listHandlers to load script file ((path to scripts folder as string) & ¬
        "List Handlers.scpt")

-- get the file

set textFile to choose file with prompt "Select a file with some words in it"

-- open the file and read its contents (up to 32KB)

set fileID to open for access textFile
set fileSize to get eof fileID
if fileSize > 32767 then set fileSize to 32767
set textData to read fileID for fileSize
close access fileID

set wordList to words of textData

-- remove the duplicates from the sorted word list

removeDuplicateItems from (listSort(wordList) of listHandlers)
```

Exercise 9 solution

```
-- Count the number of times each item occurs in a list

on countItems(L)
    set listSize to count L
    set itemList to {}    -- the resulting list of records
    set i to 1

    -- first sort the list

    set L to listSort(L) of my listHandlers

    repeat while i   listSize
        set curItem to item i of L

        -- count consecutive occurrences of curItem

        set saveI to i
        set i to i + 1

        repeat while i < listSize and curItem = item i of L
            set i to i + 1
        end repeat

        -- add a new record to the end of the list
```

```
              set end of itemList to {sItem:curItem, sCount:i - saveI}
          end repeat

          return itemList
      end countItems
```

Exercise 10 solution

As you can see from the log, what gets loaded by the `load script` command is the actual code you entered for your handlers.

Chapter 9

Exercise 1 solution

```
set eCancel to -128
set eBadNumber to -1700

set OKtoExit to false

repeat while not OKtoExit
  try
      display dialog "Enter a number" default answer "0"
      set theNumber to text returned of result as integer
      set OKtoExit to true
  on error errorMsg number errorNum
      if errorNum is eCancel then
          display dialog "Are you sure you want to Cancel?" buttons {"Yes", "No"} ¬
                  default button "No"
          if button returned of result is "Yes" then
              set OKtoExit to true
          end if
      else if errorNum is eBadNumber then
          display dialog "You entered a bad number, try running the program again" ¬
                  buttons {"OK"} with icon stop
      else
          display dialog "Error: " & errorMsg
      end if
  end try
end repeat
```

Exercise 2 solution

The answer to Exercise 1 also satisfies this problem. You may want to just change the message about running the program again because it no longer applies.

Exercise 3 solution

```
-- handler to get an integer from the user

global eCancel
global eBadNumber
```

```
    set eCancel to -128
    set eBadNumber to -1700

on getInteger(promptString, min, max)
  set OKtoExit to false

  repeat while not OKtoExit
      try
          display dialog promptString default answer (min as string)

          set theNumber to text returned of result as integer

          if min is not missing value and theNumber < min then
              display dialog "The value must be greater than or equal to " & ¬
                      min as string buttons {"OK"} default button 1
          else if max is not missing value and theNumber > max then
              display dialog "The value must be less than or equal to " & ¬
                      max as string buttons {"OK"} default button 1
          else
              set OKtoExit to true
          end if
      on error errorMsg number errorNum partial result eList from eFrom to eTo
          if errorNum is eBadNumber then
              return missing value
          else
              error errorMsg number errorNum partial result eList from eFrom to eTo
          end if
      end try
  end repeat

  return theNumber
end getInteger

-- test the handler

set numEntered to getInteger("Enter a month number", 1, 12)
display dialog "You entered " & numEntered as string buttons {"OK"} default
button 1
```

Exercise 4 solution

```
--  handler to get an integer from the user

global eCancel
global eBadNumber

set eCancel to -128
set eBadNumber to -1700

on getInteger(promptString, min, max, maxTries)
   set OKtoExit to false
   set tries to 1
```

```
            repeat while not OKtoExit and tries    maxTries
                try
                    display dialog promptString default answer (min as string)

                    set theNumber to text returned of result as integer

                    if min is not missing value and theNumber < min then
                        display dialog "The value must be great than or equal to " & ¬
                                min as string buttons {"OK"} default button 1
                    else if max is not missing value and theNumber > max then
                        display dialog "The value must be less than or equal to " & ¬
                                max as string buttons {"OK"} default button 1
                    else
                        set OKtoExit to true
                    end if
                on error errorMsg number errorNum partial result eList from eFrom to eTo
                    if errorNum is not eBadNumber then
                        error errorMsg number errorNum partial result eList from eFrom to eTo
                    end if
                end try

                set tries to tries + 1
            end repeat

        -- see how the loop was exited

        if OKtoExit is not true then
        display dialog "Too many tries, giving up!" with icon caution buttons {"OK"}
                default button 1
            return missing value
        else
            return theNumber
        end if
    end getInteger

    -- test the handler

    set numEntered to getInteger("Enter a month number", 1, 12, 3)
    display dialog "You entered " & numEntered as string buttons {"OK"} default
    button 1
```

Exercise 5 solution

This program is based on code shown earlier in the chapter:

```
try
    100 / 0
on error number N
    display dialog N as string
end try
```

Chapter 10

Exercise 1 solution

```
-- Sliding windows

tell application "Finder"
    set newWin to make new Finder window

    repeat with i from 1 to 200
        set position of newWin to ({i * 4, 800 - i * 4} as point)
    end repeat

    close newWin
end tell
```

Exercise 2 solution

On my system, I get the following for the file reference:

a.

```
folder "steve" of folder "Users" of startup disk of application "Finder"
```

```
tell application "Finder"
    tell startup disk
        tell folder "Users"
            set fileRef to get folder "steve"
        end tell
    end tell
end tell
```

b.

```
fileRef as string
```

c.

```
POSIX path of (fileRef as string)
```

d.

```
fileRef as alias
```

Exercise 3 solution

a.

```
tell application "Finder" to get size of file toDoFIleT
```

b.

```
tell application "Finder" to duplicate file toDoFIle to (path to documents folder)
```

c.

```
tell application "Finder" to set name of file toDoFIle to "ToDoOld.txt"
```

d.

```
tell application "Finder" to delete file toDoFIle
```

or

```
tell application "Finder" to move file toDoFIle to trash
```

e.

```
tell application "Finder"
    make new folder at home with properties {name: "ToDoFolder"}
    move file toDoFile to home
end tell
```

f.

```
tell application "Finder" to count (files of home whose name begins with "ToDo")
```

g.

```
tell application "Finder" to count (files of home whose name contins "ToDo")
```

Exercise 4 solution

```
-- Create an Internet location file

tell application "Finder"
    make new internet location file at desktop to "p2p.wrox.com"
end tell
```

Exercise 5 solution

```
-- Get an email for someone in the Address Book

display dialog "Enter first name:" default answer ""
set firstName to text returned of result

display dialog "Enter last name:" default answer ""
set lastName to text returned of result

tell application "Address Book"
    set theEntries to people whose first name is firstName and last name is
lastName

    -- See how many matches were found
```

```
        if (count theEntries) > 0 then
            set theEmails to {}

            -- Get the email address for each entry

            repeat with anEntry in theEntries
                repeat with anEmail in emails of anEntry
                    set end of theEmails to value of anEmail
                end repeat
            end repeat
        else -- matches is 0
            display dialog "I couldn't find " & firstName & " " & lastName
        end if

        -- Prompt if there's more than one email address

        if (count theEmails) > 1 then
            choose from list theEmails with prompt "Select an email address:"
            set theSelection to result
            if theSelection is not false then
                set selectedEmail to item 1 of result
            else
                return
            end if
        else
            set selectedEmail to theEmails
        end if

        display dialog "Email address for " & firstName & " " & lastName & " is " &
    selectedEmail
    end tell
```

Exercise 6 solution

Replace the code at the beginning of the program that sets the variables modifiedDays and backupFolder with the following:

```
set modifiedDays to missing value

display dialog "Back up files modified within how many days?" default answer "7"
try
    set modifiedDays to (text returned of result as integer) * days
end try

if modifiedDays is equal to missing value or modifiedDays < 0 then
    display dialog "I wanted a positive integer here!" with icon stop buttons ¬
        {"OK"} default button 1
 return
end if

set backupFolder to choose folder with prompt "Please select a folder:" as string
```

Exercise 7 solution

Change the backup program developed in this chapter according to the following:

```
on run
    set backupFolder to choose folder with prompt "Please select a folder:" as
string
    open {backupFolder}
end run

on open argList
    set backupFolder to item 1 of argList
    set infoRec to info for backupFolder

    if (count argList) > 1 or not folder of infoRec then
        display dialog "I just work with a single folder!" with icon stop buttons ¬
            {"OK"} default button 1
        return
    end if

    set modifiedDays to 7 * days
    set HTMLFile to (path to temporary items as string) & "backuplist.html"

    -- insert the code from the backup program in the chapter that starts with
    -- opening the temporary file (Not shown here)
    ...
end open
```

Exercise 8 solution

Change the lines from the droplet that read like this

```
    write "<HTML>
<HEAD>
<TITLE>Kids Pics</TITLE>
</HEAD>
<BODY>
<H1>Pictures of My Kids</H1>" to f
```

to the following:

```
set title to name of infoRec

    write "<HTML>
<HEAD>
<TITLE>" & title & "</TITLE>
</HEAD>
<BODY>
<H1>" & title & "</H1>" to f
```

Exercise 9 solution

Here is one possible approach to solving this problem:

```
-- Droplet to make a web page from images in folders and files

on open argList
    set fileList to {}

    -- Create a single list of all files and files in folders

    repeat with aFile in argList
        set infoRec to get info for aFile

        if folder of infoRec then
            repeat with bFile in list folder aFile without invisibles
                set end of fileList to (aFile as string) & bFile
            end repeat
        else
            set end of fileList to aFile as string
        end if
    end repeat

    -- open the HTML file for writing

    set HTMLFile to (path to desktop folder as string) & "pics.html"

    set f to open for access HTMLFile with write permission
    set eof of f to 0

    -- write HTML header info to the file

    write "<HTML>
<HEAD>
<TITLE>Pictures on my Mac</TITLE>
</HEAD>
<BODY>
<H1>Pictures on my Mac</H1>" to f

    -- process each image file in the folder

    repeat with imageFile in fileList
        set infoRec to get info for file imageFile

        if name extension of infoRec is not in {"JPG", "GIF"} then
            try
                display dialog "Can't process file " & (imageFile as string)
            on error -- if the user Cancels, clean up
                close access f
                tell application "Finder" to delete file HTMLFile
                return
            end try
        else
            write "<img border=1 src=\"" & (POSIX path of imageFile) & "\"><p>" to
f
        end if
    end repeat
```

```
    -- close the HTML file

    write "</BODY>
</HTML>" to f

    close access f

    tell application "Safari" to open file HTMLFile
end open
```

Exercise 10 solution

```
on open fileList
    set docs to (path to documents folder) as string

    set filingList to {¬
        {ext:"JPG", place:(docs & "Images:") as alias}, ¬
        {ext:"GIF", place:(docs & "Images:") as alias}, ¬
        {ext:"MP3", place:(docs & "Music:") as alias}, ¬
        {ext:"TXT", place:(docs & "Text files:") as alias}, ¬
        {ext:"PDF", place:(docs & "PDF:") as alias}, ¬
        {ext:"MOV", place:(docs & "Movies:") as alias}, ¬
        {ext:"AVI", place:(docs & "Movies:") as alias}, ¬
        {ext:"*", place:(docs & "Misc:") as alias}}

    repeat with aFile in fileList -- process each file
        set infoRec to info for aFile

        -- ignore folders
        if not folder of infoRec then -- ignore folders
            set aExt to name extension of infoRec

            -- look for matching extension or end of list

            repeat with fileTypes in filingList
                if ext of fileTypes = "*" or ext of fileTypes = aExt then
                    set toPlace to place of fileTypes
                        exit repeat
                end if
            end repeat

            -- move the file into the folder

            try
                tell application "Finder" to move aFile to toPlace
            on error
                display dialog "Couldn't file " & (aFile as string) & " in " & toPlace ¬
                    with icon note
            end try
        end if
    end repeat
end open
```

Chapter 11

Exercise 1 solution

```
set trackName to text returned of (display dialog "Type in some characters from the
        song name" default answer "")

tell application "iTunes"
    set trackList to search first library playlist for trackName only songs
    if (count trackList) is 1 then
        set trackToPlay to item 1 of trackList
    else if (count trackList) > 1 then
      -- make a list of track names, artists and albums for the user to choose from

        set trackChoiceList to {}

        repeat with aTrack in trackList
            set end of trackChoiceList to name of aTrack & " -- " & artist of ¬
                aTrack & " -- " & album of aTrack
        end repeat

        choose from list trackChoiceList with prompt "Pick one:"
        set resultList to result

            if resultList is false then -- User canceled?
            return
        else
            set trackSelected to item 1 of resultList
        end if

      -- now find the selected track from the list

        repeat with i from 1 to (count trackList)
            if trackSelected = (item i of trackChoiceList) then
                set trackToPlay to item i of trackList
                exit repeat
            end if
        end repeat
    else -- no matching tracks
        display dialog "I couldn't find any tracks containing " & trackName & ¬
                " in their titles" with icon note buttons {"OK"} default button 1
        return
    end if

    -- finally, play the track

    play trackToPlay -- AppleScript doesn't wait for the song to finish!

    display dialog "Playing " & name of trackToPlay buttons {"OK"} with icon ¬
        note default button 1 giving up after 3
end tell
```

Exercise 2 solution

Replace the line from the applet that reads

```
set trackList to search first library playlist for trackName only songs
```

with the following lines:

```
if trackName = "*" then
    set trackList to some track of first library playlist as list
else
    set trackList to search first library playlist for trackName only songs
end if
```

If a "*" is typed, a one element list is created from a randomly-selected track. (It's made into a list here so that no other lines in the program have to be modified.)

Exercise 3 solution

Replace this section of code from the applet:

```
set trackName to text returned of (display dialog "Type in some characters from the
    song name" default answer "")

tell application "iTunes"
    set trackList to search first library playlist for trackName only songs
```

with the following code:

```
display dialog "Type in some characters to identify a song" default answer "" ¬
        buttons {"Title", "Artist", "Album"} default button 1

set theResult to result
set searchString to text returned of theResult
set searchType to button returned of theResult

tell application "iTunes"
    if searchType = "Name" then
        set trackList to search first library playlist for searchString only songs
    else if searchType = "Artist" then
        set trackList to search first library playlist for searchString only
artists
    else
        set trackList to search first library playlist for searchString only albums
    end if
```

Exercise 4 solution

Change all the lines from the applet that follow this line

```
-- finally, play the track
```

to the following code:

```
    -- See if the "Play Just One" playlist exists and clear it if it does
    -- create it if it doesn't

    if exists playlist "Play Just One" then
        delete tracks of playlist "Play Just One"
    else
        make new playlist with properties {name:"Play Just One"}
    end if

    duplicate trackToPlay to playlist "Play Just One"

    -- change the reference of the track to the one in the Play Just One playlist
    set trackToPlay to first track of playlist "Play Just One"

    -- finally, play the track

    play trackToPlay -- AppleScript doesn't wait for the song to finish!

    display dialog "Playing   " & name of trackToPlay buttons {"OK"} with icon note ¬
        default button 1 giving up after 3
end tell
```

Exercise 5 solution

Change all the lines from the applet that follow this line

```
    -- finally, play the track
```

to the following code:

```
    -- See if the "Play Just One" playlist exists and clear it if it does
    -- create it if it doesn't

    if (not (exists playlist "Play Just One")) then
        make new playlist with properties {name:"Play Just One"}
    end if

    -- play the track if playlist is not playing or is playing a track
    -- from another playlist

    if player state is stopped or (player state is not stopped and name of ¬
            (current playlist) is not "Play Just One") then
        delete tracks of playlist "Play Just One"

        -- change the reference of the track to the one in the playlist

        duplicate trackToPlay to playlist "Play Just One"
        set trackToPlay to first track of playlist "Play Just One"

        play trackToPlay

        display dialog "Playing   " & name of trackToPlay buttons {"OK"} with icon ¬
            note default button 1 giving up after 3
```

```
    else
        display dialog "Queueing  " & name of trackToPlay buttons {"OK"} with icon ¬
            note default button 1 giving up after 3
        duplicate trackToPlay to playlist "Play Just One"
    end if
end tell
```

Exercise 6 solution

Replace the first three lines from the iPhoto applet that read

```
-- Make a new album from a folder of images

set imageFolder to choose folder with prompt "Select of a folder of images:"

set infoRec to info for imageFolder
```

with the following lines of code:

```
on run
  set imageFolder to choose folder with prompt "Select of a folder of images:"
  open {imageFolder}
end run

on open theList
  set imageFolder to item 1 of theList

  set infoRec to info for imageFolder
  if not folder of infoRec or (count theList) > 1 then
      display dialog "The droplet needs a single folder of images" with icon stop ¬
          buttons {"OK"} default button 1
      return
  end if
```

Exercise 7 solution

Replace the lines of code from the iPhoto applet that read

```
if exists album albumName then
    display dialog "The album " & albumName & " already exists!  Change the folder
        name and try again!" with icon stop buttons {"OK"} default button 1
        return
end if
```

with the following lines of code:

```
set goodName to false

repeat while not goodName
  if exists album albumName then
      display dialog "The album " & albumName & " already exists, type a new name" ¬
          default answer ""
```

```
            set albumName to text returned of result
       else
            set goodName to true
       end if
   end repeat
```

Exercise 8 solution

Replace the iPhoto applet code from the `repeat` loop to the end of the program with the following code (added lines appear in **bold**):

```
    set photoCount to 0

    repeat with anImageFile in fileList
        set fullPath to (imageFolder as string) & anImageFile
        set infoRec to info for file fullPath

        -- import image files

        if name extension of infoRec is in {"JPG", "JPEG", "TIF", "TIFF", "GIF"}
then
            try -- we ignore errors here
                import from (POSIX path of fullPath) to album albumName
                set photoCount to photoCount + 1
            end try
        end if
    end repeat

    if photoCount is 0 then
        display dialog "No images were added, so the album has been removed" with ¬
            icon note buttons {"OK"} default button 1
        remove album albumName
    else
        display dialog "Your album  has been created!" buttons {"OK"} default ¬
            button 1 giving up after 3

        -- display the album in iPhoto

        set current album to album albumName
    end if
end tell
```

Exercise 9 solution

Replace the iPhoto applet code from the `repeat` loop to the end of the program with the following code (added or modified lines from the previous exercise appear in **bold**):

```
    set rejectList to {}
    set photoCount to 0

    repeat with anImageFile in fileList
        set fullPath to (imageFolder as string) & anImageFile
        set infoRec to info for file fullPath
```

```
        -- import image files

        if name extension of infoRec is in {"JPG", "JPEG", "TIF", "TIFF", "GIF"} then
            try -- we ignore errors here
                import from (POSIX path of fullPath) to album albumName
                set photoCount to photoCount + 1
            on error
                set end of rejectList to anImageFile
            end try
        else
                set end of rejectList to anImageFile
        end if
    end repeat

    if photoCount is 0 then
        display dialog "No images were added, so the album has been removed" ¬
                with icon note buttons {"OK"} default button 1
        remove album albumName
    else
        if (count rejectList) is 0 then
            display dialog ("Your album  has been created with " & photoCount as ¬
                string) & " images" buttons {"OK"} default button 1 giving up after 3
        else
            choose from list rejectList with prompt ("Your album has been created
                with " & photoCount as string) & " images. These files were not added
                    to the album: "
        end if

        -- display the album in iPhoto

        set current album to album albumName
    end if
end tell
```

Exercise 10 solution

To change the applet into a droplet, you can add a run handler like this to your code:

```
on run
    set imageFolder to choose folder with prompt "Select of a folder of images:"
    open {imageFolder}
end run
```

Then, you can encapsulate your code from the original applet inside an open handler. The handler should take an argument, which is a single folder. To see how that's done, refer to the answer for Exercise 6.

Exercise 11 solution

```
-- Make a new DVD from a folder of images

on iTunesPick() -- get a track from iTunes
    tell application "iTunes" to get location of some file track of first ¬
        library playlist
end iTunesPick
```

```
(* Insert the getAlbum handler code here *)

set photoAlbum to getAlbum()
tell current application to activate -- bring current app back to the front
set projectLoc to choose file name with prompt "Select a name for your DVD
project:"

tell application "iPhoto"
    set albumName to name of photoAlbum
    set photolist to photos of photoAlbum
end tell

display dialog "Creating DVD from images..." buttons {"OK"} default button 1 ¬
      giving up after 2

tell application "iDVD"
    activate

    -- start a new project and select a theme and background pic

    try
        new project name albumName path (projectLoc as string) save current "no"
    on error
        display dialog "I couldn't create a new iDVD project!" with icon stop ¬
            buttons {"OK"} default button 1
        return
    end try

    set motion mode to false
    set assigned theme of current menu to "Transparent Blue"

    -- set properties of the menu

    set menuName to "Menu1"
    set name of current menu to menuName
    set title of current menu to albumName

    -- create a new slideshow

    make new slideshow at end of slideshows of current menu
    set the label of first button of current menu to "Slides!"
    set name of first slideshow of current menu to "Slides!"
    set transition type of first slideshow to cube

    set backgroundSet to false

    -- now add each photo to the slide show

    repeat with aPhoto in photolist
        tell application "iPhoto"
            set pPath to image path of aPhoto
            set photoName to name of aPhoto
        end tell

        -- import image files
```

```
            if not backgroundSet then
                set background asset of current menu to pPath
                set backgroundSet to true
            end if

            try -- we ignore errors here
                make new image at end of images of first slideshow with properties ¬
                    {name:photoName, path:pPath}
            end try
        end repeat

        set transition type of current menu to page flip

        -- select background music for the slide show and main menu

        set background audio of current menu to my iTunesPick()

        set motion mode to true
        set duration of current menu to 30 -- can't go any higher?

        set background audio of first slideshow to my iTunesPick()

        display dialog "Your DVD project has been created!" buttons {"OK"} default ¬
            button 1 giving up after 3
    end tell
```

Chapter 12

Exercise 1 solution

```
script countMe
    property X : 0

    set X to X + 1
    log "I've been called " & (X as string) & " times"
end script

repeat 10 times
    run countMe
end repeat
```

Exercise 2 solution

```
on surfaceArea given radius:r
        return 4 * pi * r * r
end surfaceArea
```

Exercise 3 solution

```
on rectangle given width:w, height:h
    script
        property width : w
        property height : h
```

```
            property origin : {0, 0} as point

            on area()
                return width * height
            end area

            on perimeter()
                return (width + height) * 2
            end perimeter

            on setOrigin given x:x0, y:y0
                set origin to {x0, y0} as point
            end setOrigin

            on getOrigin()
                return origin
            end getOrigin
        end script
end rectangle

on square given side:s
    script
        property side : s

        on area()
            return side * side
        end area

        on perimeter()
            return side * 4
        end perimeter
    end script
end square

-- test the new origin methods

set R1 to rectangle given width:10, height: 20
setOrigin of R1 given x:100, y:200
getOrigin() of R1
```

Exercise 4 solution

You can't use the store script command because you want to store handlers and not a single script by name into a file. (*Note:* you could encapsulate both the rectangle and square handlers inside a script compound statement and then write that script out to a file.)

```
set shapes to load script file ((path to scripts folder as string) & "rects.scpt")

set myRect to rectangle of shapes given width:15, height:20
set mySquare to square of shapes given side:12

log area() of myRect
log perimeter() of mySquare
```

Appendix A

Exercise 5 solution

```
on makeDict()
    script
        property localDict : {}

        -- this is a method used by other methods
        -- it returns the index of the specified key in the dictionary

        on findEntry given key:theKey
            repeat with i from 1 to count localDict
                if first item of (item i of localDict) is theKey then
                    return i
                end if
            end repeat

            return missing value -- not found
        end findEntry

        -- set an entry in the dictionary

        on setEntry given key:theKey, value:theValue
            set i to findEntry given key:theKey -- first look it up

            -- add the new entry if it's not there
            -- otherwise, just change its value

            if i is missing value then
                    set end of localDict to {theKey, theValue}
                else
                    set item 2 of item i of localDict to theValue
                end if
        end setEntry

        -- get a value given a key

        on getValue given key:theKey
            set i to findEntry given key:theKey

            if i is missing value then
                return missing value
            else
                return item 2 of item i of localDict
            end if
        end getValue

        -- delete an entry given a key

        on delEntry given key:theKey
            local i
            set i to findEntry given key:theKey

            if i is not missing value then
                -- following is the code to remove an item from
                -- a list.  You can use the handler you
```

```
                    -- created in Chapter 8 here
                if i = 1 then
                    set localDict to rest of localDict
                else if i = (count localDict) then
                    set localDict to items 1 thru -2 of localDict
                else
                    set localDict to (items 1 thru (i - 1) of localDict) &
                            (items (i + 1) thru -1) of localDict
                end if
            end if
        end delEntry

        -- return a list of all the keys

        on listKeys()
            set allKeys to {}

            repeat with E in localDict
                set end of allKeys to item 1 of E
            end repeat

            return allKeys
        end listKeys
    end script
end makeDict
```

Chapter 13

Exercise 1 solution

This answer uses the say command with the Bells voice. An iTunes solution is not shown here, but it is something you may want to try on your own to get authentic sounding chimes.

```
-- Big Ben!

set theTime to time string of (current date)
set theHour to first word of theTime as integer
set theMinutes to second word of theTime as integer

set theHour to 3
set theMinutes to 45

-- Get the hour

if theHour is 0 then
    set theHour to 12
else if theHour is greater than 12 then
    set theHour to theHour - 12
end if

set theChime to theMinutes div 15
if theChime is 0 then set theChime to 4
```

```
-- Ring the chimes: once for 15 after, twice for 30,
-- three times for 45 and four times on the hour

repeat theChime times
    say "do do di da" using "Bells"  -- ok, so maybe this is a little lame!
end repeat

-- Strike the hour!

if theMinutes is 0 then
    delay 1

    repeat theHour times
        say "ding" using "Bells"
    end repeat
end if
```

Here's what your entry in the crontab would look like to run your Big Ben program every 15 minutes:

```
*/15    *       *       *       *       "/Users/steve/Big Ben.app"
```

Exercise 2 solution

```
-- B&N price quote

display dialog "Enter your ISBN number" default answer ""
set theISBN to text returned of result
set theResult to missing value

tell application "http://services.xmethods.net:80/soap/servlet/rpcrouter"
    try
        set theResult to call soap {method name:"getPrice", method namespace ¬
                uri:"urn:xmethods-BNPriceCheck", parameters:{isbn:theISBN}}
    end try
end tell

if theResult is not missing value then
    display dialog "The book is selling for " & theResult as string buttons {"OK"} ¬
            default button 1
else
    display dialog "I couldn't get a price for " & theISBN buttons {"OK"} default ¬
            button 1
end if
```

Note that the method returns 10.0 in many cases as the result when given an invalid ISBN number. The program has no way to distinguish that from a true price of $10.00. Also, the program does not format the price with two decimal places. See the example in the chapter of the do shell script command using printf to format a number.

Exercise 3 solution

In the Rotate90 program shown in the chapter, first change the dialog to indicate you are scaling files and not rotating them. Then, replace the command that rotates the image

```
rotate thePic to angle 90
```

with this command to scale the image by 50%:

```
scale thePic by factor .5
```

Exercise 4 solution

The droplet from Chapter 10 only requires two simple changes. The first line that reads

```
on open fileList
```

should be changed to

```
on adding folder items to theFolder after receiving fileList
```

and the last line that reads

```
end open
```

should be changed to

```
end adding folder items to
```

Then, be sure to follow the steps outlined in the chapter to attach a script to a folder:

1. Save the file as a script file in ~/Library/Scripts/Folder Action Scripts.
2. Create a new folder called File Me on your desktop.
3. Right-click that folder and select Attach a Folder Action from the contextual menu.
4. Select the script you just created to attach it to the folder.

That's it! Now drag some files into your File Me folder and see how they get filed!

Exercise 5 solution

You can just substitute different applications for the TextEdit application shown in the example. For example, the following works to copy the text from Safari's frontmost window to the clipboard:

```
tell application "System Events"
    tell application process "Safari"
        set frontmost to true
        click menu item "Select All" of menu "Edit" of menu bar item "Edit" ¬
                of menu bar 1
        click menu item "Copy" of menu "Edit" of menu bar item "Edit" of menu bar 1
    end tell
end tell

delay 1
the clipboard
```

Chapter 14

Exercise 1 solution

Use the Info panel for the UI elements to change their properties. You can also change the label's title in the interface window by double-clicking the element.

Exercise 2 solution

In this exercise, you need to define one text field for input and two for output. If you name the three fields `radius`, `circumference`, and `area`, respectively, here's what your `clicked` handler might look like for the Calculate button:

```
on clicked theObject
    try
        set r to contents of text field "radius" of window "main" as number
    on error
        error "Please enter a number in the radius field!"
    end

    set contents of text field "circumference" of window "main" to 2 * pi * r
    set contents of text field "area" of window "main" to pi * r ^ 2
end clicked
```

Language Reference

This appendix contains a summary of AppleScript operators, classes, statements, and commands. It has been organized for quick reference. Please refer to the text for a more detailed explanation of any of the topics summarized here. This reference is based on AppleScript version 1.9.3.

Operators

The following table summarizes the various AppleScript operators. These operators are listed in order of decreasing precedence. Operators grouped together have the same precedence.

Operator	Operator	Associativity
`-` `+`	Unary minus Unary plus	—
`^`	Exponentiation	Right to left

`*`
`/`
`div`
`mod`
	Multiplication
	Division
	Integer division
	Modulus
		Left to right

`+` `-`	Addition Subtraction	Left to right
`&`	Concatenation	Left to right
`as`	Coercion	Left to right
`<, ≤, >, ≥`	Relational	—
`=, ≠`	Equality / Inequality	—
`not`	Logical negation	—
`and`	Logical AND	Left to right
`or`	Logical OR	Left to right

As an example of how to use the table, consider the expression

```
b < c + d * e
```

The multiplication operator has higher precedence than both the addition and less-than operators because it appears above both of these in the table. Similarly, the multiplication operator has higher precedence than the addition operator because the former appears above the latter in the table. Therefore, this expression is evaluated as

```
b < (c + (d * e))
```

Now consider the following expression:

```
b mod c * d
```

Because the modulus and multiplication operators appear in the same grouping in the table, they have the same precedence. The associativity property then comes into play. For these operators, the associativity is listed in the table as left to right, indicating that the expression would be evaluated as

```
(b mod c) * d
```

When using the logical and operator, you are guaranteed that the second operand will not be evaluated if the first is false; and in the case of or, you are guaranteed that the second operand will not be evaluated if the first is true. This fact is worth bearing in mind when you form expressions such as the following:

```
if  dataFlag  or  checkData() then
    ...
end if
```

In this case, checkData is called only if the value of dataFlag is false.

For another example, if L is a list, then the if statement that begins

```
if n ≥ 0  and  n ≤ (count L)  and  (item n of L) = 0 then
    ...
end if
```

references the item in the list only if n is a valid item number in the list.

English Equivalents of Relational Operators

The following table summarizes the English words that can be used instead of symbols for the relational operators. Some words are not listed in the table because they are changed after the program is compiled. For example, you can write isn't equal to, but it gets changed to is not equal to after the program is compiled.

Symbol	English Equivalent
<	is less than is not greater than or equal to comes before
≤	is less than or equal to is not greater than does not come after
=	is equal to is
≠	is not equal to is not
>	is greater than is not less than or equal to comes after
≤	is greater than or equal to is not less than does not come before

Containment Operators

The following table shows the containment operators that can be used with lists, records, and strings. Items in a record are not ordered, so the first two entries in the table do not apply to records. Because lists are ordered, checking for containment of one list inside another requires that the items appear consecutively and in the same order.

Operator
begins with starts with
ends with
contains
does not contain
is in is contained by
is not in is not contained by

Built-in Classes

The following table summarizes the classes that were covered in this text, plus a few additional ones. Many others that are not listed here are defined in the AppleScript dictionary. In some cases, they're listed in the dictionary but are not implemented in any useful way. For example, the AppleScript dictionary contains a linked list class. However, the language gives no particular support for this class.

Class	Meaning	Properties
alias	Identifies a file regardless of its location	POSIX path
anything	A particular value you can assign to a variable that won't match any other value you can assign to it	
boolean	A logical truth value of either true or false	
bounding rectangle	A list of four numbers typically used to specify the bounds of a window on the screen	
character	A single character	
class	The class a value belongs to	
constant	A constant value	
data	A raw data value written as «data type...»	
date	A value containing the date and time	date string, day, month, short date string, time, time string, weekday, year
document	A document	modified
double integer	A 32-bit integer	
file	A file reference	POSIX path
file specification	A reference to a file by its name and location	POSIX path
handler	An Applescript subroutine	
integer	An integer number	
item	An object of any type	id
list	An ordered collection of items	length, reverse, rest
machine	A value which identifies a particular computer	
missing value	A value assigned to a variable or property to indicate no value has been supplied	
number	Synonym for integer or real	

Class	Meaning	Properties
paragraph	A sequence of characters up to the end of the string, a return, or a linefeed character, whichever occurs first	
point	A list containing two numbers	
POSIX path		
real	A real number (that is, can contain decimal places)	
record	An unordered collection of property name/value pairs	length, and the names of all the items in the record
reference	A reference to another object	
script	A script object	name, parent
small integer	A 16-bit integer	
string	A sequence of characters	length, quoted form
styled text	Text with font, size, and style information	
text	Synonym for string	
text item	A sequence of characters delimited by the characters specified by text item delimiters; with the default setting, a text item is a single character from a string	
Unicode text	Text stored in Unicode format (multibyte characters)	
URL	A URL path	properties, name, scheme, host, path, user name, password
version	A string indicating the version of the application	
window	A window	bounds, closeable, titled, index, floating, modal, resizable, zoomable, zoomed, visible
word	A contiguous sequence of letters, numbers, commas (between digits), periods (before digits), currency symbols, percent signs, apostrophes (within sequences of letter or numbers) and hyphens	

Classes of Weights and Measures

The following class of weights and measures are defined in AppleScript. Note that the British spellings are not listed (for example, you can write either metres or meters) because they are changed to the American spelling at compile time.

Category	Class
Distance	inches feet yards miles meters centimeters kilometers
Area	square feet square yards square miles square meters square kilometers
Liquid Volume	liters gallons quarts
Cubic Volume	cubic meters cubic centimeters cubic inches cubic feet cubic yards
Weight	kilograms grams ounces pounds
Temperature	degrees Celsius degrees Fahrenheit degrees Kelvin

Lists

This section summarizes properties of list object and element specifiers.

List Class Properties

The following table provides the properties for the list class.

Property	Meaning
length	The number of items in the list
reverse	The list with its items in reverse order
rest	Items 2 through the end of the list

Element Specifiers

The following table summarizes the ways to specify items in a list.

Item Specifer	Meaning
first item, second item, third item, ..., tenth item	A specific item by number
1st item, 2nd item, 3rd item, ...	A specific item by number
item 1, item 2, item 3...	A specific item by number
item -1, item -2, item -3	An item relative to the last item; where -1 references the last item
beginning	First item
last item or end	Last item
some item	A random item
middle item	The middle item; item (n +1) div 2, where n is the size of the list
every item	All items
items	Same as every item
items *m* through *n* or items *m* thru *n*	Items *m* through *n*; can use beginning for *m* and end for *n*

Records

The following section summarizes the properties of record objects.

Record Class Properties

The following table lists the properties of a record object.

Property	Meaning
length	The number of items in the record
property names	Each unique name in a particular record is a property of the record

Strings

This section summarizes properties, escape characters, and the ways to identify elements when you are working with strings.

String Class Properties

The following table provides the properties for the string class.

Property	Meaning
length	The number of characters in the string
quoted form	The string inside a pair of single quotes, with embedded single and double quotes preceded by a backslash character

Predefined String Properties

You can use the predefined properties shown in the following table when you work with strings. You can changes these values, but I don't recommend doing so.

Property	Value
return	return character
tab	A tab character
space	A space character
text item delimiters	Used to delimit text items in a string and to delimit items converted from a list into a string; set to the null string by default

Escape Characters

The following table summarizes the special escape characters you can use inside a string.

Escape character	Meaning
\r	end of line character
\n	line feed character, often also referred to as the newline character
\t	tab character
\"	double quote character
\\	backslash character

String Elements

You can reference string elements by using the following element specifiers. You can specify elements by number, by a range, or by every. Refer to the table earlier in the "Lists" section.

Element	Meaning
character	A single character
paragraph	A sequence of characters up to the end of the string, return, or linefeed character, whichever occurs first
text	A sequence of characters
text item	A sequence of characters delimited by the characters specified by text item delimiters; with the default setting, a text item is a single character from a string
word	A contiguous sequence of letters, numbers, commas (between digits), periods (before digits), currency symbols, percent signs, apostrophes (within sequences of letter or numbers) and hyphens

Dates

This section summarizes the properties and classes for the date class.

Date Class Properties

The following table lists classes you use like properties when working with dates. The first five properties can be assigned values.

Class	Description
weekday	day of the week (with the value Sunday, Monday, ... Saturday)
month	month of the year (with the value January, February, ... December)
day	day of the month (1 – 31)
year	Four-digit year number
time	integer time in seconds since midnight
date string	string in the format "Weekday, Month day, year" or a different format depending on the International settings in System Preferences
time string	string in the format "hh:mm:ss AM or PM" or a different format depending on the 24-hour clock and Region settings in System Preferences
short date string	string in the format "mm/dd/yyyy" or a different format depending on the International settings in System Preferences

Predefined Properties for Working with Dates

The following predefined properties can be used when you work with dates. You can changes these values, but I don't recommend doing so.

Property	Value
minutes	60
hours	3600
days	86400
weeks	604800

Compound Statements

A compound statement is one that encloses a block of statements and is terminated by an end statement. In the case of the if and tell, you can also use one-line versions of these statements.

considering

General Format

```
considering attributeList
    programStatements
end considering
```

attributeList consists of one or more attributes from the following table. Multiple attributes are comma- separated, with the last one preceded by `and`, as in `considering case, diacriticals,` and `expansion`. You can also add a `but ignoring` clause.

Attribute	Meaning	Default
`case`	upper and lower case letters	Ignored
`diacriticals`	diacritical (accent) marks	Considered
`expansion`	ligatures (æ, Æ, œ, Œ)	Considered
`hyphens`	A hyphen (dash) character	Considered
`punctuation`	The characters . , ? : ; ! \ ' " `	Considered
`white space`	space, tab, return and newline character	Considered

A `considering application responses` block can be used inside an `ignoring application responses` block to wait for events sent to applications to respond.

if

General Format 1

```
if booleanExpression then programStatement
```

General Format 2

```
if booleanExpression then
    programStatements
end if
```

General Format 3

```
if booleanExpression then
    programStatements
else
    programStatements
end if
```

General Format 4

```
if booleanExpression  then
    programStatements
else if booleanExpression then
    programStatements
    ...
else if booleanExpression then
    programStatements
else
    programStatements
end if
```

ignoring

General Format 1

```
ignorimg attributeList
    programStatements
end ignoring
```

attributeList consists of one or more attributes from the table shown under the considering statement. Multiple attributes are comma-separated, with the last one preceded by the word and, as in ignoring case, diacriticals, and expansion. A but considering clause can also be added. Ignoring and considering blocks can be nested.

General Format 2

```
ignorimg application responses
    programStatements
end ignoring
```

AppleScript does not wait for replies from events sent to targeted applications inside the block.

repeat

General Format 1

```
repeat n times
    programStatements
end repeat
```

General Format 2

```
repeat
    programStatements
end repeat
```

General Format 3

```
repeat with var from start to end by incr
    programStatements
end repeat
```

General Format 4

```
repeat with var in list
    programStatements
end repeat
```

General Format 5

```
repeat while booleanExpression
    programStatements
end repeat
```

General Format 6

```
repeat until booleanExpression
    programStatements
end repeat
```

An `exit repeat` command can be used to terminate execution of a repeat statement.

tell

General Format 1

```
tell target to programStatement
```

General Format 2

```
tell target
    programStatementss
end tell
```

try

General Format 1

```
try
    programStatements
end try
```

General Format 2

```
try
    programStatements
on error [string] [number smsllInt] [partial result list] [from object] [to object]
    programStatements
end try
```

using terms from

General Format

```
using terms from applicationObject
    programStatements
end using terms from
```

with timeout

General Format

```
with timeout n seconds
    programStatements
end timeout
```

The default time to wait for an application to respond to an event is 60 seconds.

with transaction

General Format

```
with transaction
    programStatements
end transaction
```

Commands

The Standard Suite of commands is listed in the following table. This suite includes commands that you typically send to other applications to execute, so you should consult the application's dictionary to find out if they're implemented and to what extent.

Command
class info
close
count
data size
delete
duplicate
event info
exists
make
move
open
print
quit
reopen
run
save
select
suite info

Other suites, such as the Text Suite, are not covered in this section.

The following sections summarize AppleScript's commands. They are listed alphabetically for quick reference. The Standard Addition commands are included in this list and denoted by an asterisk.

The following table summarizes the notation used to denote specific types of values required by each command. In many cases, if you don't provide the correct argument type, the command tries to coerce the supplied value into the proper type.

Notation	Meaning
Boolean	A true or false value
filelist	A list of file aliases
fileRef	A number returned by the open for access command, a file specification, or an alias
folder	An alias for a folder
path, prompt, title	A string
n	An integer
char	A string consisting of one character
number	A real or integer value
offset	A double integer representing a file offset
smallInt	A small integer
stringlist	A list of strings

In the list that follows, optional parameters to a command are enclosed in brackets.

activate

General Format

```
activate
```

Activates the targeted application, launching it if necessary, and bringing it to the front.

*adding folder items to**

General Format

```
adding folder items to folder after receiving filelist
```

Calls your handler attached to open folder *folder* when files in *filelist* are added to it.

ASCII character*

General Format

```
ASCII character smallInt
```

Returns the ASCII character for *smallInt*.

ASCII number*

General Format

```
ASCII number char
```

Returns the integer equivalent for the character *char*.

choose application*

General Format

```
choose application [with title title] [with prompt prompt] ¬
        [multiple selections allowed Boolean] [as rtype]
```

Provides a dialog for the user to select an application, using the prompt *prompt*. The window's title is *title*. Multiple selections are allowed if *Boolean* is true. The default is false. The application's return type is specified by *rtype* as either application (the default) or alias.

choose color*

General Format

```
choose color [default color RGBcolor]
```

Prompts the user to select a color, returning the selection as an RGBcolor value. If specified, *RGBcolor* is the default RGB color to use.

choose file*

General Format

```
choose file [with prompt prompt] [of type typeList] [default location alias] ¬
        [invisibles Boolean] [multiple selections allowed Boolean]
```

Prompts the user to select a file, using the prompt *prompt*. The starting location for the dialog can be specified by using the default location parameter. If invisibles is true (the default), hidden files are shown. If invisibles is false, hidden files are not shown. Multiple selections are allowed if multiple selections is true (the default is false). An alias to the selected file, or a list of aliases if multiple selections are allowed, is returned.

choose file name*

General Format

```
choose file name [with prompt prompt] [default name string] [default location alias]
```

Prompts the user to select a new file name, using the prompt `prompt`. The default name can be specified by the `default name` parameter. The starting location for the dialog can be specified by using the `default location` parameter. An alias to the selected file is returned.

choose folder*

General Format

```
choose folder [with prompt prompt] [default location alias] ¬
        [invisibles Boolean] [multiple selections allowed Boolean]
```

Allows the user to select a folder, returning an alias to the folder or a list of aliases if multiple selections are allowed. If `invisibles` is `true`, hidden files are shown. If `multiple selections allowed` is `true`, the user can select more than one folder.

choose from list*

General Format

```
choose from list stringlist [with prompt prompt] [default items stringlist] ¬
        [OK button name string] [cancel button name string] ¬
        [multiple  selections allowed Boolean] [empty selection allowed Boolean]
```

Presents a list of choices to the user. The result is a list — even if `multiple selections` is `false` — of the choice or choices selected. Returns `false` if the user cancels the dialog.

choose URL*

General Format

```
choose URL [showing servicelist] [editable URL Boolean]
```

Presents a list of services that the user can select from. The list can be filtered to show just the services in `servicelist`, which can consist of one or more of the following: `Web servers`, `FTP servers`, `Telnet hosts`, `File servers`, `News servers`, `Directory services`, `Media servers`, and `Remote applications`. If `editable URL` is `false`, the user cannot key in his own URL. The default value is `true`. The command returns a URL.

clipboard info*

General Format

```
clipboard info [for type]
```

Returns a list of two-item lists, each describing the type and size of each item on the clipboard. The `for` parameter returns only items of the specified `type`.

close access*

General Format

```
close access fileRef
```

Closes file identified by `fileRef`.

closing folder window for*

General Format

```
closing folder window for folder
```

Calls your handler attached to `folder` after the folder's window gets closed.

continue

General Format

```
continue cmdHandler
```

Executes `cmdHandler` in the parent script object. The argument `cmdHandler` is a command or a handler call, complete with arguments.

copy

General Format

```
copy expression to variable
```

Copies `expression` to `variable`. New copies of a list, record, or script object are made with this command. Multiple copies can be made by specifying a list of expressions and corresponding variables.

count

General Format

```
count object [each type]
```

Returns the number of elements in `object`. If the `each` parameter is specified, just the elements of type `type` are counted.

current date*

General Format

```
current date
```

Returns the current date and time as a date object.

delay*

General Format

```
delay n
```

Pauses program execution for *n* seconds (*n* is actually optional, in which case the command does nothing).

display dialog*

General Format

```
display dialog string [default answer string] [buttons stringlist] ¬
    [default button button] [with icon icon] [giving up after n]
```

Displays a dialog to the user. If default answer is specified, input is requested from the user and the specified string is used as the default value. Up to three buttons can be shown with labels indicated in *stringlist*. The default button is a string specifying a button name or a number giving its relative position in *stringlist*. If buttons is not specified, *button* can be Cancel or 1 for the Cancel button or OK or 2 for the OK button (the default). The icon can be specified either by a name or ID, or it can be either stop, note, or caution. The giving up parameter specifies how many seconds to wait for the user to click a button before closing the dialog.

do shell script*

General Format

```
do shell script string [as type] [administrator privileges Boolean] ¬
    [password string] [altering line endings Boolean]
```

Executes the shell command line specified by *string*, returning the output as Unicode text, or as *type* if specified. If administrator privileges is supplied and true, the command is run with those privileges. In that case, if the password parameter is specified, a dialog asking you to enter the administrator password is bypassed and the supplied password is used instead. If altering line endings is true (which is the default), line endings are converted to return characters (most Unix commands produce output that ends with newline characters) and the last newline character from the output is also removed.

error

General Format

```
error [string] [number smsllInt] [partial result list] [from object] [to object]
```

An error is generated, normally causing program termination unless the error is caught. The following table lists some common error numbers.

Error Number	Meaning
–34	Disk <name> is full
–37	Bad name for file
–39	End of file error
–43	File <name> wasn't found
–44	Disk <name> is write protected
–47	File <name> is busy
–48	Duplicate file name
–49	File <name> is already open
–61	File not open with write permission
–120	Folder <name> wasn't found
–128	User canceled
–1700	Can't make <data> into a <type>
–1708	<reference> doesn't understand the <commandName> message
–1712	Apple event timed out
–1728	Can't get the specified item
–1730	Container specified was an empty list.
–2701	Can't divide <number> by zero
–2702	Result of a numeric operation was too large
–2703	<reference> can't be launched because it is not an application
–2704	<reference> isn't scriptable
–2705	Application has a corrupted dictionary
–2708	Attempt to create a value larger than the allowable size
–2721	Can't perform operation on text longer than 32K bytes
–2753	Variable <name> is not defined
–30720	Invalid date and time <date string>

exit repeat

General Format

```
exit repeat
```

Terminates execution of the enclosing `repeat` statement.

get

General Format

```
[get] expression [as type]
```

Gets the value of *expression* (which can be a reference to an object), coercing it into a value of type `type`. The resulting value is stored in the special `result` variable.

get eof*

General Format

```
get eof fileRef
```

Returns a double integer representing the size of the file referenced by `fileRef`.

get volume settings*

General Format

```
get volume settings
```

Returns a record containing the input, output, alert volume settings, and a Boolean indicating if the output is currently muted.

handle CGI request*

General Format

```
handle CGI request [searching for string] [with posted data string] ¬
    [of content type string] [using access method string] [from address string] ¬
    [from user string] [using password string] [with user info string] ¬
    [from server string] [via port string] [executing by string] ¬
    [referred by string] [from browser string] [using action string] ¬
    [of action type string] [from client IP address string] ¬
    [with full request string] [with connection ID integer] ¬
    [from virtual host string]
```

This command is executed to process a CGI request sent to your application, enabling you to write AppleScript programs that can function as CGI applications. The handler you define is expected to return a string representing an HTML web page. Consult the Standard Additions dictionary for more information about the various parameters.

info for*

General Format

```
info for fileRef
```

Returns a record containing information for the specified file, folder, or disk.

launch

General Format

```
launch
```

Description

Starts the targeted application.

list disks*

General Format

```
list disks
```

Returns a list containing aliases of the currently mounted volumes.

list folder*

General Format

```
list folder folder [invisibles Boolean]
```

Returns a list of names of the items in the specified `folder` (as Unicode text). Default is to list invisible files.

load script *

General Format

```
load script file
```

Reads and returns the script from the specified file as a script object.

log

General Format

```
log string
```

Adds the specified string to the Event Log.

mount volume*

General Format

```
mount volume string on server string [in AppleTalk zone string] ¬
    [as user name string] [with password string]
```

Mounts the specified AppleShare volume on the specified server.

moving folder window for*

General Format

```
moving folder window for folder from boundRect
```

Calls your handler attached to open folder *folder* when the folder gets moved. The location it was moved from is specified by the bounding rectangle *boundRect*.

offset*

General Format

```
offset of  Ustring1 in Ustring2
```

Returns the position of the first occurrence of Unicode string *Ustring1* inside Unicode string *Ustring2*. If the string is not present, returns 0.

open for access*

General Format

```
open for access  fileSpec [write permission Boolean]
```

Opens *fileSpec*, which is a file specification or alias. The default is to open to file for reading only. To write to the file, specify `write permission true`. If the file doesn't exist, it is created, even if the file is opened only for reading. The command returns a small integer value that can subsequently be used to identify the file for other file commands. Note that `open for access` also accepts a file specified as a string.

*open location**

General Format

```
open location string [error reporting Boolean]
```

Opens the URL specified by `string` using the default browser. If `error reporting` is `true`, errors that occur are reported in a dialog.

*opening folder**

General Format

```
closing folder window for folder
```

Calls your handler attached to folder `folder` after the folder's window is opened.

*path to**

General Format

```
path to name [from domain] [as type] [folder creation Boolean]
```

Returns an alias to the application or folder specified by `name`, in the domain `domain`, with the result coerced into the type specified by `type`, which can be either `alias` (the default) or `string`. If the specified folder doesn't exist, it is created for you (if you have the proper permissions), unless the `folder creation` parameter is supplied with the value `false`.

The possible values for *domain* are: `system domain`, `local domain`, `network domain`, `user domain`, and `Classic domain`.

The possible values for *name* are: `application string`, `application support`, `applications folder`, `desktop`, `desktop pictures folder`, `documents folder`, `favorites folder`, `Folder Action scripts`, `fonts`, `frontmost application`, `help`, `home folder`, `internet plugins`, `keychain folder`, `library folder`, `modem scripts`, `movies folder`, `music folder`, `pictures folder`, `preferences`, `printer descriptions`, `public folder`, `scripting additions`, `scripts folder`, `shared documents`, `shared libraries`, `sites folder`, `startup disk`, `startup items`, `system folder`, `system preferences`, `temporary items`, `trash`, `users folder`, `utilities folder`, `voices`, `apple menu`, `control panels`, `control strip modules`, `extensions`, `launcher items folder`, `printer drivers`, `printmonitor`, `shutdown folder`, `speakable items`, and `stationery`.

*random number**

General Format

```
random number [ulimit] [from lower] [to upper] [with seed seed]
```

Returns a random real number between 0 and 1. If the number *ulimit* is specified, the random number is between 0 and *ulimit*. If *ulimit* is an integer, so is the random number. If the from and to parameter are used, the random number is between *lower* and *upper*, inclusive. If both *lower* and *upper* are integers, the random number is an integer. The seed for the generator can be set with the parameter with seed to the number *seed* for repeatability of the random number sequence.

read*

General Format

```
read  fileSpec [using delimiter char] [using delimiters list] [as type] ¬
    [for length] [before char] [until char]
```

The contents from the current location in the file until the end of the file are read and returned. The optional parameters to the read command can be used to alter this behavior and are summarized in the following table. An error occurs if you try to read from a file that has already reached the end of file.

Parameter	Meaning
for *length*	read *length* bytes from the file
from *offset*	read from file starting at byte *offset*
to *offset*	read from file up to byte *offset*
before *char*	read bytes from the file up to, but not including, the character *char*
until *char*	read bytes from the file up to, and including, the character *char*
using delimiter *char*	use the character *char* as the delimiter character read
using delimiters *list*	use any character in *list* as a delimiter character
as *type*	convert the data that is read to *type*

removing folder items from*

General Format

```
removing folder items from folder after losing filelist
```

Calls your handler attached to open folder *folder* when files in *filelist* are removed from it. For an item that has been permanently deleted, the corresponding reference in *filelist* is a string and not an alias.

return

General Format

```
return [expression]
```

If executed inside a handler or script object, returns execution immediately to the point where the handler was called or the script was run. The value returned is the value of *expression* if supplied. Otherwise, the value returned is the result of the last statement executed before the `return`. When executed from your top-level script object, terminates execution of the program.

round*

General Format

```
round real [rounding direction]
```

Converts the real number *real* to an integer, using the rounding method specified by *direction*. Possible values for *direction* are up, down, toward zero, to nearest (the default), and as taught in school. See the description of this command in the text for a description of these various rounding directions.

run script*

General Format

```
run script script [with parameters list] [in string]
```

Runs the script specified by *script*, which can be a script object, an alias, or file that contains a script. The parameters listed in *list* are parameters to the script's run handler. The string *string* specifies the scripting component to use.

say*

General Format

```
say string [using string] [waiting until completion Boolean] ¬
    [saving to file] [displaying string]
```

Speaks the specified string using the default voice, or using the specified voice if the using parameter is provided. The program normally waits until the speaking is done, unless you specify waiting until completion with a false value. The sound output can be captured in a file using the saving to parameter. Here *file* is an alias, file reference, or string specifying an AIFF file. If speech recognition is on, the text specified with the optional displaying parameter is displayed in the feedback window.

scripting components*

General Format

```
scripting components
```

Returns a list of strings indicating the installed scripting components.

set

General Format

```
set variable to expression
```

Sets the variable or property specified by `variable` to the value of `expression`. If `expression` is a list, record, or script object, a new copy of the object is *not* made.

Multiple variables and properties can be set at once if `variable` is a list of variables or properties, and if `expression` is also a list of values.

set eof*

General Format

```
set eof fileRef to offset
```

Sets the size of the file referenced by `fileRef` to `offset`. Setting the size to 0 truncates the file. Setting the size greater than its current size extends the size of the file, which is padded with zeroes.

set the clipboard to*

General Format

```
set the clipboard to anything
```

Copies `anything` to the `clipboard`.

set volume*

General Format

```
set volume number
```

Sets the sound volume to `number`, which is in the range of 0 through 7, inclusive.

start log

General Format

```
start log
```

Resumes logging of AppleEvents in the Event log.

stop log

General Format

```
stop log
```

Suspends logging of AppleEvents in the Event log.

*store script**

General Format

```
store script [script] [in file] [replacing flag]
```

Stores the script object *script* in the file or alias indicated by *file*. If the file already exists, a dialog asks if the file should be replaced. If the `replacing` parameter is supplied, *flag* can be `ask` (the default), `yes`, or `no`. If *script* is not provided, a dialog asks for the script name. If the `in` parameter is not supplied, a dialog lets you select the file to store the script in.

*summarize**

General Format

```
summarize textRef [in n]
```

Returns a string summarizing the first *n* sentences of the text object or text file specified by *textRef*. If the parameter `in` is not provided, the entire text is summarized.

*system attribute**

General Format

```
system attribute [string] [has n]
```

Gets the Gestalt value or the environment variable specified by *string*, returning a string or integer. The `has` parameter specifies specific bits to test. If *string* is not provided, a list containing the names of all environment variables is returned.

*the clipboard**

General Format

```
the clipboard [as type]
```

Returns the items on `the clipboard`, or just items of the specified *type*.

*time to GMT**

General Format

```
time to GMT
```

Returns the number of seconds between the current time zone and Greenwich Mean Time.

*write**

General Format

```
write anything to fileSpec [starting at offset] [for length] [as type]
```

Writes the data specified by `anything` to the file identified by `fileSpec` starting at the current offset in the file. The meaning of the optional parameters is summarized in the following table:

Parameter	Meaning
`starting at` *offset*	write to file starting at *offset* bytes from the beginning of the file
`for` *length*	write *length* bytes of data to the file
`as` *type*	convert the data to *type* before writing

C

Resources

This appendix contains a selective list of resources you can turn to for more information. Some of the information may be on your system, online at a website, or available from a book. If you can't find what you need, send me an e-mail at `steve@kochan-wood.com` and I'll try to help you out.

Errata, etc.

You can visit the book's companion website at `www.wrox.com` to get errata and download the programs from this book. For more details on how to get to the source code and errata, see the specific sections on those topics at the end of this book's Introduction.

AppleScript Books

A number of books are out there on the topic of AppleScript. Following is a list of some selected titles:

❑ Apple Computer, Inc., *AppleScript Language Guide*, Apple Computer, Inc., May, 1999.

This guide is available for download in HTML and PDF formats. As you might be able to tell from the date, this document does not cover all the newer features of AppleScript.

Go to this URL to download the HTML version `developer.apple.com/documentation/AppleScript/Conceptual/AppleScriptLangGuide/index.html`

Go to this URL to download the PDF version: `developer.apple.com/documentation/AppleScript/Conceptual/AppleScriptLangGuide/AppleScriptLanguageGuide.pdf`

❑ Soghoian, Sal. *AppleScript 1-2-3*, New Riders Publishing, October, 2004.

This book was written by Apple's AppleScript product manager but was not available for review at the time of this writing.

❏ Neuburg, Matt. *AppleScript, the Definitive Guide,* O'Reilly & Associates, Inc., November, 2003.

This book explores many of the intricacies of the AppleScript language and is the recommended follow-up to the book you hold in your hands.

Websites

Many websites that are not listed here also address AppleScript. However, the bigger portal sites have been listed. You can usually find what you're looking for by first going to one of these sites and checking their Links or Resources.

❏ `www.apple.com/applescript`: The main website provided by Apple for AppleScript. From here you can find links to other information, such as sample code, documentation, other websites, training, and so on.

Under the Applications tab you can find a variety of scripts for download that are organized by application. This is a good place to learn by example how to talk to many of Mac OS X's built-in applications, such as iTunes, QuickTime Player, and Mail.

The Resources tab provides good links to other information, but it is not quite as extensive as the site at macscripter.net.

❏ `www.macscripter.net`: The premiere website for AppleScript. It has an excellent archive of AppleScript scripts that you can search, in addition to providing AppleScript news and an active bulletin board where you can ask questions or find answers to some of your scripting questions.

Macscripter.net is a good place to look up AppleScript dictionaries to see the type of AppleScript support provided by an application. Check out its AppleScript Books section for a good summary of available books. Finally, this website contains a great links page to guide you to other places that may be of interest.

❏ `www.scriptweb.com`: A portal site that contains links to other sites. Here you can find links to AppleScript products, news, training, and books (among other things).

❏ `www.blankreb.com/studiolog.php`: Part of the Blankrebel Productions website devoted to AppleScript Studio and Cocoa programming.

❏ `www.malcolmadams.com/itunes/index.php`: Doug's AppleScripts for iTunes site contains hundreds of scripts for working with iTunes and iPods. This is a great site!

❏ `www.xmethods.net`: Primary website for SOAP services, which were described in Chapter 13.

❏ `www.applemods.sourceforge.net`: Good place to find AppleScript libraries.

Mailing Lists and Newsgroups

Here are some AppleScript-related lists and newsgroups that you might want to check out:

❏ `lists.apple.com/mailman/listinfo/applescript-users`: You can join the applescript-users mailing list and get e-mails sent to you whenever a message is posted to this mailing list.

You can get on the mailing list by going to this URL. Also at this address, you'll find a link to the mailing list archives, where you can search and view previous messages.

❑ `discussions.info.apple.com`: This is the Apple bulletin board website (called Apple Discussions). Click on AppleScript under Software Product Forums on this page to get to the AppleScript discussions.

❑ `macscripter.net`: This site was mentioned under websites, but I mention it again here because of its extensive bulletin board about AppleScript.

❑ `www.lsoft.com/scripts/wl.exe?L1=MACSCRPT&H=LISTSERV`: An AppleScript mailing list maintained by Dartmouth College.

❑ `alt.comp.lang.applescript`: A newsgroup devoted to the AppleScript programming language. A good way to get access to this newsgroup is through `http://groups.google.com`.

Development Tools

The following sections provide references to development tools mentioned in this book if you want to look into any of them in more detail.

AppleScript Studio

As I note in Chapter 13, AppleScript Studio is an interactive editing and debugging environment for working with AppleScript programs. It also gives you the capability to create graphical user interfaces like those you see in many Mac OS X applications. The following sections provide some resources to help you learn more about AppleScript Studio.

Books

For additional help with AppleScript Studio, you might want to refer to the following book:

❑ Ross, Charles, *Absolute AppleScript Studio*, No Starch Press, June, 2004. This book was not available for review at the time of this writing.

Websites and mailing lists

As you delve further into AppleScript Studio, you might find the following websites and mailing lists helpful:

❑ `www.apple.com/applescript/studio`: Apple's main website for AppleScript Studio. Here you'll find examples, links to documentation, other websites, training, and so on.

❑ `http://developer.apple.com/documentation/AppleScript/AppleScript-date.html`: A direct link to the main Apple page for documentation related to AppleScript and AppleScript Studio.

❑ `www.lists.apple.com/mailman/listinfo/applescript-studio`: Here's where you can join the applescript-studio mailing list.

Script Editor

This is the most commonly used application for AppleScript program development, and I used it extensively throughout this book. Script Editor is bundled with your Mac OS X system. You can get more information about Script Editor, including a tutorial on how to use it, from Apple's website at www.apple.com.

Smile

Smile is an excellent development environment for writing and debugging AppleScript programs. One of its neatest features is the capability to work interactively in text windows and to enable you to execute AppleScript statements on a line-by-line basis just by pressing the Enter key.

Also included as part of Smile and available for separate download is a scripting addition containing commands to handle regular expressions and perform folder backups. It also includes a set of mathematical functions and commands to enable you to efficiently work with lists, arrays, and numeric matrices.

Smile is available for no charge from www.satimage-software.com.

Script Debugger 3.0

This is the best debugging utility for AppleScript programs, and it is available from www.latenightsw.com. This powerful, interactive debugger enables you to trace the execution of your program, insert breakpoints and watchpoints, and dynamically monitor your variables. The utility also provides a nice graphical presentation of dictionaries, as I illustrated in the text of this book.

Index

E

F